BITS AND PIECES

of a Psychiatrist's Life

Barry Blackwell

To order additional copies of this book, contact:
Xlibris Corporation
1-888-795-4274
www.Xlibris.com
Orders@Xlibris.com
77935

BITS AND PIECES
of a Psychiatrist's Life

CONTENTS

PART TWO: PROFESSIONAL

PIECE 17. THE BREAD AND BUTTER OF PSYCHIATRY 375

PIECE 18. SPIRITUAL PILGRIMAGE 410

PART THREE: PERSONAL

DEDICATION

This memoir is shared with affection and gratitude for my family, friends, and former colleagues or companions. They have bestowed upon me much love, joy, and generosity. In return, I offer this volume in lieu of a funeral, a memorial service, or, God forbid, a eulogy or epitaph. All you folks will remember my penchant for having . . .

The Last Word

Read between the lines,
Perhaps you'll catch a glimpse of
What remains behind.

ACKNOWLEDGMENTS

The Web discovers, stores, and distributes knowledge, channels communication, and herds people into social networks, breeding consensus. It also names things, but "self-publishing" is not what it claims to be. It was not a solitary exercise because, while the author had fun, others worked hard to turn writing into reading.

The "Others" are the following:

Kathy Malec was my secretary and assistant thirty years ago in 1982 after we came to Milwaukee. Marriage to a military man took her away for a while till she returned to work for many years as administrative assistant to my wife, Kathie, director of the Milwaukee County Behavioral Health Division. After Kathie left to become president of Saint John's Retirement Community, Kathy followed a few years later and worked here until we all three retired. When we joined together to put this book to bed, Kathy typed, organized, collated, and corrected; crossed every *t*, dotted every *i*, and uprooted every dangling participle. Our book is an epitaph to this lifelong collaboration.

Jessie Blackwell designed the book's cover while raising our grandson, Oliver, and giving birth to his sister, Amelia. Jessie is an amazing mother and a talented graphic artist.

Kris Alberto, our ambassador to the publisher, **Xlibris,** shepherded the book from pen to press with patient persistence over several long years despite the author's episodic irascibility and dilatory writing habits.

Kathie Eilers, thrice wed to me, was kind, patient, considerate, and supportive, as always. She encouraged me to do my thing knowing, but never saying, this memoir would yield neither fame nor fortune.

And lastly, to **Ollie**, who kept us all happy while watching him grow along with our book. He deserves a T. rex dinosaur drawing from his mother's pen and his Yappa's heart.

Caveat: There is, however, one way in which "self-publication" is an accurate label; the publisher takes no responsibility for the content, style, or opinions expressed. The book is published "as is" without any attempt to improve or embellish the narrative. This makes it easy (inevitable) for the author to accept responsibility for anything the reader disagrees with or finds objectionable. I do so willingly.

Part One:
Preparation

1. Literary Considerations

The Writer

It is unusual enough for a seventy-eight-year-old man to attempt to write a book, but when its style and format deviate from the norm, that demands an explanation. So first about my muse and then how I have chosen to express it.

My Muse

England and America are two countries separated by a common language.

—George Bernard Shaw

I was born British and moved to America in 1968 at age thirty-four. Our educational systems were different. In the USA, children were coached in copperplate script and examined by multiple-choice questions; in England, your handwriting mattered less than the essays you wrote. I never saw a multiple-choice question until I took the test that allows foreign medical graduates to practice in America.

All tests in Britain required essays. Perhaps I went overboard. At Cambridge University, my anatomy tutor (who had the splendid English name of Max Bull) noted my florid answers to mundane questions. My essay in response to the question "Describe the structure and blood supply of the uterus" led him to predict that "Blackwell, one day you'll end up writing for the *Reader's Digest*."

That never happened (not yet), but it is true that I began publishing scientific articles as soon as I qualified as a doctor at age twenty-six. I was the first in my class to do so, and three years later, as a psychiatric resident, I was writing anonymous leading articles for *The Lancet*, Britain's premier medical journal. By the time I was forty, I had published about a hundred articles, reviews, editorials, book chapters, and book reviews. When I retired for the first time, at age sixty-four, the total had doubled and included several books, none of which made any money.

But scientific writing is constrained by tradition in ways that stifle artistic elements in the muse. That component of my muse surfaced in late midlife. To understand why and when that aspect was let loose is a compelling question. Important because age augers ill for a bard. Of the fifty-one poets anthologized in an edition of *Contemporary American Poetry*, only three celebrated three score years and ten. The unlucky thirteen who were already dead averaged barely fifty-five years, and none achieved their biblical quota.

My first poem was penned when I was going on fifty. By that age, Shakespeare was about over and done with, but Grandma Moses had hardly begun. Why? D. H. Lawrence, who wrote early and painted late, was more enigmatic than explanatory when he described his own artistic development: "Things happen, and we have no choice." I doubt if it is so simple or so obscure.

As a prepubescent boy, I played a courtesan in the school production of *Hamlet*. There were no real women in my boarding school except a starched and remote matron. The gentler distaff side of nature was subordinated to the command of bells, routines, and time tables. A struggle for dominance was acted out in elbow-jostling competitions on muddy playing fields and in tidy classrooms. D. H. Lawrence's indictment of our culture was an apt epitaph for my education: "We *know* so much, we *feel* so little." This void created an echo that urged me to enter medicine and cater to the needs of others in ways I had lacked myself. The tools I had sharpened were obsessive and mindful.

Throughout medical training, these traits allowed me to endure the meat grinder of massive fact, to master the technology, and to preserve a safe distance from those who suffered in order to keep my own pit-stomach fears at bay.

By the time I was ready to embark on a career, the hatches were battened down on a below-decks ferment. For several years, I wavered between medicine and psychiatry, from science to art, and from cure to comfort. The choice was more distinct in Britain where psychiatry was organic and pragmatic, hardly influenced by the poetic insights of psychoanalysis. In America, it was different. Freud was king. The egalitarian ideal that everyone can overcome their origins was coupled with the affluence to afford therapy. I was not converted, but by osmosis, the significance and awareness of emotion welled up. The veneer began to strip, peeled away, in part, by the psychological sensitivity of my American wife, Kathie.

What was happening to me was occurring in society. The public knew medicine had become too technical, dehumanized, and inaccessible. In the mid-1970s, a move began to open medical schools that would spawn a new breed of doctor, more humanistic, less elite, and willing to practice in communities away from urban academic ivory towers. As an educator in one of these new and developing schools, I helped introduce literature into the curriculum and back into my life. Poetry began to bubble up, in the medical journals and at the tip of my own pen.

For good reason Apollo, god of poetry, was father to Aesculapius, god of healing. The two are of the same flesh, linked in the way they must coexist for emotion and intellect, mind and body to meld and become whole. Among physician writers, this union has been consummated at different times. Keats endured his apothecary's training but quit medicine at once to write poetry. William Carlos Williams did both passionately throughout an exhausting professional life. Richard Seltzer waited till he was past forty to turn from his surgeon's talent for mending the foot to his writer's eye for the footprint.

After we moved to Wisconsin in 1980, I began to attend evening classes in writing and poetry. Later, at age sixty-four, the time felt right to hang up my shingle and move a step closer to the source. My atheism collapsed as the cynicism that had supported it melted in the warmth of my wife's sustaining love. I entered our Catholic seminary as a lay student and busied myself advocating for those I once ministered to as a physician. Spiritually handicapped, poetry remained an easier channel to the soul than prayer or contemplation. As my interests shifted in later life, it was less a crisis and more a coming together. Perhaps Anne Sexton, who ended her own life and poetry writing at an age before I began, has plotted the course more clearly:

> There was life
> with its cruel houses
> and people who seldom touched—
> though touch is all, but I grew.
> like a pig in a trench coat
> and then there were many strange apparitions,
> the nagging rain, the sun turning into poison
> and all of that, saws working through my heart,
> but I grew, I grew,
> and God was there like an island I had now rowed to,
> still ignorant of Him, my arms and legs worked,
> and I grew, I grew,
> I wore rubies and bought tomatoes
> and now, in my middle age,
> about nineteen in the head I'd say,
> I am rowing, I am rowing.

—Excerpt from "Rowing" by Anne Sexton

I knew it was late, and I would have to row fast.

The Book

Finally in Florence in 1904, I hit upon the right way to do an autobiography: start it at no particular time in your life; wander at your free will all over your life; talk only about the thing which interests you for the moment; drop it the moment interests threaten to pale, and turn your talk upon the new and more interesting thing that has intruded itself into your mind meantime.

—Mark Twain
Cited by Mark Powers in *A Life of Mark Twain* (p. 621)
Free Press, 2005

My title, *Bits and Pieces*, has dictated the format of the book and was chosen for good reason. Some years ago, when I read Mark Powers's biography of Mark Twain, the approach he advocated sounded appealing. At least it would eliminate all the dull interludes that occupy most of a person's life. But Powers adds some cautionary comments about the lack of success of the unadulterated approach which Mark Twain espoused. It yielded an enormous amount of rambling material which was chronologically incoherent and baffled several editors who attempted to place it in book form. In 1967, the Mark Twain Project was founded by the Bancroft Library to "create a comprehensive critical review of everything Mark Twain wrote." Over forty years later, in 2010, the first volume was published. It is 736 pages long and a very dense read!

So I have chosen to borrow Mark Twain's central idea of focusing only on the interesting, entertaining, or educational highlights but to retain a chronological approach overall. This means there are no traditional chapters; instead there are themes I call "pieces" which flow in a logical sequence from past to present. Each piece contains autobiographical material, but it is placed in a broader context. For example, the twin pieces, "What's in a Name" and "Family Matters," are not simply an effort to trace my own family heritage but a reflection on the role that heredity and environment (nature and nurture) may play in shaping personality as well as a consideration of the nuances and potential pitfalls in the popular sport of genealogy. This leads naturally into the next piece, which deals with what I consider to be the most important environmental influence, "Boarding School." Once again, this is set in the broader context of literature and poetry written about the topic.

Within each theme or piece are the "bits"; these include my short stories, essays, poems, a few philosophical reflections, and some scientific articles carefully selected because they have broad social interest and will be easily understood by lay readers. Those that include patient material are modified so as not to reveal any individual's identity. For those that have been published previously, the source is identified.

A word about poetry. Every poet has their own "voice." Sometimes it takes time to find. I enjoy experimenting with both novel and classical forms because I feel challenged by the tension between creativity and compulsive conformity to rules. When appropriate, I include a comment or explanation of either the form or the content of the poem, hoping this adds interest for the reader. But explaining a poem has the same risks as explaining a joke! I am not shy to use rhyme, meter, alliteration, or assonance which some may consider old-fashioned. But so am I.

None of my poetry is so metaphorical as to be opaque or obscure. Poetry is meant to be shared and enjoyed, not to bewilder, confuse, or amaze. This swims against the current tides of literary criticism, but I am comforted by remembering that Shakespeare wrote to entertain and attract large audiences at a time when the average Englishman had little formal education.

Finally, let's be honest. Most books are written to relieve the author's itch. Very few attract a sizeable readership, and almost none make any money. My message to the chosen few who stumble across this volume is to wish that you enjoy the reading as much as I have enjoyed the writing. The first bit is a haiku which says in poetic form what I have just explained in prose. Take your choice! It is followed by two very short prose bits—both published in *Jazz Street*, the University of Wisconsin, Milwaukee (UWM) student literary magazine.

Haiku Poetry

Deceptively simple, the haiku form of poetry has a long and complex history, stemming from the seventeenth century, and possibly before, in Japan. In later centuries, the form was borrowed by poets everywhere and, like ethnic foods, shaped to the taste of new audiences and cultures. The haiku retains its basic structure of three lines with five, seven, and five syllables. Originally its subject was nature, especially the seasons. Now anything goes, even sex. There is no requirement for rhyme, and I have no idea if that is possible in Japanese. But if it sounds right in English, why not? Inevitably, a short poem with only seventeen syllables invites pithy and even paradoxical insights to complex themes. So here it is for the first time.

"Buy Mine!"

Authors who write books
feel the need to scratch an itch—
readers can decline.

—Barry Blackwell, May 2010

The Writer Bit: Lesson One

Published in *Jazz Street*, Vol. 1, 1984:

Writer's Repair Shop is more than the catalogue claims. By any other name, it is sometimes a support group. For a psychiatrist who is learning to write, that bit is a busman's holiday. So I play fly on the wall, listening a lot, contributing little.

As usual it's taken time to get here. We are the remnant. Others flashed their talent and left. One-night stands. Thanks, but no thanks.

The course is five evenings old, close to its end. True confession time. Jim, our after-hours English teacher, nudges, nurtures, and cajoles. If I were doing this, I'd charge more and give less. I often do.

Tonight's big question is, "Why write?"

Jerry says money. He hasn't any. Sharp face, sharp wit, he has ten years of blunt prose stored in shoeboxes. He remains undaunted and unpublished except for the official record of his last cruise on a navy ship. "A bit like a high school yearbook," he quips and we laugh.

Madge says fame. Grandmotherly and past seventy, she devours other authors' books while waiting patiently to produce her own. Next week we get to discuss her novel, meticulously researched, about men in submarines. We will be its first eager audience and maybe its last.

Today Penny tells us what works. The lily in our weed patch, she has her third children's book in press. Bubbling over, she reads the story of how she became an author. It was commissioned by *Milwaukee Magazine*. We try not to let envy mar her honeymoon. After it is published, we will tell our friends which comma we helped move.

For me it's not money. Doctors don't starve. It isn't adulation either. The shelves in my office are stacked with scientific papers I've published. Reprint requests are foreign stamps now, not fame. So what is this writing mania? It won't sell, and I can't stop. Nobody reads it, and I don't care. If you believe that, you should see a psychiatrist. Meanwhile I'm looking for a new class. This one ends next week.

The Writer Bit: Lesson Two

Published in *Jazz Street,* Vol. 2, 1985:

I'm still struggling at the edges of the literary world, wondering if I belong there and trying to infiltrate. But I've forgotten how to behave as a beginner. A good place to start seemed to be the student writing association. They sent back my first short stories because I wasn't a full-time student but softened up after I attended some workshops. Finally they said they'd publish one in their new magazine provided the professor who taught my evening course wrote a note to say I really was a student. Then I knew at least I was back in school. I took the proofs proudly to an afternoon workshop and felt flattered when the editor asked if I'd like to present the story at a poetry reading that evening.

I've given scientific talks to large audiences but this felt different. When I present my own research, it is pasteurized, sanctified by scientific etiquette, and stripped of me. Reading a story to strangers would be a different kind of encounter, risky and maybe more rewarding. But not too dangerous I hoped. The poets I'd met so far were sometimes angry at the world but always kind to each other. Like nudists in a colony, they've learned how to admire one another without becoming overly aroused.

Between the afternoon workshop and the evening reading I returned to the hospital to attend a special session of the Medical Executive Committee convened to consider the appeal of a physician denied privileges to practice surgery. The room was set up like a tribunal; the table for the plaintiff, a lawyer and court reporter faced the table at which I sat, next to the Chief of the Medical Staff and the Hospital President, flanked by the other Chairmen of Departments and members of the committee.

As the meeting dragged on, my Type A clock began ticking inside my head, telling me I might not make it to the poetry

—

meeting on time. If I wanted to leave, and my departure destroyed the committee's quorum, I would have a tough choice—doctor or writer?

The plaintiff's pleading got short shrift, but the meeting went to the brink as I made it back to the University Center with only two minutes to spare. Trotting from the parking lot to the coffee shop, I tugged off my tie and turned off my pager. It was bad enough to be wearing a jacket and not jeans. If I couldn't pass for a student, at least I didn't need to look like a doctor.

I paid my two dollars at the door and signed the list of poets waiting to present. There were already eleven names ahead of mine although only a few people were seated in the darkened room, and it was hardly time to begin. Obviously the organizers had front loaded the list with their own names and poems. Feeling surreptitious, I chose a solitary seat and slid inconspicuously into its contours. The last time I visited a university bar with my son's girlfriend we overheard someone ask, "Who is that old fart with the good-looking broad?"

The stage stayed empty as students slowly filtered in. The bar hadn't been stocked, and it took fifty minutes to find the beer. The band began to play cool jazz for openers. At around nine, the first poet stepped on the stage. Giggling nervously, she picked up speed and confidence fast. One poem, then a second, then another. After about twenty she ran dry and left to a flutter of applause. It made me wonder if I'd be brave enough to read a poem as well as the story.

Time wasn't rationed and the audience was kind. Three or four more poets in assorted sizes, sexes, and shapes came and went. My doubts began to germinate. Anger, bawdy humor, and revolution were the themes. Crooked stanzas, daring line breaks and stark metaphors were the medium. I began to feel old in art and body, past my prime and bedtime. If I could leave and not look as if I were escaping, I would. Instead, I bolstered myself with beer and waited.

—

Past ten o'clock, the poets took a break and the band played again. Half an hour later, they joined in with poems set to music. Then there were more pure poets. I lost count and began to wonder if they had forgotten me and my short story. It was almost eleven thirty and the audience was drifting away. The band were packing up their instruments, the organizers chatted cozily in a corner, and only a few half listening couples were left. The stranger sitting next to me leaned across to ask the title of my story, so he could introduce me next. The last poet was almost done. He was a Native American wearing a headband and had a homespun talent who would be a hard act to follow. Nobody had read a story and I wondered if anybody wanted to hear one.

The poet was working his cadences to a climax when my student sponsor put his hands on my shoulders and whispered softly in my ear from behind the chair. "Security says we must shut it down. I'm sorry we won't have time for your story." "Fine," I said, making it sound as if I was mature enough not to mind. Nobody knew me well enough to say good-bye, so I left the coffee shop and slunk past the night owls and drunks back to the parking lot. I climbed up into my van, put it in gear, and backed it into a concrete pillar with a scrunch of metal on stone and a tinkle of shattered glass.

Too dejected to examine the damage I drove home to a dark house where everyone was already asleep. The mail on the kitchen table included the course catalogue I had requested from the University two months earlier. Too tired to read it, I crept upstairs and into bed. I wasn't ready to laugh yet and I didn't want to wake anyone.

Next morning, I went outside to assess the damage to the van and came back in to read the catalogue. The dent would cost about as much to repair as a three-credit course in poetic form. It's expensive to get an education these days.

Apologia

The bits in this book accumulated over a fifty-year time span and the memoir itself was assembled over four years. Not surprisingly, there is a limited amount of repetition some might consider redundant. In my own defense, I offer the following haiku:

Duplicate or Propagate?

Why repeat myself?
Like books on a library shelf
Ideas propagate.

—Barry Blackwell, June 2012

2. THE BLACKWELL NAME

Family Matters

Every family pattern has its own costs and benefits, its own internal contradictions, its own concerns about the gap between the ideal and the real.

—Arlene Skolnick

The English language is a joy—a subtle, complex fusion of ancient dialects producing words that rhyme readily and often have multiple meanings. Take "matters" as it qualifies "family." The noun has five distinct definitions and is derived from Old French via the Latin *materia*, meaning "discourse" and further back from *mater*, for "mother." In the plural form, "matters" means "the present state of affairs." So, in this piece, starting with my mother (and father), we have discourse on how my immediate family past illuminates the present.

My father, Vernon Blackwell, was born in the second month of the new millennium, on February 10, 1900, shortly before the Wright brothers first took flight. My mother, Nancy Valentine Dale, as her name suggests, was born on February 14, 1906.

Both families lived in the suburbs of Manchester, where my father won a scholarship to Manchester Grammar School. The school was endowed by Henry VIII in AD 1515 and founded by Hugh Oldham, bishop of Exeter, who was a graduate of my alma mater, Queens' College, Cambridge, four hundred fifty years before I matriculated.

—

Manchester Grammar School is the largest independent boys' school in Britain and a breeding ground for the nation's leading universities. My father's achievement was the crucial step elevating our family above its blue-collar origins.

The family finances probably dictated my father's immediate entry into the workplace as a junior executive with a leading insurance company in Manchester. My mother was his secretary. They married when he was twenty-three and she was seventeen. Today, in America, he might have been considered guilty of sexual harassment or even branded a sexual predator for corrupting a minor!

Within a short time, my father joined the Brooke Bond Tea Company where he remained for the rest of his working life. When my only brother, Clive, was born in 1926, my father was already a branch manager and the family had moved to Bebington in the Wirral of Cheshire. A few years later, he was promoted to a larger branch in Birmingham where I was born in 1934.

My father was a talented businessman and excellent manager, clearly on the fast track for further promotion. In 1937, he was sent to India on trial as a sales manager, did well, was confirmed in the post, and returned to England to collect my mother and me. We set sail for India in September 1938, exactly one year before war with Germany erupted.

Clive, who was twelve at the time, was left behind at Merchant Taylor's boarding school in Liverpool after a token father-son fishing trip in a rowboat on the Mersey River. Founded in AD 1620, the school has a distinguished academic record and several noteworthy alumni (an archbishop of Canterbury, the second engineer on the Titanic, and playwright Terence Rattigan who taught classics at the school and wrote the well-known play *The Winslow Boy*). Unfortunately, during the war years, all the talented teachers joined the armed forces, and Clive became one of a small band of boys separated and stranded from parents by the hostilities. He did not see his mother for five years or his father for seven. Apart from brief visits to his maternal grandparents, he lived, year-round, at school.

My entire childhood contains only sketchy memories of my parents. From ages five to eighteen, three-quarters of every year was spent in boarding school. The portraits my mind carries of them are vague and maybe inexact.

My father was a self-contained, reserved, and unsentimental man. He was not unkind but largely inaccessible. I cannot remember a hug or an emotionally inquisitive conversation, and he showed little interest in my academic or athletic accomplishments. Although a lifelong atheist, he was scrupulously honest and ethical but not given to social causes or philanthropy. I suspect his dour demeanor derived from a strict upbringing and rigid home life where children were "seen but not heard." He never talked about this, but my brother remembers occasional visits to the family home where he would be left alone to read *The Children's Newspaper* while the adults went about their business.

Later in his life, my father owned a motorboat he named *Sarah* after his granddaughter, and he liked to take the kids fishing. Occasionally we played golf, but he was a far better player than I and impatient with my lack of talent. He was an avid gardener who paid me to pull weeds from the lawn and collect horse manure by following the milkman's horse-drawn cart with a bucket. When I got into legal trouble on a rugby tour of Cornwall by letting air out of a taxi driver's tires, he hired a lawyer, paid my fine, and was not judgmental. I admired and respected his success in business. Eventually he became the director of world sales and a member of the board of directors. He contributed many innovative ideas to marketing, including the first use of chimpanzees. At Christmas 2003, my children gave me a framed eulogy my daughter Sarah found on the Internet describing my father's advertising accomplishments.

In perspective, my father's major contribution to my own development is probably genetic rather than personal or psychological. On the Myers-Briggs personality inventory I am an INTJ—intellectually rather than emotionally driven and on the cusp between extroversion and introversion.

My father barely outlasted his biblical quota of "three score years and ten," dying at the age of seventy-one. He outlived my mother by ten years and dwelt in comfortable retirement by the sea and close to a golf course where he played almost daily. He lived alone, cared for by a housekeeper, and had a girlfriend. One week before his death, we returned to visit him from America for the first time and were joined by Clive for a family reunion. Like so many grown children, my brother was unhappy our father had found a replacement for his mother and angry words were exchanged. A week later, after we had returned to America, Clive phoned to tell us my father had died. The housekeeper arrived in the morning to cook his breakfast and found him sitting in his armchair, facing the television, with a glass of whisky and half-smoked cigar beside him.

My mother also remains something of an enigma. Superficially, she was an outgoing, outspoken, happy-go-lucky person who was generous, kind, and loving. But she was an addictive chain smoker and closet alcoholic who kept a bottle of gin hidden behind the kitchen curtain or under the sink. My father turned a blind eye and angrily rejected Clive's suggestions she might need help. Although Alcoholics Anonymous was founded the year after my birth (1935), twenty years later alcoholism was still viewed as a moral rather than a medical issue, and medical schools found no place for it in the curriculum. All this contributed to my mother's early death at the age of fifty-six, an event in which I played a significant role. (See "Dream Doctor" in "Piece 14: Medical Education.")

Again, I have no sense that my psychological development was moderated by my mother, except in a hereditary manner. I do share her mild hysterical traits and lack of social tact. I have a liking for rum and good wine but have a severe phobia of smoking. Freud noted that children had only two opposing ways to respond to parental role modeling, "identification" (doing the same) or "reaction formation" (doing the opposite). Why alcohol would provoke the first and nicotine the second illustrates how psychoanalysis can never be a science; the same stimulus can provoke diametrically opposing behaviors.

Finally, I suspect by inference only, my mother may not have been a comfortable caretaker of babies or young children. There is a family rumor she had a backstreet abortion after Clive was born that led the police to make inquiries based on the abortionist's list of clients. (It was a crime in Britain at the time.) Perhaps I owe my existence to that.

—

All in all, I believe that, apart from heredity, my personality was shaped more by the experience of boarding school, positive and negative, than by parental modeling or home life. There was not much of either.

What's In A Name?

The further backward you can look, the further forward you are likely to see.

—Winston S. Churchill (1874-1965)

Most people are interested in their ancestors and heritage. Apart from mere curiosity is the intriguing question of whether there are recognizable personality traits passed on from one generation to another. During the first half of the last century, popular opinion tilted more toward nurture than nature. Influenced by Freud's psychoanalytic theories, the prevailing belief held that the child was father to the man, molded primarily by parents and the environment. In the next fifty years, evidence has swung back in a biological direction. We become what our genes dictate. The die is cast when sperm meets egg. Identical twins are more alike than nonidentical twins even when they are separated from each other and their parents at birth or adopted out. Family trees and genetic studies confirm that a majority of medical and mental illnesses are inherited.

Any doubt that personality traits and behavior patterns also breed true evaporated when I became a dog owner. Choosing a breed educated me to the significant differences between them. Sheep dogs herd people at cocktail parties, Labradors love to plunge into your swimming pool, hounds slip their leash to pursue a scent, bird dogs bark at crows and helicopters, corgis can be mean to kids and hate to swim. All these complex, breed-specific behaviors are manifest after puppies are separated from their litter but long before they witness any parental role modeling.

The name "Blackwell" is among the oldest on record and prominently represented in telephone directories everywhere in the world. Its lineage extends back centuries to the earliest records. The reason is not hard to find.

Family names were first derived from geographical features where people dwelt; rivers, hills, meadows, forests, and the like. Rural life in general, and agriculture in particular, demanded water; rain, rivers, and wells. There were no pipes, conduits, or sewers. Wells were ubiquitous. Often deep and sometimes dark. There are nine hamlets, villages, and small towns named Blackwell scattered through five counties in England. Their inhabitants identified themselves by coupling their given name (John, Sarah, Robert, Margery) with their place of origin. The practice of naming a person or family with a surname derived from a place is called "toponymic" by genealogists. That's from the Greek *topos*, "place" + *anoma*, "a name."

Because the Blackwell name is so old, it has been the subject of extensive genealogical research and a number of published databases. Particularly informative is the *Blackwell Newsletter* discovered by my daughter, Sarah, while at college in Canada. It was edited in Ontario by a John D. Blackwell, a doctoral student doing graduate work on Canadian, British, and Irish history. The newsletter was published once or twice a year from 1979 to 1985 and contains large amounts of information on the family name. The newsletter later joined the Guild of One Name Studies, a genealogical organization of over four hundred projects devoted to tracing individual family names. Included in the *Blackwell Newsletter* during the six years of its existence were a number of subsidiary databases as well as individual efforts to trace lineage by a large number of families from around the world.

Because place names preceded family names, the first Blackwell mentions appear in documents that list property. A convent of Blackwell was endowed by King Alhedus in AD 778, captured by the Danes, restored to the English by the Earl of Mercer, and listed by King Edgar in an inventory of church property (the Church Hundred) in AD 964. After William the Conqueror overran England (AD 1066), he compiled a census of property in the Doomsday Book which includes the village of Blackewelle.

Cited in the newsletter is the work of Lt. Commander Philip Blackwell (1899-1978) who was a member of the Society of Genealogists in London. He compiled a forty-five-page manuscript that listed all the

—

individuals with the Blackwell name in England from public records up until 1700. Over a thousand names are included; among the earliest were Galfredo de Blakewell (1272) and Margery de Blackwelle (1273).

The village of Blackewelle in the Doomsday Book gave its name to an important lineage of ancestors who built Spouston Hall in Taddington, Norfolk (close to Blackwell). Sir John Blackwell (1307-1337) was awarded a coat of arms by King Edward II that has a shield with a lion and a family motto of *Petit Ardua Virtus*: "Courage aims at hard things." In Taddington Church, there is a sixteenth-century brass of Sir Richard and Lady Agnes Blackwell. Another ancestor in this line, John Blackwell, was a "gentleman of the Board of Green Cloth to King Charles I" and high sheriff of the County of Surrey in 1657. He fathered seventeen children and his grandson, Sir Lambert Blackwell, had a distinguished career as "knight harbinger" to King William and envoy to the courts of Tuscany and Genoa before returning to England to serve as a member of Parliament and be made a baronet by King George I.

A second distinguished branch of Blackwells was located at Ampney Crucis in Gloucestershire. They too were granted a coat of arms in 1494, comprised of a shield with the image of a greyhound. This lineage led to Sir Basil Blackwell, the owner of Blackwell's Bookstore in Oxford, known as the "best-read man in England" and one of the largest book distributors and publishers in the world.

Because Britain was the hub of an empire, the Blackwell name spread quickly around the globe. Included were the adventurous, the persecuted, and the criminal element. But the first to leave were those suffering religious persecution. The Puritans first sought refuge in Holland and from there would eventually board ship for America.

In 1614, Elder Francis Blackwell assumed leadership of a group of almost two hundred pilgrims in Emden, Holland. Two years later they planned to sail to New England but were delayed finding a ship and eventually sailed in the winter of 1618, too late for a safe voyage. The ship ran off course with passengers "packed together like herrings" (*Mayflower* by Nathaniel Philbrick, Viking Press, 2006). They ran out of fresh water, disease erupted, and one hundred thirty passengers died

—

and were buried at sea, including Frances Blackwell. Only fifty reached Virginia alive. Almost two years later, the *Mayflower* set sail on September 6, 1620, and met a better fate, but without a Blackwell aboard. In 1637, the Blackwell name resurfaced in Sandwich, Massachusetts, where Sarah Warren, granddaughter of a *Mayflower* passenger, married John Blackwell.

Forty years after the *Mayflower*, Robert Blackwell arrived in New Jersey in 1661. His family had acquired Blackwell Manor in 1573, which traced its existence back to William the Conqueror. In 1676, Robert moved to New York and married Mary Manningham whose stepfather had willed her Manning's Island; formerly known by its Dutch owners as Hog's Island. Robert changed the name to Blackwell's Island and members of the clan lived, farmed, and quarried the land for the next one hundred fifty years until New York City purchased the island in 1828 for $32,500. In 1921, the name changed to Welfare Island and, finally, in 1973, to Roosevelt Island. The original Blackwell house has been restored and refurbished as an historical site.

As might be expected, the Blackwell name spread rapidly throughout the United States. American place-name records show that there are nineteen populated locations named Blackwell, a majority in Virginia (three), Missouri (two) and Georgia (two). The Blackwell name is also attached to twenty-four cemeteries, fifteen rivers, eight lakes, eight dams, and a handful of oilfields, swamps, mines, and forests as well as a glacier and a mountain.

Not surprisingly, the predominance of southern states has created an historical link to a significant African-American lineage coupled with the Blackwell name. An African-American genealogist, Thelma S. Dowell, whose mother was named Blackwell, has done considerable research on black ancestry and its origins. In 1735, a woman from Senegal named Ama was sold at a slave auction in Yorktown to Robert Blackwell. One of her descendants, Jenny, married a Sauk Indian named Mika who had no surname and so adopted Blackwell. In 1780, Samuel Blackwell of Virginia wrote a will bequeathing six named Negro slaves to his wife, Elizabeth. Just as Europeans assumed the names of places, slaves took the names of their owners.

—

There is much mundane and tedious material in the Blackwell genealogy but also some "bits" of interest and amusement. Here are a few:

When Australia was a penal colony to which England exported its criminals (until 1853), no less than sixteen convicts with the Blackwell name were transported by ship to the small island of Tasmania (home to a strange creature known as the Tasmanian devil).

Stephen Blackwell from Trenton, New Jersey, traveled as a passenger on the *Titanic*'s maiden voyage and went down with the ship in 1912. He was last seen smoking a cigar with the captain in the first-class lounge, but those who escaped reported that he and a friend were heroes who scorned seats in the lifeboats and helped others leave the sinking ship. He was the son of a former state senator and was reported to have had more life insurance than any other passenger.

Richard Blackwell, the well-known fashion designer, famous for his annual list of the "Worst Dressed Women," is not a Blackwell. He was born Richard Selzer and changed his name to further an early attempt at an acting career in Hollywood.

Jacob Blackwell served as a colonel in the Newtown militia but sided with the revolutionaries in the War of Independence. His house was confiscated by the Crown and the "privations and pecuniary losses" inflicted contributed to his early death in 1780.

The town of Blackwell in Oklahoma is named after an adopted citizen of the Cherokee nation. Many of the greyhounds seen on American tracks were bred and trained there in the Blackwell kennels. Any association with the greyhound on the English coat of arms is unclear.

W. T. Blackwell founded the town of Durham in North Carolina and built its fortunes on the Blackwell Tobacco Company, which sold the famous Bull Durham brand of tobacco in the late nineteenth century.

George Blackwell was the Catholic archpriest in England, appointed by the pope in 1598. He was serving on November 5, 1605, when Guy Fawkes and his Catholic co-conspirators attempted to blow up the

Houses of Parliament while King James I was addressing its Protestant members. Father Blackwell admonished his Catholic flock to avoid all disloyalty or violence toward the monarchy, but Guy Fawkes was tortured and burned at the stake, an event still celebrated annually with fireworks and bonfires. (See *The Gunpowder Plot* by Antonia Frazer, 1996.)

Blackwells fought on both sides in the American Civil War. After the defeat of the South, Major John Lindsay Blackwell, a Confederate cavalry officer, sought refuge in the Everglades where he was attacked by a giant alligator that he successfully fought off with a wooden pole.

A Blackwell ancestor was the co-founder of the wholesale grocery company, Crosse and Blackwell. Addicted to its well-known "Branston Pickle," I once consumed an entire jar for a bet in the junior doctors' dining room.

Otis Blackwell was a famous composer of over 1,000 popular songs that sold over 185 million copies. His hits, written for leading artists, included "Don't Be Cruel," "Return to Sender," and "All Shook Up" for Elvis Presley, "Great Balls of Fire" and "Breathless" for Jerry Lee Lewis, and "Fever" for Peggy Lee. Otis sang his songs for the performers before they were recorded and some believe his style influenced Elvis Presley's. We can claim no genetic linkage to this talent. The choirmaster wrote on my school report, "Has a good voice when he sings in tune."

The occupations of earlier Blackwells are diverse and include priests, preachers, scholars, authors, military men (including a distinguished officer in Napoleon's army and a humble archer at Henry V's battle of Agincourt), musicians, politicians, mayors, and a major league baseball pitcher.

Of personal interest are several physicians. Included is Major General William Blackwell, an Irishman who served as honorary physician to King George V. Dr. Alexander Blackwell of Scotland was a talented linguist who worked as a printer, went bankrupt, studied medicine and agriculture, and eventually became physician to the king of Sweden. Involved in an unspecified political intrigue, he was tortured, refused to confess, and was beheaded in 1747 without a trial.

—

A Famous Blackwell Clan

It's not only a man's ancestry but also what he considers his ancestry to have been that conditions his life.

—Benjamin Disraeli (1804-1881)

It is certainly desirable to be well descended, but the glory remains to our ancestors.

—Plutarch

Faced with such a numerous, diverse, and ancient ancestry makes me aware of how foolish it is to expect sufficient uniformity or consensus of character, occupation, or lifestyle to resonate with my personal or family circumstances. That is what we, who engage in genealogy, hope for. But it is highly unlikely.

From the beginning of the name Black-Welle, there have been numerous bloodlines, each with its different geologic origin and distinct genetic makeup. Every issue of the *Blackwell Newsletter* included dozens of requests seeking information about ancestors. The four hundred "single name" genealogy studies are testament to the archetypal desire for retrospective affirmation or prophetic insights. Even more confounding than this diversity is that only the heroes and villains are chosen for interest and sharing. The vast majority of ordinary folk remain unremarkable and unremarked.

Like the inkblot test in psychology, a family tree is a visual invitation to fantasy and wish fulfillment.

With that as caveat, I shall indulge myself some more; this time by selecting a single family whose accomplishments and attributes I envy enough to admire, covet, and would like to emulate.

Samuel Blackwell was born in 1790 and married his wife Hannah at Saint James Church in Bristol, England, in 1815. Both were deeply religious but also liberal and socially active. All of their nine children, boys and

—

girls, were encouraged to study mathematics, science, literature, and foreign languages as well as to participate in their parents' political and social activities. Samuel was a sugar refiner who was strongly opposed to slavery. He tried to refine sugar from beets to avoid British dependence on cane sugar grown in the slave plantations of the West Indies. When his business failed during a recession in 1832, he and his family sailed for New York on the ship *Cosmos*. They lived for several years on Blackwell's Island where Samuel attempted to reestablish his sugar business but he contracted malaria and, when his factory burned down, the family moved to Cincinnati.

The story of this family is told in several places and ways including, *Those Remarkable Blackwells* (Hays, 1963), *The Feminist Papers* (Rossi, Bantam Books, 1973), *Loving Warriors* (Wheeler, Dial Press, 1981), an autobiography by one daughter (Elizabeth), and a biography about another (Emily). The reasons for my interest in the family will become apparent but stem from their pioneer contributions to anti-slavery, feminine emancipation, and women's earliest contributions to medicine, religious ministry, and evolutionary theory. My admiration is also due, in small part, to my own family's experience and beliefs. One hundred thirty-six years after Samuel and his family immigrated to America and settled in Cincinnati in early midlife, my family and I did likewise.

The Ohio River divides the seven hills of Cincinnati from the horse country of Kentucky. In 1820, Congress approved the Missouri Compromise which extended the Mason-Dixon Line from Pennsylvania and Maryland westward along the Ohio River to the Mississippi. The original purpose of this demarcation was to resolve a boundary dispute between the states, but now it separated the slave states of the South from the free soil states of the North. When Samuel and his family arrived in 1837, Cincinnati was already a main stop on the underground railway for slaves escaping to the North. This may have influenced Samuel's decision to move there because the family continued to be involved in abolitionist and emancipation causes at a time when the oldest children were impressionable adolescents.

But, in less than a year after arriving, Samuel died of malaria at age forty-eight, leaving his wife, five daughters and four sons to fend for

—

44

themselves. Impoverished, the family survived by operating a small school out of their home.

Our story involves not only the Blackwell children but also the wives of two of the sons, Henry and Samuel Jr. Oberlin College, farther north from Cincinnati and founded in 1833, was the first institution in America to open its doors to women and blacks. It was also a station on the underground railway. It became the alma mater of Lucy Stone, who married Henry Blackwell, and her roommate, Antoinette "Nettie" Brown, who married Samuel Blackwell Jr. Both these women and their Blackwell husbands made unique contributions to the abolition and emancipation movements.

Lucy Stone was an only daughter whose father paid to educate his two sons but refused to pay for his daughter's college. He reluctantly loaned her seventy dollars to pay the first month's tuition at Oberlin College where room and board was an additional dollar a week. Lucy made do by cooking her own meals and washing dishes for three cents an hour in the Ladies Dining Hall.

When Oberlin was founded, women were not allowed to take full course work to protect their "weaker intellects." This was revoked before Lucy's time but, when she was chosen by her class to read an essay at commencement, the faculty insisted that a male professor read it for her. Lucy declined. After graduation, she became an active participant and frequent speaker in the women's emancipation and abolitionist movements, working as a salaried employee of the Massachusetts Anti-Slavery Society.

Henry Blackwell and Lucy Stone had a protracted courtship due to a number of impediments. Henry was seven years her junior, she traveled the country, incessantly speaking out for abolition and emancipation, and, most of all, she was protective of her independence. They met in 1853 in Cleveland at the Fourth Annual Women's Rights Convention where Henry was elected secretary of the convention and made a spirited speech, "The interests of the sexes are inseparably connected and in the elevation of the one lies the salvation of the other." The address was generally considered "very fine" but the *Cleveland Plain Dealer* made the snide comment, "Mr. Blackwell spoke too long. He forgot it was a women's convention." Lucy also spoke and expressed her outrage about the forced return to the South of a captured slave and she demanded that the "Union be dissolved."

Henry continued to display his devotion to Lucy and approval of her causes in practical ways. In the summer of 1854, he participated in the rescue of a young slave girl returning to the South by train with her master after the Ohio Supreme Court had ruled it was legal to free slaves passing through the state. In the South, he was indicted for kidnapping and in Memphis, a reward of $10,000 was offered for his capture, "dead or alive."

Faced with Henry's obvious devotion and persistence, Lucy capitulated, and they were married in May, 1855, but only after they read a joint declaration of protest against the contemporary marriage laws which "refuse to recognize the wife as an independent, rational being, while they confer upon the husband an injurious and unnatural superiority." Lucy kept her own name after marriage and for many years, women who did likewise were called "Lucy Stoners." When my wife, Kathie, and I were married in Cincinnati over thirty years ago, she chose to do the same.

Lucy, Henry, and their daughter, Alice, remained active in their causes throughout their lives. Lucy died of cancer in 1893 and her last words to Alice were, "Make the world better." Newspapers throughout the country remembered her as "one of the noblest women of the century." Henry continued to edit *The Women's Journal* and never missed an annual meeting of the Women's National Suffrage Association. After Henry's death in 1909, Alice continued to edit the journal until after the ratification of the Nineteenth Amendment when she organized the Massachusetts League of Women Voters.

Lucy's Oberlin roommate, Nettie Brown, had an equally distinguished career (*Great Women of Christian Faith*, Edith Deen, Barbour, 1959). Together, Lucy and Nettie founded the first women's debating society at Oberlin, which met in secret to avoid scandal and criticism. She was the first woman student in the theology class of 1850 and wrote her

—

graduation essay on the biblical injunction, "Let women keep silent in the churches." She based her exegesis on translation of the Greek word *alein*, as "inconsequential gossip" as contrasted with the serious discourse of the ancient priestesses. Like Lucy, Nettie refused to have a male professor read her essay and, as a result, she was forbidden to graduate. Nevertheless, she was ordained the first woman minister in America (perhaps in the modern world) for the Congregational Church in South Butler, New York, in September 1853 when the officiating Methodist pastor (the Congregational priest declined) preached his sermon to the text, "There is neither male nor female for ye are all one in Jesus Christ" (Galatians 3:28). Henry's brother, Samuel, visited Nettie's church at Henry's suggestion in 1854 and began a courtship that ended in marriage in 1856. Unlike Lucy, Nettie took the Blackwell name but kept Brown as her middle name.

Now that Lucy and Nettie were both married, Susan B. Anthony wrote them reproachful letters for relinquishing spinsterhood and abandoning her. Lucy wrote back, telling her not to be absurd, for, "if you were ever married, you will find there is just as much of you as before."

Nettie eventually left her church to become a Unitarian and continued a lifetime of devotion to the same causes as Lucy. In addition, she wrote a book, *The Sexes Throughout Nature* (1875), in which she challenged Charles Darwin's claim that the male was the superior of the species. She derided the lack of any psychology of womanhood and accused Darwin of using a "veneer of science" to protect "the moss-grown foundations of ancient dogma." Beyond the hyperbole was a cogent disciplined critique of Darwin's thesis about male superiority.

In some ways, Nettie's life was even more remarkable than Lucy's. She lived to be ninety-six, visited the Holy Land at seventy-six, was granted a belated doctorate of divinity by Oberlin in 1908 (at age eighty-three) and preached her last sermon at age ninety. She raised six daughters and, at the time of her death in 1921, there were three hundred ordained women in the United States. Although Samuel also espoused his wife's causes and supported her in them, he was less actively involved politically than Henry but provided more of the child and domestic care. He died in 1901 at age seventy-eight, twenty years before Nettie.

—

The Blackwell sisters were as socially and politically involved as their brothers' wives. Elizabeth Blackwell was born in 1821, the third of nine children. Like her mother and older sister, she began life as a schoolteacher helping to support the family. At age twenty-four, she returned from a teaching assignment in Kentucky to visit a friend dying from a painful gynecological disorder. The friend pointed out that her worst suffering involved the lack of a female physician and suggested that Elizabeth consider the profession. Elizabeth's immediate response was negative; "I hated everything connected with the body and could not bear the sight of a medical book." This distaste for physical contact extended to intimacy. Later in life she would admit, "Whenever I became sufficiently intimate with any individual to be able to realize what a life association might mean, I shrank from the prospect." Paradoxically, this was one factor that increased her motivation for medicine; "I felt more determined than ever to become a physician and thus place a strong barrier between me and ordinary marriage."

Also important to Elizabeth was the challenge to become the first woman to obtain a medical degree in an entirely male-dominated profession. She began the search for a school willing to take her in 1847 and was turned down by twenty-eight medical schools, including all the leading institutions, until Geneva Medical College in upstate New York accepted her, but only after the faculty asked the students to vote. (They approved, thinking it was a joke.) Faced with initial discouragement and disparagement, Elizabeth's ability and persistence won over the faculty and students and she graduated first in her class two years later.

After graduation, Elizabeth undertook a midwives' course in Paris (where an infection caused the loss of sight in one eye that prevented her from becoming a surgeon). From there, she went to London for orthopedic training where she befriended Florence Nightingale. Returning to New York in 1851, she was shunned by hospitals, refused lodging or office space, and eventually bought her own house to set up a practice for women and children. She lectured on public health and hygiene and published a book in 1852, *The Laws of Life*. The following year, she opened a public dispensary in the slums of New York and was joined by her younger sister, Emily, who had also graduated as a physician.

In 1859, Elizabeth went on a year-long lecture tour of England and became the first woman on the British Medical Register.

She returned to work in the dispensary and during the Civil War was asked by Dorothea Dix, superintendent of women nurses, to help train nurses for work with the Union wounded. Her political reply (she was now an administrator) was, "not in my hospital, but at Bellevue, so that the male surgeons may take credit."

After the war ended in 1868, Elizabeth and Emily opened a women's medical college they planned with Florence Nightingale. The following year, Elizabeth moved back to England and opened the London School of Medicine for Women. In 1875, she was appointed professor of gynecology at the London School of Medicine for Children, where she remained until her retirement in 1907. When she died in 1910 at eighty-nine, there were 7,000 women physicians in America.

Emily, Elizabeth's younger sister, was equally frustrated by the constraints of the nineteenth century feminine role; "I am full of furious bitterness at the constraint and littleness of the life I must lead." When she decided to follow in Elizabeth's footsteps, she was turned down by twelve medical schools (including her sister's alma mater) before being accepted by Chicago's Rush College in 1852. She did well in her studies, but the following year was refused permission to return because the Illinois State Medical Society was strongly opposed to women practicing medicine. She transferred to Western Reserve University in Cleveland and graduated with honors in 1854. Emily obtained further surgical and gynecological training in Scotland, London, Paris, Berlin, and Dresden before returning to America to join Elizabeth in New York.

Emily is described as a superb clinician and inspirational teacher, and both she and Elizabeth strove to practice at a standard that would inspire respect for women in the profession and stifle disapproval. Their patients were charged according to ability to pay; four dollars a week if they could afford that, and less or nothing if they could not. They began teaching programs for nurses and medical students as well as the first in-home medical social work program in the United States.

When established medical schools refused to accept their trainees, they founded and accredited their own, graduating three hundred sixty women physicians before Emily retired. Emily also died in 1910, three months after Elizabeth.

The Blackwell family members were not without their idiosyncrasies. The word "clan" conveys their lifelong closeness to one another, their voluminous correspondence (much of it published) and their fondness for family visits and joint vacations on Martha's Vineyard. But none of the five sisters married nor did their four paternal aunts. In *The Feminist Papers* Alice Rossi writes, "The Blackwell sisters showed great capacity for work but not for love." She speculates, "Their psychological antipathy toward marriage caused them to seek out careers." Both Elizabeth and Emily kept diaries and recorded their loneliness and need for family. In 1854, Elizabeth adopted a seven-year-old girl, Kitty Barry, from an orphanage. Kitty was both a companion but also a domestic helper and though she lived with Elizabeth for fifty years she never called her "mother" but only "doctor." Four other Blackwell siblings (Emily, Ellen, Henry, and George) adopted orphans, none legally. After these children were grown, all five Blackwell sisters became devoted to dogs which caused their niece, Alice (Lucy and Henry's daughter), to comment on her aunts' "hereditary tendency to an excess in dogs." Clearly, the Blackwell women craved intimacy but only within safe and asexual limits.

Our Modern Roots

The only history that's worth a tinker's damn is the history we make today.

—Henry Ford

Amateur genealogy is not an easy hobby. A family's interest in its roots is often delayed until the children grow up and ask questions about their ancestors that can't be answered, or when adults, aware of life's transience, seek a sense of permanence in their heritage. By that time, the people most likely to be a reliable source of information are often dead or have disappeared. When this happened to us in America, both sets of grandparents were deceased, my parents had also died, I was divorced, and my only remaining relative in England was my older brother, Clive.

A distinguished lineage, like the Blackwell clan, may leave behind correspondence or diaries, but most average folks find little worth communicating to posterity. In a secular society, like Britain, with dwindling church going, family Bibles or baptismal and marriage certificates issued by a priest or pastor are becoming a rarity. This leaves the government registrars to provide birth and death certificates which include skimpy information about date and place along with the father's or deceased person's occupation. The only good news is that, until the invention of cars and airplanes, families remained close to their roots. Unless, like so many Blackwells, they took ship for foreign shores.

The most we can say is that both my father's lineage (the Blackwells) and my mother's (the Dales and Arrowsmiths) have names that indicate antiquity. The families had probably lived for generations in the Manchester region of Lancashire, although the earliest birth certificate we could trace was from 1879. They were of working-class stock, but since the Industrial Revolution, public education began to interact with intelligent genes to encourage upward social mobility. My maternal grandfather manufactured raincoats and was reasonably well-off until the Second World War when the government rationed rubber, provoking him to burn down his factory for the insurance. Family myth has it that grandfather Dale's wife said she could "put the bugger in jail for his arson" if he misbehaved. I cannot recall ever meeting my paternal grandfather, but his children's birth certificates record their father's blue-collar jobs: factory warehouse foreman and commercial clerk.

Coincidences or Chromosomes?

Genealogy: Tracing yourself back to people better than you are.

—John Garland Pollard

So far, we've considered three aspects of the Blackwell genealogy. Selections from a generic overview going back over 1,500 years, involving hundreds of folks bearing the Blackwell name, an in-depth look at one famous Blackwell clan, and, finally, our family's own immediate roots.

What does it add up to? An honest answer must be "not much." The overview provided a large assortment of mostly ordinary men and women with a sprinkling of heroes and villains. The clan was inspiring and a little flawed, with no evidence that their lineage is linked to ours. Our personal, bare-bones roots are undistinguished and suggest only that we are temporarily climbing the social ladder.

Still, there are a few intriguing resonances we might cautiously point to. My wife is a modern-day "Lucy Stoner" with an independent and distinguished career in the medical field (nursing), a fierce sense of family loyalty, and a record of involvement in not-for-profit ventures that benefit the needy in society. But the genetic credit is due to the Eilers' chromosomes, not the Blackwells'. The only credit we can claim is that, like Henry and Samuel, I knew a good thing when I saw one.

Elizabeth Blackwell was the first woman physician and Nettie Brown Blackwell the first woman minister. As a physician and a late-life seminarian, I pursued both medical and spiritual pathways. But, again, half the credit belongs to the Browns, and none of the Blackwells have been first in anything (not an easy thing to be this far along in history).

My youngest son, Adam, while in medical school, enjoyed gynecological surgery and considered it a career option. But he learned from his mentor that women now dominate the field, and it is slim pickings for men. He can thank Elizabeth and Emily for that. Perhaps his genes created the impulse to follow them although they might not approve.

There does seem to be a common commitment to social justice in our two clans. In the nineteenth century, this focused on abolition and emancipation, today on a more diffuse desire to help the needy. (Unless you count abortion and pro-life.) But the modern Blackwells lean toward atheism and pro-choice. There is my work with the homeless, people with mental illness, and female prison inmates. My daughter, Sarah, is a lawyer providing help to immigrants seeking citizenship or asylum. All

—

the children, including my three sons, side with the underdog against authority (as I do) but that buys us trouble in organizational hierarchies. Not a trait that would have allowed Elizabeth and Emily to be the politically savvy administrators they obviously became.

Lastly, we are devoted to dogs but not orphans!

My conclusion is that while we can admire potential ancestors, we cannot take credit for them. We only own what we accomplish ourselves.

Poetic Postscripts

Poetry is the spontaneous overflow of powerful feelings.

—William Wordsworth

The Blackwell clan was made up of passionate people. Both Henry and his father wrote poetry, but I have not been able to find any that is published. After I wrote this prose section, I realized I had three poems relevant to its themes, two written long before I decided to write this book. The first is a haiku; the other two are written in the classical style of a Shakespearean sonnet. One is about cloning; the other concerns the vicissitudes of adoption.

Nature and Nurture

What matters most is
Kind hosts and loving homes for
Family chromosomes.

—Barry Blackwell, April 2010

Mutant Sonnet

Technologies such as human cloning have raised our awareness of the profound ethical and moral issues we face.

—Bill Joy

Published in *Perspectives in Biology and Medicine,* Vol. 30, No 1, Autumn 1986:

Life's Rosetta stone, the double helix,
Kept the secret of its hieroglyphics
Within a spiral code, until unfurled,
The pairs of matching molecules revealed
Its building blocks and templates of the mind
In elegant simplicity aligned,
Transcribing messages on R.N.A.
That replicate the past today.
Before the syntax of the cell is known
Impatient scientists who try to clone
Another Hemingway, a new Shakespeare,
May breed instead a mutant demagogue; I fear
 Genetic engineers will play roulette
 Like monkeys spelling with the alphabet.

—Barry Blackwell, 1986

Birthchoices

Adoption is not about finding children for families, it's about finding families for children.

—Joyce Maguire Pavao

Published in the *Crazy Shepherd, Poetry Circuit,* Vol. 4, No. 5, December 1984:

Birthmother

This is the product of our conception
That multiplies in fluid nurtured gloom
Outlasting love, growing to perception
Unwanted but protected in its womb.
Shall we destroy what we so briefly wrought?
Before our secret reaches other eyes?
Or shall we parent it ourselves? And ought
We live the lesson of our loving lies?
It could be cheaply done and quickly gone
Scraped clean and emptied out within a week.
There's no real pain they say, this early on.
No one will know and even we won't speak.
    But unsure lives ought never end another,
    We should seek a loving barren mother.

Adoptive Mother

You were born to us without conception
The unloved product of another womb.
Can this longed for heir to our reception
Be so deformed to make us search for whom
To blame? Your twisted genes or our dry hearts?
Were we too hopeful of our good intent?
Will extra effort mend your broken parts?
Make you the child of whom we dreamt?
When parents, brothers, sisters, church and schools
All fail to curb your hurt or build your trust.
Can tender limits, pleas or tougher rules
Give birth to love? Or lacking it we must
      Surrender you to what the world will do
      Because we nurtured you and nothing grew.

The Child

A full term failure of contraception
I was implanted in an alien womb.
I don't care who fucked whom. The deception
Taught me early on, there is no real room
In life for me. Dry breasts and unsure hands
Told me the rest. I somehow got the sense
Of early transience, like one night stands.
I grew to be a token recompense
Who fed your middle class nobility,
And purged your conscience of its social sins.
I even cured your infertility
So your real kids could grow in white clad skins.
      You wonder why I feel so black and small
      That I might one day want to end it all?

—Barry Blackwell, 1984

"Birthchoices" is a sonnet ("little song"), a form that originated in Italy in the thirteenth century and is attributed to Giacomo da Lentini. A sonnet typically has fourteen lines, each of which has ten syllables where alternate syllables are stressed and unstressed, creating a lilting rhythm known as iambic pentameter. There is also a defined rhyme scheme in which the end words of the alternating lines rhyme with each other. The last two lines are a rhyming couplet set back from the margin to provide a concluding emphasis to the poem's theme. There are occasional deviations from this strict form but probably the best known classical author is Shakespeare who wrote 154 sonnets independent of the plays, many with themes of love.

3. India

Time and Place

When my parents moved to India in 1938, taking me with them but leaving my brother behind, we settled into a large house on Short Street in Calcutta, close to the headquarters of Brooke Bond Tea Company. There were several servants, a cook, cleaners, a manservant (bearer) who went on field trips with my father, and an Indian nanny (*ayah*) who taught me to count to ten and swear in Hindi. The house was cooled by large overhead fans (*punkas*) and boiled drinking water was stored in empty gin bottles. One day I mistakenly downed a swig of gin and developed a "one trial" lifetime aversion to it. My parents soon adopted the expatriate life style of Empire: golf, bridge, mahjong, cocktail and dinner parties.

Soon after settling in, I contracted amebic dysentery. The cure, before antibiotics, was a strict diet of bananas and apples. I recovered, but my parents were advised that the city was unsafe for a five-year-old, and I was packed off to boarding school in the hills. My first school was in Darjeeling, surrounded by tea estates, close to Tibet and within sight of Mount Everest. This was a school for younger children of expatriate army officers and businessmen, and my only memories were of food. I remember a "tuck box" filled with a three-month supply of supplementary candy and cookies, kept in a locked room to which kids had supervised access once daily. The cooks occasionally served artichokes to which I developed a lifelong aversion. At breakfast we had oatmeal (a.k.a. porridge), garnished with brown sugar and a dollop of cream. I habitually consumed the oatmeal from the edge to the center, saving the best till last, until one morning a maid whipped away my almost empty plate. After that, I ate the cream and sugar first.

Later, I moved to a second school for older boys at Coonoor in the Nilgri Hills, several hundred miles south of Calcutta. My mother and I traveled three days and nights by train before she dropped me off. Three months later, she returned to take me home for the vacation. My only memory of this school is of getting into trouble with the headmaster for filling a water pistol with pee and dousing another pupil. An analyst might speculate that these selective memories reflect the transition from an oral to a genital stage of development!

During holidays, I had no friends, so I spent most of my time hanging out with adults and servants. I learned to play mahjong, sipped lemonade while they consumed Pimm's No.1, and accepted raffle tickets bought for me at the Grand Hotel during cocktail hour. I remember winning a woman's bra and throwing a tantrum. Occasionally, I amused myself painting my mother's toenails and anointing her bunions. This was when I first developed the idea of becoming a doctor. It was prescient because when I completed my psychiatric training in England, I was awarded a DPM degree, which stood for a Diploma of Psychiatric Medicine but in America was awarded for podiatric medicine!

This unusual childhood came to an unexpected end around the time of my ninth birthday. The Japanese had conquered Burma and reached Imphal, striking distance from Calcutta. Every Sunday my father drove a 1914 World War I armored car through the streets of Calcutta, preparing to repel the enemy. Occasionally he took me along for a ride before we returned home for a bacon-and-egg breakfast. The Japanese were close enough to bomb the city while we took shelter in slit trenches. This led to a decision to evacuate the women and children back to England. Mid-1943 was the turning point in the war; the Japanese were pushed back, and we began to reoccupy Burma and prepare to invade Italy. But it was also the height of the German U-boat offensive, the worst time to board ship for a month-long journey around the Cape of South Africa, out west to the Azores and over the north of Ireland to Liverpool. We traveled in convoy with destroyer escort on a Dutch mail steamer, the *Dempo*, filled with repatriated wounded soldiers. Several ships in the convoy were sunk.

—

My mother and I arrived in England to be greeted by the German V1 and V2 rockets. Just as disease made Indian cities unsafe, these weapons led to an exodus of children to the countryside. For me, this meant a return to life in boarding school until after the war ended, when I became eighteen and old enough to be drafted into the army for two years of national service.

India Redux

In 2002, Kathie and my youngest son Adam (now aged twelve), made a return trip to India so we could visit all the places I had known as a youngster. It was a magical time, during which we toured my father's business offices in Calcutta, met the man who now had his job, and, later on, at the hotel where my parents dropped me off to boarding school in Darjeeling, we fortuitously met the wife of my father's former co-director in Pakistan. Years previously, she and her husband had spent time with my parents in England.

Reprise

This India is,
and yet is not,
the place where I grew
from four to nine years old.
Transported by sea,
then trapped by war.
With peace declared
my father and the Raj
went home to England,
leaving Muslims and Hindus
to vent their sacred rage.
The jewel was sliced apart,
the crown thrown out;
Mahatma Gandhi sacrificed,
New India's gentle Oedipus.

* * *

In Calcutta, Chowringee
remains a honking concourse
dividing Banyan trees and cricketers
from crumbling concrete.
The Grand Hotel still stands,
owned now by Oberoi,
ornate as memory tells it stood
in nineteen thirty-eight.
Inside, modern trends intrude;
Jalapeno poppers, not cocktail canapés,
margaritas, not pink gin,
discotheques, not string quartets,
polite address now sir, not sahib.

* * *

In Darjeeling,
India's ceiling to the world,
tea gardens still glisten green
on the slopes of Tiger Hill.
But the boarding school
I was banished to,
a refuge from city dysentery,
has vanished.
This time a bug
travels with me
to Hotel Windemere,
keeping me in bed
before the same coal fire
that warmed my mother
when she dropped me off,
kissed, then said "good-bye,"
for three months, more or less.

* * *

In India now, everywhere,
things are mostly as they were.
Old monuments to Mogul power,
seething masses in poverty,
a brown spectrum of humanity.
Sacred cows, hens, stray curs and pigs
crammed in dusty streets,
one multicolored blur of cloth,
flesh, feather, skin and hide
pressed close to mother earth
and tightly knit together.

* * *

My present is different from my past
but India's child is much the same.

—Barry Blackwell, 2002

* * *

In grateful memory

Vernon Blackwell, 1900-1971
Nancy Valentine Blackwell, 1906-1961

* * *

The Dempo

Sixty years after my mother and I returned to England on the Dutch mail steamer, Kathie and I were on a cruise to South America on the Holland America line. At the captain's cocktail party, we met his first officer, who was Dutch, and told him the story of the *Dempo*. After dinner, we returned to our cabin to find an old photograph of the ship pushed under our door!

—

Fallout?

On the morning after September 11, 2001, I drove from Milwaukee to Madison to attend a meeting. During it, I began to have trouble with paying attention and memory and wondered if I was having a stroke. I remember nothing of the next sixteen hours but later learned I was taken by ambulance to the university emergency room and admitted to the neurology ward after a normal CT and EEG of my brain. My wife was called and spent time trying to communicate with me, but I kept repeating the same things over and over, not remembering what I had just said. I finally came to at three in the morning and found myself watching reruns on the TV above my bed of the planes hitting the Twin Towers and their eventual collapse. A nurse explained I had experienced an episode of "transient global amnesia" from which I would make a full and complete recovery apart from the residual sixteen hours of total memory loss. Later that morning, the neurologist told me this was an extremely rare but benign condition, the cause of which was unknown. It occurs only once in a person's lifetime and never repeats. It is sometimes called "Agatha Christie" syndrome because the famous British author of detective stories suffered an episode during her divorce when she disappeared for forty-eight hours and eventually "came to" in a country inn. Nobody mentioned "stress" or asked me any questions about it. Had they done so, I would have denied experiencing any. But perhaps that is the point. I have since wondered if the continuous threat of Japanese bombs, German submarines, and then German rockets, sensitized a nine-year-old mind to "play possum" in response to sudden unpredictable overwhelming trauma later in life. It's an untestable hypothesis.

Jay Bhore

My acquaintance with India was extended in an unexpected manner after we moved to Milwaukee in 1980. As the academic chairman of psychiatry at an inner city hospital, I experienced the conventional "town and gown" competitive relationship with psychiatrists making their living in private practice at the same institution. Would the faculty upstage them, outwit them, and edge them out of practice? Why did the administration appear to cater to our needs and wishes more than to theirs when they brought in the paying patients while faculty took care of the poor and indigent? Would people prefer our services because we taught and published? Would the young residents we trained become their future competitors?

An exception to these unwelcoming attitudes was a five-foot, wiry, hyperactive Indian psychiatrist. As soon as he knew about my childhood in his mother country, he befriended me. Jay Bhore worked long hours and took all comers at any hospital that needed or welcomed him. (Not all did.) Before long, he invited Kathie and me to an Indian dinner at his home, cooked by his wife, Mary, a former social worker he met and married in Chicago. An inveterate and unstoppable raconteur, Jay told his life story. He was born in a small rural village in mid-India, into the "untouchable" caste. Jay grew up in a mud-and-straw hut outside the village wall, destined for his predetermined life task of removing the Brahmin upper caste night soil and waste. Fortunately, he attended a school run by Christian missionaries for outcasts, where his native intelligence and energy quickly asserted themselves. First, he went to nursing school and then to medical school, finally working for the Indian government as a surgeon.

Like many Indians in the days of the British Empire, Jay learned to speak English, and his medical education was from texts in that language. This enabled him to move to England for further training, then to Canada and finally to Chicago. When he was unable to obtain American accreditation in surgery, he switched to residency training in psychiatry and then moved to Milwaukee to practice.

Jay was contemporary in age to my father, born around 1900 and, despite lifelong diabetes, he lived to be over a hundred, into the early twenty-first century. Jay's practice thrived and since the couple lived an austere Christian lifestyle, he quickly accumulated a sizeable fortune together with a large life insurance policy. Jay placed his wealth in a not-for-profit foundation dedicated to supporting the poor and untouchables in his native and surrounding small villages. His brother in India assessed the local needs and distributed the foundation's earned interest.

—

As I listened to Jay's stories and learned of his philanthropic intentions, I became attracted to the idea of helping him achieve them. Every week, for almost a year, we met in his living room where I listened to his stories and then translated the oral tradition into written form. Eventually the stories were published by a vanity press in a book entitled *Untouchables of God.*

I also joined the board of the Bhore Foundation in America to help manage the 501(c)(3) and its resources. This had a less happy outcome. Despite Jay's remarkable life story, he was capable of making bad or stubborn choices and cutting corners in his drive to achieve goals. The Bhore Foundation and its 501(c)(3) were poorly thought through; mismanaged by an incompetent and perhaps dishonest attorney, they were soon out of compliance with IRS regulations. Jay avoided or ignored the board's input and alienated his family in India who would have obviously preferred to inherit his wealth. Until Jay, and eventually Mary, developed dementia, matters were mostly covered up until after Jay's death when his estate and the foundation ended up in federal court and were placed under legal administration to bring it into compliance with IRS guidelines. A new board was convened and new problems emerged. None of its members, except me, had ever visited India or were familiar with its problems, language, or customs. Communication with the Bhore family and its foundation in India was difficult, and compliance with IRS regulations even more difficult, particularly in the wake of September 11 and caution about international transfer of funds. In addition, the stock market and real estate collapse eroded the assets of the foundation and hindered sale of Jay's property.

Faced with these difficulties and the lack of understanding in India of IRS constraints, I and one other board member flew to India for a week to conduct a site visit of the villages and ongoing projects. We arrived at monsoon time, which this year was mercifully late. My childhood experience of India was based on upper-class, wealthy city living; this time I saw India from the bottom up, a poor rural area two hundred miles south of Bombay in the midst of a transition from agrarian to an industrial culture with strong residual religious tensions between Christians and Hindus as well as the various castes.

—

We were welcomed by Jay's nephew, both an entrepreneur and minister, married to a school principal and with two lively teenage children, all of whom spoke fluent English. Pradeep had already established a school of nursing, some of whose students were recruited from the local villages in the region. We toured the school, met with faculty and students, and then visited three of the villages, including Kavalpur, where Jay was born.

The foundation had established a highly innovative program throughout the twenty or so villages. In each village, a woman inhabitant had been identified to fulfill three tasks. First, to find every child in the village who failed to attend school or had dropped out and persuade both parents and teachers to enroll them as soon as they learned to read and write. This was accomplished by classes of ten or more children held each afternoon on the mud floor of a village hut. We were welcomed by the children with flowers, examples of their work, and prepared speeches, followed by group photographs.

The second task was to identify any child or adult in need of medical treatment, advice, or rehabilitation and link them to a government-run clinic. We met with several villagers, from a woman in need of birth control advice to an open-heart patient for rehabilitation.

The third objective was to ensure that all teenage girls attended classes and talks at the nursing school on marriage, child rearing, birth control, and women's legal rights and protections.

The women responsible for these three tasks, including teaching the literacy classes, were paid five dollars a month!

In one village, we were invited to a meeting of the village elders (all men) and visited their Hindu temple followed by a welcoming party in the village hall, ending with a ceremony at which we were crowned with a colorful honorary turban!

At the conclusion of our visit, we developed plans and protocols to ensure better communication and agreement on future goals which included the need for a small hospital with enough beds to train the nursing students and ensure accreditation.

—

On our return, it was impossible for me not to be aware of the discrepancy between the efforts and accomplishments in India and the functions of the board in America where the assets were continuously drained by legal and brokerage fees. We met once every three months, sometimes for only an hour, and paid ourselves each $200 every time. My personal conviction was that Jay, albeit out of the kindness of his heart, had stubbornly created an unworkable and unjust system of control that frustrated and obstructed the family in India from achieving its goals. If he had received better or more competent legal advice or had lived long enough to recognize the accomplishments in India, Jay might have bequeathed his estate (worth two to three million dollars) directly to his heirs.

I am not a fan of not-for-profit boards. Members are often seeking to pad a resume with charitable causes, seldom want to work hard, and frequently are out of touch with the benefactor's original intentions or misinterpret them to fit their own ideology. At the first board meeting after our return, I suggested that our site visit had confirmed the integrity and goals of the Bhore family in India and that it was not too late to dissolve the 501(c)(3) in America and distribute the remaining assets to the Bhore Foundation in India. The board declined, and I resigned.

Quick Thinking

Like many raconteurs, Jay's anecdotes were retold often and elaborated on equally often, usually in minor ways. Here is one I heard several times and always enjoyed. Though the setting and dialogue might differ, Jay's quick wit and clever mind never varied. This version is told in *Untouchables of God* (2002). It takes place after Jay and Mary's return from Canada to the United States and, this time, places the event during his psychiatric training as a resident in Chicago, before he moved to Milwaukee.

> I'd been told to do a mental status exam on a 70-year-old delusional man just admitted to the inpatient ward. When I entered his room I first noticed the patient's stance—he stood with his back to the wall, keeping the bed between us. He seemed engrossed with the partially opened suitcase on the mattress in front of him.

"I'm Dr. Bhore," I said. "What can I do to help you?"

"You can return my wife, that's what!" he rasped. "Bring her to me!"

"Your wife? Sir, I don't . . ."

He reached into his suitcase and with one smooth motion produced a sawed-off shotgun and aimed the muzzle between my eyes. I was looking down the barrel of a cannon. I felt a bead of perspiration snaking down my neck. He was going to blow my brains out.

"Sir, your wife . . . I'll bring her to you immediately . . . but only I know where she is. If you kill me you'll never see her again."

I darted from the room, called a security guard, and ran from the hospital.

4. Boarding School

The Institution

Life was hierarchical and whatever happened was right. There were the strong, who deserved to win, and there were the weak, who deserved to lose and always did, everlastingly.

—George Orwell, in *Such, Such Were the Joys*

The boarding school is an institution invented to cater to the English upper class. Its alternative name, "public school," is a misnomer. Never intended for the public at large and certainly not funded from the public purse; the name contrasts communal learning at a distance from home to the private tutoring of privileged heirs in their ancestral homes. Because the intellectual and pedagogic elite were rare and often confined to religious cloisters, it was more practical for pupils to commute even if this meant separation from home and paying a premium for "room and board."

The goal of these schools was to ensure that these scions of the aristocracy and nobility rubbed shoulders with their peers, were educated to enter university, and tutored in a disciplined environment, protected from sowing adolescent wild oats.

Over time, this gold standard depreciated as peripubertal boarding school became an aspiration of the middle classes moving up the social scale. Public schools morphed into "major" and "minor" based on reputation, antiquity, and cost. Major, like Eton and Harrow, minor, like the schools I attended. But, like most social institutions, boarding schools would not have survived unless they were successful in achieving their goal of graduating alumni who became priests, lawyers, doctors, politicians, and civil servants.

The earliest known public school, and still in the upper echelon, is King's School in Canterbury. Its origin is tenuously attributed to Saint Augustine from the time of his arrival in England in AD 597. It was more formally founded in 1541 by King Henry VIII after he separated from Rome, founded the Anglican Church, and disestablished the monasteries. Perhaps as recompense, he endowed fifty "King's Scholars" and the school became closely aligned with Canterbury Cathedral and its archbishop. By way of contrast, my own "minor" public school, Kent College, was situated two miles away on the hill looking down on the city and its cathedral.

In the nineteenth century, many minor public schools fell into disrepute. When Charles Dickens wrote his third novel, he situated its central character, Nicholas Nickelby, as a pupil at Dotheboys Hall, an all-male boarding school with its tyrannical headmaster, Wackford Squeers. Preparing for the novel, Dickens visited several of the more infamous schools, and in the preface, he describes them as "traders in the avarice, indifference, or imbecility of parents and the helplessness of children . . . to whom few considerate persons would have entrusted the board and lodging of a horse or dog." This harsh opinion is echoed by George Orwell, who described his own experience of boarding school in the quotation from his essay, *Such, Such Were the Joys,* at the beginning of this piece.

To be fair, there are also idealized and idyllic accounts of boarding school derived from biographical sources. In *Goodbye, Mr. Chips,* written in only four days by James Hilton in 1934 (the year of my birth), the novel is set during wartime when Mr. Chips comes out of retirement to replace the teachers called up during World War I. The plot is based on the author's own experiences as a pupil at the Ley's School in Cambridge (my Cambridge roommate's alma mater). The story had great popular appeal and was made into a film in 1939 (when Robert Donat won the

—

Academy Best Actor Award for his lead role) and again in 1963 (when Peter O'Toole won the Golden Globe Best Actor Award).

Dead Poets Society, written by Tom Schulman, was also based on personal experience of his prep school in Nashville, and it too became a film in 1989. (Robin Williams was nominated for both the Academy and Golden Globe Best Actor Awards.)

The existence of such vividly contrasting views of all-male boarding schools, from punitive to redemptive, suggests they may reflect archetypal themes of childhood, puberty, and adolescence. Preeminent among them is the teenage struggle for individuation and the significance of good or evil role models in its successful accomplishment. My own experience matches this point and counterpoint in the two boarding schools I attended in England between 1944 and 1952.

In 1943 and 1944, after returning from India, my mother and I spent a brief spell at my Grandfather Dale's house in Manchester. My mother and her sister, Molly, kept house for their father after their mother died in 1942. I soon acquired a Lancashire accent, was learning very little at the local council school, and the German rockets continued to land around us. This became adequate reason to seek a safe and socially acceptable boarding school in the countryside, but we had no idea how to choose one. In *Nicholas Nickelby,* Dickens describes the seductive prose used by Wackford Squeers, luring parents to send their children, "Youth are boarded, clothed, booked, furnished with pocket money, provided with all necessities, instructed in all languages, living and dead." Knowing, as I do, the outcome of our choice, it is only fair to say that my mother delegated the final decision to her ten-year-old son.

I chose Chard School in Somerset. It was founded in 1671 by William Syme, a local squire and landowner "for the education and bringing up of youth in virtue and good learning." Among its earliest alumni was the Duke of Monmouth, illegitimate son of Charles II. He aspired to the throne, led the Monmouth Rebellion against the king, and was defeated and beheaded on July 15, 1688. Despite its ancient origin, Chard did not become a public school until 1890, and it closed in 1971 to become a day prep school for young children.

—

When I arrived at Chard in September 1944, the war was still going on, the best teachers were all gone, there was no Mr. Chips, and the school was run by an eccentric, middle-aged bachelor with a shiny bald head who the boys nicknamed "Peanut." He had turned his study into a playroom for the younger boys, and he seemed to enjoy bathing them at bedtime, an activity that might arouse concerns today if anybody was looking. The classrooms were cold, stone-walled enclosures with oak beams, filled with ancient wooden desks on which generations of bored pupils had carved their initials. Absent any visible adult supervision, discipline was imposed by older boys named "prefects" who were empowered to cane anyone for whatever they considered an infraction. Those selected to undergo this ritual (I was a frequent participant), formed a line on the dark uncarpeted stairwell that led to the prefect's study. Called forth, we entered the room one at a time, bent over, received the punishment, and left quickly to conceal any tears from those behind us.

Cruelty spread like a contagion in this environment. I recall a tall spindly youth with an obvious developmental handicap who was a regular subject of torture. One day, some older boys tied a rope under his armpits, hauled him off his feet, and suspended him from a wooden beam while he begged for mercy. I was not a popular child; my nickname (we all had one) was "Inkwell." I received my share of bullying, and it was not long before matters came to a head when I was buried up to my neck in the school "Victory Garden"—a plot of land behind one of the classrooms where boys were encouraged to grow vegetables to supplement wartime rations. After I extricated myself, I wrote and mailed a letter home asking to be rescued. Next day, feeling like a coward, I sneaked out to the post office with just enough money to send a telegram to my mother that read, "Don't open letter written in red ink." Naturally she did, she came, took me home to Manchester, and next time my parents picked the school.

In September 1945, the war was over and I began a seven-year stint at Kent College, Canterbury. I never asked how my parents chose this school, but it was a wise decision. A Methodist school, founded in 1885, it was originally named "Wesleyan College" after Charles and John Wesley. By the time I arrived, it had changed its name and achieved minor public school status. It had an excellent principal and mostly competent teachers with a diverse student body, many from overseas.

—

All boarding schools conform more or less to a common prototype. The students are segregated in "houses," each with its own dormitories that sleep from ten to thirty boys of a similar age. Each house has its own name (at Kent College they were the English royal houses: Windsor, Neville, and Godwin) and each is presided over by a housemaster (usually a bachelor). The houses compete with each other in sports and social events. Baths were taken and clean clothes distributed twice weekly in rotation. The day is divided into routine segments announced by bells: wake up, mealtimes, class periods, evening homework time, and bedtime. Chapel was twice a day. Wednesdays and Saturdays were half days with afternoons devoted to team sports. Sundays were for church attendance; pupil's choice in the morning (Methodist, Anglican, Jewish, etc.) and school chapel in the evening. Sunday afternoon was divided into writing letters home followed by free time for walks. All the teachers were male, and the only female on site was the matron who usually wore a starched apron and cap. Discipline was maintained by older boys appointed as prefects and consisted of a point system for minor infractions (talking in line, being late, untidy appearance, etc.). The points were added up weekly and posted on the school notice board if they exceeded a threshold, resulting in detention. (Sitting silently at a desk for an hour or more depending on the point total.) Meals were served three times daily to a rather predictable menu, with pupils seated at tables for twelve, each supervised by a prefect. In addition to sports, there was voluntary participation in a school choir, school orchestra, and annual plays. Boys were allowed to go into town with permission from the housemaster on Saturdays when pocket money was also distributed.

I flourished academically and athletically in this environment. It was predictable, orderly, and reasonably benevolent. I became an excellent student, well toward the top of each class and, at age fourteen, passed the national junior certifying exams with credits and distinctions. My only failure was in carpentry class where my innate (lifelong) clumsiness caused me to weep at an inability to produce a straight mortise and tenon joint. On the playing fields, I excelled at rugby, field hockey, swimming, and athletics, becoming the school captain in each of these sports. Eventually, I was chosen as the head prefect responsible for much of the discipline and minor administrative tasks affecting student life.

This is the kind of outcome that perpetuates the British public school system but not without some hidden costs. Based on my experience and the literature, there are good and bad schools. Some of the bad can be attributed to poor administration and inadequate teachers, particularly in wartime when the rationale is more toward safety than academic excellence. But there are other subtler, psychological influences that can damage some children in less obvious ways.

George Orwell implies that boarding school can segregate the strong from the weak, accentuating assets but worsening weakness. Boarding school is competitive, but so is life in general and in a family. At home, siblings compete for parental approval; in boarding school for peer and teacher acknowledgement. Perhaps it is more persistent, less personal, and less benevolent in the school setting. Despite personal success, I made no close friends in boarding school, and I doubt any of my teachers loved me. Some children need love to thrive. It is more often, but not always, available at home than it is in boarding school.

Age must also be a factor in the cost-benefit equation of boarding school. Particularly in America, it is common to hear school or university referred to as "alma mater." This means "a source of nourishment," or, more literally, "generous mother." A rebellious adolescent may well find school preferable to home and discover nurturing qualities in peers or staff not perceived in parents. But a five-, or even nine-year-old, separated in the same way does not have the emotional capacity to absorb the change or loss of parents and may react to boarding school with anger or sullen withdrawal. I may not have been in an emotional position to benefit from the first three boarding schools I attended, but did it matter? I caught up in the end. I believe it matters in only one way. As an adult, I have suffered from incapacity to tolerate abandonment—real or perceived. As a psychiatrist, I am painfully aware of the difference between insight and behavior change—knowing what the problem is versus doing something constructive about it. This particular vulnerability was laid down at a sufficiently young age that my adult reactions are so strongly reflexive, they are sometimes impervious to reason. So for about twelve to twenty-four hours I feel so bruised and hurt, I become sullen and withdrawn—we call it a "micropsychosis"—and I learned to wait it out. All in all, it's not a big price to pay for an excellent education!

The last flaw in boarding school education is the most obvious, the least discussed, and may no longer be an issue. Until the mid-1970s, almost all boarding schools were single-sex. Kent College became coeducational in 1975, and most others are now the same. There are two aspects to this, one far more important than the other. The absence of a feminine presence in life, at any stage, is a severe deprivation for intellectual and emotional reasons. As we live in an increasingly gender-equal environment, understanding one another is more and more significant for respectful, collaborative lives. Living in a family without sisters, separated from my mother for long periods, and confined to all-male schools most of my early life constituted both a handicap and a deprivation.

Less important now (but not then) is the sexual aspect. Awareness began as "wet dreams" (a.k.a. nocturnal emissions) and soon demanded more active relief. "Special friendships" are always a possibility in single-sex environments (prisons, convents, boarding schools) but they were never for me (this was just another form of intimacy I shunned). All my activities were solitary and required only access to the illegal trade in nudist magazines (pornography was an adult entertainment, and the Internet was not yet invented). It wasn't harmful, but I did feel guilty and realized it was "abnormal." Only after I became a psychiatrist did I learn that until well into the twentieth century, most of my profession believed that masturbation caused schizophrenia. To my credit, I decided to confront the difficulty with the headmaster and requested official approval to date a local girl. This was someone I had flirted harmlessly with outside the school boundaries on Sunday afternoon walks. The headmaster was surprisingly tolerant, perhaps because I was now the head prefect. He agreed, subject to my parents' approval in writing, and his knowledge of the girl's name. During the summer vacation, I invited Margaret to make a day trip from Canterbury to London to meet my parents and submitted her name to the headmaster. Unfortunately our friendship was brief, which meant I had to submit another name soon afterward! Several years later, at an alumni meeting, I learned Margaret had married a fellow prefect, and they were now the parents of several children.

Boarding School Poetry

Everything here measures; weight, effort, sin—and everything costs in this seclusion . . .

—Claudia Emerson, "All Girls School"

There is a substantial genre of poetry about boarding school. W. H. Auden, who attended Gresham's School in Norfolk, published his first three poems, anonymously, in the school magazine at age fifteen (discovered posthumously). His later autobiographical comments tell how boarding school and its "honor code" shaped his worldview and sexuality. Claudia Emerson, the Pulitzer Prize winner for poetry in 2006, published her latest book, *Figure Studies* (2008), which begins with twenty-five lyrical poems about a boarding school for girls based on her own experiences (cited above.)

Here are two unpublished poems of mine. The first is a narrative poem describing the events you have read in prose form:

Boarding School

Parents learn
On the job,
Too late to return
Kids they don't enjoy.

Kids they'd like to sell
Or send away.
Out of sight, out of mind,
Don't ask, don't tell.

I was four the year
Dad went to India,
Taking Mum and me,
Leaving Clive behind.

My older brother,
Alone in boarding school,
Bereft, expecting us
To come back soon.

Instead of that,
War erupted;
It trapped us,
Half a world apart.

So he waited
More than five years,
From '38 to '43
Before we reunited.

In Calcutta, a year later,
Amebic dysentery
Escaped the gutter
And attacked my gut.

Before antibiotics;
Apples, bananas,
Pediatric narcotics,
Achieved a cure.

When schools sprouted
For army brats and invalids,
Parents uprooted kids
To tea estates, safer places.

The train traveled
Through rural stations,
Three days and nights
To its destination.

We kissed farewell
My mum and me,
Goodbyes which spelled
Three months apart.

When Japan took Burma,
Then bombed Calcutta
They sent us home in '43
Just Mum and me.

Aboard a troop ship,
We dodged U-Boats,
Rounded Good Hope,
Docked at Liverpool.

Nazi V1 and V2 rockets
Greeted us, creating
A new rationale
For boarding school.

A sixteenth century
Stone antiquity, staffed
By military rejects
And sadistic prefects.

Bullies buried me alive
In Victory garden soil;
I survived, my parents
Found a better place.

At that enlightened
Minor public school,
I didn't just survive,
I thrived at everything.

Head Prefect, captain
Of every major sport,
Thirsty to learn,
Tutored for University.

My older brother
Served the Queen,
In war, Royal Marine,
In peace, Colonial police.

The moral of my tale,
When all is told;
Parents may get it right,
Kids may feel they failed.

—Barry Blackwell,
April 2010

Happily Ever After

Widowed solitude spread in her
like a virus breeding resistance.
She sold the cows, the fields, the farmhouse
down to their antique silver spoons.
Beggared, persuaded by the culture,
she bought five years of boarding school.
As the train shuffled out, she shouted,
"Be good, I love you dearly, son."
Bereft, feeling alone, he doubted that.

Her sacrifice minted tougher coin
in all male routines, incessant bells,
cruel classrooms, muddy football fields.
Calloused, his ambition seeded
inside a carapace. He left equipped
to climb the twisted vine of business.
There was plain terror on the way up
plotting takeovers, forcing mergers,
toppling corporate giants. He reached the top.

Past forty, he paused. Eligible, unwed,
her provider and protector.
Only hers. A fairy tale come true.
Safe at last, united with a man,
expressing joy not felt before,
she flung her arms about his neck
but sensed the reflex pulling back
and looking deep into his face
she softly said, "Don't you love me, Jack?"

—Barry Blackwell, circa 1990

This poem was written almost twenty years ago, probably for one of my first poetry classes. It comes more from the heart and the gut than from the head.

5. In Time Of War

Men at Arms

Wars may be fought with weapons but they are won by men.

—General George S. Patton

Members of my immediate family participated in World War I (my Grandfather Dale in France and my father, briefly, in Ireland during "the troubles"), World War II (my Uncle Ewart), and the Korean War (myself). My grandfather survived three years of trench warfare in France and was wounded twice, my uncle Ewart (my father's younger brother) died for his country in North Africa, and I never saw a shot fired in anger but left the army wiser than when I was recruited. Here are the stories:

Grandfather

Frederic Dale was working as a midlevel executive in the Cavalier Waterproof Company in Wigan, Lancashire, when he volunteered to join the Manchester Regiment as an infantryman and private on August 26, 1914. He lied about his age in order to be able to enlist, claiming to be only twenty-six when he was thirty-five. He left behind his wife, Annie, my mother, Nancy (aged eight), and her sister, Molly (aged four). His recruitment papers state he was enlisted for "three years, unless the war lasts longer." It did.

In less than a month, he was promoted to lance corporal and after another month to corporal. His battalion sailed for France on July 15, 1915, with thirty officers and 975 other ranks. Three years later, over a thousand had died and countless others were gassed or wounded. Grandpa Dale was wounded for the first time, in the stomach, six months after arriving in France, was promoted to lance sergeant a month later and full sergeant in April 1916. He was wounded for the second time in 1916 and commissioned in the field as an officer in May 1917, reaching the rank of captain before he resigned his commission and was discharged on November 15, 1918, a few days after the armistice with Germany was signed. My grandfather never spoke openly about his military service although he was quite close to my brother, Clive, during the years our parents were in India. We know he was awarded three medals, the 1914-1915 Star, the British War Medal, and the Victory Medal. Perhaps his major accomplishment was that he served in every rank from private to captain and survived an astonishing rate of attrition in the trenches. My brother tells a tale of uncertain authenticity suggesting my grandfather, based on his civilian occupation, was responsible for the design of the waterproof cape that soldiers also used as a ground sheet in their bell tents, laying them side by side with the neck toward the center pole, thus creating a dry floor for the squad to sleep on.

I only got to know my grandfather for the short time we lived with him in Manchester after we returned from India when, after his rubber factory burned down, he worked as an accountant at a local Royal Air Force establishment. Clive joined us for a few months after leaving boarding school and served in the local Home Guard before enlisting in the Royal Marines in May 1944. I recall he amused me by firing a round from his 303 Lee Enfield rifle through a dustbin lid in our backyard!

After the war had ended and India gained independence from Britain in 1952, my father returned home. My aunt Molly insisted it was her sister's turn to care for Grandpa Dale, but by now we lived in London, opposite Lord's Cricket Ground and close to my father's office headquarters. Grandpa's hygiene had deteriorated (like my mother, he was fond of liquor; in his case, port) and his aim for the toilet was erratic. My father, unsentimental and pragmatic as usual, declined to have him move in with us but paid for him to live in a nursing home in Tunbridge Wells, close to

Molly but a safe distance away and somewhere we never visited. He died at the age of seventy-seven of a pulmonary embolus, a complication of prostate cancer, two days short of my twenty-second birthday. My mother had his ashes buried beside her mother's grave in Manchester.

Uncle

My Uncle Ewart was eleven years younger than my father and aged twenty-eight when war with Germany began in September 1939. He was engaged to his fiancée Lillian, and a formal wedding had been planned but was abandoned for a quick, quiet ceremony before he joined his reserve army unit in Yorkshire—the Forty-Fifth Battalion (Leeds Rifles) of the Royal Tank Regiment. The Leeds Rifles were formed in 1859 at a time when there was the strong fear of a French invasion and the plentiful recruits were obliged to buy their own rifle and uniforms as well as to pay one guinea (a coin worth a pound and a shilling) for the privilege of joining up. The Tank Regiment was formed in 1936 and equipped with Valentine tanks in which they trained for two years until, in May 1942, they were inspected by King George VI before embarking for North Africa. Somewhere along the way, the outdated Valentine tanks went astray and were replaced by modern Sherman tanks. Ewart was the gunner in one of the sixteen tanks in "A" squadron, commanded by Major Flatow, who was subsequently awarded the Victoria Cross at El Alamein for "an example of leadership and bravery that inspired the whole battalion."

General Montgomery had set zero hour for the battle of El Alamein to commence at 2200 hours on October 23, 1942. An enormous artillery barrage signaled the start of the battle. The Germans were equipped with 88-mm anti-tank guns that were accurate and lethal. The Forty-Fifth Battalion's advance was blocked, and they were forced to retire behind "Kidney Ridge." Two days later, they had regrouped and began to engage the enemy at 11:30 a.m. on October 25. The Germans had tapped into the British radio frequencies and were taunting the tank crews in mock English accents, "It's the Forty-Fifth—they come from Lancashire and Yorkshire . . . they can't do anything against the German artillery . . . these 88 mm are so accurate . . . I don't know what they're fighting for." Ewart's tank was in reserve behind "Snipe Ridge" but

—

the Sherman tanks had high turrets that created an easy target for the German artillery. What happened next is described by Major Flatow in the official regimental history:

> We were killing Germans for the first time but unfortunately they were also trying to kill us—the first squadron casualty was from the ricochet of a dud shell which bounded along the ground at an angle and took off Corporal Blackwell's leg. Now Corporal Blackwell had just come back to No. 3 Troop from Headquarters Troop at my request and he was a first-class man, in fact he had been in A Squadron since Farnley Park and I had promoted him to Corporal. I will never forget this poor fellow being wounded. I was up on the ridge in Attila [Major Flatow's tank] drinking a cup of tea my driver had made by revving up the engine to boil our tin on the exhaust when Sgt. Bell came in through the cupola on top of me (the shelling was very heavy now) and nearly spilt my tea. He was in a hell of a state, as pale as death, and told me what had happened. I got hold of the Colonel on the air and he called the Medical Officer. Apparently Blackwell had also been "brewing up" tea when the dud shell came in at an angle and hit him when he was standing near Captain Daniels behind their tank. Blackwell died the next day, October 26, at the Company Clearing Station.

Ewart's grave is in the El Alamein War Cemetery at Mersa Matruh, west of Alexandria, which contains 7,239 burials of which 814 are unidentified. His grave reference number is XI.D.8. A major goal of the North African campaign was to protect access to the Suez Canal. In 1950, my father visited Port Said on business and took my mother and me along. It was the closest we came to Ewart's final resting place, but I cannot recall his name being mentioned.

So I have a grandfather who survived three years of brutal trench warfare in World War I and an uncle who was among the first to die in the battle most consider to have been the turning point in World War II. My own army career was more mundane and free from danger though it lasted longer.

—

Myself

I was drafted in 1952 after completing high school and during the Korean War. Cambridge University had deferred my admission until I completed my military obligation, a policy designed to allow a student to mature. Although I might have applied for officer training in the infantry, I decided the Royal Army Medical Corps (RAMC) was more relevant, and I was posted to Aldershot for boot camp. Within a couple of weeks, I was promoted to "local, acting, unpaid lance corporal" and assigned the duty of writing letters home on behalf of several illiterate men in my squad.

I was an ungainly soldier, clumsy and uncoordinated with a lopsided stance which drove our drill sergeant crazy. I was unable to get my boots to shine (perhaps my spit was defective) and bribed a fellow soldier to buff them. But I did learn to sew on buttons and produce razor-sharp creases in my khaki uniform.

After a few more weeks, I was approached by the sergeant in charge of unit athletics who informed me that the RAMC was in the finals of the army novices boxing championship. Would I be willing to box heavyweight? I had never boxed in my life, but the inducement was a forty-eight-hour weekend pass to return home. The rules of amateur boxing are an invitation to recruit cannon fodder. A team is awarded two points for a win and one point for putting a fighter in the ring but no points for failure to find a willing sacrifice. The good news is that the contest only lasts for three two-minute rounds. This limits the risk of damage which, in the heavyweight division, is not inconsiderable. I accepted and was knocked out in the first round after a few clumsy jabs.

Shortly after I had returned from my weekend reward and recovered from concussion, the trainer approached me again. The RAMC was also in the real (not novices) final, and would I oblige again? We would be fighting the Royal Army Ordinance Corps, and I would be matched against a man named Henry Cooper. I agreed and returned to tell my fellow squad members the news. A few of them were acquainted with boxing, and after a hushed silence, I learned that Henry Cooper was a first-class opponent (he subsequently became the world heavyweight champion). Fortunately fate intervened. Henry was boxing for the British against the German Army, and I would face his backup.

The fight was scheduled in a vast auditorium in the center of Aldershot before several thousand spectators. The bell rang, and I backpedaled fast enough to survive the first round, but the crowd, disappointed at my abject cowardice, began to boo. I came out swinging wildly and missed, and the next thing I knew I was flat on the canvas, the count was over, and so was my brief boxing career.

When I graduated from boot camp, it was time to choose a military job and undergo further training. I decided on "hygiene assistant," the army's polite designation for a civilian sanitary inspector. There were several attractions. After graduating, you were given a motorcycle and promoted to corporal. The job involved travel to inspect cookhouses and latrines in different military installations. Training included the detection and elimination of infestations (rats, cockroaches, fleas), the nuances of waste disposal, the construction of field latrines, and the mechanism of water closets.

After three months, I was relieved not to be posted to Korea but to the reserve army training camps on Salisbury Plain, close to Stonehenge. Each month, I visited about ten camps, wrote detailed reports, and dropped them off at Headquarters Southern Command in Wilton, a famous carpet weaving community close to Salisbury and its magnificent cathedral. The town dates from the eighth century and the carpet industry from 1741 when the Earl of Pembroke imported two French weavers to teach their trade to the local craftsmen.

The officer to whom my reports were directed was a crusty, ginger-haired, Irish colonel who was the deputy director of army health for Southern Command. Colonel Keatinge took an immediate liking to me. I believe he approved of having an assistant who was a rugby-playing future medical student. So he offered me the job with an automatic promotion to sergeant and a comfortable room of my own in the brand-new sergeant's mess where I was the only drafted, nonregular army occupant. My job was to serve as his secretary-assistant which required I learn to type—a skill, like bicycle riding, which lasts a lifetime and stood me in good stead when computers arrived on the scene twenty years later.

I still have my discharge papers (Army No. 22727636) which include the following handwritten reference from Colonel Keatinge:

> Sgt. Blackwell has served directly under my command as my assistant at Command Headquarters. During that time he has given me the most valuable, loyal service. He very quickly picked up the extra knowledge required. He is a man of pleasing appearance, tall, strong and of marked personality. He has a very pleasant, correct manner and is easy to work with. Keen, hard working, with an elastic mind he uses initiative governed by common sense and is equal to any problems that may arise. He plays an excellent game of rugby.

This ended my draft experience but not my military career. I rejoined the medical corps after I graduated as a doctor and received my commissioning document signed by Queen Elizabeth II. I served as a medic in a reserve army field ambulance for five years until I emigrated to the United States when I resigned with the rank of major, having served in every rank below that in the British Army (like my grandfather before me).

I have spoken to many men in both Britain and America about their experience of being drafted into the armed forces. With only one exception, they were universally positive. Developmentally, the bridge between adolescence and adulthood (eighteen to twenty-two) can be a wasteland of aimless drifting. I appreciated mingling with peers from very different backgrounds, life experiences, and viewpoints. It was structured time with exciting opportunities to obtain work outside the norm. How many psychiatrists know the inner workings of their toilet? The army also offered disciplined teamwork with affirmative oversight. It helped me grow up and learn more about who I am.

In retrospect, doing this before medical school and not as an officer were added advantages. The one person I know with a bad experience was a psychiatric resident, drafted under the Berry Plan in America, who was placed in moral dilemmas by the conflicting roles of trying to be an empathic psychiatrist but required to enforce military discipline on his patients. He became embittered and disgruntled and came close to being sanctioned himself.

War Talk

Christian, Muslim, Jew
Use God's name in vain for war.
Why blame Him? It's you!

—David Taylor and Barry Blackwell, March 2011

Guns and the Draft

The only way to control handgun use in this country is to prohibit guns. And the only way to do that is to change the Constitution.

—Michael Gartner

A young man who does not have what it takes to perform military service is not likely to have what it takes to make a living.

—John Fitzgerald Kennedy

To think about war and military service brings to mind guns, the uses to which they may be put as well as the draft and its necessity. After I left Britain for America, friends often asked what the differences between cultures were. Early on, I was careful to say that there were indeed differences but they were not better or worse, just different. Forty years later, and now an American citizen, I feel less complacent.

Among the biggest differences is America's infatuation with firearms and the mayhem they cause. Death rates due to accidents, suicides, or murder are far higher this side of the Atlantic. Four times higher for murder, which includes the death of four of our presidents, including two of our best (Lincoln, Garfield, McKinley, and Kennedy). There are more gun-related deaths in many cities in America in one month than in the whole of England in a year.

In America, 25 percent of adults and 40 percent of households have a total of 192 million firearms. (One-third are handguns, and this was before concealed carry laws.) Gun ownership in England is mostly an upper-class attribute confined to shotguns for killing grouse on the family moors. Even the police are not routinely armed. There is no "open carry" and the constitutional right to own a lethal weapon ended with the bow and arrow. The best way to acquire a firearm is to join the military. Belonging to a "militia" is not an option. But who needs a militia anyway when there is an active and a reserve army? Who are the enemy? Ourselves? The government?

Paradoxically, even when we have an enemy, the eagerness to own and use a weapon does not result in a universal draft. Now that America has an increased appetite for war (Korea, Vietnam, Iraq, Afghanistan), a draft might not be a bad idea. Not because it would feed our bloodlust, but because it would spread the trauma of war across the entire population and douse our cultural hubris to democratize the world. It would also reduce the personal burden and cost of caring for the psychological fallout of war like PTSD (posttraumatic stress disorder) which the Veteran's Administration in now attributing to a "preexisting condition." This is not an entirely ridiculous assertion because in an all-volunteer army, those willing to be recruited are often vulnerable individuals most in need of a job and willing to kill for one.

What would the framers of the Constitution make of our contemporary interpretation of a 1791 amendment intended to confer the right of self-defense against foreign invaders now parsed as an instrument of civilian mayhem? The founding fathers were imbued with wisdom and common sense when they designed a Constitution for both their present and our future. What would they think of a rigid, gun-crazed interpretation of their Second Amendment, which condemns us to keep looking backward and never forward?

—

Disposing of Royalty and Presidents

Literary hyperbole outstripped my knowledge of history when I intimated that Americans were more likely to shoot at our presidents than Brits were to take potshots at their royalty.

A recent book (*Shooting Victoria* by Paul Thomas Murphy, Pegasus), catalogues eighteen attempts to assassinate Queen Victoria in the sixty-four years of her reign (1837-1901). After the first attempt in 1840, the queen resolutely refused to curtail her public appearances and seems to have led a charmed life attributable to a combination of primitive weaponry and incompetent assassins.

On the last attempt in 1882, when she was traveling to Windsor Castle, two schoolboys from nearby Eton public school spotted the assassin waving a gun and beat him into submission with their umbrellas. There were no secret service men in those days!

In medieval times, British kings were disposed of on the battlefield using ancient weaponry; Harold at Hastings with an arrow in the eye and Richard III by battle-axe at Bosworth Field. Once guns became available, the British failed miserably with Queen Victoria and have never tried to rid themselves of royalty since. American assassins, on the other hand, have fared better, perhaps because they were better armed and more proficient with firepower. Thanks to the NRA?

6. CAMBRIDGE UNIVERSITY

Much learning does not teach understanding.

—Heraclitus

Academic and Other Affairs

It is strange but fortunate that, as the first of my family to attend a university, I was accepted by Cambridge, the fourth oldest university in the world (founded in 1209) and currently ranked the second best, just a hair behind Harvard. I suspect I may have been the first pupil from my high school to achieve that goal. Certainly luck or good fortune was involved. Although I excelled as a young student, I barely scraped through premedical exams in physics, chemistry, and biology, my brain addled by puberty and not helped by mediocre upper-level teachers in high school.

I cannot recall why, out of over twenty colleges, I went to Queens'. Perhaps it was just the luck of the draw. Certainly it is one of the loveliest, nestled on the "backs" (the banks of the River Cam), its medieval red brick Cloister Court and President's Lodge connected to them by "Newton's Bridge"—a wooden structure allegedly designed by the legendary scientist without benefit of nails.

My admission was delayed until I completed the military draft in 1954; a wise pause allowing for some emotional maturity, though hardly enough.

There is a Queens College at both Oxford and Cambridge, but they differ; Queens' Cambridge was endowed by two queens and has the apostrophe after the *s*, Queen's Oxford by only one. In 1448, Margaret of Anjou, the eighteen-year-old queen of Henry VI, petitioned her husband to allow her to found and become patroness of a Cambridge college. Her motives, recorded by the university historian, will appeal to feminists:

> This Queen, beholding her husband's bounty in building King's College, was restless in herself with holy emulation until she had produced something of the like nature, a strife wherein wives, without breach of duty, may contend with their husbands in pious performances.

When the War of the Roses erupted, the House of Lancaster defeated the House of York, Henry lost the crown, and Margaret retired to France while her former lady-in-waiting, Elizabeth, became the queen consort to Edward VI. Elizabeth was gracious to her former mistress and agreed to succeed her as patron, placing the apostrophe after the *s* in recognition of their dual roles as founders of the college.

Another prominent benefactor of the college was King Richard III who bestowed his boar's head emblem for college use. In our final year, my roommate and I found a stuffed and mounted boar's head in a local antique shop that decorated our room and became a trophy for special occasions.

From their inception, both Oxford and Cambridge Colleges were places for students to eat, sleep, and recreate while they attended classes under a broad university umbrella. Each college took students in a variety of disciplines (law, medicine, religion, music, philosophy) although some colleges specialized in a particular field. While students attended generic classes at the university, they were tutored in small groups by the fellows of their own college. The segregation of residential and recreational from academic activity is mimicked by the American Greek system of fraternities, but the American system is exclusive and optional while in England it is inclusive and obligatory.

The recreational activities were diverse and comprehensive, covering intercollegiate sports of every kind and a spectrum of societies for just about all leisure activities including debating, music, drama, religion, dining, career choices, and (of course) carousing. Some of these, particularly drama and debating, were replicated at the university level. The academic year ended each June with the oddly named "May" balls and intercollegiate rowing ("bump") races on the Cam.

When I "went up" to Cambridge in 1954, the colleges were still segregated by sex; now they are almost all integrated. Queens' had about a dozen medical students out of several hundred undergraduates. When attending lectures in town and dining in college, we were required to wear short black academic gowns. The college gates were locked at 10:00 p.m., after which it was necessary to climb over the metal fences and avoid the dark-suited, bowler-hatted porters who patrolled the boundaries after dark. During the day, the town streets were policed by "bulldogs," fit and swift young men, similarly attired and hired to suppress riotous undergraduate behavior. On several nights a week, we were required to eat dinner in the college dining hall, a beautifully decorated medieval structure with long tables and benches set below a raised dais at which the president and fellows dined and supped wine, following a Latin grace we jointly said aloud.

During our first year, students slept in rented accommodations in the town a short bicycle ride from the college. My future roommate and lifelong friend, Wally, lived a few doors up from me, over a corner grocery store where he introduced me to the jazz music of Fats Waller. Wally was a foot shorter than I and among the first to survive open-heart surgery for a narrowing of the aorta at the age of sixteen. For the remaining three years, we shared rooms in college assigned by lottery. Our last room was in Old Court and dated from the sixteenth century with solid stone walls several feet thick, narrow slits for windows, and a small gas fire for toasting crumpets. There were no modern conveniences so, after dark, we fertilized the rose beds. The room was cleaned and beds made by "bedders," middle-aged women from the town, hired by the college.

—

I suspect there is a sharp divide among Cambridge undergraduates; those who take advantage of its outstanding academic milieu and others, like myself, who indulge in its social and collegial opportunities. This almost cost me dearly early on. To pursue medicine required passing organic chemistry before being able to enter the second year of study. I had already failed in high school and took the exam again at the end of my first year at Queens'. The subject baffled me; its logic and relevance to medicine eluded me (and still does). Organic chemistry is the trip wire most notorious for flunking future physicians. I knew I had failed. This left one final opportunity; returning to Cambridge for a cram course during the summer. That required permission from my college tutor. Sitting me down, Dr. McCullough began, "Blackwell, I know you failed, but they published your name in the pass list. I think you'll make a good doctor, so I don't propose to say or do anything." This gracious, generous act saved my career. A year later, my tutor, in young middle age, suffered a fatal stroke, taking our secret to his grave.

Perhaps my good fortune should have transformed my study habits, but I continued to pursue athletic ambitions at rugby and rowing. As a second row forward, I aspired to play rugby for the university; at home I had played for the Saracens, a prominent London club, and now among the leading professional teams in Britain. But I had picked a bad time; two of my fellow Queens' teammates played second row for England's international team. So I was relegated to the university second team (the Sixty Club), and the only time I wore the light blue and white-striped university jersey was for a photograph before the Cambridge-Oxford game at Twickenham, in case one of my two rivals was injured!

Despite my bad luck, our presence together at Queens' almost certainly saved my career a second time. Drunken young men, primed with beer, are capable of behaving as mindless vandals in ways that are, in sober retrospect, incomprehensible and virtually unforgivable. Toward the end of the rugby season, the Cambridge Colleges compete in an intercollegiate "Cuppers" competition. Queens' was matched against St. Catherine's (known affectionately as "Cats"), an adjacent college whose forecourt faced the sandstone façade of Christ's College. My international rivals decided to conclude an evening of drunken revelry at the Anchor Pub by leading members of the Queens' rugby team to that sandstone wall where we painted, in black creosote, the slogan, "Cats for Kippers." It seemed hilariously funny. But centuries-old sandstone absorbs creosote like a sponge soaks up water, creating graffiti that is virtually indelible.

Within a very short time, Dr. Armitage, the president of Queens', was demanding the identity of the culprits and a guilt-fed confession soon followed. Summoned to the President's Lodge, we gathered to hear our fate. A just one might have been to "send down" (expel) the entire team. But this would deprive the university of its two star international players. Instead we were fined, confined to college ("gated") for the rest of term, and forbidden to attend the May Ball. Compared to our crime, it was a light punishment.

My remaining athletic and social accomplishments included two trophy oars acquired in the May bump races, my fiancée, Mavis, and a lifetime friendship with Wally and his future wife, Joanna, that lasted longer than my own marriage. My academic accomplishments were meager. I graduated with an indifferent second-class degree but sufficient to go on to medical school with a bachelor's degree in natural science that automatically upgraded to a master's degree after one year, a peculiarity due to an ancient university's hubris.

The Prodigal Son

Nine years after I concluded my undistinguished academic career, I returned to Cambridge to receive a doctoral degree. Although my research was in pharmacology, a discipline ironically linked to organic chemistry, the degree itself was in medicine. Unlike America, where every physician has an MD, in Britain the graduate medical degree is a Bachelor of Medicine (MB) and a Bachelor of Surgery (BChir). The MD is a relative rarity awarded by thesis and oral examination for scholarly research in a discipline related to medicine. In America, my degree would have been equivalent to a PhD in pharmacology.

—

The degree was awarded in an impressive ceremony in one of the university's oldest buildings, the Senate House, presided over by the president of the university and an assembly of distinguished dons and fellows. The degrees are awarded in sequence starting with the oldest professions, religion, law, and medicine. The MD gown is a resplendent scarlet and pink with a black silk cap.

I processed down the aisle, accompanied by faculty, and knelt before the university president to be hooded. Glancing up I recognized the former president of Queens', now Lord Armitage. As he placed the hood over my head and shoulders, he leaned forward and said in a low voice, "Blackwell, I didn't expect to see you back so soon."

I believe I was the first member of my class to receive a doctorate. The prodigal had returned!

X Trumps Y Chromosome

My daughter Sarah's child, Jessica, graduated from high school in America (Shorewood in Milwaukee) and was the first student from there accepted to Cambridge University where she studied French and Spanish. She was an undergraduate at Sidney Sussex College, where Oliver Cromwell's head is buried under the chapel floor.

She not only played rugby—an unheard of sport for women in my day—but represented Cambridge against Oxford, was on the winning side and was awarded her university "blue" (the equivalent of an American "letter"). During her final year, Jessica was the president of the women's rugby club and still graduated with a better degree than mine! We went to the ceremony in the same Senate House where I received my degrees over half a century earlier.

A Naked Truth

Medicine's unique rite of passage, its sacrament, is to dissect the human body, laid naked on a cold slab. The corpse I was assigned belonged to an obese eighty-year-old physician. In the summer of 1954, the anatomy lab lacked air conditioning and adequate ventilation. The air was perfumed with formalin, astringent and penetrating; an odor that clung to the skin long after a day's dissection was over.

Like every student, I came equipped with my personal cutting kit: scissors, scalpel, tweezers, and probes as well as *Cunningham's Manual of Dissection* with instructions on what, when, and where to cut. At the end of each day, whatever remained of the body was returned to a large lead-lined tank to float alongside its brethren, male and female. This task was performed by the curator of corpses; a friendly fellow with spiked hair that looked like barbed wire and a face pockmarked with erupting acne. But Ron went out of his way to ease our discomfort.

Born clumsy, I hacked away, separating fat and fascia from muscle, bone and nerves. Once in a while, an anatomy docent stopped by to quiz or encourage me. As the body dwindled and the summer heated up, formalin-resistant maggots invaded the body to speed my dissection with decomposition.

With no desire to become a surgeon, I thought then, and still believe, my labors were a redundant waste of time, like much else in medical education. But there were exams to pass, and I began to have a lifelong recurring dream of failing my anatomy finals. I shared my fears with Ron who offered me an unexpected opportunity to perfect my skills during the coming winter vacation. Floating in the tank was the surplus corpse of a small infant. Would I like to take it home to dissect at leisure?

When the lab was empty, I arrived with my carryall; we wrapped the small body in a cloth and tucked it under my rugby kit. When I arrived home, my horrified mother watched me unpack the baby and place it in the sink in my bedroom. It remained there until spring when I returned it to Ron, undefiled and pristine. A few weeks later, I passed the anatomy test, calmed by the token presence of an unnamed infant.

—

Cambridge Redux

Reminiscences make one feel so deliciously aged and sad.

—George Bernard Shaw

Forty-four years after I graduated from Cambridge University in 1957, my granddaughter Jessica graduated from Sidney Sussex College in 2011. Attending her graduation ceremony provided an occasion to attend the Queens' College May Ball with my wife, Kathie, and our lifelong friends, David Taylor and his wife, Karin. The memories came flooding back, embroidered by the differences. What evolved was the following poem, "Going Back."

Going Back

I bought four years
From seven centuries or more
And thought I owned the place
Until I ventured back.

Ancient spires and stone quads,
Cloisters cool and dank,
The river flowing dark and slow,
Where daffodils adorn its banks.

Past illusions faded fast
As eclipses dim the sun;
When orbs diverge and light returns
Fresh sights and scenes emerge.

In times long gone young men in mini-gowns
Paraded through the streets to lecture halls.
Now Town and Gown are all an urban coalition,
Blurred beyond distinction.

—

Today the genders share fun and space,
No longer housed like monks and nuns.
When College gates were locked at ten
Scaling rails and getting in were venial sins.

My peers did proper things, in proper ways,
Bred in public schools, an upper crust elite,
Predictable in musts and mores,
Marching to the same familiar beat.

Now diversity is flavor of the day,
Income, accents, skin color, class,
Sexual orientation, every perversity.
Stereotypes dissolved and swept away.

Women play rugby, men crochet,
Blazers and college tankards are outré,
But some traditions do persist;
Drunks and pranks still exist.

Flat bottomed punts with poles
Cost shillings an hour to rent.
Tourists now aboard have spent
Pounds the students can't afford.

Don't call your University "Alma Mater,"
Bricks and mortar stay, but students alter;
Forget that truth and then repent,
You didn't own the place, you only rented.

—Barry Blackwell, June 2011

7. Guy's Hospital

I'm always amazed when people rank medical schools; it's not what the school gives you but what you put into your education.

—Leo Hollister
(Pioneer U.S. psychopharmacologist, 1999)

Medical Student

In 1957, Cambridge University had no affiliated teaching hospital, so graduating premed students headed for the dozen or so hospitals in London. My roommate opted for Guy's Hospital where the world-famous surgeon Sir Russell Brock had operated on the congenital defect in his aorta; ultimately Wally would become his former surgeon's house officer. Absent any personal or family connection, Guy's was also a logical choice for me, certainly by reputation the equal of any other teaching hospital but also home to the oldest rugby club in the world. However scant my academic attainment, my reputation on the rugby field guaranteed acceptance.

Guy's Rugby Football Club, founded in 1843, was one of the thirteen clubs that formed the original English Rugby Football Union, establishing the competitive framework for "a ruffian's game played by gentlemen." During the 1920s and 1930s, Guy's was the most formidable team in Britain, fed by medical student athletes from South Africa of the caliber portrayed in the movie *Invictus*. Its teams won the United Hospitals

Challenge Cup thirty-two times. When I joined the club and eventually captained the team, it was far from its former self but still playing an elite fixture list of the country's leading clubs and almost inevitably losing to them. My suggestion that we voluntarily weaken our fixture list created outrage but later was inevitable when rugby became a semiprofessional sport. Jessica's boyfriend, Tom, a Cambridge rugby Blue, was recently offered about two hundred dollars a week (in pounds) to play for a London club—something I did for fun.

The hospital itself was founded over a hundred years earlier, in 1721, by Thomas Guy, ironically a publisher of Bibles who made his fortune in the "South Sea Bubble." This was the English precursor to many subsequent stock market crashes based on wild speculation and public hysteria in response to dubious marketing ploys.

Guy's was established to care for "incurables" and is one of the oldest hospitals in the capital, situated next to London Bridge, Southwark Cathedral, and Shakespeare's Globe Theater. Its distinguished alumni include Thomas Addison, who discovered the disease of the adrenal gland named after him; Thomas Hodgkin, who discovered lymphoma; Richard Bright, who discovered Bright's kidney disease; Sir Alexander Fleming, who discovered penicillin; Sir William Gull, who described both myxedema and anorexia nervosa; Humphrey Osmond, the psychiatrist who did pioneer work with psychedelic drugs; and John Keats, the poet who abandoned medicine as soon as he was eligible to practice it.

The move from premed to medical student marked an end to dead bodies and dull, often irrelevant, texts and sparked an intense curiosity about the human condition and its ailments. I proudly acquired the paraphernalia of the profession, including a shiny new stethoscope. My first task was to obtain surgery so that it would fit into my cauliflower ears, the consequence of calcified hematomas from squeezing my head between the buttocks of burly front-row forwards in rugby scrums. The operation was successfully performed, gratis, by Guy's Hospital's leading plastic surgeon.

In England, at midcentury, medicine was still taught at the bedside with a focus on detailed history taking matched to the natural history of the diseases and diagnosis derived from skillful physical examination without precipitous resort to laboratory tests of the kind seen on today's TV drama, *House*. As students we rotated at intervals through each specialty at random; medicine, pediatrics, obstetrics, psychiatry, surgery, anesthesia, and emergency room. Assigned to consultant teams, we paraded daily through large open wards containing up to thirty beds, separated only by curtains, accompanied by a bevy of consultants, senior and junior registrars, house officers, and medical students. As we entered each ward, named after distinguished alumni (Addison, Bright, Gull, etc.), the team was greeted and escorted by the sister in charge, wearing her dark blue dress with starched white cap and apron. Scattered throughout the ward, junior nurses attended to their chores, each level of seniority distinguished by a unique headdress. The cutest was a "butterfly" with a bow tied beneath the chin.

At selected bedsides, the procession halted, the consultant greeted his patient, and a member of the team presented a brief history and progress report. At the end of each "rounds," the clan gathered in a side room or around an empty bed to answer questions and debate the diagnosis or treatment. The primary documentation of each "case" was the responsibility of a student, including a history, physical findings, differential diagnosis, the consultant's words of wisdom, and sometimes embellished by diagrams or drawings. These became part of the official hospital record, available at any subsequent admission or outpatient visit and a source of personal pride for the student.

On medicine and surgery, teams were assigned their turn on "intake" when routine and emergency admissions for twenty-four hours would be the responsibility of the members. This meant sleeping and eating in the hospital with evening rounds to review each day's intake. At the end of the day, the team would gather to cook and share a meal.

During the rugby season (September to April), weekends were devoted to sport, and those of us who played for the hospital often traveled out of town to compete against teams as far away as Wales, several hours by train. For those who were married, this was an added burden on spouses and children.

—

Only much later in my career did I become aware of how different my experience was compared to a medical student's life in America. This was the time in England when Richard Gordon was publishing his books in the *Doctor in the House* series, several of which became movies. They portrayed medical students as riotous, fun-loving, beer-swilling, and flirtatious, quite different from the tense and competitive lifestyle of our Yankee counterparts. One obvious cause for this difference was that after Britain adopted a National Health Service (1948), the state paid for our entire medical education, and health care was free. We were only responsible for our own living arrangements, mostly an apartment only a short train, bus, or underground trip from the hospital. Even our rugby travel and out-of-town accommodations were paid by the hospital. Today, in America, my youngest son, Adam, pays almost $40,000 a year in tuition and $900 a month for family health insurance. A student can accrue up to a quarter of a million dollars in debt. No wonder rivalry is fierce to gain good grades as many compete for the few highly competitive and lucrative "procedure-oriented" specialties that yield the highest practice incomes.

Choosing Psychiatry

It was as a final-year medical student that I made my decision to become a psychiatrist. Even today, many students will tell you this is a "pariah" specialty to choose. Not only is the profession stereotypically "weird," but it is low on the totem pole financially. Our only procedure, electroconvulsive therapy (ECT), is not exactly popular and we spend most of our lives in the least remunerative activity of all, listening and talking. We are on the bottom rung with family practice and pediatrics. Nevertheless, I took perverse pride in my choice, perhaps because it was not what people expected from a rugby-playing "jock."

The incident that determined my career choice took place on the obstetric rotation. I was assigned a young woman in her first pregnancy who told me she had no idea how she became pregnant. She was terrified of anything entering or leaving her vagina, so neither could she contemplate how she might give birth. First, I requested a psychiatric consult, with which the consultant obstetrician disagreed, and then I suggested a Caesarean section which was ignored. The woman was induced (forced) into labor with an intravenous drip that stimulated the uterus to contract. I held her hand and tried to comfort her as she screamed throughout the delivery.

Two weeks later, *The Lancet*, a leading British medical journal, published an article by a professor of obstetrics at another London teaching hospital titled "Human Relationships in Obstetrics." Outraged by my experience, I wrote a letter to the editor of *The Lancet*. On May 21, 1960, it was published as the first letter in the correspondence column of the journal over my name. Here it is, entitled:

Human Relations in Obstetric Practice

Sir, it is hard to see how anyone could possibly detract from the observations and conclusions expressed by Professor Morris—so broadly and humanely are they based.

The problem is clearly not due to a few frustrated spinsters who administer barbaric rituals, but is the outcome more probably of factors inherent in obstetric practice itself, which cause the average "normal" midwife and doctor to fail in their personal relationships with their patients.

Obstetrics appeals to many because it is a practical specialty productive of a guaranteed end-product far more tangible than the patient's gratitude. Unlike medicine and surgery, all the patients suffer from the same "disease"; they all follow the same natural history, and are subject to the same complications. Such patients tend to become units devoid of identity.

Every known obstetric hazard is expressed as a percentage. Small wonder then that a practical person working upon stereotyped materials, with statistics as his master, seldom allows his imagination to wander above the fundus. The very risks which we wish to avoid are the only ones not expressed in figures. Patients who develop one-child frigidity, marital estrangements, or varying degrees of depression and fear seldom complain and never die. They simply remain "primips."

"Maternal distress" only catches the obstetrician's eye as a rising pulse-rate. Even if he does notice something overtly amiss he will not summon expert aid for two reasons. In medicine every man is his own psychiatrist. He can no more admit to a failure in human relationships than he can admit to being a bad driver. Secondly, everyone knows that most psychiatric conditions are incurable. The obstetrician, so consistently producing results, forgets that most doctors cannot hope to cure, but only to comfort their patients. Nonetheless, when palliation is called for, he sends for the radiotherapist. Why not the psychiatrist?

The midwife is subject to the monotony of normal labour without even the occasional abnormal case to leaven the dough. She resents the doctors who "pinch all the best cases," or "rush in at the last moment to pull the baby out." These feelings communicate themselves.

She forgets that the patient is not used to appearing unclothed in an undignified attitude, performing a function akin to defaecation. Endless reiteration lays calluses on her emotions. When kindness is most needed she is capable only of exhortation. Intent on five minutes' juggling at the perineum she overlooks the fact that, for the patient, this moment represents a unique end to nine months of anxious waiting.

After labour is over the midwife's task finishes where the mother's begins, and when the patient is most demanding of sympathy and explanation she is least likely to obtain it. She may even have her baby's weight kept from her to "stop her worrying." The patient's worries at this time are, in fact, like an iceberg, and it requires both imagination and insight to detect the larger submerged portion. Worse still, it takes time and patience to dissolve them. Such worries should be intelligently anticipated, not dextrously avoided.

The cure must lie with the people involved. If the obstetricians cannot accept the psychiatrists, they must cultivate, as part of their equipment, the psychiatric approach. For midwives what is needed is a correct psychiatric training, the temperament to accept it, and the time to apply it.

Very little can be done about obstetrics itself. There is only one way to have a baby, and most women need help.

Barry Blackwell, Guy's Hospital

Sophomore's Disease

Doctors quickly become acquainted with patients who are "symptom sensitive" and acutely aware of sensations in their bodies. They are frequent visitors to the office, seeking examinations or tests but, most of all, reassurance. By and large, our profession is remarkably insensitive to their appeals, labeling them "crocks" or "hypochondriacs." This is surprising because most medical students have undergone a similar personal experience but, presumably, have forgotten it. A short while after starting to read textbooks about disease and seeing patients who have them, students often begin to experience the symptoms they are learning to recognize. Which disease they imagine they might have ("Sophomore's Disease") will depend on their unique individual vulnerability, perhaps a family member with a particular illness or caring for an unusual or tragic patient.

In my case, the predisposing factor was a guilty conscience. I became attracted to one of those nurse "butterflies" and violated my marriage vows. Soon after, I began to experience symptoms that suggested I might have contracted an infection. The more I worried, the worse the sensations became. Convinced, I visited the student health clinic and confessed my concerns to a kind and wise senior registrar. He took a careful history, did a thorough examination, and reassured me that I was disease-free after explaining Sophomore's Disease. My symptoms disappeared immediately and never came back. It was a lesson that stood me in good stead my entire career.

Payback Time

In the fall of 1960, I had completed my two years of clinical training, and it was time to take the qualifying exams that would make me a doctor. The MB and BChir (Bachelor of Medicine and Bachelor of Surgery) was conferred by Cambridge University which required that I return there to take the exams. I learn better by experience than from books, so I was more prepared than as an undergraduate although a poor memory and exam phobia left room for doubt.

Things went well until the obstetric oral exam, which took place in a patient's hospital room. In those days, there was no anonymity. I was "Mr. Blackwell, from Guy's Hospital," the same student who had written that letter to *The Lancet* pillorying the obstetric profession. After greeting me by name, the examiner invited me to perform a vaginal exam on the patient. It was not a procedure I had practiced; in those days, there were no "surrogate" patients or life-sized anatomical models. My anxiety escalated as I struggled to pull size seven rubber gloves onto my size-eight hands. The examiner spoke, "I can see you don't put gloves on very often, Mr. Blackwell." Now I was in meltdown mode. My thoughts became scrambled and virtually incoherent. I don't remember the rest of the encounter.

Several days later, it was time to go to the Senate House where the exam results were posted by name in alphabetical order. There was no

Blackwell on the pass list. I later learned that I had passed every part of the final exam with the exception of obstetrics. At Cambridge, an examiner had the right to "ring" someone whose performance in their subject was sufficiently poor. This meant the student would have to spend an entire six months studying that single subject before retaking the exam. There was no appeal.

In the spring of 1961, I finally took and passed the exam, knowing more about obstetrics than I wanted or needed.

House Officer

There have been some medical schools in which, somewhere along the line, a faculty member has informed the students, not so much by what he said but by what he did, that there is an intimate relation between curing and caring.

—Ashley Montague II

Medical licensing laws in Britain require a year of supervised experience as a hospital house officer before entering independent practice. Only a few selected graduating students are invited to become house officers at their own teaching hospital. Despite my failure to graduate on time, I was fortunate. Perhaps my rugby reputation saved me, or my mentors saw something in me that I had not yet perceived myself. But becoming fully responsible for the fate of patients transformed my performance and unleashed my curiosity and creativity. For the rest of my fifty-year career, I never took a position without asking questions and seeking answers (also called doing research and writing papers).

My first job was a three-month stint as a house officer in the emergency room (ER). I am not particularly comfortable with blood and guts or high-drama situations in which technical competence trumps empathy. But I was surprised to find that a significant proportion of people who came to the ER were local citizens with relatively minor ailments. This was unexpected, because in the British system of universal health care, everyone had a family doctor. Why did they come to the ER and not

—

go to their family doctor? The chief of the ER was the plastic surgeon who had reamed out my ears, and he encouraged me to find out. I began to collect information. The outcome was a paper with the title "Why Patients Come to an Emergency Room." I submitted it to *The Lancet* and was astonished and delighted when the editor wrote back accepting it for publication. I believe I was the first person in my Cambridge class to have an article in a major medical journal.

The main answer to the question was that worried people seek what they perceive to be the most accessible and competent answers to their concerns. An emergency room in a neighborhood teaching hospital fits the bill and competes successfully with the crowded waiting room of an overwhelmed and harassed family doctor whose office may or may not be open. Published fifty years ago, this topic still raises questions in America where emergency rooms are obligated by federal law to provide aid to the uninsured and absorb the cost, passing it on indirectly to those with insurance. Any efficient and cost-effective system of universal health care will have to solve the problem of how to use primary care physicians to control access to expensive emergency rooms by educating the public and gaining their confidence and compliance. In America today, we have hardly begun to address that problem.

My next house officer rotation was another three-month stint, this time in medicine, under the mentorship of the consultant, Charles Baker, a crusty bachelor, who lived in the hospital's gatehouse on campus. I took to this like a duck to water. The responsibility to greet and settle the patient with the first opportunity to make a diagnosis satisfied both the caring and curing side of my temperament. Asking the right questions, doing a thorough physical examination, and then (and only then) requesting confirmatory lab work was exciting, rewarding, and reinforcing.

During this rotation, I encountered more of one of medicine's most puzzling and frustrating clinical dilemmas: patients who are addicted to hospitals and gain admission to them by simulating disease. I had already seen three of these individuals in the emergency room, and over the next nine months, in medicine and surgery, I saw another seven. Ten years earlier, in 1951, this problem had been named "Munchausen's

—

syndrome" by Richard Asher, a gifted internist with a literary talent for interesting labels. (He also described the dementia associated with hypothyroidism as "Myxoedematous Madness.") My adventures with this syndrome are described in one of the bits that follow this piece.

My final six months as a house officer were spent on surgery working for Sir Headley Atkins, a world-renowned breast surgeon whose success allowed him to live in Charles Darwin's former house. Given my constitutional clumsiness, surgery was a surprising and challenging assignment. Fortunately, the surgical expectations were minimal. Once in a while, I was asked to sew up the wound after a mastectomy, watched by a cadre of nurses eager to escape but unable to leave the operating theater until I had fumbled my way through the number of surgical knots necessary to close. I regret the jagged scars I inflicted on those unfortunate patients.

My main tasks were more mundane. Twice a week I was called on to assemble the operating schedule by culling the waiting list from the basement files. A lump in the breast always took precedence while hernias, varicose veins, and hemorrhoids waited months and occasionally years. After the lucky patients were admitted, my task was to make sure they were prepared for surgery, which involved confirming the diagnosis, assessing any complicating factors, and performing simple tests on blood and urine to rule out conditions such as anemia or diabetes while ensuring that blood was crossmatched to meet the patient's type and postoperative needs.

Several months into the rotation, I admitted a young woman with a lump in the breast for surgery, performed a few days later. Everything seemed normal, and Sir Headley proceeded to remove the lump and send it to the pathology lab for a frozen section to determine its malignancy. Meanwhile, as customary, he removed the breast while waiting for the pathology to determine how radical the procedure should be. The phone rang, and the lab technician reported that the lump was not cancerous but, instead, was a leukemic deposit. This was shattering news with dire consequences. What had I missed, and how could this happen? The patient was quickly stitched up and returned to the ward. Within forty-eight hours, she began to bleed from the wound site and all

—

her orifices. She exsanguinated and died a short time later. There were no recriminations, although fifty years later, in America, it could have initiated a career-ending lawsuit. Instead, I was encouraged to write up the event as a cautionary tale that was published in the *British Journal of Surgery* with the title "Acute Leukemia Presenting as a Lump in the Breast."

Before the rotation ended, Sir Headley and I would share in an unexpected personal tragedy. My father, living with my mother in the suburbs of London, called to tell me she was experiencing severe abdominal pain, which the family doctor thought was due to intestinal obstruction, the result of adhesions from a poorly performed hysterectomy some years previously. Sir Headley agreed to operate, and she was admitted to Guy's by ambulance. I "signed off," and my mother was assigned to another team member. What I did not reveal was that my mother had become a closet alcoholic, consuming large amounts of gin, which she hid under the kitchen sink or behind the curtains. When my brother tried to intervene, my father told him to mind his own business. This was a time when alcoholism was a moral, not a medical issue, Alcoholics Anonymous was still relatively unknown, and medical school curriculum contained no mention of the problem. At surgery, the adhesions were severe and little could be done; after the anesthesia wore off my mother went into full-blown alcohol withdrawal (delirium tremens) from which she never recovered. Her body was cremated, and her ashes scattered in the crematorium grounds. I wrote to my brother in Africa, breaking the news.

My mother and the woman with leukemia returned to haunt my dreams many years later. (See "Dream Doctor" in "Piece 14: Medical Education.")

My year as a house officer ended with the surgical rotation. To mark the end of our year, the house officers traditionally produced an annual musical in which the consultants were the mythical characters, impersonated by their former students. Our play was *Doom at the Top* and my role was Sir Deadly Ratkins. The music, songs, and script were all written by house officers, and the quality was surprising. Sir Headley had a mildly aristocratic and pompous demeanor I was called on to mimic

—

and for which I think he forgave me; he certainly wrote me a flattering reference for my next position, a six-month junior registrar position in neurology at the Whittington Hospital in North London that would prepare me to begin psychiatry.

Munchausen's Syndrome

My interest in this syndrome began as a house officer and continued until I left for America in 1968. I had originally published case histories of the ten individuals I had seen in the *Guy's Hospital Reports* in 1965, and my final article, which included a seven-year follow-up of one case, was published in the *British Journal of Hospital Medicine* in October 1968, a month after I arrived in America.

Before Richard Asher named the syndrome, these patients had attracted a number of pejorative names, including hospital hoboes, hospital addicts, hospital frauds, wandering Jews, and peregrinating problem patients. Asher chose his name because, "Like the famous Baron von Munchausen, they have always traveled widely, and their stories, like those attributed to him, are both dramatic and untruthful." The original German author, Raspe, had published his book of stories in 1786. Asher's choice of Munchausen had been criticized on the grounds that the fanciful tales had not involved sickness and the character had never troubled doctors. But when I obtained a copy of Raspe's original text, the frontispiece included an etching of an escapade in which Munchausen demonstrated his aggressive feelings toward doctors by surprising the college of physicians "feasting sumptuously" and "hoisted them to an immense height" attached to a balloon where he kept them "upwards of three months." There could hardly be a better metaphor of taking doctors for rides!

I first met Victor in the emergency room at Guy's when he was admitted semicomatose. He had scars on his belly and over every superficial vein in his body and a half-empty bottle of barbiturates that explained his condition. He was already well-known and in the hospital's "black book" of repeat offenders. I next met him in the emergency room at the Whittington Hospital after Victor had just left another hospital fifty miles away clad in a suit of clothes provided by a social worker. I admitted him

—

overnight, and the next morning he discharged himself after accusing the nurses of rifling through his belongings. Later the same day, he came back, semicomatose and with a new box of barbiturates. The next day, he tried to extort a pair of shoes from the social worker before leaving London to visit his family in Liverpool.

It so happened that my wife's mother also lived close to Liverpool, and we were shortly to visit her on vacation. I obtained a map of England and drew a straight line between London and Liverpool, noting all the hospitals in between. I wrote a letter to their emergency rooms asking them to notify me if Victor showed up. When he did, I asked them to admit him until we arrived by car. Victor was surprised to see me, but when I asked him to visit me on his return to London, he agreed. He showed up a couple of months later, and I had him admitted to the local psychiatric hospital. Meanwhile, I had written to the records departments of every hospital in Britain. In less than ten years, Victor had been admitted to eighty-nine hospitals on 188 different occasions, visiting all the London teaching hospitals at least once and some hospitals as often as nine times. In one brief spell, he spent forty-eight out of sixty nine consecutive days in nine different hospitals, traveling three hundred fifty miles to do so. I personally visited him in four different institutions, and for a brief while, he became a patient of mine when I was a psychiatry resident. I once bumped into him in Piccadilly Circus when he was panhandling on the pavement!

I kept track of Victor's travels through the social security system, which administered his army pension. Eventually, after seven years, I received news that Victor had died as he had lived. He boarded a London bus and "collapsed," complaining of chest pain (he had an old infarction on his EKG). When the ambulance took him to the nearest hospital, he was dead on arrival.

A Teaching Moment

Several years after I went to America, I was passing through O'Hare airport in Chicago on my way to give a lecture. As I crossed the concourse, I heard myself being hailed. "Dr. Blackwell!" I turned to face the person calling, whom I didn't recognize. "You won't remember me, but I was a student on the surgical rotation at Guy's when you were the house officer and we were on call. I'll always remember what you taught me." I felt flattered and enquired what that was. "You taught me to cook rice. Exactly seven minutes in fast-boiling water after rinsing off the flour. It works every time." Amused and deflated at the same time, we parted company.

Out of the Mouths . . .

My eldest son, Simon, was nine years old when we took an extended vacation between my first and second jobs in America. We rented a trailer and began a cross-country tour that would last several weeks and take in some of our famous national parks. An adventurous boy, and later an Eagle Scout, he went scrambling up a cliff face before falling off and fracturing his ankle. It was acutely painful and extracting him over a stream and rough terrain made matters even more painful and difficult. Eventually the fracture was set by a small-town general practitioner who doubled as the local surgeon. Between jobs, we had no health insurance, and he waived his fee in those days when "professional courtesy" was still a generous reality. We continued our trip and arrived back home several weeks later. Simon was at an age when the joints between parts of developing bones (the epiphysis) begin to fuse. We decided to obtain an orthopedic opinion about whether the ankle had been properly set so as to avoid any possible deformity.

We took Simon to see two orthopedic surgeons just to be sure we got the best advice. The first surgeon was brusque, matter-of-fact, and impersonal. The second was friendly, showed Simon the x-rays, and engaged him in conversation, both social and surgical. Back home we asked, "Which of the two doctors would you prefer?" He replied, "I'd like the first to operate and the second to look after me afterwards."

As a house officer, I came to know the difference between curing and caring and the way in which circumstances can alter the balance between the two. I had worked hard to learn what my nine-year-old son knew intuitively.

A Bit of History

It is possible to be in the middle of a cultural or scientific revolution and not know it. In retrospect, there was a remarkable synchronicity between the milestones of my early career, an evolving understanding of brain chemistry, and the discovery of drugs to treat mental illness. Although my choice of psychiatry was reactive to psychological factors, I would soon be drawn into the center of a new scientific and pharmacological era by coincidence and serendipity. This "Bit of History" provides a background to understand how this happened.

The year I matriculated and began premedical studies at Cambridge University (1954) was shortly after chlorpromazine (Thorazine) was discovered. A French anesthetist who was using chemical analogues of antihistamines to calm patients before surgery discovered a compound that was particularly potent. He shared this finding with a psychiatric colleague who gave chlorpromazine to agitated patients with schizophrenia to discover it alleviated many of their symptoms. With dramatic speed, this new treatment spread around the world to replace insulin coma, ECT, and barbiturate induced sleep, all dangerous and dubious treatments.

Three years later, in 1957, I began medical studies at Guy's Hospital. In that year, infectious disease doctors began treating tuberculosis with a new drug, iproniazid (Marsilid), that had fewer side effects than its predecessors. They soon realized that some of their patients became less depressed, and they passed this information on to psychiatric colleagues in America. They confirmed that it was the first effective antidepressant and suggested this might be because, in animals, the compound inhibited an enzyme present in the brain, monoamine oxidase, that controlled the turnover of norepinephrine, a neurotransmitter possibly involved in elevating mood. For the first time, the clinical effect of a drug on human emotion was linked to a potential biochemical cause.

By the time I graduated from Guy's Hospital in 1961, study of neurochemistry and the synthesis of new compounds was in full swing. We now had the additional category of tricyclic antidepressants (imipramine, Tofranil, and its analogues), a drug for anxiety and insomnia

—

113

(meprobamate, Milltown), and on the immediate horizon the "minor tranquilizers" called benzodiazepines (first Librium, then Valium), much safer and less lethal than the barbiturates. The number of monoamine oxidase inhibitors (MAOI) had increased and the two most popular were tranylcypromine (Parnate) and phenelzine (Nardil).

When I began psychiatric training in 1962, these new drugs were in widespread use; the pharmaceutical industry was expanding rapidly and aggressively marketing its products, while a new breed of psychopharmacologists was banding together to form national and international societies like the American College of Neuropsychopharmacology (ACNP) and the Collegium Internationale Neuropsychopharmacologicum (CINP). Their mission was to foster interdisciplinary dialogue between clinical and basic scientists; the goal was to find new or safer drugs to treat mental illness and elucidate their mechanisms of action.

This was the state of affairs as I completed my medical and neurology internships and prepared to begin a four-year training program in psychiatry at the Maudsley Hospital in London. It would influence my career in ways I never imagined or anticipated.

8. The Maudsley Hospital

The most exciting phrase to hear in science, the one that heralds new discoveries, is not "Eureka" (I found it) but, "That's funny."

—Isaac Asimov

The Maudsley History

Because the brain is the center of the nervous system and the seat of emotion, it seemed appropriate to spend six months as a neurology intern before beginning my training as a psychiatrist. It might also improve my chances for acceptance as a registrar (resident) at the Maudsley Hospital, which was the most prestigious training program for psychiatry in Britain and set the bar high for applicants.

It almost certainly helped. During my time at the Whittington Hospital in North London, I published another two papers on psychiatry in the emergency room and on Munchausen's syndrome. I also won the hospital's annual research award with a study on the management of barbiturate overdose. In 1961, barbiturates were still commonly prescribed for anxiety and insomnia and were the most frequent means of attempted suicide, particularly in women. The task of keeping patients alive to survive their drug-induced coma fell to neurology.

The surest way to obtain acceptance to the Maudsley was to have completed training in internal medicine and obtained membership in the Royal College of Physicians. This was an exacting task that took several years to accomplish, so there were always residual openings for those, like myself, who lacked this distinction. This created the basis for a virtual two-class system of "A" and "B" stream candidates.

To enter the B stream still required some other mark of distinction, broadly interpreted as any unusual academic, athletic, or artistic accomplishment. The papers I published, the prize I had won, a Cambridge degree, and a successful rugby career probably weighed in the balance. That I played an indifferent double bass in my school orchestra certainly did not. Others were talented musicians and athletes or had some unusual accomplishment. One resident in my class, an Australian, had been a world-class heavyweight wrestler and a member of a scientific expedition to the South Pole.

Altogether, our entering class in the summer of 1962 was made up of a dozen or so very bright, competitive, ambitious, and accomplished individuals. Our other common denominator was height. We were almost all over six feet tall and became known as "The Guards Brigade."

"The Maudsley" is the simple identifier of a complex institution. It is also the London University Institute of Psychiatry, affiliated with King's College Hospital on the other side of Camberwell High Street and situated in the Elephant and Castle region of South London. It is not one hospital but two, with several hundred beds and a large, active emergency room. The Maudsley component and all its substantial research departments (Psychology, Pharmacology, Pathology, and Neurosurgery, etc.) are located in Camberwell. The Royal Bethlem Hospital is south of London, about a forty-five-minute drive away.

The names of the two hospitals tell a story. Henry Maudsley graduated as a physician in 1857 after winning ten gold medals as a student. At age twenty-three, he was medical superintendent of the Manchester Royal Lunatic Asylum and later became the preeminent psychiatrist in Britain, author of several major textbooks (including *The Physiology and Pathology of the Mind*) and also editor (from 1862 to 1878) of the *Journal of Mental Science* (predecessor to the *British Journal of Psychiatry*). Maudsley was a friend of Charles Darwin, who quotes his opinions in *The Expression of Emotion in Man and Animals* (1872).

In 1907, Maudsley donated funds to endow a hospital named after him which opened in 1915 after an act of Parliament made voluntary treatment of the insane possible. Maudsley died three years later and, in 1948, when the National Health Service began, the Maudsley merged with the Bethlem Royal Hospital.

The Bethlem Royal Hospital has an ancient and checkered history. Originally a priory for the brothers and sisters of the Order of the Star of Bethlehem, it became a hospital in 1337 on the site of Liverpool Street Station and took its first patients with mental illness in 1357. Two hundred years later, it became a "royal" hospital controlled by the city of London. It housed twenty to thirty severely disturbed inmates, often restrained or chained to the walls, whose loud and aggressive behavior coined the term "bedlam." In 1620, the inmates (not "patients" until 1700) submitted a "Petition of the Poor Distracted People in the House of Bedlam" to the House of Lords and, in 1675, the hospital moved to new buildings in Moorfields, now the site of the Imperial War Museum.

In 1725, patients were subdivided into "curable" and "incurable" and the public were allowed to come and peer at them for a penny a day; in a single year there were 96,000 voyeurs. Patients fortunate to recover were sometimes licensed to beg with a tin cup; in Shakespeare's *King Lear*, the Earl of Gloucester's son assumes the role of a "Bethlem beggar" to remain undetected after he is banished from the realm.

In 1815, Bethlem moved to Southwark, close to Guy's Hospital, and in 1930 to Beckenham in South London where it was situated when I was a resident. Throughout the centuries, there have been many famous patients, including artists, authors, and painters. Playwright Nathaniel Lee, incarcerated for five years, wrote, "They called me mad, and I called them mad, and damn them, they outvoted me." Other notables included two men and a woman who attempted to assassinate King George III at the time of the American Revolution (perhaps they were American spies?).

—

117

The Modern Maudsley

The Maudsley was transformed into Britain's leading center for psychiatric education and research during the tenure of Sir Aubrey Lewis from 1936 until his retirement in 1966. He was appointed the founding professor and chair of psychiatry in 1946 when the hospital came under the auspices of the University of London and shortly before the founding of the National Health Service and its merger with the Bethlem Royal in 1948.

Lewis is credited with establishing the institute's international reputation and attracting the best and brightest faculty and students from Britain and around the world. Under his leadership, the stature of psychiatry as a scientific discipline increased significantly and graduates from the program went on to distinguished academic careers and chairmanships of departments in Britain, Canada, America, and Australia.

An Australian by birth and anthropologist by early training, Aubrey Lewis's psychiatric formation included time in America and Germany before settling in Britain. He was influenced by Adolf Meyer's emphasis on family origins but less impressed with Freud and psychoanalysis. Above all, Sir Aubrey stressed accurate description and careful classification of mental phenomena. Therapeutically he was a minimalist, some might say nihilistic. Late in his career, when psychiatry was in the throes of a pharmacologic revolution, he was modest in his expectations for its accomplishments.

As a person, Sir Aubrey was short, with a shiny bald pate and a rim of black hair, with piercing eyes framed by old-fashioned spectacles. An austere demeanor and a critical mind concealed a kind and humorous persona known only to his family and a few intimates. The climate he created was intellectually challenging and industrious; an ideal environment in which to mature, supported by a talented multidisciplinary faculty.

Without the imprimatur of board certification in medicine, I inevitably joined the B stream, assigned to the Bethlem Hospital in the country, where the tempo was slower but the climate still rigorous. My first patient greeted me with the news she had forgotten to bring her toothbrush. Young, attractive, and seductive, she wondered if I might run an errand to fetch her one. I did, exposing myself to good-hearted ridicule from my new colleagues and unflattering interpretations from my mentors.

These were the days when Saturday was still considered part of the work week, and on that morning, every trainee and faculty member attended a professorial conference at headquarters. Each week, residents took it in turn to present a clinical case of their own choosing. It was a competitive forum where we went to significant lengths to impress Sir Aubrey by selecting unusual or interesting topics we had studied in great depth and detail. He was our probing but benevolent inquisitor.

My Australian friend spoke fluent German and had worked at the Burgholzli Hospital in Zurich under Manfred Bleuler, one of Europe's leading psychiatrists. George chose to present an account of the famous hospital, which was celebrating its centennial anniversary. During the presentation, he attributed an opinion to Bleuler. Sir Aubrey pounced. How could George possibly know what Bleuler thought? My friend was so anxious that the odor of his sweat permeated the conference room. With hardly a pause, he explained that he had flown to Zurich at his own expense to conduct a personal interview. Even Sir Aubrey was impressed. Later George, who had a lifelong inferiority complex about his writing skills, invited me to coauthor his paper, "The Burgholzli Centennial," which we published in the *Journal of Medical History*.

When my turn came, I chose to present a rare case of myoclonus epilepsy, misdiagnosed as hysteria and sent to us for a second opinion. I persuaded the hospital's audiovisual technician to make an 8-mm film of the patient's bizarre and explosive movements. At the conclusion of my presentation, I awaited Sir Aubrey's inevitable comeback. "Had I by any chance read the recent Japanese accounts of the disorder?" No I had not. A week later, I stopped by Sir Aubrey's office and spoke to Miss Marshall, the guardian at Sir Aubrey's gate. I learned Sir Aubrey had taken the Japanese journal out on loan from the library and only just returned it. Checkmate?

A Bit of Cheese

It is not enough to know that cheese is a bad article of food in that it gives pain to anyone eating it in excess, but what sort of pain and why, and with what principle in man it disagrees.

—Hippocrates
(cited by Brock, A. J., in *Greek Medicine*, Dent & Sons, 1929)

Here we interrupt the Maudsley piece in the same manner that cheese created a break in my psychiatric training and changed the course of my professional life. This is the story:

In the fall of 1962, a few months after I began my psychiatric training, I was eating lunch in the Bethlem Hospital cafeteria when I heard residents at an adjacent table talking about a young woman patient who had just suffered a cerebral hemorrhage. My ears pricked up. During my recent neurology internship, the chief resident insisted I take a careful drug history from any patient who was admitted with a cerebral hemorrhage. He had recently published a letter in *The Lancet* describing a patient taking Parnate, a new MAO inhibitor antidepressant, who had suffered an episode of high blood pressure causing a subarachnoid hemorrhage. I did as he requested, but with no positive results.

Excited, I leaned over to ask my colleagues if their patient was taking any drugs. She was. Parnate! I went to the library to look through recent issues of *The Lancet*. There were six letters in the last twenty months describing an association between taking Parnate and sudden headache and severe hypertension. At about that time, I ran into my family doctor and, when I told him what I was interested in, he explained he had been called out twice in the previous week to see the same thing.

So I wrote my own letter to the editor of *The Lancet* suggesting that this side effect might be much more common and serious than previously thought. It was published in *The Lancet* in January 1963. A week or so later, I received a letter from a hospital pharmacist in Nottingham who went to the public library regularly to read the medical journals. He described two episodes of sudden severe headache his wife had suffered

—

while taking Parnate and after eating cheese. He described these in detail and went on to write:

> Could there be a link between the effects and the amino acids of the cheese? No effects are caused by butter or milk. Although treatment has continued, no further episodes have occurred. If cheese is indeed the factor, it could perhaps explain the sporadic nature of the incidence of the side effect. I hope my comments will be of some use to you in your investigations. (G. E. F. Rowe)

This was an astute, scientific analysis of the situation, but I was naïve and arrogant enough to find it amusing and share it among my fellow residents. A week later, I also showed it to Gerald Samuels, the local representative of Smith Kline and French, the manufacturers of Parnate. He had heard of similar cases as well as a death at a research unit where they were studying the combination of MAO inhibitors with amino acids. He suggested I take the letter seriously and look into the composition of cheese.

The first thing to do was to see if we could find out what our own patient had eaten. She was a vegetarian and the hospital menu for the meal before her hemorrhage had been a cheese pie. The next obvious but foolhardy thing to do was to see if I could provoke the side effect myself. So a fellow resident and I took Parnate for a week, bought and ate some cheddar cheese from the cafeteria, and sat down to see what would happen. Nothing! We were disappointed but lucky.

The cheese idea was beginning to attract ridicule from my fellow residents when coincidence stepped in to play its part. As a cash-strapped resident with a wife and two (soon to be three) children, I supplemented my income by serving as a medical officer in a field ambulance. I had recently received my commission as a captain, signed by Queen Elizabeth. My commanding officer was also a family practitioner for whom I moonlighted on weekends. One evening, I was called by the husband of a patient whose wife was suffering from a sudden severe headache. She had recently been prescribed an antidepressant and had just eaten a cheese sandwich for supper. I jumped in my car and did a

—

home visit to find her in the midst of a severe hypertensive crisis, from which she made a rapid and complete recovery.

Was there something that made people with depression vulnerable while my colleague and I were immune? So I persuaded myself it might be ethical to repeat the experiment in a patient and approached a woman on the ward who was already taking Parnate. After explaining my plan to both her and the husband, I bought a piece of cheese from the cafeteria and watched her eat it. For two hours I sat by her bedside, monitoring her pulse and blood pressure while nothing happened. So I left the ward but within minutes was paged by a nurse to prescribe the patient "aspirin for a headache." When I arrived at her bedside, the patient was in the throes of a hypertensive crisis. An hour later, her blood pressure was normal and her headache gone.

Evidence was mounting to support the connection with cheese and one further coincidence confirmed it. I was working late at the hospital one night when the registrar on duty passed me in the corridor en route to see two patients taking Parnate on the psychotherapy ward in adjacent beds. Both were suffering from sudden severe headaches, and both had just returned to the ward after supper where cheese had made its weekly appearance on the menu. I experienced the "Eureka syndrome."

In the nine months after my letter to *The Lancet*, I collected twelve cases of hypertensive crisis of which eight had definitely eaten cheese. The data were published in *The Lancet* in October of 1963 entitled "Hypertensive Crisis Due to Monoamine Oxidase Inhibitors." There were immediate responses in the correspondence columns of the journal. A patient wrote to say she had known of the association for several months but "doctors laughed at the idea." The medical director of the pharmaceutical manufacturer said my findings were "unscientific and premature." Another doctor had treated hundreds of patients and never seen a severe headache. (Headache occurs at least once weekly in a third of the population.)

Doubt disappeared a few weeks later when a team at another London teaching hospital discovered the causative component in cheese to be tyramine and published its findings in *The Lancet*. Tyramine is derived from the amino acid tyrosine by bacterial action during the maturation of cheese. Both were first discovered in cheese and named after the Greek word for cheese, *tyros*. Hippocrates was right!

It is not uncommon for serious side effects to be discovered several years after a drug is approved for marketing. In many cases, this is because the number of patients studied in early controlled trials is relatively small (in the hundreds) and the trials last only long enough to show statistical efficacy (usually six to eight weeks). A contributory factor in this case is that cheese is a very common dietary item, and headaches are frequent in the population. It is a truism that "everyone eats cheese." The fact that the side effect was relatively rare and that many who suffered an attack ate cheese again without incident served to obscure the cause-and-effect relationship. An analogy might be drawn to sex and pregnancy. The two are undoubtedly connected, but the first is common and the second is relatively rare. This is because there are many intervening variables between the act and the outcome.

It would soon become my responsibility to identify these variables. *The Lancet* article attracted considerable attention, not least of all at the Maudsley. I had accomplished the work unaided and unfunded during my first year. My reward was immediate promotion to the A team, which meant that my next rotation was as a team member of Sir Aubrey Lewis's professorial unit. This was the only unit at either hospital where we were expected to wear a white coat.

Toward the end of my six-month rotation, Sir Aubrey took me aside. Was I by any chance undergoing an analysis? Generally speaking, this was not considered a good thing at the Maudsley, so it had never crossed my mind. Why I had come under suspicion was unclear and unspoken. Perhaps because I did show an unusual amount of interest in the potential origins of a patient's illness and relatively less on its phenomena. I denied the charge. In which case, Sir Aubrey informed me, it would be a good idea if I got some rigorous training in research. He would assign me to work under Professor Marley in animal pharmacology where I could study the variables involved in the cheese reaction for up to two years. It was not an offer I could refuse, and it came without a pay increase.

—

"Ted" Marley was a delightful man and kind mentor. He presided over a one-person program (himself), aided by David, a lab tech, housed in an old army Nissen hut on the extreme edge of the Maudsley campus. The walls were lined with cages filled with three kinds of animals, cats, rats, and baby chicks. My work would be primarily with rats, the least expensive of the creatures. I would learn to "pith" them by administering ether on a cloth and then inserting a long metal probe alongside the eyeball and down the spinal cord. This preserved the blood pressure mechanisms intact, which I measured by inserting a catheter into the carotid artery before attaching it to the recording arm on a smoked drum. I also developed a technique for inserting homogenized cheese into the rat's duodenum. On rare occasions, we sacrificed a cat when we worked together on an important experiment. The friendliest cats were always spared, and after a year, I took one home as a pet for my children (Moppet).

One potential reward associated with this work was the chance to obtain a doctoral degree in pharmacology from Cambridge University. My application was rejected by the university on the grounds that I lacked the training and facilities to accomplish the goals of the research proposal. Ted intervened and advocated successfully on my behalf. Two years later, I was awarded my doctoral degree in medicine. (In the U.S., this would be the equivalent of a PhD in pharmacology.)

In those two years, we accomplished a great deal. Our first task was to define the pharmacologic effects of cheese and its tyramine content on blood pressure in rats and cats using traditional laboratory techniques. Before we began this work, we had visited the pharmaceutical company, met with their pharmacologist, and agreed to share our findings and publish them simultaneously. Several months later, we received a phone call from the editor of *The Lancet* to tell us that the journal had received a submission in violation of that agreement. He gave us a month to finish and submit our findings. Working day and night, we accomplished the goal; early in 1964 the two papers were published back-to-back in the same issue of *The Lancet*.

–

After about a year working with Ted, I received a phone call from a well-known family physician in London. He had a patient who had experienced the cheese reaction and stopped eating it but had started to use a yeast product as a substitute. Marmite is a sticky brown substance, made from brewer's yeast, which contains large amounts of B vitamins. It can be spread on bread or dissolved in hot water as a drink and is popular with invalids. In Britain, it often appears on hospital tea trolleys. The patient had begun to experience headaches and hypertension after eating or drinking it. Because it is soluble in water, it was easy to inject into a pithed rat and, sure enough, it caused hypertension and was subsequently shown to contain large amounts of tyramine.

To better understand the presence of tyramine in cheese and Marmite, we collaborated with a scientist at the National Institute for Research in Dairying who analyzed samples of both foodstuffs, some of which were salvaged from patients who had eaten them and suffered the consequences. The patient who had first eaten the Marmite volunteered to be admitted to the Maudsley Hospital Metabolic Unit, where I was able to carry out a series of experiments demonstrating the relationship between drug dosage and regimen on the size of blood pressure responses and their relationship to headache.

During this time, Ted, our collaborators, and I published nine articles in leading medical, pharmacological, food science, and psychiatric journals. But all was not plain sailing. Born clumsy, I was ill-suited to the fine finger work and coordination needed to perform animal experiments. I broke innumerable expensive glass syringes and smudged endless smoked drums. Before the work was finished, I knew basic pharmacology would not be my future; this was a disappointment to Ted who had waited a long time for an apprentice to follow in his footsteps. It was also necessary for me to return to the Maudsley mainstream to complete my psychiatric training.

Adumbration
(*adumbrare,* Latin: "cast a shadow")

What is originality? Undetected plagiarism.

—Dean Inge

Scientific discoveries often appear original and unannounced but are frequently foreshadowed by long-forgotten facts, buried in books. To that extent, we are all plagiarists.

Because Sir Aubrey was also a Greek scholar, I learned that Hippocrates thought cheese was a "bad article of food." This quotation became the preface to my Cambridge doctoral dissertation. As I delved into microbiology and food science, I learned that cheese was packed full of protein and bacteria that converted it first to amino acids and then, over time, to amines. Both tyrosine and tyramine were first discovered in cheese in the nineteenth century, and both were named after the Greek word for cheese, *tyros.* In 1909, Sir Henry Dale, the British physiologist, demonstrated that tyramine was a pressor substance, capable of raising blood pressure. Two years later a physician, Findlay, used tyramine to deliberately increase blood pressure while he was developing and calibrating the sphygmomanometer, an instrument to measure blood pressure. He expressed concern that the sudden severe increases tyramine produced might cause subarachnoid hemorrhage.

In the late nineteenth century, the German biochemist, Metchnikoff, suggested that the colon was a "putrefying sac" from which toxic amines in foods might be absorbed into the bloodstream. Queen Victoria's surgeon, Sir Arbuthnot Lane, subscribed to this belief and made a fortune removing the colon for constipation. In 1906, Bernard Shaw wrote his play, *The Doctor's Dilemma,* which parodied this practice but concealed the perpetrator by calling him Sir Colenso Ridgeon and naming the offending organ the "nuciform sac." The controversy surrounding this became the subject of a special conference convened by the Royal Society of Medicine in 1913, during which headaches were among the offending symptoms and cheese a potential toxic foodstuff.

Science added to these speculations in 1952, when a prominent biochemist, Blaschko, identified large amounts of an enzyme, tyramine oxidase, in the gut and liver, and speculated it was there to deny the access of amines in foodstuffs to the circulation. The name of the enzyme was subsequently changed to monoamine oxidase when other substrates were recognized.

In 1955, a British physician, Ogilvie, studied the first MAO inhibitor, iproniazid, in the treatment of tuberculosis. Four out of forty-two patients in that study developed sudden severe throbbing headaches and hypertension for which no precipitant was found.

By the time cheese was identified in 1963, forty deaths due to the side effect were recorded in the literature.

An Ethical Conundrum

Those experiments that can only harm are forbidden. Those that involve no foreseeable harm are "innocent" and therefore permissible. Those that may do good are obligatory.

—Claude Bernard (1813-1878)

This quotation was the preface to an article in *Time Magazine* in July 1966 on "The Ethics of Human Experimentation." It was published about the time I was conducting my experiments with Marmite on the metabolic ward at the Maudsley.

I remember the name of the first patient who agreed to eat cheese and who suffered a hypertensive crisis but not that of the woman who willingly volunteered to participate in the Marmite study. This seems surprising, given that we were involved in experiments on a daily basis for at least two weeks. By that time, we knew that tyramine caused the problem, I had calibrated the amount present in the sample of Marmite we were using and, based on the animal experiments, we knew how to block blood pressure effects if necessary. So the procedures were significantly safer and involved minimal risk. In addition, the information I was seeking about the relationship between drug dosage and timing with food ingestion could only be obtained by this type of carefully planned and monitored experiment.

So, in terms of Claude Bernard's aphorism, this was a relatively "innocent" procedure. More questionable is whether it was "good." The knowledge it yielded would really have no impact on routine clinical practice with these drugs and revealed no useful advice about how to avoid an interaction with food. But the shortcoming of the aphorism is in a lack of precision in defining "good." In the short term, the only good accruing to the patient was the attention and interest coincident with her participation and the vague concept she might be "furthering scientific knowledge." One possible long-term benefit she was offered was continuing therapy for depression, but she declined.

But there was another long-term adverse outcome I never anticipated and which she never revealed (assuming she knew it at the time). Some months later, I learned from her family doctor that she had died suddenly and unexpectedly. The autopsy revealed a subarachnoid hemorrhage. The patient left no note. But had she used the knowledge gained in our experiment to end her life?

Whose Discovery Is It?

Conflict over priority has been an integral part of relations between scientists.

—Robert Merton, 1957

Conflicts over priority and disputed ownership of discoveries are common. They are engendered in part by the depersonalized etiquette of scientific publications which cleave to evidence and shun romance. Contrast Crick and Watson's terse and sparse description of DNA in *Science* with Watson's book, *The Double Helix*.

Examples exist in every scientific field, including psychiatry. Freud's biographer, Ernest Jones, makes the erroneous statement that Freud was "never interested in questions of priority." Robert Merton identified one hundred fifty examples from Freud's own work to dispute this. Included is a dream that Freud interpreted himself as an expression of regret that he lost priority about the discovery of cocaine to his colleague Koller because he postponed some experiments in order to visit his fiancée.

In the case of cheese, there are plenty of people among whom to spread credit. To the woman patient who recognized the reaction which physicians ignored, to the pharmacist's brilliant analysis of his wife's headaches, to the pharmaceutical representative who knew of other cases and urged me to take them seriously. To mentors and colleagues like Gerald Russell and David Taylor, who encouraged and assisted my inquiries, to Sir Aubrey who opened the door to research, to Ted Marley who endured my clumsy efforts at basic research and pled my case in Cambridge. To the female colleague and two women patients who volunteered to be experimental subjects, to the microbiologist who analyzed cheese for us and educated us in food science. To the scientists at another hospital who identified tyramine in cheese and gave the story credibility.

Perhaps two people have reasons to feel slighted. G. E. F. Rowe deserves full credit for the first documented mention of a link between cheese and sudden severe headache while taking an MAO inhibitor. My first article confirming this relationship in 1963 did not make attribution, but every subsequent publication has done so. My recollection is that I sent him all of our papers at the conclusion of the research, but this is contested. By an odd coincidence, I attended my former roommate's memorial service in Britain in 2010 where I met a family member who is a pharmacist and had been taught by Rowe in Birmingham. She remembered him as an excellent mentor. I can believe it.

The second person, Gerald Samuel, complained more vociferously and continuously. Three years after we first met and he encouraged me to pursue the contents of cheese, we met again when he visited me at the Maudsley in his role as a pharmaceutical company representative. I learned how bitter he was at not being acknowledged in any of our

—

publications. Feeling his resentment was justified, and wishing to make amends, I suggested we write a joint article describing his role and contribution. This was published in 1968, with Gerald as first author, in the *Journal of Hospital Medicine*. As an expression of gratitude, he gave me a cheese board engraved with the words, "Everyone Eats Cheese."

I assumed we were reconciled, but about fifteen or so years later he published an angry letter in the *British Journal of Psychiatry*, again complaining bitterly. He had contacted Mr. Rowe and alleged he was similarly aggrieved and had never heard from me. I decided not to respond, feeling that there was nothing further I could do to assuage such deep-seated and long-lasting emotions.

Back in the Mainstream

Returning to the role of a regular student, I had to take myself down a peg or two; cheese had earned me a reputation and made me a leader in the "publish or perish" stakes. I had also been invited to America to present our research at an international conference. Meanwhile, I had begun to write anonymous leading articles and annotations for *The Lancet* on a wide variety of psychiatric topics. How this happened, I am not sure. Perhaps it grew out of my published articles or maybe Sir Aubrey put in a good word. If so, we never spoke of it, although he must have known. Every several months, the deputy editor of *The Lancet* treated me to lunch at the prestigious Athenaeum Club. To reach our table in the dining room, we sometimes passed Sir Aubrey reading *The Times* in front of the fireplace.

During this time, I began a lifelong friendship with my fellow resident, David Taylor. Residency is a time of rivalry and bonding when kindred spirits find allies to mitigate the stress of heavy workloads, high expectations, and unrelenting oversight. David worked on the neurosurgical unit, documenting the outcome of temporal lobe surgery for epilepsy, a topic about which he became a world-renowned expert. In 1971, he achieved eponymous distinction by describing a unique tumor of the temporal lobe, focal cortical dysplasia of Taylor (FCDT), the outcome of research begun as a resident at the Maudsley.

—

David plays an accomplished mouth organ, speaks Welsh, paints with talent, draws amusing cartoons, pens wicked satire, cooks creatively, lectures with panache (except when I am in the audience), and has an encyclopedic memory for life's finer moments, Greek mythology, and classical poetry. What we have in common is a quirky worldview, contrarian "outside the box" opinions, disrespect for bureaucracy, and an insatiable curiosity for the complex ways in which individuals adapt to disease and disability.

Our career trajectories differ; scientists who accomplish much take one of two distinct pathways. Some, like David, stick to their last; focusing their energy on a chosen field—in his case, the borderlands between neurology, pediatrics, and psychiatry. My interests are more scattered and diverse as reflected in the "pieces" or themes in this book. Fame and reputation favor the first path. Persistence is rewarded with depth, and repetition builds recognition. "Jacks-of-all-trades" often remain beneath the academic establishment's radar.

Fifty years ago we, typically, chose to collaborate on an unusual form of inquiry. The MAO inhibitors were the dominant drugs of choice for the milder forms of depression seen in outpatient clinics. The prevailing Maudsley format for research was to define a hypothesis and test it in a tightly controlled group of subjects under highly artificial constraints. The double-blind study was the "flavor du jour." Instead, we chose to study the records of all the outpatients taking MAO inhibitors treated by the different consultants. We were looking for the outcome of treatment in its natural setting through the wrong end of the telescope, without a hypothesis in mind.

Today it is easier to see the virtue of this approach now that the failure of rigidly controlled studies to illuminate the real world is apparent. Theories abound, but half a century later, we still do not know which drugs work or why. Trial and error dictates choice. Experts have learned to distinguish between "efficacy" (a drug is statistically better than a sugar pill over a short time span in a small group of a highly selected sample) and "effectiveness" (a drug produces more benefit than its side effects in a diverse, real world population, even though half of them may not take the medication "as directed").

—

We presented our results at the Royal Society of Medicine and published them in the proceedings of that prestigious organization. They were largely ignored. But here are several things we noticed worth knowing that, even today, are not in the literature:

Different consultants obtained markedly variable results. Those who used MAO inhibitors a lot obtained better results. They used the drugs as "first choice" treatments, gaining the advantage of spontaneous remission, drug-naïve patients, and their own enthusiasm, which probably inflated the placebo response. Cautious or skeptical consultants only prescribed MAO inhibitors to people who had failed previous treatments or experienced side effects. This was a population of drug-resistant, side-effect sensitive patients less likely to show a spontaneous remission or placebo response. Poor outcomes reinforce therapeutic pessimism but may be due less to the properties of a drug than to the manner in which it is used.

Most contemporary controlled studies require the inclusion of patients selected to conform to the "Chinese menu" criteria of the DSM system (*Diagnostic and Statistical Manual*) based on a person's symptoms. But symptoms are almost certainly unrelated to any underlying biochemical disorder in the same way that pain, fever, or cough tell nothing about a specific medical diagnosis. Reliance on symptoms creates a spurious homogeneity in the study population that encourages physicians to believe they are treating a discrete entity and discourages them from looking for individual patterns of response. The benefit of looking at an unselected population treated by different psychiatrists is that it does not exclude the possibility of subtypes of depression linked to an underlying biochemical disorder, not simply to symptoms.

Take, for example, the psychiatrist in our study who wrote in the chart, "Although this patient never looked depressed before, she looks less depressed now." To our regret, David and I lacked the time to study the possibilities this observation suggests. No clear distinctions had been drawn yet between people who responded to MAO inhibitors or tricyclic antidepressants (like imipramine or Tofranil). There was a suggestion, later substantiated by another researcher, that MAO inhibitors were more effective in "atypical" depression—defined as someone who ate and slept

—

excessively with some features of a (undefined) personality disorder. In hindsight, this is the type of depression that had previously benefited from amphetamine, perhaps due to its effects on appetite, sleep, and certain types of inadequate or avoidant personality. Unremarked and overlooked is the fact that the most widely prescribed MAO inhibitor (Parnate) was structurally very similar to amphetamine, had mild stimulant effects, and was abused in rare instances. In retrospect, our study suggests that assumptions about the similarity or homogeneity of both diagnosis and drug categories may contribute to lack of progress in the field.

Lastly, the results of traditional controlled trials are based on once-weekly ratings of selected symptoms, made by a researcher, for only as long as it takes to establish statistical superiority over a sugar pill (usually six to eight weeks). The problem with this method is that it is an infrequent, secondhand measurement of limited symptoms for a relatively brief period. To overcome this drawback, we asked a small number of people to evaluate their own choice of symptoms on a daily basis. An example of what we discovered is a successful middle-aged businessman who was only sad on the weekends. An in-depth inquiry revealed why. He was impotent. Concerns only surfaced when he was not at work, where his performance and mood benefited substantially. On weekends, an MAO inhibitor may have increased his desire but failed to improve his performance. Parnate was not Viagra! In a traditional drug study, measurements made only on weekdays (researchers don't work on weekends) would judge the drug a success. The patient's opinion might be more nuanced but never understood.

Fifty years later, David and I still think of this study and regret we were unable to pursue its implications in more depth. It generated hypotheses but didn't prove or disprove any. So we and the field moved on, but not necessarily ahead.

By the time I reached the end stages of my psychiatric training, took and passed the final exams, I was, not surprisingly, identified as a budding psychopharmacologist. I was offered a research fellowship working with Michael Shepherd, the number two professor and, some feared, the possible successor to Sir Aubrey whose retirement coincided with

—

my graduation in 1966. Shepherd was a highly intelligent, somewhat acerbic, and therefore not very popular individual with a major interest in epidemiology. I was sufficiently assertive and self-confident to withstand his temperament, and we spent a productive year in which we published two articles in *The Lancet*, one of them highly controversial.

By the mid-1960s, the pharmaceutical industry had awoken to the profit potential in psychiatric drug development. The hunt for new, better, and safer drugs was on. The discovery of the "cheese reaction" and the dietary restrictions it imposed placed a damper on the MAO inhibitors. The other category, the tricyclic antidepressants, also had many undesirable side effects, which were often fatal if the patient became suicidal and took an overdose.

When Professor Shepherd was approached by a pharmaceutical company to study a new drug with money to help support my salary, the temptation was irresistible. We learned the hard way how difficult it was to accumulate an adequate number of willing recruits. Women of childbearing potential were excluded for fear of fetal abnormalities. So were the elderly and those suffering from significant physical disorders. Concurrent medication was forbidden. Patients who were obvious treatment failures, unlikely to comply with medication, unwilling to sign an informed consent or fill out rating scales were also excluded. Added to all that was the natural reluctance of consultants to relinquish control of their patients and refer them to a drug study.

After struggling for some months, we abandoned the project but, in true Maudsley fashion, salvaged a paper entitled "A Trial that Failed." Perhaps the most important lesson, not emphasized at the time, was what this revealed about the artificial nature of such studies.

The second project we undertook brought significant controversy and animosity. It was also, in many ways, typical of what others viewed as the Maudsley's scientific nihilism. Two Scandinavian psychiatrists had published an article in *The Lancet* on their studies and experiences with the use of lithium to treat and prevent relapses in recurrent manic depressive (bipolar) disorder. This was an important claim for several reasons. "Prophylaxis," or the ability to prevent the recurrence of a disorder, was a novel idea. There were no such treatments for a condition that affected a group of creative people who were frequently normal and productive between episodes but could become wildly and dangerously impaired when manic, sometimes without realizing it.

Lithium is not a manufactured drug but a naturally occurring substance (*lithia* is the Greek word for "stone") with a history of medicinal uses going back centuries. Earlier in the twentieth century, it was used as a salt substitute in cardiac conditions but caused several deaths due to overdose. The recent discovery of an accurate way to measure it in the blood facilitated its reintroduction into psychiatry.

Shepherd was familiar with the Scandinavian work, probably through his involvement in a new international society of psychopharmacologists (the CINP). He suggested I analyze the study and prepare a critique of its claims. It was not difficult to find flaws in the research. Some of the subjects clearly had recurrent depression, not bipolar disorder. The statistical analysis was questionable and undermined by a phenomenon known as "regression to the mean." Anytime you have a condition that waxes and wanes in severity, and you start to study it at its worst, there is a strong likelihood it will improve on its own, independent of treatment. Anything new will seem to "work." Finally, one author's belief in lithium was influenced by successfully treating a relative, thus introducing an element of enthusiasm and potential bias into the analysis.

In order to be more certain of our concerns, I found a cohort of Maudsley patients who met the same criteria but had been treated with a standard tricyclic antidepressant. Analyzing the outcome using the identical flawed statistics showed that the antidepressant produced the same degree of benefit as lithium.

Putting together my critique with these results in support, we submitted an article to *The Lancet* provocatively entitled "Prophylactic Lithium: Another Therapeutic Myth?" This aroused controversy that persisted for many years, deeply offended the Scandinavians, and evoked significant name-calling.

—

The controversy is still not fully resolved by research because of the difficulties involved. Nevertheless, my own clinical experience, and that of many others, supports the conclusion that lithium is indeed an effective treatment for bipolar disorder, both in the control of manic episodes and also in the reduction of recurrences. It is just that what may be obvious clinically cannot always be convincingly proven scientifically or statistically. This issue is discussed in more detail later. (See "Learning from Lithium," "The Book Review," and "Nathan Kline" in "Piece 12: Psychopharmacology: Then and Now.")

With this rousing conclusion, my career at the Maudsley came to an end. What happened next was a mystery to many, not least to me.

Back and Beyond

We swam upstream, against an ebbing tide,
Trained alongside each other. Idealists and alienists
We shunned the mob, the go-alongs, the look-alikes,
Consensus chaps and bureaucrats who clung to status quo.
Oft unsung among our mainstream brothers, outliers at odds,
We seldom hesitated or paused o'er long to deviate.
(Nor ever reached the topmost rung of academic ladders!)

Zodiac twins, crabby Cancer clones,
We sifted shoals of scientific sand,
Panned silt to mine un-minted flecks of psychic gold.
Chance, wed to firm intent, birthed novel testaments midst old ideals,
From which we toiled to teach a worthwhile truth or two;
Aspired to leave behind fresh footprints on a virgin beach,
Bequeathed into an ebbing tide, washed out to sea.

—Barry Blackwell, June 2012

This poem is dedicated to my friend and colleague David Taylor. (See "Back in the Mainstream" in "Piece 8: The Maudsley.") The poem's theme is a poignant and ironic resume of our mutual career trajectories, distilled from fifty years of delightful conversations on both sides of the

Atlantic. The poem's form, as usual, combines traditional and free-form elements.

Flabbergasted

A creative man is motivated by the desire to achieve, not to beat others.

—Ayn Rand

This eighteenth-century English word of unknown derivation expresses how "greatly surprised" I was when I recently received unexpected feedback from fifty years ago. It had passed through several hands, but its provenance was impeccable.

From the time of the Maudsley's preeminence, the chairmen of academic departments of psychiatry in Britain have met regularly to exchange views and share information. Sir Aubrey attended, as did Gerald Russell, the academic dean of the institute and also head of the metabolic unit where I conducted clinical experiments on Marmite. Today, Sir Aubrey's position is taken by his successor, Sir David Goldberg, also a friend of David Taylor and contemporary of both of us. We were residents and rivals at the Maudsley.

Like all humans, even distinguished academics gossip. Toward the end of his tenure, Sir Aubrey was asked to name his favorite trainee. He mentioned my name, coupled with the rationale that I had "discovered something useful." The news of Sir Aubrey's accolade passed from Gerald Russell via Sir David to David Taylor and hence to me. This was a generous act, given a lifetime of covert but friendly rivalry.

Hearing this, I was overwhelmed by mixed feelings; surprise, pleasure, pride, and sadness, to the point of tears. I had felt affection and gratitude toward Sir Aubrey and, though I suspected he liked me, we had never had an intimate conversation nor did I feel singled out by him in any way. This was fair and just, given the Institute's exacting standards and the outstanding qualities of our entire class. Praise was not a required or necessary ingredient to motivate us.

But it was not praise I lacked or needed; rather it was advice, mentoring, and encouragement. Absent that, my own stubborn independence, bred in boarding school, influenced my next career decision. I quit psychiatry and went into family practice.

Part Two: Professional

9. FAMILY PRACTICE

Breadth or Depth?

It is much more important to know what sort of patient has a disease than what sort of disease a patient has.

—William Osler, MD (1849-1919)

My decision to leave psychiatry for family practice was both intellectual and emotional, but I doubt if I understood it fully at the time. It was also impulsive. Intellectually, I valued the depth of psychiatry but was not ready to give up the breadth of medicine. I now realize that is a somewhat spurious distinction; there is plenty of medicine in psychiatry and more than enough psychiatry in medicine. Perhaps that is why Sir Aubrey preferred trainees who had already served an apprenticeship in medicine.

Emotionally, I needed to be needed. Who doesn't? Ken Walker was not just my reserve army commanding officer but also a friend. He was running a well-established suburban solo practice with over 3,000 patients and wanted a partner. The academic medicine ladder thrives on patronage and, despite or because of my success, no one at the Maudsley seemed eager to mentor me after my innate clumsiness, and preference for humans cut short any animal pharmacology career aspirations.

The transition was made easier because Michael Shepherd and David Goldberg recognized my move created an epidemiologic research opportunity that would enable me to maintain some psychiatric

—

connections. This was not a major determining factor but would become a significant source of satisfaction.

The increasing availability of drugs to treat mental illness was coupled with the knowledge that many patients and family doctors did not recognize the problems or shunned psychiatric referral and treatment. This created a compelling need for ways to help identify mental disorders in a primary care setting.

I soon settled into a new routine of morning and late-afternoon surgery hours, seeing each patient for up to fifteen or twenty minutes. In between the two sessions, I drove around the neighborhood doing up to half a dozen house calls, stopping to chat with the local pharmacist and share a cup of tea.

I developed a special interest in weight loss and started a weekly clinic run on behavioral principles. People kept a daily log of their calorie intake, which we reviewed weekly after they were weighed, adjusting the target intake commensurate with change in weight. This was simple and highly successful, with some individuals losing as much as sixty pounds or more over several months. Of course, as often happens, some gained the weight back, but others learned a life-changing lesson.

Used to hour-long interviews in psychiatry, I sometimes felt frustrated by the brevity of visits but soon realized that primary care is a sequential experience in which knowledge and trust build over time, facilitated by careful record keeping that always included personal information relevant to the patient's day-to-day life. For people who needed more, I set aside an afternoon a week with longer time slots. Of course there were still people who, after a careful history and examination of their initial complaint, would be about to leave and say, "Oh, while I'm here, could you . . ." Aware of the crowded waiting room, this could be aggravating, but it happens in psychiatry as well; perhaps more often.

There were simple procedures that didn't tax my lack of dexterity: minor cuts to be stitched, sprains to be bandaged, splints to be changed, and ear wax to be removed—a remarkably simple but rewarding task! There were amusing moments; an attractive young French exchange student who spoke no English came with symptoms suggestive of appendicitis. How to explain I needed to do a rectal exam? Reaching back to high school pidgin French I said, "*Il faux que je vous examinez en arriere.*" She understood at once!

There was even some time to dabble in research. I recognized a number of patients treated for depression with tricyclic antidepressants who complained of word-finding difficulty and described this in a letter to *The Lancet.* In retrospect, this was probably due to the drugs' anticholinergic side effects, mimicking a cardinal symptom of Alzheimer's disease, perhaps due to the same mechanism.

During this time, urine pregnancy tests became available for use in a doctor's office. My partner and I published a small study in *The Practitioner* on the reasons women were anxious to obtain early confirmation of a possible pregnancy.

Undoubtedly, David Goldberg's research was the most innovative, interesting, and time-consuming project. David had designed a sixty-item survey instrument, the General Health Questionnaire (GHQ) to identify the possibility of a psychiatric disorder in patients attending a family practitioner's office. The questions were intended to measure "How your health has been in general over the past few weeks?" Each question was answered as "better," "same," "worse," or "much worse" than usual. Examples include, "Have you recently: been feeling run-down and out of sorts?" "Lost much sleep over worry?" "Found everything getting on top of you?" "Felt on the whole you were doing things well?" The questions were easy to understand, quick to respond to, and most avoided an overt implication of mental illness.

Patients completed the survey in the waiting room before coming to see me for the standard fifteen-minute visit. I behaved entirely as their family doctor dealing with their complaints (usually physical) and their treatment. After the patient left, without seeing the questionnaire, I made my own quick rating of any possible mental illness. Following my interview, David, in an adjacent office, did an hour-long psychiatric interview on a random sample of the patients I had seen, making a formal psychiatric diagnosis when relevant.

—

Based on this data, we were able to compare the ability of the GHQ and a family doctor (myself) to agree with a psychiatrist (David) on the presence of a mental illness. This was a unique design because we were both identically and fully trained psychiatrists, but I was operating as a family practitioner under the usual constraints of time and purpose. The fact that I had to focus almost entirely on physical symptoms and their treatment in a quarter of the time led me to miss one-third of the psychiatric cases identified by David.

David undertook a sophisticated statistical analysis of the data to determine the specificity, sensitivity, reliability, and validity of the GHQ in the detection of a mental illness in primary care. Together we coauthored two articles in the *British Medical Journal*. David, as first author, dealt with the GHQ and its measurement characteristics while I described the clinical nuances that influenced and complicated accurate psychiatric diagnosis in primary care.

My involvement with the GHQ ended with the project, but the instrument became the keystone to David Goldberg's distinguished career in social and academic psychiatry. He shepherded it through numerous revisions and reductions in the number of items (sixty, thirty, twenty-eight, and twelve) of which the twenty-eight-item version is the most widely used. Its reliability and validity were confirmed in many different populations, and it has been translated into thirty-eight languages, making it possibly the most widely used measure of mental well-being and vulnerability in use today, forty years after our initial study.

I quickly learned how much hospital practice differs from family practice. In both psychiatry and medicine, hospitals are places for well-defined, severe, and often end-stage disease. Family practice is where disease begins, often vague, with its margins blurred by the fears or beliefs of the patient and doubts or beliefs of the doctor. In Britain and all countries with universal health care (but not in America), the primary care physician is responsible for detecting and referring patients in need of specialty care to experts trained to provide it. Wealthy individuals, with supplementary private insurance, may bypass this process that is designed to curb costs by curtailing unnecessary and expensive "fee-for-service" procedures which inflate the specialist's income.

The burden of making referral decisions in a timely and cost-effective way can be heavy. Family physicians know that vague symptoms can get worse, stay the same, or get better. And, because most pathology in primary care is early or mild, much does indeed get better. Time heals. This seductive truism encourages a "wait and see" tendency, sometimes with unintended adverse outcomes.

Having been trained exclusively in hospitals, family practice opened my eyes to the early manifestations of mild mental illness and its treatment, almost exclusively anxiety, depression, or both. Until recently, anxiety had been treated with barbiturates and depression with amphetamines, both with potentially serious side effects. Barbiturates could be addictive or lethal in overdose, and amphetamines were also addictive and could cause a paranoid psychosis, indistinguishable from schizophrenia.

By the time I joined the practice, we now had the benzodiazepines (Librium or Valium) for anxiety, safer but still mildly addictive in vulnerable individuals. For depression, the tricyclic antidepressants (Elavil or Tofranil) were not addictive but still potentially lethal in overdose.

The addictive tendency of drugs is often blamed on their withdrawal effects, which make it difficult to stop taking them. But the real problem is at the front end: on the streets or in the doctor's office. All the addictive street and prescribed drugs share the common property that they produce an immediate effect, altering mood either up or down, often in minutes. This includes alcohol, nicotine, caffeine, marijuana, amphetamine, cocaine, heroin, and benzodiazepines. The striking distinction between these agents and modern drugs resides in the fact that the newer drugs have a delayed onset (days or weeks) and offer no immediate gratification.

It took me almost a year to absorb these lessons and limitations of family practice; by then I realized I must return to psychiatry. There were too many intriguing questions that needed time to answer in dealing with individuals and in understanding the broader issues at the interface between medicine and psychiatry, between the effects of disease and peoples' unique responses to illness and its treatment. The way ahead soon declared itself.

—

145

A Maudsley contemporary had recently returned from a lecture tour in America. He was interested in appetite control and wanted to see my weight clinic. In America, he had consulted with a pharmaceutical company that marketed an appetite suppressant drug. They were looking to expand into the larger psychopharmacology arena and wanted to recruit a director of psychotropic drug research. Was I interested? Within weeks, I was flown to Cincinnati, interviewed, and offered the job at four times my current salary. I did not need a license to practice in industry, and I would have a day a week to teach medical students and psychiatric residents at the University of Cincinnati. I accepted.

Twice in a While

The desire to take medicine is perhaps the greatest feature that distinguishes man from animals.

—William Osler, MD

Published in *Wisconsin Medical Journal*, October 1986, Vol. 85:

In every age there are medicines of the moment that divide doctors and patients down the middle. In the eighteenth century it was opium; in the nineteenth, bromides; and in the early twentieth century, barbiturates. The 1960s ushered in the benzodiazepines (like Valium) in an era of John Kennedy's Camelot. By George Orwell's *1984* it was clear that some people were more equal than others and that these drugs were prescribed unequally often to women, the indigent, the elderly, and the maimed.

These new drugs were so safe that they could be used more often and for less reason, raising hackles on segments of the public. Were mind-tampering drugs being used to correct a social or chemical imbalance? Were doctors dabbling in existential predicaments beyond their bailiwick? Was there a medicine for mother-in-lawness or a pharmacologic lid to Pandora's Box?

These are all appropriate questions to be asked in an age that has amplified "anxiety" and invented safer "tranquilizers" to treat it. But the problem is broader and older than that. It has existed as long as there have been panaceas, a physician to prescribe them, and a public eager to seek such comfort. Even if the correct agenda is caretaking and not chemicals, the drugs often help in uncertain ways.

Which drug it is doesn't really matter. But how it happens does. It could be (and has been) various tonics, liver extract, Vitamin B12 shots, iron tablets, or thyroid pills. They are given to patients who visit doctors when life events have loaded up on them. Often these are symptom-sensitive people with the amplifier turned up on their autonomic arousal. They voice distress in body language and invite doctors to collude with diagnoses and prescriptions.

After they leave the office, life subsides or the pills placate them. A cycle is set. Next time a spouse leaves, a job ends, or a child sickens they return expectantly for more. "Those pills you gave me really helped," they say.

Doctors disagree about all this. Prescribers are "chemophilic hedonists" say the withholders. Withholders are "pharmacologic Calvinists" say the prescribers. My partner and I sit in friendly disagreement on opposite sides of this rhetorical fence. She is younger and knows where the benzodiazepine receptors are in the brain. When her patients see me, we talk briefly about their troubles. Some, in a minor way, seem more tranquil. Others sense the skepticism with which I write their refills.

"There isn't any harm," they ask, if I just take them once in a while?" "The only risk," I reply, "is twice in a while."

A Trivial Complaint

To do nothing is also a good remedy.

—Hippocrates

This bit of ancient wisdom is the siren song of family practice. Sometimes it is wrong.

In the autumn of 1967, a middle-aged man I had not seen before came to the surgery early on a weekday morning. His folder was bare; he was not a chronic complainer, and he suffered from no recorded diseases. Sitting across from me, he looked like your average suburban business executive, wearing a suit of expensive dark cloth with a herringbone pattern, set off by a regimental tie. He had probably stopped by on his way to corporate headquarters in the city.

As usual, I began with a few personal questions. Lifestyle can breed disease. He was married, two teenage kids doing well in school; he didn't smoke, drank moderately, no family history of chronic conditions, both his parents were still living. What was his job? Vice president for sales in a large multinational food conglomerate. Now that he was visibly relaxed, I asked why he had come to see me.

Pain in the right calf; he gestured toward his lower leg. When he was comfortable on the examining table, I prodded and poked the area; he grimaced slightly. It hurt "a bit" when he walked, and the ache was enough to make him restless last night. There was no bruising, perhaps a little swelling, not enough to justify the tape measure. The knee and ankle flexed easily without pain.

Did he have any explanations himself; had he done anything unusual; did he exercise regularly? He worked out three times a week in a local gym, but not for two weeks. He had just returned from a business trip to India, uncomfortable in economy (the corporation was tightfisted) but no accidents or falls.

148

Short of a diagnosis, I recommended heat pads if possible at work, but certainly at home in the evening. His wife was a former nurse and would know what to do. He might stop at the local pharmacy on the way to the commuter train for a mild analgesic. Call me next week or stop by the surgery again if it still bothered him or was any worse. Probably a pulled muscle.

Fifteen minutes later, he left for work, seemingly satisfied.

Two days later, his wife called our receptionist while I was seeing patients and left a message. Her husband had dropped dead while dressing for work. The coroner was doing an autopsy. She thought I would want to know.

Postscript: Over forty years later, six months after my hip replacement, I returned from a flight to England and a week later developed pain and swelling in my calf. My primary care doctor diagnosed a deep vein thrombosis and anticoagulated me before a lung x-ray revealed an asymptomatic pulmonary embolus. I had dodged the same bullet that killed my patient long before doctors knew or medical students were taught that prolonged air travel could cause blood clots and lethal emboli.

Wisdom always needs an update.

Elavil Deficiency?

Better Living through Chemistry

—DuPont corporate slogan, 1960s

Once David Goldberg became familiar with the patients he was interviewing in our practice, he noticed how many were being treated with Elavil, an antidepressant. "Was there an Elavil deficiency in the practice?" he asked with a smug smile.

At the Maudsley, I had been used to seeing people with severe (major) depression who had "classical" symptoms: hopelessness, lack of energy, poor concentration, severe sleep disturbance, early-morning ruminations (the ceaseless round of painful thought), suicidal ideas, and complete lack of pleasure (anhedonia). They deserved and received large doses of Elavil and had to tolerate the dry mouth, constipation, blurred vision, and urinary hesitancy as the price to pay for recovery.

In family practice, I saw a different picture. Like a thirty-year-old mother of two young children burdened with household chores and an unhelpful husband. Reluctantly she complained to me of being irritable, easily angry at the kids but quickly guilty afterward. She had difficulty falling asleep, woke feeling tired, and reluctantly admitted she had lost all interest in sex. This story wasn't in the textbooks nor was her reluctance to consider a psychiatric diagnosis (and certainly not referral to a psychiatrist). She wasn't keen on medicines either, especially one that had all the side effects I catalogued that might come on immediately when I couldn't promise benefit in less than three weeks. How would she be able to do the chores and care for the children?

So I became cunning, like a drug salesman. I selected a low dose, just enough to help her fall asleep without side effects. I explained this wasn't a sleeping pill which worked immediately but would take two to three hours to kick in. I quoted Shakespeare's *Macbeth*, "'Tis sleep that knits the raveled sleeve of care," and explained this benefit occurred after the first dose and would help her cope better with the kids and her husband. Interest in sex would certainly return, but perhaps not for a few weeks. When it did, it might help to recruit a babysitter and plan a night out on the town. I would see her again in a couple of weeks to see how things were going. She thanked me and managed a smile.

10. AMERICA

Then, Now, and Next

America: Love it or leave it.

—Popular saying

I have lived in America for forty-four years and been a citizen for twelve. It is no longer the same country it was when I arrived in 1968. I am too old at age seventy-eight to return where I came from, and the future here is uncertain. This is that story:

From Immigrant to Citizen

When you leave one country for another, you can expect advice, opinions, and questions. The professor of psychiatry at Guy's Hospital asked how old I was and felt that at thirty-four, I "might just make it." The year was 1968, the time of the urban riots in America, widely reported in the British press, stirring the concern of family and friends. Once we arrived, people often asked why we had come and seemed surprised to hear they "lived in the land of opportunity."

It was not unusual for academic physicians to spend a year or so in America before returning to resume their careers in Britain, but we certainly felt we were stepping into the deep end, headed for a job and a place about which we knew almost nothing. We traveled three days by sea to New York on a French luxury liner, were issued our green alien cards by immigration, and flew to Cincinnati where we were crowded into a small single hotel room because no one had remembered to book more comfortable accommodations; two crotchety adults and three exhausted children, aged nine, eight, and five.

I don't recall feeling nervous or overwhelmed. It was too new and exciting. Moved to more comfortable accommodations, we bought a used car and a Cape Cod house in the northern suburbs, with a large yard backing onto a horse farm, which we furnished from scratch. Everything seemed large and inexpensive compared to Britain; gas was twenty-odd cents a gallon, and folks were friendly in a time when immigrants were mostly legal and welcome. Perhaps a white skin and British accent helped, though the latter could be ambivalent, uppity, or distinguished, depending on the ear of the audience. And we had to learn to adjust our nouns: yard for garden, trunk for boot, gas for petrol, and tomato spelled the same but pronounced differently.

Domestic life for an immigrant, without family or friends, vacillates from tranquil to boring, but there were a few highlights worth mentioning about our assimilation into American culture as we adapted to its customs, mores, and norms over the ensuing months.

Americans are great fixer-uppers I sought to emulate. Eager to please the kids, I struggled to overcome mechanical ineptitude and put together a primitive tree house in the lower branches of the large oak tree in our backyard. The day after it was complete, a Midwest twister blew through the neighborhood, ripping it apart, scattering the components far and wide, but sparing the house. God had spoken; I was not designed to create things, only purchase them. From then on, my tool kit consisted of nothing more than a hammer, concrete, and super glue.

Apart from God's messenger, the weather, religion is a huge distinguishing feature between our transatlantic cultures. Britain is a secular nation with a state religion; America is a religiose republic whose Constitution forbids one. Both my parents were atheists, and so was I. In 1968,

—

America's places of worship were full, while in Britain they were empty and decaying. Even so, in those days, before prolife and gay marriage, nobody cared where you went on the Sabbath; religion meant minding your own business, not anybody else's.

Religion only mattered once, after my oldest son joined the Boy Scouts and I was recruited to be the scoutmaster, an unlikely role for someone unable to tie knots, pitch a tent, or believe in God. I muddled along until Simon, who later became an Eagle Scout, needed to acquire the religion merit badge. We were unable to meet the worshipful requirements, and my apostasy was revealed when I suggested a secular alternative. Consternation spread among the parents of the troop. Our phone rang at night as they tactfully explored the depth and strength of my unbelief. But, in the end, nobody else was willing to do the job of scoutmaster, and I ended up keeping it. This included presiding over the opening ceremony at our weekly troop meeting when I led the scouts in the pledge of allegiance, "one Nation under God . . ."

Some sports were an enigma. Nobody who grew up playing rugby could understand the nuances of American football. Fast and complex, it baffled my untutored eye; but the dancing elusive quarterback and floating thrilling throws were enough to lure me to the Sunday couch and glue me to the TV, but not the stadium. Baseball was an easier transition, mentored by an American spouse who is addicted to the game. Cricket is a poor cousin by comparison, slow, tedious, and prolonged, sometimes lasting a day or more, and lacking the athleticism, energy, and drama of baseball; the rowdy crowds, the peanuts, the beer, the brats, the tailgates, and the friendly banter between seatmates. Sometimes it seems as if the spectators, not the players, are on steroids, especially when the Brewers play our despised neighbors, the Cubs. So now we have season tickets.

America is a country that runs on credit, and credit cards are its currency. I never owned one in England, but I caught on quickly. A year or so after our arrival, I was flying to a conference, in the days of civilized travel, when the stewardess announced over the intercom that the passenger with the most credit cards would win a bottle of wine. That was me—total fifteen!

—

The Tipping Point

The events in our lives happen in a sequence in time but in their significance to ourselves they find their own order . . . the continuous thread of revelation.

—Eudora Welty

I had been in America for five years and was now acclimated to my role as an academic psychiatrist at the University of Cincinnati when former friends and colleagues in England notified me that the chair of psychiatry at Guy's Hospital was vacant and advertised. Why not apply?

During my time at Guy's as a student and house officer, the chair of the department was occupied by a charismatic psychiatrist who had published a book about mental illness for the public and also hosted a popular TV show on the same topic. Also a strong supporter of the Guy's rugby team, he invited me to take part in an episode; a healthy young athlete who was nevertheless susceptible to hypnotic suggestion.

I was ambivalent about returning to Britain, although I felt assured of local support, had a credible academic resume, and was confident I stood a chance. But things were also going well for me in America and the family was now settled. Why uproot them?

The lure of becoming top dog in my own teaching hospital prevailed; I also realized that to remain in America, I would soon need to take the accreditation exam for foreign graduates to obtain licensure. It was time to decide where I belonged.

So the British health service flew me to London for the interview and allowed time for preliminary talks with colleagues and inquiries of my own. My major rival for the post was a contemporary from the Maudsley Hospital. We knew each other well; I had been a volunteer subject in his dissertation study exploring Freud's Whore-Madonna Complex—the dichotomous masculine opinions about which female physical characteristics best match the role of an ideal wife or mistress.

154

This was to be accomplished by assigning a numerical rank to a series of carefully chosen photographs that ranged from romantic to pornographic. Our responses were analyzed to determine the extent to which each of us tended to integrate or segregate the characteristics into stereotypes.

The end result was to rank the volunteers from most to least inclined to stereotype the two distinct roles; wife-Madonna or whore-mistress. The reason I remember this well is that the two of us, now rivals for this leading academic teaching post, were tied at the top of the list.

What this study might mean I never questioned, but I had a suspicion that youthful incarceration in all-male boarding schools, lacking any female influence or presence (while exposed to illicit masturbatory magazine images), might encourage the development of stereotypic sexual role models.

If the interviewers were to ask each of us about our dissertation topics, I wondered how cheese would compete with sex. Certainly, it would divide the biological from the psychodynamic among both candidates and committee members.

One other prelude to the selection committee was an opportunity to meet the current acting chair at Guy's Hospital. This psychiatrist had been a faculty member during my time and must have known about my research as a house officer on psychiatry in the emergency room and Munchausen's syndrome. But he had no interest in this or any other aspect of my career. Instead, he immediately announced he had a candidate of his own and would pursue that person's appointment with vigor. He gave no reasons and entertained no discussion. I was berated and dismissed.

Understandably, my confidence was badly shaken; I had no certain idea why this had happened or what to do about it, although I suspected my perceived status as a protégé of his former chief might play a role. How ironic that the psychiatrist who predicted I "might make it in America at age thirty-four" was succeeded by another who made certain I wouldn't make it back to Britain at age thirty-nine! Today I would have filed a

—

personal grievance, but in the early 1970s, things were different; this kind of autocratic behavior and blatant patronage were tolerated and another reason why I left Britain. Seldom do three psychiatrists agree on one thing. I belonged in America.

The selection process itself was swift and certain. Four male candidates sat together attired in their Sunday best, engaged in uneasy conversation as each awaited a summons to meet the committee. After about twenty minutes of questions, each returned to the room to await the outcome. The chosen one was invited back and the rest were dismissed. It was not I; it was my former fellow resident and cowinner of the Whore-Madonna stakes!

This experience was the tipping point. I never again contemplated a return to Britain; instead, I took and passed the American licensing exam and two years later was appointed chair of psychiatry in a brand-new medical school.

It is forty years since fate launched the careers of two academic leaders on opposite sides of the Atlantic. We had participated in a thought-provoking study capable of spawning a testable hypothesis and, perhaps, a publication: *The Role of the Whore-Madonna Complex on Marital Stability*. Neither of us had the guts or resources to do the necessary research. But my first marriage fell apart within two years of this interview while my second has lasted thirty-five years. I learned, but I didn't teach.

Becoming a Citizen: Act One: Sixteenth Century Law

When I arrived in America in 1968 at the age of thirty-four, I viewed myself as a temporary immigrant, trying out the culture. But after ten years, married to an American wife and with an established professional identity, it was time to embrace citizenship. So I applied. This bit tells the story of why it was twenty-two years before the goal was accomplished, and I finally took the oath of allegiance.

Back in the 1970s, an aspiring citizen was required to appear before a circuit-riding legal adjudicator, accompanied by two witnesses of at least five years' acquaintance who could testify to the applicant's character and worthiness.

At the appointed hour, I arrived with two faculty members, my vice chair (a psychoanalyst) and the director of medical student education (a female psychologist and friend). I was immediately ushered into the investigator's office while my two colleagues were told to wait outside.

My inquisitor came quickly to the point, "I see you've been married twice; could you tell me the name, address, and phone number of your former spouse?" His second question aimed for the bull's eye, "Did you by any chance have sexual intercourse with your present wife while still married to your first?"

I was sufficiently acculturated to ask, "Could I plead the Fifth?" Yes, but if my application proceeded, I would have to answer the same question asked by the judge in open court.

I surrendered and withdrew the application. "What would happen next?" I asked. Helpful, he told me, "Immigration law dates from the sixteenth century, and there is a three-year statute of limitations. Then you can apply again."

I stood, thanked him, turned, and left in a hurry, tail between my legs. My colleagues were surprised to see me back so soon and to learn their testimony would not be needed.

Becoming a Citizen: Act Two: Room 102

There are eight of us seated opposite one another in a narrow corridor with a wooden bench and five plastic chairs on each side. We are around a corner and out of sight from others, although the scenery from where we sit is magnificent. Inside the impressive façade of the federal courthouse is a soaring atrium supported by red and gray-green marble columns with shiny matching floors and walls decorated with Grecian motifs.

We are an ethnic smorgasbord of Asian, Hispanic, and Caucasian descent, most dressed casually in sneakers, T-shirts and skirts or jeans. Men outnumber women, and a majority is middle-aged. Shortly we are joined by a father and son dressed in Muslim attire, the older with a white beard and walker. Another Asian man arrives, carrying a small baby girl with a tuft of hair tied in a topknot by a rubber band.

Everyone stays silent, but a diminutive Hmong man with a goatee and drooping mustache paces nervously. A younger Caucasian lad with a cell phone, who seems to be his helper, reassures him.

My appointment is for eight-fifty, but with a fetish for punctuality, I am ten minutes early. The massive door to the left of us is closed but its sign says, "U.S. Immigration and Naturalization Service—Examination Branch." Beneath, in smaller letters, is the statement, "Individuals with scheduled interview appointments should report here." Next to the impressive lintel is a metal frame with the plastic numbers 1, 0, and 2.

The bolder folks and those who have been to Room 102 before know to open the door. Inside is a small room, on the right wall of which is the INS seal with its motto, *Qui Pro Domine Justitia Sequitur*. To the left is a glass partition behind which one would hope to find a receptionist, but it is boarded up, and in front of it is a tray with an invitation to "place your interview letter here." I do so and go back outside to sit down. By nine-ten, fourteen of us are gathered, and two people have been called by a disembodied voice that shouts out a name from around the corner. Those called for enter through a back door with an opaque glass panel that is kept firmly locked.

By now it is obvious we are in for a long wait—at nine-thirty-five, a man in a red shirt with a Mexican logo reenters the small room and returns with the news that all our letters are still stacked up in the tray. There is an air of submission—even subjugation. It is another five minutes before I summon the courage to check for myself. Sure enough, my letter is where I left it but now buried under ten later arrivals. This seems the perfect Catch-22—the earlier you arrive, the later you will be seen. As a former physician, I am painfully aware of the logic of block booking—everyone else's time is less valuable than yours.

With little else to do, I begin to ruminate about my experiences with the INS.

It is thirty years since I came to America. It still delights me when I am asked why. "Because it's the land of opportunity," I say—a fact that most second-generation Americans have forgotten. Still, it was a long time before I felt I belonged and wanted to become an American. Three years ago, when my career as a psychiatrist began to wind down, I applied for citizenship. In the early months, I called an 800 number in Nebraska often to hear an automated voice report the lack of progress on my application.

It was a year before I heard anything, and then it was a request for fingerprints. The local police station obliged, but the FBI rejected the prints—I went back for a second set, which were also rejected in spite of a letter explaining that perhaps the problem was mild eczema of the fingertips. Now the INS wanted a third set taken by "an FBI expert." I called the FBI, but they had never heard of such a person. Eventually, I was referred to a local Hispanic community center where a third set was taken.

Meanwhile I had been scheduled for my citizenship test and was studying hard from the standard texts available—helped by a list of the one hundred most often-asked questions published by the *New York Times*. This was my first visit to Room 102. It lasted only about an hour and was anticlimactic. The "test" consisted of a mimeographed sheet of ten multiple-choice questions. The first was, "How many stars are there on the American flag? a) ten, b) twenty, c) forty, d) fifty." I finished in less than two minutes with a score of ten out of ten.

The examiner assured me that I could expect to soon be called for the swearing-in ceremony. It was eighteen months since I filed the application, so I hoped to be done within two years. But it was not to be. I received a letter informing me that the third set of prints was not acceptable, and I

—

should present myself in three months' time for a fourth attempt—but this time at the federal courthouse. This was my second visit to Room 102. A militaristic young man in a white coat wearing rubber gloves saw me. He made three attempts, discarded them all, and finally came up with a fourth set which he "hoped would be good enough." They were not. Months later, I received yet another letter asking me to return for a fifth attempt.

I now decided to seek the help of a local congressman. A liaison person expressed her own frustrations at dealing with the INS. They were chronically underfunded and poorly staffed, a reflection of the contemporary anti-immigration sentiments and the lack of will by Congress to improve the agency. Waits of two to three years were not unusual. The reason for a fifth request for fingerprints was an INS rule that two failed tests must occur within six months before any alternative action could be considered to rule out a criminal background. Another Catch-22. The slower the system operates, the more likely you will have to do things over. Fortunately, the congressman's office did have a contact at the INS, and after a few weeks, a letter arrived, canceling the fingerprint appointment. No reason was given, and no alternative indicated. A month or so later, I received a summons to appear at Room 102 six days hence—the day after the Memorial Day weekend, which conflicted with a long-planned visit to my son in New Jersey. I was forced to cancel and waited another three months to be rescheduled.

Ruminating on all this helped pass the time. Outside Room 102, it was now well past ten o'clock. It also made me irritated—clearly people arriving after me had been called. The man next to me sympathized—he also had been in America thirty years (from Mexico) and had failed the fingerprint test four times. His wife had passed but had been awaiting the swearing-in ceremony for ten months. I decided to complain. But how to do so was unclear. The doors were all locked. INS correspondence lists no phone numbers and agents are careful not to give out names.

I waited for the next name to be called, shot round the corner and accosted the name-caller. He was distinctly dour and unfriendly, scuttling quickly back behind the door he had just unlocked and attempting to shut it in my face. He threatened to call security when I requested the name of a supervisor, so I placed my foot in the door space to keep the dialogue alive. He gave me a name and I let the door close. Two minutes later a woman appeared asking if I had "tried to kick the door down" and complaining that she had little time to deal with complaints because she was "on a conference call." She wore a neat, peach-colored suit that set off her light tan complexion. I wanted to ask if she was an immigrant and how long it took her to become a citizen but decided this was not the time. She did explain that there were only two examiners on duty and each had seventeen appointments booked at fifteen-minute intervals. Unfortunately, I was in the slow lane. But I was next.

My fellow immigrants seemed heartened by this assertive display but uninclined to join in when I suggested we celebrate by singing "God Bless America." Another fifteen minutes passed, and I was finally called at eleven o'clock—two hours and ten minutes after my appointment time.

The agent who saw me was charming and in her twenties. She normally deals with adopted children and orphans but had been drafted because of the backlog. She ushered me into her cluttered cubicle and apologized for the delay. I learned again about the frustrations and low morale of an overburdened staff. I swore an oath, testified to my lack of a criminal record, and was told that my file would be complete as soon as I produced a letter from the local police confirming this. Of course, I could have brought this with me if asked. The nice young lady stated that all I now had to do was be sworn in—but it might be a year from now and four years since my application was filed. As she escorted me out, I noticed a Post-it stuck on her side of the door. It read, "Keep Door Locked."

Calling the congressman's aide to report progress, I learned of yet another step in the process—a final "quality control" check of all "completed" files to ensure they are complete.

Still curious about the motto on the INS seal, I consulted a friend and Latin scholar. It means, "He who is with the Lord follows justice." It seems a strange maxim for an agency that now processes so many Muslims, Buddhists, and Hindus. But whatever the deity, today's mills do grind exceedingly slowly.

—

When I brood about my experiences with the INS and Room 102, I think about the signers of the Declaration of Independence who went to war with my British ancestors because of the injustice they felt about taxation without representation. I have paid taxes for thirty years and only hope I get to vote before I die. If not, my estate will be taxed at higher rates because death came faster than the INS.

Postscript: On Thursday, January 27, 2000, I took the Oath of Allegiance to the United States before a federal judge in the atrium of the federal courthouse, across from Room 102. There were sixty-seven immigrants from twenty-four nations gathered for the ceremony. It was three years and two months since my second application was filed, and thirty-two years after I arrived in America.

Nonassimilation

Man in a crowd is a quite different creature than man acting alone.

—William Jennings Brown

According to the Myers-Briggs Personality Inventory, I am an INTJ—on the cusp between extroversion and introversion. Anyone who plays rugby, carouses with teammates, and sings bawdy songs is assumed to be an extrovert. But boarding school trimmed my sails. Everything there was communal; nothing was individual, private, or personal. So I tend to avoid "belonging" to organizations or, when I do, I swim against the current. It is not a popular or wise strategy, nor does it foster career development where "networking" and "going along to get along" are the alleged keys to success. My kids are like that too, so I suspect a genetic "Blackwell" component (via my father's side) that favors the underdog over authority and solitude over crowds.

Switching countries at age thirty-four was certainly not helpful either. Bonding is strongest in the early stages of a career. In America, those destined for distinction in psychiatry are groomed at the National Institutes of Health (NIH), are board-certified examiners, and card-carrying members of the American Psychiatric Association (APA).

I indulged in the latter but neither of the former. I should and could have proved myself by taking boards in my specialty, but stubborn hubris and exam phobia kept me from doing so, comforted by the assumption I didn't need to in order to progress up the academic ladder. This excluded me from convivial and influential influence makers. It was not helped by my late arrival at the table and lack of psychoanalytic training. But independence, the "man acting alone," has intrinsic rewards also.

America is xenophobic toward other countries' credentials. Once I decided to stay in America and practice here, I had to take an exam that allowed me to prove I still knew the fundamentals of medicine. I did. To practice in Wisconsin, I was also required to show I could speak fluent English. I mailed the licensing board a few of my publications and threatened to sue them if they denied me a livelihood. They backed down!

While my story as a psychiatrist in America unfolds, readers may decide for themselves about the price paid or benefits incurred by "nonassimilation" with my profession.

2010 Redux

2010 was a year of mindless ignorance spreading through the land like a plague. Perhaps it was an outbreak of undiagnosed mad cow disease or epidemic hysteria. Our president was a "Muslim or Nazi," evolution and global warming were "myths," and the federal budget could be balanced without raising taxes or reducing services. The Tea Party surfaced as the recurring cultural manifestation of angry "know nothings" with Sarah Palin as its standard bearer. The public preferred to risk being blown up in midair to security screening on terra firma.

With a metal hip, I am among the two percent of travelers routinely "patted down." This is mildly intrusive, time-consuming, and irritating, but someone who mistakes a "pat down" for a "grope" has either a deeply deprived or wildly imaginative libido. The idea that a bored TSA worker of your own gender might be aroused by a blurry image of your private parts amounts to phallic or mammary narcissism.

—

The End of Camelot

The 2010 election raised serious concerns about the state of our democracy in my own mind and that of others. How had we gotten to this point of political and social unease?

Britain and America have each made mistakes at opposite ends of the socioeconomic spectrum. Britain, an ancient culture, used to compromise and caring, has overextended its entitlement programs, while America, a new republic, proud of individual autonomy and skeptical of government, has overvalued unregulated commerce, embraced greed, and neglected the sick and needy. In both cultures, the crisis drives a wedge between conservative and liberal ideologies, exaggerating fear-driven remedies that undermine bipartisan compromise.

The fear and rage now engulfing the United States is an emotional, preintellectual awareness that America is quickly becoming a second-class nation and that political gridlock is preventing timely remedial action. A democracy or a republic cannot function without an informed electorate willing to vote and elected representatives able to compromise and develop consensus on behalf of the people who elected them, without undue fiduciary influence from special interests. When this system breaks down or becomes dysfunctional, it threatens the ideals of democracy, the identity of the country, and dreams of a future for its citizens and their children. When people fail to understand or lose influence, scapegoats proliferate; big government, illegal immigrants, taxes, homosexuals, socialism, Islam, outsourcing. This is a visceral reaction that comes from the gut, not the head.

Citizen anger is directed to politicians of both parties in a frenzy of "throw out the bums." Political preferences are based on idiosyncratic or irrelevant issues because what has not yet emerged is a thoughtful analysis of the root cause and an alternative solution. Muted murmurs of armed insurrection by civilian militias offer only anarchy which could destroy democracy. These are rightly and recurrently identified as "know nothing" movements.

What is necessary for real change is the recognition that economic recession is not the root source, but a symptom, of our malaise. Anger and fear is deflected onto the sources of pain rather than diagnosing the cause.

Two fundamental but intertwined factors contribute to this source; an increase in income disparity, and greed with a dysfunctional political system leading to gridlock. The next bits elaborate on these themes.

Ill Fares the Land

Ill fares the land, to hastening ills a prey
Where wealth accumulates, and men decay.

—Oliver Goldsmith, *The Deserted Village* (1770)
Quoted by Tony Judt, 2010

It is only when you look back over a lifetime that you can see clearly the changes that have taken place. So it is with my time in America. This bit amplifies and clarifies the political commentary in the preceding bit, "Then, Now, and Next," with some redundancy and repetition for which I ask forgiveness. Two years separate their creation, and my old brain is still absorbing new information!

When I landed on these shores in 1968, the tectonic plates of social and political change were just beginning to shift. The decades before and after the Second World War stood in stark contrast; from the depths of the Great Depression to the expansive, optimistic years of the Eisenhower presidency; from income disparity to a more equitable distribution of wealth. In this climate, citizens were generally cheerful, hopeful, unafraid, and generously inclined.

But the year I arrived, 1968, was also a moment of civil unrest with inner-city riots; it seemed to be a civil rights upheaval, but, in retrospect, was probably prodromal of much more to come.

165

What that might be became clearer when a friend suggested I read Tony Judt's book with the same title as this bit, taken from the poem cited above. These words are from a four-hundred-thirty-line epic poem by the British author and poet, Oliver Goldsmith. Goldsmith was born around 1730, ten years after the South Sea Bubble had burst, making citizens aware of the dangers of unbridled greed and capitalism.

Oliver was a dilettante who led a chaotic and somewhat debauched life but with a kind gentle heart and a philosophical frame of mind. Educated at Trinity College, Dublin, he barely scraped a liberal arts degree before going on to study but fail in medicine (at Edinburgh University), law, and religion. After he was turned down for ordination, he began a successful career as a writer; he was author of the much admired *Vicar of Wakefield* (1766). A friend of Dr. Samuel Johnson and Horace Walpole (British politician, playwright and author), the latter described Oliver as "an inspired idiot." Oliver, at one time, planned to migrate to America but characteristically "missed his ship." He died young at age forty-six.

The Deserted Village describes the demolition of an ancient mythical village, sweet Auburn, in order to clear space for the private garden of a wealthy landowner. It contrasts the tragic impact on the villagers with the privileged life of their nemesis:

> Amidst thy bowers the tyrant's hand is seen,
> And desolation saddens all thy green.
> One only master grasps the whole domain . . .

Like myself, Judt was born and educated in Britain at Cambridge University, then lived in America and was a university professor (at New York University). He died of Lou Gehrig's disease in 2010, the year his book was published. He is described as an outstanding historian with a clear-sighted view of international politics and a "fearless critic of narrow orthodoxies and bullying cliques" (Obituary, *The Guardian*, August 8, 2010).

Judt uses the subject matter of *The Deserted Village* as a metaphor for our current sociopolitical climate, focusing on the huge and growing income disparity, in both Britain and America, its cause, impact, and possible future outcome.

He captures his readers' attention by focusing early on the impact of income inequality in a nation and its citizens with three graphs which show a statistical correlation with poor health, mental illness, and crime in the Western nations. While statistical correlation does not prove causation, the USA is a startling outlier in all three outcomes related to income disparity.

Judt goes on to catalogue evidence for the gap increasing between what he calls "private affluence and public squalor" since the late 1970s, between conspicuous consumption and accumulation of excessive assets by the wealthy compared to failing schools, collapsing infrastructure, lack of health insurance, underwater mortgages, and bankruptcies that impact the poor and middle class.

He contrasts the current situation with the post-World War II period between 1945 and 1980 when faith in capitalism had been eroded by the prewar Depression while faith in government was enhanced by the evils of fascism and communism and victory in the war.

At this time, there developed almost universal belief in the benevolence of the democratic state with policies governed by a moral imperative to provide for the poor, needy, sick, elderly, and unemployed. This involved progressive taxation, government regulations and restraints, the GI Bill, publicly supported education, pensions and health care for the elderly, and education for the young. In Europe, even public ownership of essential industries and universal health care were included. All this resulted in broad-based upward social mobility and an expectation that children could surpass their parents on the economic ladder.

Judt summarizes this state of affairs as follows: "For three decades following the war, economists, politicians, and citizens all agreed that high public expenditure, administered by local or national authorities, with considerable latitude to regulate life at all levels, was good social policy."

—

After distinguishing where we are now with what went before, Judt examines the sociopolitical forces that sustained such an apparently ideal system among and between different Western nations. First, he identifies the need for trust between citizens as essential to common purpose and chooses taxation as an example; that money would be fairly raised and wisely used for the common good without scofflaws or loopholes. At this time in history, the Judeo-Christian ethic was widely accepted by the American public in an uncomplicated way—free of political, fundamentalist, or bizarre creedal overtones: "For unto whomsoever much is given, of him shall much be required; and to which men have committed much, of him they will ask more" (Luke 12:48).

Judt points out that comity is easier in small, culturally homogeneous nations and names the Scandinavian countries, the Netherlands, and Austria as examples. By contrast, America is a vast domain with no single ethnic or religious majority, flooded with immigrants like myself who have diverse economic, cultural, and religious backgrounds.

An important impact of the Second World War was Roosevelt's insistence on "shared interests and purposes and needs of *all* Americans."

To sustain common purpose in a democratic society requires a commitment to compromise and avoidance of demagoguery while preserving civilized dissent. Beginning in the 1960s, there was a diminution of collective purpose in favor of individualism; the rights of segments of society; women, patients, consumers, and homosexuals, over the common good. During this period, the iconic figures of social democracy died or were assassinated—John and Robert Kennedy, Martin Luther King, and Lyndon Johnson. They were replaced by right-of-center politicians like Ronald Reagan and Margaret Thatcher. Government became identified as the problem and not the solution, and taxation became demonized as no longer for the common good but as a personal affliction to be avoided if possible.

The unifying ideals of the Sermon on the Mount, like the concept "Love thy neighbor as thyself" supported by a personal commitment of time, treasure, or talent, were replaced by self-referent and divisive ideologies like abortion, contraception, and gay marriage that demanded little personal sacrifice beyond a loud voice and a large placard. Simultaneously, it became fashionable to question evolution, global warming, or the need to conserve natural resources.

Deliberate underfunding or privatization of communal or government resources in favor of for-profit entrepreneurs occurred in prisons, energy utilities, higher education, transportation, and postal services as federal and state tax support dwindled. Moral obligations changed along with this shift in ownership. The profit motive and insatiable greed drove up prices, leading to unsupportable debt and bankruptcy in home ownership and educational loans.

The idea of providing services for the public good was extinguished. Judt comments: "The result is an eviscerated society. From the point of view of the person at the bottom seeking unemployment pay, medical attention, social benefits, or other officially mandated services, it is no longer to the State, the administration or the government that he or she instinctively turns." Even our military is supported by thousands of private contractors. Later, Judt notes the paradoxical outcome: "The loss of social purpose articulated through public service actually *increases* the power of the over-mighty State."

This decline in community consensus and a lack of commitment to the instruments of democratic government have been associated with an erosion of the process itself. Turnout at elections has declined as citizens realize their vote is subordinated to financial lobbies and to the advertising impact of anonymous super PACs fueled by profit-making organizations and billionaires. The voting process itself is being stifled by redistricting and impediments to voting imposed by the unsubstantiated possibility of fraud.

Finally, as Judt comments, the contemporary cohort of politicians "convey neither conviction nor authority." He goes on to say that "the institutions of the republic have been degraded by money. Worse, the language of politics itself has been vacated of substance and meaning." Partly this is due to what Judt describes as "the suppression of genuine debate"; the replacement of civilized discussion by demagoguery. He says of the Tea Party: "Far from opening debate they shut it down." The

—

recent development of rigorous fact-checking reveals the depressing news that many, perhaps the majority, of politicians' statements, when independently examined, are partial or total falsehoods. Among them is the American conviction that "socialism" is the demon responsible for Europe's debt crisis and to be avoided at all costs. Judt's opinion is far more nuanced; he points out that Europe has long since moved beyond the kind of radical attempt to replace capitalism in Britain after World War II. There is now a much more balanced blend of capitalism with what he prefers to call "social democracy." What he does not say, but may well be so, is that melding together so many disparate cultures into a single Eurozone may have eroded the comity necessary for success and bred the dissension and dysfunction that is undermining the enterprise.

When Judt arrives at the point where he writes hopefully of "the shape of things to come," his focus becomes the need to revive a sense of common purpose and social justice, which succeeded in banishing income inequality for a quarter of a century. Standing in the way is the fear that accompanies economic instability. "We are assuredly less confident of our collective purpose, our environmental well-being or our personal safety than at any time since World War II. We have no idea what sort of world our children will inherit but we can no longer delude ourselves into supposing that it must resemble our own."

Globalization is forcing America into the same kind of uneasy collaborative relationships with cultural strangers that threaten the Eurozone.

What is currently lacking in America is a commitment to a blend of capitalism and social justice that constitutes "social democracy." Instead, we are locked into a false "either-or" debate and have lapsed back into a polarized "know nothing" advocacy for "American exceptionalism," "big government" disparagement, and anti-tax sentiment, an environment in which the rich get richer and the poor go to the wall. One thing we have learned is that greed is an insatiable urge, and that, for its victims, there is never enough. It cannot go unregulated because it will not regulate itself.

—

I have gone to some length to summarize and parse Tony Judt's ideas because they resonate with my own experiences, told in these bits and pieces. America is no longer what it was when both of us, born and educated in Britain, migrated to this country. As a physician, I have lived through the changes described so eloquently by this distinguished historian and wish, like he does, that it is not too late to turn things around.

In the end, Judt remains hopeful but offers no specific solution. He notes that "grotesquely unequal societies are also unstable societies." They generate internal division and, sooner or later, internal strife—usually with undemocratic outcomes.

On the eve of the 2012 presidential election, America stands at a tipping point. Tony Judt exited this life before the outcome, still hopeful but leaving a sharply divided citizenry, a gridlocked Congress, and two parties in a bitter battle to the death between capitalism and social democracy with no compromise in sight.

My best hope is that one or other party will gain control of both the legislative and executive branches, accept the need to compromise, and lead the country in the direction of a social democracy in the way Tony would have wished.

My worst fear is that this may not happen, and America will confront the lessons of history.

Throughout the ages, intractable income disparity has brought down kings, governments, nations, and empires beginning with the English Magna Carta, Europe's peasant revolts, the Roman Empire, the Russian revolution, Gandhi's peaceful civil disobedience in India, and today's Arab spring.

If the political parties remain obdurate, special interests, lobbyists, and PACs continue to wield sufficient influence to suborn democracy and citizens remain apathetic, America could become the first democratic republic to bring about its own destruction.

—

There is no more odious tyranny than income disparity and the evil it imposes on the least of its citizens; worse than war, it destroys its own kith and kin from within.

Manifesto for a Democratic Republic

We, the people, endorse capitalism without greed with safety nets for the poor and needy free from fraud and undue dependency.

We expect politics without corruption and civilized, truthful debate that facilitates compromise and leads to consensus.

We accept taxation sufficient to ensure the fair distribution of wealth throughout society and regulations adequate to stifle abuse while encouraging entrepreneurship and economic growth.

Amen.

Greed: The Deadliest Sin

Greed is expansive; it feeds on itself at the expense of principal. There is never enough. It betrays family, friends, colleagues, and fellow citizens. Greed is corrosive; those that succumb to its lure no longer work for pleasure, no longer teach for joy, or perform research with integrity or for the thrill of discovery. Greed is infectious; it spreads from person to person and place to place, bred in environments that lack intellectual, emotional, and spiritual rewards. Greed takes over whenever science becomes mundane, repetitive, boring, or duplicative. Greed perpetuates itself, producing nothing innovative, creative, or unique; it cultivates its own sterile, infertile seedbed. Greed is cunning; it hides behind platitudes, excuses, rationalizations, and deceit. Greed is ubiquitous in industry, finance, politics, medicine, education, and entitlement programs, its tentacles spread throughout society. Greed is tenacious; it can destroy cultures, institutions, nations, organizations, and individuals. Civilization rests on the triumph of generosity over greed, of equity over avarice.

Not between conservatives or liberals, democracy or dictatorship, deism or atheism, constitutions or commandments. Today, the outcome is in doubt.

Is Greed an Addiction?

Humans are the only animals, outside the laboratory, that abuse their own appetites and can become addicted to their sources of gratification. Drugs (including alcohol and nicotine), sex, money, and foods are included, defined as compulsive activities an individual is unable to stop abusing despite negative consequences.

In recent years, America has seen an upsurge in food addiction, resulting in an epidemic of morbid obesity and its medical complications. The addiction already associated with money is gambling, also on the rise. Sixty percent of the population gambles in any given year using casinos, lotteries, the Internet, card rooms, and bingo halls. Out of that number, 1 percent are addicted and 3 percent are problematic. Some segments of the population are at increased risk; teens and college kids showed a six hundred percent increase in four recent years (2001-2005), while adults in Utah are twice as likely to be problem or pathological gamblers (6 percent of the population).

Undoubtedly, most addicts outrun their resources or incur complications of their addiction; almost half (48 percent) consider suicide and 13 percent attempt to kill themselves.

It seems logical to consider the possibility that addiction to money is not confined to casinos and may have spread to corporate headquarters and the boardroom. Greed is defined as "intense and selfish desire for wealth, power or food" (OED). Greed feeds its own appetite. For food, this is often in takeout or fast-food chains, "all you can eat" buffets, and obscene portion sizes; for money, addiction may be reinforced by stock options, bonuses, and salary increases not linked to productivity.

In 2008, the highest-paid CEO in America made over $700 million. The next person in line took home $556 million despite a 21 percent drop in the corporation's stock price. The bottom CEO of the top ten earned a meager $72 million—$60 million of that in stock options, during a year when the price of the corporate stock dropped 70 percent. This suggests a questionable relationship between performance and reward. The amounts involved are so beyond the common person's experience or imagination, they must inevitably call into question what possible motives require them.

With this kind of money, few, if any, of the normal checks and balances exist that keep addictions at bay, including shame, bankruptcy, declining health, stigma, and family concerns. On the contrary, families feed from the same trough, corporate health benefits are princely, and lobbyists bribe politicians to avoid or minimize regulations that might curtail free market conditions or check profit margins.

In Greek mythology, King Midas of Phrygia came to rue the god-given ability that turned everything he touched into gold because it included the food he attempted to eat and his own daughter. Starving to death and grieving for his child, Midas begged the gods to cancel his golden touch, and they generously obliged.

In today's nonmythic world, money addicts have no reason to seek relief but can gloat in private over their growing hoards. The only people held responsible for this largesse are those of us who feed the beast by buying what is offered. The doctrine of *caveat emptor* (Latin for "Let the buyer beware") was established in U.S. law with a Supreme Court decision written in 1817 by Chief Justice Marshall. It states that a buyer is responsible for assessing the quality of a product or service before purchasing it. Over the years, this ruling has been modified by consumer protection laws and regulations against fraud. But anyone who has bought a used car from a slick salesman or stocks from Bernie Madoff knows this is still a bumpy road to travel.

Greed may not be bloody or lethal and is not a capital crime, but it deserves credit as the deadliest sin because it is so pervasive and insidious. It can operate whenever goods and services are sold for profit, and it frequently corrupts those government agencies charged to define standards or protect the public from fraud. Witness the SEC's (Securities and Exchange Commission) failure to investigate Madoff.

—

Greed is also enabled by politicians who claim that competition always drives down costs. This may be true for everyday products like clothes, computers, and cars, but is seldom true for those who want to enhance or extend quality of life, seeking health care, education, safety, or a home of their own. When a buyer wants the best in these arenas and the seller knows that, the table is set for excessive lending and profit, usury, price fixing, or fraud. The end of that story is already told in underwater mortgages, crushing college loans beyond hope of redemption, and untreated illness leading to foreclosure, bankruptcy, and death.

If, as a society, we decline to set standards or limits on how much wealth is enough, we will inevitably enable a growing addiction to greed. Today's numbers suggest it is thriving, is unrestrained, and is increasing. It is upsetting the balance and distribution of wealth in our civilization and could destroy it.

The normal addict, like Midas, places his own life at risk. The greed addicts, like Madoff, Wall Street CEOs, and the barons of Big Pharma gamble for higher stakes; blind to the welfare of others.

Welcome to the world of the morbidly wealthy!

A Constitutional Conundrum

We have always known that heedless self-interest was bad morals; we now know it is bad economics.

—Franklin D. Roosevelt

America needs a united citizenry with the desire and determination to elect a government that can develop a plan and implement a strategy to meld together capitalism without greed and social welfare without dependency. Can the Constitution Americans are justly proud of accomplish that?

Those who crafted the Constitution were wealthy, white landowners but, unlike the lord of sweet Auburn, their struggles with mentally handicapped

George III and his recalcitrant Parliament sensitized them to the needs and rights of people like the unemancipated villagers. In the age of a dawning Enlightenment, the framers of the Declaration of Independence saw the justice of "liberty and freedom for all" even though blacks, women, and poor whites would have to survive a brutal Civil War and long-delayed constitutional amendments to await their turn.

Today the picture has shifted. Entitlement programs for the elderly (Social Security), the handicapped and needy (Title 19 and Medicaid), or medical needs of the old (Medicare) have ballooned due in part to poverty, lack of health care, and an aging population.

Working among the inner-city poor, the homeless, and the mentally ill, I know there is overuse, fraud, and abuse in these programs. I am also aware of serious attempts to curb and restrain these. My patients with severe mental illness sometimes became homeless, were often without health care, frequently incarcerated in (expensive) prisons and, when they applied for Title 19 or Medicare, were routinely rejected on repeated occasions for unjust reasons.

On the other hand, my work with illness behavior and psychosomatic medicine taught me how difficult it is to treat or deter those who seek or have found refuge from a hostile environment in a sick role endorsed by softhearted or gullible health care providers.

If I imagine an economic balance sheet between corporate greed and welfare abuse, it tips heavily toward the dark side of unfettered capitalism. As I suggest in the preceding bits, greed is insatiable and currently unregulated or unstoppable. It has corrupted any proposed constitutional restraints by using its ill-gotten gains to lobby and bribe senators and congressmen, influence elections (with Supreme Court help), depress voting rights, and evade regulations. Worse still, it has undermined faith in government, disparaged as "big," as well as the social purposes and moral foundation for a progressive income tax used to fund the social safety nets.

Our War of Independence from Britain was fueled by a deep resentment against "taxation without representation." The Constitution substituted our democratic system where the amount and use of tax dollars were set by a government elected by and responsible to its citizens. There was consensus about how progressive taxation would be and how wide the safety net.

This is no longer true; a corrupt legislative branch, in thrall to special interests, an ideological judiciary whose votes are predicted prior to argument, and an impotent executive branch have created a loophole-ridden and increasingly unprogressive tax code. The middle income and poorer folks would like to see this reformed but have lost their capacity to influence events. This is a modern version of "taxation without representation" imposed from within, not from abroad.

No wonder every politician of either stripe panders to the anger this creates with perpetual promises to never raise taxes, increasing stress on the safety nets, and fueling public concern about their integrity. This is the perfect Catch-22, a product of political gridlock and stubborn rejection of political compromise.

Consider the following unintended outcomes of our Constitution and the need for change:

- The ideal of free speech condones political advertisements, half of which are, at best, half truthful. As a result, most elected politicians appear to be confirmed liars.
- The ideal of individual liberty underestimated human nature and the influence on it of unregulated greed (Wall Street, Big Oil, Big Pharma, disproportionate distribution of wealth).
- It overvalued the merit of legislative procedures that allow opinionated minorities to obstruct reasoned consensus (Senate filibuster rules).
- It overestimated the ability of the populace to understand complex issues (deficits, immigration, and evolution) and the willingness to vote wisely to solve them (low voter turnouts and "know nothing" movements, driven by passion for a simpler past).
- It failed to anticipate the difficult balance between unrestricted, abused, or unwisely used entitlement programs (food stamps,

—

unemployment, Social Security, Medicaid, Medicare) and the moral imperatives of a society to care for those in most need (the homeless, those without health care, the inner-city poor, and children left behind). Attempts to reconcile this conflict are derisively labeled "socialism" and rejected or ignored.

- It did not recognize that a society that valued individual accomplishment and independence might empower the "haves" to turn their backs on the "have-nots."
- It created ambiguity about the role of religion in government, opening the door to the role of faith over reason in policy making (abortion, stem cell research, prohibition, women's emancipation).
- It failed to define the destructive potential of unlimited access to firearms used to intentionally or accidentally kill one another rather than defend the nation from nonexistent foreign invaders, despite the existence of a fully armed standing army and a reserve.
- It legitimized ways to cull the poorest and sickest members from the population (a "volunteer" army, absence of a draft, no health care for the poor, and prison for the mentally ill).
- It anticipated the need for constitutional amendments but made the criteria and process deliberately difficult. Today's adversarial political climate makes it impossible to achieve consensus for change when a sizeable portion of the electorate looks backward, not forward, or is apathetic.
- The House of Representatives has two-year tenure which demands incessant fund raising and allows special interests to preempt voters' wishes. This also allows well-heeled incumbents to cling to office. Now the public demands change but, driven by recession and fear, is unwilling to wait for it, electing presidents who promise change but voting out their representatives two years later.

If the founders of the nation and framers of our constitution were resurrected, they might welcome the opportunity to contribute their wisdom to do what they never anticipated might become necessary. Human nature simply has not achieved what their idealism anticipated. Here is a suggestion:

—

Vague promises of "change" cannot solve this problem. Only specific, honest, and common-sense remedies will suffice, formulated by new and trustworthy leadership and made available to everyone in easily understandable language, independently vetted for accuracy and truth. Endorsed by a national plebiscite, the plan would then be implemented by a coalition, nonpartisan government, elected for a single ten-year term. Its primary purpose would be to fuse the best attributes of capitalism and social welfare but purge each of greed and dependence. Ample resources to rebuild our nation would be made available by ceasing all military attempts to build other nations. The United Nations would nominate China to replace America as the world's "philanthropist-in-chief."

If there is truth in satire, America may be committing slow cultural suicide driven by competing political ideologies, unwilling to revise our Constitution to frame a tougher, less idealistic version of democracy. As citizens, we seem no longer able to use the freedoms we were granted in a generous, wise, or productive way. Our founders and the framers must be turning in their graves and even the God so many believe in must be grumpy.

Proxymoron

Red States will either
Shoot to kill or vote pro-life.
Blue States do neither.

—Barry Blackwell, 2006

Mammon and Modern Medicine

Mammon is an archaic word of uncertain, possibly Aramaic, origin. In the Bible, it refers to a deity personifying greed or avarice but no such god has been uncovered. I like to imagine Mammon was the twin brother of Midas, cornering the market on creating money and hoarding it. The M & M twins?

In contemporary usage, devotion to Mammon conveys the antithesis of charity and benevolence, so it is often invoked to imply the responsibility of individuals to maintain a balance between acquisition of wealth and generosity toward others in need. The corresponding community implication is a moral and ethical imperative to ensure an equitable distribution of wealth across all citizens and to care for the needy.

In America today, this is a hard-fought-over concept pitting those, usually Republicans, who preach the gospel of "exceptionalism" and vigorously defend the unbridled wealth of individuals against those, often Democrats, who defend a more equitable distribution of assets, the Buffet Rule.

Since I came to America forty-four years ago, the distribution of wealth has tilted toward Mammon, the so-called "top one percent." While physicians are very seldom, if ever, members of that elite, they do accumulate in the economic upper crust. They are not immune from the epidemic of greed that has engulfed the rest of society.

Two years after I arrived in America, a move from industry back to academia created a one-month summer hiatus between two jobs. So I purchased a camping trailer and our family set out across country from Cincinnati to San Francisco via several national parks. Deep in the heartlands, my nine-year-old son fell off a cliff face and fractured an ankle; it was set and put in a cast by a kind rural family doctor who doubled as the local orthopedic surgeon. Accustomed to British universal health care and naïve about medical insurance, I had failed to cover the lapse in coverage between jobs. The doctor-surgeon insisted on giving us "professional courtesy" and waived the entire fee.

In the late 1970s, as founding chair of psychiatry in a new medical school, allegedly devoted to humanitarian ideals, I ministered to the emotional ailments of several fragile students. It was part of my educational obligation, and no money changed hands.

When I moved to Milwaukee in the early 1980s, I, like several of my medical peers, volunteered to provide pro bono care at a homeless clinic. But then the climate changed. Bed occupancy at my hospital plummeted, financial support for faculty salaries dwindled, and the need to earn more money in practice escalated. "Professional courtesy" between colleagues disappeared almost overnight, along with Christmas gifts from patients.

I experienced this at both ends; as a provider of services and as aging recipient in need of care. In the mid-1990s I acquired a kidney stone, too large to pass, which required the services of an itinerant community lithotripter. Awaiting my turn in the hospital, the urologist inserted a stent in my ureter, creating free passage for the coming fragments of stone.

Soon after discharge, still recovering from a savage attack of gout and wrapped in a protective diaper, I visited the urologist's outpatient clinic. The office was festooned with notices warning patients of dire consequences for unpaid bills. An hour later, a nurse shunted me into an empty cubicle where I stripped naked and robed myself in one of those scanty and revealing hospital gowns. After a significant time lapse, I was ushered into the urologist's suite; he was absent, but I climbed onto the metal operating table with my legs placed in stirrups ready for the scope to be inserted into my penis to withdraw the stent.

At this moment, the nurse, previously silent, thrust a sheet of paper into my hands, instructing me to read and sign it. But I had left my glasses behind with my clothes. So I invited her to do the reading for me. In a voice filled with purpose but devoid of feeling she said, "If Medicare refuses to authorize the procedure the urologist is about to perform, I acknowledge full responsibility for the cost." Realizing I could not live with a stent in my ureter for life, I did my best to append my signature without my glasses and, like any other patient, kept my mouth shut. You don't want to piss off your surgeon as he is about to perform a delicate procedure.

Final verification that professional courtesy and benevolence toward the needy were lost causes in modern medicine came when my youngest son began medical school. The entrance to his medical school is a veritable temple to Hippocrates whose life-size statue faces incoming students on their way to the library and lecture halls.

—

181

Reciting the Oath of Hippocrates is traditionally a rite of passage for students, usually at graduation. In its classical form, translated from the Greek, Hippocrates's opening statement reads, "To hold him who has taught me this art as equal to my parents and to live my life in partnership with him, and *if he is in need of money to give him a share of mine*, and to regard his offspring as equal to my brothers in male lineage and to teach them this art, if they desire to learn it, *without fee and covenant*" (italics added).

Toward the end of the nineteenth century, as science advanced, the apprenticeship model of medical education began to disappear, a scientific curriculum evolved (the Flexner Revolution), and the number of accredited medical schools decreased dramatically. Wealth in society at large was increasing and frontiers were opening up. Mammon was doing well in the run-up to the Great Depression. Against this backdrop, many medical schools chose to drop the Hippocratic Oath and any mention of fiscal generosity to the needy, including fellow practitioners and students.

Some schools substituted the Oath of Maimonides which includes this statement, "May the love of my art activate me at all times, may neither *avarice nor miserliness* (italics added), nor thirst for glory, or for a great reputation engage my mind."

Another substitution was a so-called "Modern Version," developed in 1964 by Lou Lasagna, father of modern clinical pharmacology and dean of medicine at Tuft's University. This leaves out any mention of a financial obligation to peers or students but does state, "I will remember that I do not treat a fever chart or a cancerous growth but a sick human being whose illness may affect the person's family and *economic stability*" (italics added).

In 2010, when I edited Volume 7 (Special Areas) in the *Oral History of Neuropsychopharmacology*, I dedicated the volume to Lou Lasagna, president of the ACNP in 1980. (See "Piece 12: Psychopharmacology: Then and Now.") I wish Lou were alive today to become involved in this debate.

When my son became a medical student, I was deeply concerned about the debts he might incur and the influence this could have on his choice

—

of specialty. The annual cost of tuition alone was very close to $40,000. In 1992, the average debt of a new doctor was only around $25,000, but by 2010, it had risen to $160,000, and a quarter of students owed over $200,000. During this period, tuition increased at almost twice the rate of inflation.

This was added to any additional debt incurred during undergraduate training prior to medical school. This was especially burdensome for mature "nontraditional" students like my son who had graduated *magna cum laude* in politics, philosophy, and economics before deciding on a medical career. This also meant he was too old to qualify for coverage on his parents' insurance (increased to twenty-six years of age under Obamacare).

Finally, most egregiously, the medical school provides no health coverage for students despite the fact it has a well-developed network of providers, many of whom are faculty members who would almost certainly be willing to provide free medical care for students in need. For my son to obtain coverage for himself, his wife and, infant son would have added an additional $10,000 to his annual debt. In the end, he applied for and obtained Medicaid (BadgerCare) and food stamps, passing the burden on to the Wisconsin taxpayer.

Attempting to research this problem, I could find no published information on how medical students in America deal with their health care. What does seem to be accepted is that debt-burdened students tend to avoid low-paying primary care specialties and opt for those that are procedure-oriented and offer far higher incomes. This is at a time when there is an urgent, unmet need for more well-trained primary care physicians.

My own attempt to deal with this problem was to extend my career, until age seventy-seven, for the four years of my son's training. During this time, I earned enough to cover most of his tuition costs. Twice in the year since he graduated, we have been solicited by the medical school for donations, principally to support research goals. Each time we responded with modest donations to support needy students and included a plea to consider offering health coverage to students. Both times, we requested a reply from the dean. It never happened.

—

Two Sides of the Same Coin

Published in the *Wisconsin Journal of Medicine*, March 2012:

Separated by the Atlantic Ocean, but united by a common heritage, Britain and America share a pressing problem on which they disagree fundamentally about a solution.

This is the fact that health care costs are escalating alarmingly due to scientific and technological advances, the biggest contributor to which are resources spent in the last six months of life, mostly on vain attempts to prolong it.

Each culture has a different viewpoint and advocates for it demonize the other. The British, with an (almost) free-for-all system that is derided by Republicans as "socialist," have aggressively addressed this problem by drawing a harsh line between end of life "care" and "treatment." Decisions and response to expectations for treatment are made by administrators and physicians according to clinical guidelines, castigated by American critics as "death panels."

America, on the other hand, boasts a two-tier system. In the first five decades of life, it is a "free-for-all" in another sense. Politicians, who are given it, often claim it is the "best in the world." This may be true for those who can afford or are fortunate to obtain it; if not sickness may bankrupt or kill you. But, in the sixth decade, everyone is eligible for government-run Medicare; comprehensive, almost free, and eagerly utilized by a society that believes in heaven but does everything it can to defer going there. This is abetted by a relatively unregulated, misnamed "not-for-profit" health care industry and a market place in which promiscuously prescribed pills and procedures are viewed and advertised as commercial products, like cars and clothes. This is sustained by the myth that competitive forces will constrain cost and make distaste for the afterlife affordable. But there are no fire

—

sales or bargain basements in health care. Folks who willingly wear jeans and drive small cars demand Cadillac health care.

This rather abstract and philosophical debate between our two nations recently became personal and relevant in my own life.

Now an American citizen, beyond age seventy-seven, I visited my internist for an annual medical exam. Newly retired, several deferred decisions were addressed. Twenty youthful years of playing rugby and pushing in the scrum had wreaked havoc with my joints. I have had a hip replaced (followed by a pulmonary embolus), both knees are arthritic, and I suffer from spinal stenosis, severe on x-ray but mercifully asymptomatic. In addition, I have an ataxia of undetermined origin so my gait resembles an inebriated penguin walking on stilts. My eligibility for safe surgery is compromised by atrial fibrillation and anticoagulants. Despite this depressing litany, both my internist and orthopedist contemplated bilateral knee surgery, separated and followed by several months of prolonged rehabilitation at an estimated cost probably in excess of $100,000. The alternative, a gradual progression from cane to walker to wheelchair eased by palliative analgesics, might cost $5,000.

Next, I had previously undergone two colonoscopies, five years apart. Despite best practice guidelines that suggest colonoscopy after age seventy-five is unproductive (even if positive you are more likely to die of something else), the gastroenterologist sent me a reminder for a repeat procedure and my internist felt I should go ahead, "just to be safe." I scheduled the colonoscopy but, on second thoughts, cancelled the procedure, presumably saving Medicare a significant sum while shortchanging the hospital and gastroenterologist.

Finally, a new concern raised its head. My platelet count was marginally low for no apparent reason (140,000). One possible cause was my Churchillian propensity for heavy social drinking, to which I willingly confessed. Might an enlarged and dysfunctional liver be suppressing splenic function? Perhaps I needed a nuclear medicine scan of both organs at the same time as a repeat platelet count. The latter came back normal, but the scan was already scheduled. It was reported as showing a liver and spleen both "twice the normal size." This led to scheduling a chest x-ray and CT scan of the abdomen and pelvis for a more definitive view of the liver. Alarmed, I embraced total sobriety during the three-week hiatus before the results came back; they were normal. My internist concluded that the false positive scan was not likely due to my rigorous sobriety but to "an inexperienced radiologist." I estimate the cost of these procedures must have exceeded $10,000. (I was told that the brand-new CT scanner, of which the hospital has three, cost over a million dollars.)

At exactly the same time these events occurred, my eighty-four-year-old brother in England viewed the reverse side of the coin. I knew this from an early morning phone call the day after I learned of my normal liver and spleen.

A former Royal Marine and retired superintendent of police, he is legally blind, physically handicapped, totally housebound, and completely dependent on his eighty-one-year-old wife for support. I had visited them five months before and found them well-stabilized, but in the three weeks preceding their phone call, his wife had suddenly developed severe back pain and become bedridden. The pain had not responded to several painkillers and muscle relaxants and failed to benefit from two sessions of physiotherapy and a visit to a chiropractor. The local GP had conducted a brief home visit and examination but made no definitive diagnosis and declined to request an x-ray. Concerned, my brother called the National Health Service regional hotline resulting in a phone diagnosis of "probable sciatica" and a prescription for Valium. When this failed to improve matters, he called the local hospital to suggest admission and request an x-ray but was turned away and told there were no x-rays available on weekends.

—

My brother's true predicament was that they had been shunted into the "care" continuum. So the issue became disposition, either in-home care or a long-term facility, rather than diagnosis or treatment, now deemed irrelevant. This was the responsibility of social workers, not doctors, and of a new "for-profit" industry providing in-home assistance for from fifteen to thirty dollars an hour. The only thing delaying this option was the fortunate fact that my brother's middle-aged son was laid off work and able to temporarily assume their care.

My first response to all this was stereotypically American; it was outrageous that a more aggressive attempt had not been made to reach a definitive diagnosis. No x-ray, no CT scan, no referral to an orthopedist, just symptomatic treatment and disposition, all ineffective. But then I began to recall my early days as a family doctor in Britain and weigh the odds. Statistically, by far the most common cause of sudden onset back pain in a healthy eighty-one-year-old woman would be musculoskeletal. Even if it was something more sinister, perhaps a metastatic lesion, the treatment was likely to be palliative. Hadn't we been taught that when scanning the diagnostic parking lot a Ford was far more common than a Rolls Royce? The reality of my brother's total disability and dependence on his wife, as well as their ages, made a move into a long-term care facility seem inevitable. Why not sooner than later? Even without a job, Clive's son had an independent life to lead. The psychiatrist in me wondered if part of the predicament and lack of recovery might be due to carrying a burden of care his wife no longer felt able or willing to bear. I sensed my brother already knew this and was beginning to accept its implications.

Back in America, my anger melted, transformed into more support and less advice. But the policy implications lingered; as with so much these days, the issues seem inflated by political rhetoric focused on exaggerating differences rather than attempting compromise.

In Britain, it might help to pay empathic and more nuanced attention to accurate diagnosis, easing acceptance of disposition before crossing the Rubicon from cure to care. In America, we might learn that not everybody can have everything, especially immortality. Clinical guidelines, firmly applied, might rationalize the fair distribution of resources and feel less like rationing, which Brits are culturally inclined to accept but Yanks fiercely resist.

Overall, Britain appears to be holding the fiscal line while, in America, costs are escalating out of control in an aging population even though Medicare pays physicians less than market rates and politicians are debating radical change.

Postscript: This was the text submitted to the editor but not the one published. Without any communication or opportunity to discuss, review page proofs, or approve changes, all standard procedure, the essay appeared in print. The revised text accorded me a title I did not possess (emeritus professor), included a typographical error ("scrum" was misspelled), and removed three entire paragraphs (two, three and four) which contained much of the cultural and economic background to my concerns. I suggested this was censorship, not editing, and requested a correction in the next issue. The editor never replied! My fifty-year career included over two hundred publications, many in the world's leading journals, but this was the first and only time a text appeared without any personal communication with an editor or my prior approval. Changing mores, ageism, or my own senile thin skin?

"Your money or Your Life!"

—The demand made by English highwaymen of the
seventeenth century to the occupants of stagecoaches.

I was reminded of these words on the final day of what may prove to be my last visit to England by the banner headlines of national newspapers on display in the departure lounge at Heathrow Airport.

They announced an impending twenty-four-hour strike by the country's general practitioners (GPs) set for the following day.

This would abort over a million patient visits or appointments and tens of thousands of hospital procedures. The strike, the first in nearly forty years, was planned by the British Medical Association. Widely condemned by the public and press, it also divided the doctors themselves with an increasing majority promising to opt out and less than a quarter firmly committed to the stoppage.

The crux of the conflict, created by the Eurozone crisis and subsequent recession, was a proposed increase in doctors' contributions to their pensions coupled with a rise in the age of retirement, akin to similar adjustments across the spectrum of public employees in other national economies.

In 1967, the year before I left Britain, I earned 5,000 pounds annually as a GP. In 2004, the British Labor Government (post-Thatcher), implemented a controversial deal with GPs which doubled the annual salary to 110,000 pounds. It also allowed GPs to opt out of all evening and weekend calls without penalty and outsourced these responsibilities to fly-in doctors from other Euro countries. GPs were also allowed to supplement salary by providing "optional" services such as cancer screening and minor surgery. The top income earner makes in excess of 700,000 pounds a year.

The editorial page of one newspaper (*The Daily Mail*) carried a banner headline in half-inch capital letters, "HOW TRAGIC IF THE SACRED BOND OF TRUST BETWEEN G.P.s AND PATIENTS IS DESTROYED BY NAKED SELFISHNESS."

But perhaps the damage is already done. The harm inflicted by a one-day deprivation of service hardly bears comparison to the existing inability to contact a personal physician outside regular office hours, even in a life-threatening situation.

The essential, almost unique, benefit of "primary care" is the ability to forge and sustain a prolonged and incremental relationship of trust between doctor and patient based on intimate knowledge of one another. This is what I meant by the term "primary care psychiatry." (See "Primary Care Psychiatry" in "Piece 14: Medical Education.") All my patients had both my office and home phone number (also in the phone book) and were free to call in times of need. Nobody abused that privilege, and many deferred out of respect for my privacy.

When it was time for our dog to die, I took him to our vet who had cared for him over seventeen years and stroked Stanley's head while he was put to sleep. When his eyes closed, my own shed tears. People deserve as much.

Highway Robbery

The doctor you trust
With your life just threatened it;
"Pay more or I'll quit."

—Barry Blackwell, June 2012

End Times

Beg Republicans to desist,
Gridlock isn't politics
It's Apocalypse!

—Barry Blackwell, May 2012

11. The Pharmaceutical Industry

Director of Psychotropic Drug Research

The desire to take medicine is perhaps the greatest feature which distinguishes man from animals.

—William Osler, MD

I now had two cultures to accommodate to: America and the pharmaceutical industry. Make no mistake—industry is about profit and pleasing its shareholders. There is an innate tension between science and commerce; between what is proven true and what is possibly profitable.

I arrived in Cincinnati to join the Wm. S. Merrell Company (later Merrell Dow) in September 1968, when this truism had become powerfully apparent. Merrell had marketed Thalidomide as a safe drug to treat insomnia, only to discover that it produced fetal abnormalities in some pregnant women that were of a particularly repugnant kind: phocomelia or deformed limbs. Congress had recently passed the Harris-Kefauver Amendments mandating that all new drugs approved by the FDA must be both safe and effective. A zealous FDA physician, Frances Kelsey, had detected flaws in Merrell's new drug application and had blown the whistle, leading to the criminal indictment of Merrell scientists for falsifying data.

It was hardly the best of times to become an industry physician, for both pragmatic and professional reasons. In self-defense, Merrell had "lawyered up." Everything the scientists wanted to do was legally adjudicated—with an understandable but stifling effect on innovation. Professionally there was an aura of stigma that made me feel subtly ashamed of my new role as director of psychotropic drug research. If my recruitment was part of an image campaign, it was a secret to me.

But there were compensatory influences. The overall director of research was a hard-nosed, feisty, and ethical old-timer, willing to stand behind his employees and face up to the business administration. Merrell had also retained one of the country's leading psychopharmacologists as a consultant, available to me as a mentor. Frank Ayd was a devout Catholic and father of twelve children who had lived in the Vatican as an adviser to the Pope on ethical and psychiatric matters. Frank had also been one of the first psychiatrists in the world to study and report on the benefits of Thorazine in schizophrenia and was a founding member of the American College of Neuropsychopharmacology (ACNP) in 1961. Frank took me under his wing and introduced me to all of the leading psychopharmacologists in America. He also sponsored me as a member of the ACNP in 1970. Many years later, in 2008, I had the honor of writing Frank's obituary for the ACNP archives.

My industry job required that I work closely with the company's basic scientists and travel extensively throughout the United States, meeting clinical researchers, attending conferences, and initiating studies of new and old compounds. Some of the older drugs were beyond redemption, including a compound alleged to extinguish psychotic hallucinations and a popular tonic for the geriatric population, Alertonic, which contained B vitamins, alcohol and a small dose of an amphetamine-like stimulant. Patients loved it but not enough to show sufficient benefit to exceed the placebo improvement derived from the added attention associated with being in a research study.

I also designed and undertook preclinical studies on volunteers to establish the physiological effects and safety of newer compounds. This sometimes involved me and interested coworkers as experimental subjects as well as prison inmates in the Cincinnati jail willing to trade a prison cell for a comfortable research ward and the slight risk of ingesting a new drug for the first time. At a conference in Montana on prison research, participants were awarded a certificate making us "honorary inmates" of the state penitentiary.

I used my day-a-week academic time to begin teaching medical students and psychiatric residents at the university about the new drugs available to treat mental illness. This also allowed time for me to pursue research and scholarly writing on a variety of topics. With a colleague in another company, we wrote an article describing the "Roles and Tasks of an Industry Physician," and with Frank Ayd we designed workshops for ACNP conferences and wrote an article on the "Scientific and Ethical Problems of Psychotropic Drug Research in Prison Volunteers," published shortly before the FDA banned their involvement in drug research on ethical grounds.

Both Frank and I were involved in teaching our new discipline to public and professional audiences. Out of this came the idea of bringing together those scientists from Europe and America who had made the original discoveries in the field. The conference took place in Baltimore and the proceedings were published in 1970 in the book we coedited, *Discoveries in Biological Psychiatry*. It was among the very first books published on the topic and is still in print today.

After just over eighteen months of this dual industry-academic life, I was offered an opportunity to reverse roles; to become a full-time professor of psychiatry and pharmacology at the University of Cincinnati with one day a week consulting to Merrell. This would help support my academic salary and allow me to resume treating patients under the university umbrella without seeking formal licensure. By now, our kids were settled in school and we were becoming acculturated to life in America.

I had enjoyed and benefited from my time in industry but felt uneasy about my role. Given the competing priorities of industry and science, I knew I would be better placed as a consultant and not as an employee. When differences inevitably occurred, my judgment might be questioned but not my loyalty. In addition, my-self-image and self-esteem were tied to education and research rather than product development and commerce.

—

"Snake Oil"

A derogatory term for a quack medicine. The expression is also applied metaphorically to any product with exaggerated marketing but questionable or unverified quality or benefit.

—Wikipedia definition

By the time I arrived at Merrell, the research department was ready to give up on attempts to prove that one of its drugs, azacyclonol (Frenquel), was effective for their advertising claim that it alleviated hallucinations. To begin with, hearing voices or seeing visions are epiphenomena of a variety of psychotic conditions but not the core symptoms of any psychiatric disorder. The drug was available in both oral and intravenous forms and had the unique and bizarre claim that the dose by injection was higher than by mouth. Most persuasive was that the sales were barely sufficient to justify the costs of manufacturing and advertising. It seemed a "no-brainer" to pull the plug and withdraw the drug from the market.

This happened soon after I arrived, so one of my first jobs was to analyze the response from patients and providers who felt deprived by the decision. They needed the drug; it was the only one that helped (it was certainly a unique claim), what would they do without it, was it possible to keep on getting it? The FDA was firm. Testimonials were no substitute for evidence. There would be no "humanitarian" exceptions.

I had a trip planned for New York and decided to call on one of these vocal supplicants. The office where the cab let me off in Greenwich Village was next to a homeless drop-in center. The doorbell was answered by a polite, casually dressed, older physician who greeted me and ushered me into a room in the basement furnished more like a family doctor's office than a psychiatrist's den. In the center of the room stood an examining table rather than a reclining couch with an attached shiny aluminum tray on which lay a large syringe containing a colorless liquid I assumed was Frenquel.

Sitting on the table, legs dangling and wearing a brightly colored, mildly revealing dress, was an attractive young woman. Almost before I could take in the scene, she leapt to the floor, faced me, and began to shout, "So you're the f—ing drug company man that's going to ruin my life!"

The doctor moved quickly to take her arm, guided her back to the table, and did his best to calm her. She settled down and lay back, still eyeing me furiously, pulling up the sleeve of her dress to expose the veins in the hollow of her arm. This was obviously a well-practiced routine, which the doctor performed often. He inserted the needle and gently pushed the plunger as the patient closed her eyes and appeared to drift into a light sleep. Visibly relieved, the doctor removed the needle, lay down the syringe, and leaned toward her. "It's all right, Martha, you can get up now." Her eyes opened, she smiled at us, and thanked me for coming so far out of my way to help her.

Another surprise awaited me; the doctor suggested the three of us have lunch together. We walked to a nearby bistro, and, over a meal paid for by Merrell, I spent an hour in the company of two friendly, apparently normal, people. Over lunch, the doctor explained that the alcohol and drug detox clinic adjoining the homeless center used Frenquel often to help "bring down" people in drug withdrawal.

On the flight back to Cincinnati, I wrote my "trip report" explaining I had found two "off-label" novel uses of Frenquel: to calm someone who, most likely, had a borderline personality, and to facilitate drug or alcohol detoxification. I didn't suggest Merrell pursue research into these potential new indications, but perhaps I was wrong. New uses for old drugs are often discovered by chance; looking for one thing and finding another. It's called serendipity. On the other hand, it seemed more likely that everything attributed to Frenquel might be due to suggestion, the placebo response, or spontaneous remission.

Serendipity

The sort of thing that happens to you when, on a dull day collecting fossils, you find instead a beautiful woman who proves to be neither a geologist nor archeologist.

—Zebulun Column: *Serendipity,*
Archives of Internal Medicine, 1963

This charming definition from a medical journal is only correct in noting that serendipity describes an unexpected finding while looking for something else. The true original meaning comes from a Persian fairy tale, "The Three Princes of Serendip," which describes how the princes of Serendip (formerly Ceylon, now Sri Lanka) had a fortunate ability to make such discoveries. The term was introduced into popular European literature by Horace Walpole in a letter to a friend in 1754. The example he chose from the story was how one of the princes deduced that a mule, blind in the right eye, had traveled the same road frequently because the grass was eaten only on the left side of the path. All the original discoveries in psychopharmacology involved this chance process. Finding one thing while looking for another.

Panacea

A remedy for all diseases, evils or difficulties; a cure-all.
From Greek: all-healing: pan (all) + *akos* (cure).

—Dictionary definition

The mind accepts what's working well,
But resurrects our body's ills
In rituals of colored pills.

White oils the joints; green quells bad moods,
Pink stifles aches; red thins the blood,
Blue re-creates a gero-stud.

—

Despite these drugs, death reaches all.
God pulls the plug and wills us each
Eternal peace without the pills.

—Barry Blackwell, December 2003

12. Psychopharmacology: Then And Now

Early Days

Better things for better living through better chemistry.

—DuPont corporate motto, 1939-1982

A thread running through all human history has been the use of substances such as alcohol, marijuana, coca, nicotine, and mushrooms to alter the mind. In the late nineteenth and early twentieth centuries, mankind began to synthesize chemicals that mimicked naturally occurring substances, producing barbiturates, amphetamines, bromides, and hallucinogens. All of these natural and synthetic compounds shared the ability to produce an immediate change in a normal person's thinking, feeling, or behavior and, for this reason, all were potentially addictive. It was not until I was a young man, in the mid-1950s, that the new science of psychopharmacology and the modern pharmaceutical industry began to discover and manufacture drugs that altered brain chemistry in more subtle ways, taking days or weeks (not hours) to benefit mental illness. The synchronicity between these discoveries and my early medical career was related earlier. (See "A Bit of History" in "Piece 7: Guy's Hospital.")

This piece covers the forty-year interval between my return to academia in America in 1970 and my final retirement in 2011.

—

1970 also marks the year I became a member of the American College of Neuropsychopharmacology (ACNP). This organization was founded in 1961 to promote the new science and it celebrated its fiftieth anniversary in December 2011. Membership was selective and chosen to encourage communication between basic scientists working on animals and clinical investigators in the hope of discovering safer and better drugs for mental illness (translational research).

During the first years (until around 1975), Frank Ayd and I were quite involved in the annual ACNP meetings which took place in San Juan, Puerto Rico, two weeks before Christmas. This was designed as a relaxing getaway in a sunny clime intended to encourage creative dialogue between experts in the new field.

During this early period, American psychiatry was changing rapidly; the psychoanalytic stranglehold on academia was slackening as drugs for depression, schizophrenia, bipolar disorder, and anxiety were shown to be unarguably effective and superior to other forms of therapy. The pharmaceutical companies, seeking "market share," began to make major commitments to drug research in psychiatry. The federal government, through the recently created National Institute for Mental Health (NIMH), formed its own Early Clinical Drug Evaluation Units (ECDEU), which linked together existing centers of excellence in drug research and established new ones, all using common rating scales and statistical methods of analysis. The Veterans' Administration (VA) sponsored the first large-scale collaborative studies working to common protocols and sharing results. Several large State hospitals also became involved in research on their chronic populations.

The result was a dramatic shift in patterns of mental health care. The large state asylums began to empty as patients were able to be discharged back into their communities (de-institutionalization). These were often ill-equipped to absorb the large influx of chronic and still-disabled patients. Two major problems ensued; unsupervised patients stopped taking their medications, relapsed, and were readmitted—the so-called "revolving door syndrome," while others, abandoned by their families, became homeless, including numbers of returning Vietnam veterans and those with drug or alcohol problems.

—

During this period (1970-1975), my natural instinct toward the psychological and social aspects of medical care began to assert itself. I became intrigued by the many "nondrug" factors that modified the outcome of treatment. For many patients with illness behavior, medication was largely a prop to help sustain the sick role. For every patient, the placebo response, spontaneous remission, metabolism, gender, and ethnicity all played a role in outcomes. I wrote several papers on these topics but, as usual, also undertook research in the context of what I was doing as an educator.

With a pharmacologist fellow faculty member and a statistician, we designed a study to demonstrate the placebo response to first-year medical students in the pharmacology course, using them as the subjects for the study in the classroom. We designed what we told them was a "double-blind comparison between a stimulant and sedative drug." The students were randomly assigned to receive one or two, red or blue, capsules and completed a rating scale later in the class to record their responses in mood and side effects. They also worked in pairs to measure blood pressure and pulse rate.

Based on the existing research literature, we predicted the nature, size, and frequency of the "treatment" responses and sealed them in an envelope to be opened at the next lecture after the results were tabulated.

In reality, both the red and blue capsules were placebos containing an inert powder. When the results were available, and the envelope opened, every prediction was confirmed. A third of the students reported changes in mood, some had "side effects"; red capsules produced more stimulant effects, including increases in blood pressure and pulse rate, while blue capsules caused sedative responses. Two capsules produced more effects than one. Even we were surprised, and so were the students!

When the experiment was over, the chair of the pharmacology department expressed ethical concerns about the deceit involved. But the students saw the point and approved; at the end of the summer, they awarded me their "Golden Apple" as the teacher of the year. I still have it.

The article describing our experiment and results was published in *The Lancet*, Britain's leading medical journal, with the title "Demonstration to Medical Students of Placebo Responses and Non-Drug Factors."

By the mid-1970s, the national perspective on the new psychotropic drugs had consolidated among the experts at ACNP and elsewhere. Their merits and disadvantages were better defined.

The antipsychotic drugs, like Thorazine and Haldol, were capable of bringing the "positive" symptoms of schizophrenia into remission (hallucinations, delusions, and bizarre behavior), but the "negative" features of apathy, disorders of thinking, and social withdrawal often persisted and gave meaning to the older name "dementia praecox." These residual symptoms often impaired a person's ability to work and socialize, setting the stage for relapses. But the benefits of treatment were also mitigated by unwanted side effects, including sedation, sexual dysfunction, and neurological symptoms similar to Parkinson's disease. The worst of these were involuntary, often permanent, movements of the face and mouth (tardive dyskinesia).

The tricyclic antidepressants, like Tofranil and Elavil, were effective in about two-thirds of people with severe (major) depression. Their commonest side effects were dry mouth, constipation, blurry vision, and urinary retention. More serious was that an average one month's prescription could be fatal in overdose; this presented a significant hazard in a disorder with a suicide rate of fifteen percent (one in six).

By now, the MAOIs were in sharp decline, both because of side effects (including dietary restrictions) and convincing efficacy limited to "atypical depression" which included symptoms of weight gain, increased sleep, and personality disorders.

Added to the therapeutic repertoire was lithium, not a drug but a naturally occurring substance, similar to salt, and found in rocks (*lithia*, "stone" in Greek). Lithium had a long history as a panacea in medicine but was rediscovered by an Australian psychiatrist in the 1960s as a treatment for mania and then studied by Scandinavian psychiatrists who made the unusual and controversial claim that it not only suppressed manic behavior, but it prevented relapses in bipolar (manic-depressive) disorder. (See *Back in the Mainstream* in Piece 8: The Maudsley Hospital.) So lithium became the first in a new category of drugs: the mood stabilizers.

Finally, the most profound and controversial issue in the mid-1970s was the popularity and increasing use of first Librium and then Valium. These benzodiazepine compounds were highly successful at treating anxiety and, in higher dosages, sleep disorders. Their principal advantage over the barbiturates and Milltown was absence of suicide potential in overdose. At first, the drug manufacturers claimed they were also free of addiction potential but, as experience accumulated, it became clear that, like all drugs with an immediate effect on mood, they were readily abused in progressively increasing amounts. This became the root cause of the controversy over their widespread and increasing use.

As the faculty member responsible for teaching the residents psychopharmacology, I wanted to involve them in research relevant to the problems of the day and also to stimulate their capacity for critical thinking and interest in a possible academic career. This resulted in three projects, all published in leading scientific journals with residents as coauthors.

When the first of the new drugs were identified (all by chance or serendipity), the primary task was to prove they were more effective than existing panaceas or placebo. This led to the requirement for controlled studies of every drug compared to placebo, in which neither the patient nor the investigator knew which the patient was taking (hence, "double-blind"). After the Harris-Kefauver Amendments, passed by Congress in 1962, this became the gold standard, and no new drug could be approved by the FDA for marketing unless it had showed statistical superiority in two such trials.

While this requirement was essential to eliminate ineffective drugs, it had serious shortcomings that became obvious to me early in my career when I attempted, with David Taylor, to study why and how the MAOIs were actually used. (See "Back in the Mainstream" in "Piece

8: The Maudsley Hospital.") Controlled studies are highly artificial and bear little resemblance to real life. They involve small numbers of highly selected individuals, without concurrent disease and taking no medication. Excluded are fertile females (for fear of birth defects), children, and the elderly. As psychotropic drug use has become more and more common, it is increasingly difficult to find drug naïve subjects. Those who enter the study are closely observed, consistently reassured, and compelled to take the medicine.

So the first study I undertook with a resident (who is now chair of psychiatry in a leading medical school) was to review actual prescribing habits in five different city hospitals; two private practice institutions, a VA, the university hospital, and the state hospital. The drugs chosen and way they were used differed between hospitals, but a common theme was what we named the "add-a-drug" strategy. If a patient failed to get better on a particular drug, another was added, usually without discontinuing the first or increasing the dose!

At this time, a developing national interest in chronic pain coincided with our illness behavior research. Others had noted that antidepressants like Tofranil and Elavil had pain-relieving properties, but it was unclear if this was related to relief of depression (which often includes physical symptoms, such as pain) or to a direct analgesic effect. Working with two residents, we designed a placebo-controlled study in a local rehabilitation hospital for men with chronic painful disabilities. The residents paid close attention to their individual patients, rating mood and pain. The antidepressant worked well on both symptoms but so did the placebo. We concluded the therapeutic benefit was largely due to the increased amount of attention subjects received. The residents, both in analysis, were delighted that empathy trumped pharmacology!

In 1973, I had access, via my consulting work with industry, to national prescribing statistics on the use of psychotropic drugs as well as the knowledge from our local five-hospital study. It was clear that there had been a remarkable increase in benzodiazepine use for anxiety related disorders. I published my analysis of this data in the *Journal of the American Medical Association* (JAMA) in an article entitled "Psychotropic Drugs in Use Today: The Role of Diazepam (Valium) in Medical Practice." The national data showed very little change over eight years (1964-1972) in the use of antidepressants and major tranquilizers, but during this period the use of anti-anxiety drugs increased from twenty-five million to over seventy million prescriptions annually at a cost of $200 million. This increase was due entirely to one drug, Valium, which was prescribed by 97 percent of internists and general practitioners. Primary care providers far outnumber psychiatrists in overall use of these drugs. This rate of increase led me to facetiously suggest that by the year 2000, the entire population would be tranquilized.

Others began to call this period "The Age of Anxiety" and the topic became the focus of a national debate, both professional and public. "Hedonists" and "Puritans" argued over the probity of using an expensive and potentially addictive medication to quell existential angst. These concerns provoked the South Carolina Medicaid Program to ban the use of benzodiazepines. As a result, one-third of their use was replaced by cheaper but more powerful and dangerous drugs while the remaining two-thirds was unaccounted for, along with any distress the absence of treatment may have provoked.

This controversy led us to undertake a study designed to cast light on the controversy using a unique research design that has never been replicated and might be considered unethical today. There were four other authors under my direction. First was the same resident who worked on the five-hospital study; second, the head nurse on the unit (my future wife, Kathie); third, a university statistician; and finally, the pharmaceutical representative from Roche Laboratories, which manufactures Valium. Including him was a controversial step, based in part by my earlier experience with the MAOI/cheese investigation. (See "A Bit of Cheese" in "Piece 8: The Maudsley Hospital.") I had hoped this might enhance his career; instead, the marketing division was displeased about mingling science with commerce!

The study was intended to cast light on the almost universal practice of routinely prescribing Valium "when necessary" (p.r.n.) to every person admitted to an inpatient psychiatric unit. This was based on the belief that anxiety is a ubiquitous accompaniment to all psychiatric disorders as well as the stress of admission to an inpatient unit. Prescribing "when

—

necessary" gave the nurses discretion and avoided a need to contact the patient's physician at inconvenient times.

On admission, all patients were given a written invitation to talk to a staff member if they were anxious or worried; "Staff will be happy to talk to you about your feelings and to give you medication if they consider it would be helpful." In order to quantify the patient's behavior, a drug-seeking index (DSI) was derived by dividing the number of requests by the number of days on the ward.

Over six months, one hundred patients were admitted, help was requested by two-thirds of the patients on six hundred eighty-nine occasions, and Valium was given in ninety-five percent of contacts. A third of patients never sought help, and those who did averaged one request every three days (DSI of 0.33). The DSI declined with duration of stay. Over the entire course of the study, the DSI was correlated statistically with high rating scale scores for anxiety and bodily concern. Use of Valium was higher among women and white patients, lower in men and ethnic minorities. It was unrelated to psychiatric diagnosis or use of other psychotropic drugs. During the study, staff opinions became more favorable to drug use.

In commenting on these findings, the following conclusions were drawn:

> When made freely available, patients of all diagnoses seek diazepam (Valium) for the appropriate indication of anxiety and most use it conservatively . . . An important inference from the study might be that any tendency to overuse minor tranquilizers may not be due to importunate or unnecessary demands by patients.

This study was published in the *Archives of General Psychiatry* in 1974, a leading psychiatric research journal. To the best of my knowledge, the design has never been replicated but is an early example of "effectiveness" research, an attempt to study drug use in the real world as opposed to the hundreds of double-blind "efficacy" studies conducted under highly artificial conditions by the pharmaceutical industry. It is never referred to in the still-ongoing debate about use of benzodiazepine drugs where prescribing practices are determined more by attitudes than data. Finally, like almost all my research, it was not financed by any outside source. It cost only the time and effort of the authors in the everyday search for contemporary knowledge in an educational environment.

In 1974, I left Cincinnati and moved to Dayton to become chair of psychiatry at the brand-new medical school at Wright State University. My activities there and subsequently are described in "Piece 14: Medical Education." Briefly, my interests became increasingly, though not entirely, involved in nondrug and other educational issues, so for an extended period (1978-2010), I ceased being directly involved in the ACNP. Nevertheless, psychopharmacology and the ACNP continued to evolve in ways that affected my professional life and the American public. Over the next three decades, significant changes occurred in both science and commerce.

The pharmaceutical industry continued to expand in its attempts to meet the obvious need to develop and market better and safer drugs. It was enabled by two social and cultural developments. First, it perfected the art of direct advertising to the public and of manipulating physicians' prescribing practices to capture more "market share." Secondly, like other special interests during this time period, it devoted its increasing resources to aggressively lobbying Congress for deregulation and relaxed oversight. More money and less regulation gave the industry increasing power and influence over drug development and organizations, like the ACNP and the American Psychiatric Association, in the enterprise. They were further driven by a need to find new drugs because patents were expiring on the original compounds making them significantly less profitable.

This resulted, during the 1980s, in the discovery of both a new type of antidepressant (the selective serotonin reuptake inhibitors or SSRI) and the "atypical" antipsychotics. The industry launched a sustained, expensive, and creative approach to persuade the public, academia, and the scientific community of the superiority of their new compounds. The results of the mandatory controlled efficacy studies confirmed they were, indeed, equally effective compared to a placebo as the older

—

compounds, but not more so. Because these initial studies were only of brief duration (usually six weeks or less) the side effects and the safety of the new drugs were unclear, facilitated by the industry's failure to compare them directly with the older prototype compounds—for fear they might not be superior.

This lack of information was amplified because the NIMH and federal government closed down its independent clinical drug-testing program to divert resources into basic animal research, leaving control almost entirely in the hands of Big Pharma. A scientific myth, endorsed by both academia and industry, created the widely held belief that these newer, very expensive, drugs were indeed "better" than the older, cheaper, and increasingly generic compounds. While this has proven accurate for the SSRI antidepressants (compared to the tricyclic drugs), it was shown to be tragically untrue of the atypical antipsychotics when the NIMH finally reentered the scene to conduct the first "effectiveness" study comparing the newer drugs to an old standard compound in a "real life" design.

Recent Events

In December 2009, events conspired to pull me back into the center of this evolving "perfect storm." I was invited to the annual meeting of the ACNP to participate in the Oral History Project (OHP). This involved over two hundred scientists, myself included, who had made significant findings in the earliest days of the psychopharmacology revolution. Each of us was videotaped for an hour-long dialogue with a colleague in the field to relate the story of our contribution. This process has been ongoing for several years, not without difficulty.

The quality of many interviews left much to be desired. Although oral communication is spontaneous, it is usually far less organized than the written form. The language tends to be repetitive and redundant; people prevaricate, elaborate, and exaggerate from habit or nervousness. The quality of the sound and transcription was often flawed. Technical terms were sometimes not defined. Most of us still living were well past seventy, and a few had failing memories.

—

The task of turning this verbal output into written form, suitable for publication, was daunting. When I saw the transcript of my own interview, I thought it was irreparable and should be destroyed. But during my time at the meeting, I again met and spent time with the OHP series editor; an eighty-odd year-old polymath and pioneer with an encyclopedic knowledge of psychopharmacology and the people involved. We hit it off at once and shared similar views about ACNP and the field. Tom Ban also knew of my earlier work with Frank Ayd in editing our book about the first *Discoveries in Biological Psychiatry*. So I was invited to assist in editing the entire ten-volume series which included the edited interviews, a biography of each scientist, a bibliography, and interpretative commentary by the series editor.

Our collaboration lasted almost two years, conducted entirely by phone and e-mail, assisted by some support from the administrative office of the ACNP in Nashville. During that time, I edited two of the ten volumes, wrote fifty biographies of individual scientists and copyedited almost two-thirds of the entire ten volumes. For a few months, I managed the project on my own when Tom was admitted as an emergency to intensive care with a severe medical setback. From a scientific point of view, this was a trip down memory lane, reacquainting me with people, events, and topics from my career forty years before. But it was also a rapid induction into the politics and dynamics of the ACNP, where all was not well.

I was alarmed at the minimal support (secretarial and financial) the ACNP was willing to provide. Tom was devoting twelve to eighteen hours a day on the project and was totally and resolutely dedicated to ensuring that the OHP was published (in PDF on Amazon) and available in time for the fiftieth anniversary of the ACNP at its annual meeting in December in Hawaii. As the reasons behind this organizational reluctance became clear, my own interest focused on that issue and I decided to confront it. The outcome is contained in the following bit, "Sea Change or Tsunami?" This essay was formulated as an attempt to draw attention to problems confronting the ACNP and was e-mailed by me personally to every member. Enjoy!

—

Sea Change or Tsunami?

Hypothesis One: *History is more or less bunk. It's tradition. We don't want tradition. We want to live in the present and the only history that's worth a tinker's damn is the history we make today.*

—Henry Ford

Hypothesis Two: *What's past is prologue.*

—William Shakespeare *(The Tempest)*

I read the president's September 1 and earlier blogs and also received the *ACNP Bulletin* (Volume 17) describing a "Sea Change" in the format of the annual meeting. This derives from the president's mandate to the program chair to minimize the past, pay no respect to stature, rank, or seniority, and provide every opportunity to the young and inexperienced. This is consistent from the president's declared libertarian beliefs that are defined by the *Oxford English Dictionary* as "an extreme laissez-faire philosophy advocating only minimal intervention in the lives of citizens." His blogs make it clear the president attributes the ACNP's current ailments in part to a complacent oligarchy of old-timers who have stifled youth and innovation. Consequently the ingredients of the "Sea Change" are "mini-panels" devoid of discussion and a "data blitz" of apprentice investigators presenting "rigorously timed five-minute presentations." This might be a laudable experiment in normal circumstances, but current problems confronting the ACNP merit a response more appropriate to a tsunami than a sea change. To extend the maritime metaphor, it sounds like a "ship of fools" crewed by midshipmen, heading for an iceberg. Will the officers remain on the bridge and go down with the ship?

Satire aside, there are serious concerns about what this belief system and its simplistic solutions have drowned out. As a Life Fellow since 1970, I was active in the ACNP's earlier years but drifted away to pursue other interests before returning over two years ago to assist in work on the *Oral History of Neuropsychopharmacology* during which time I copyedited, read, or edited nine of the ten volumes, and wrote over fifty biographies of the early pioneers. This complemented my earlier work when, in 1970, with Frank Ayd, we coedited *Discoveries in Biological Psychiatry*, first-person accounts of the discovery or development of all the first-generation psychotropic drugs by the clinicians and scientists who made them.

In both of these databases, most of the pioneers were experienced clinicians with long exposure to large populations with untreated severe and persistent mental illness, mostly in a variety of nonacademic settings including the VA, state hospitals, and private practice. They became motivated by the dramatic changes they saw in people never previously exposed to effective treatment, and they quickly developed valid, reliable rating instruments and research protocols. They also recognized, from the start, the need for close collaboration and communication with basic scientists in an extended environment conducive to translational dialogue. This is how the ACNP was born in 1961.

For the first decade (1962-1972) this was a fruitful enterprise driven by intellectual curiosity and a profound desire to help people with severe mental illness return from asylums to life in community. They succeeded, but this atmosphere, its motivations, and rewards were quickly and progressively eroded and no longer exist. Over the next four decades (1972-2012), the complexity of mental function and the difficulty of translational dialogue became increasingly clear.

Receptors, enzymes, and transmitters, often with manifold functions, were modulated by multiple messengers. Genes, like Shakespeare's sorrows, came "not as single spies, but in battalions," expressing themselves in uncertain ways and frustrating fifty years of wasted effort on the DSM fantasy that phenotypes, derived by political consensus, might be linked to drug function and specificity.

In short, neuroscience prospered while psychopharmacology dwindled. The only truly innovative drug discovered in forty fallow years of research was Viagra. Decades after chlorpromazine, serendipity still colludes with science in unexpected ways and places!

While worthwhile improvements in clinical care were minimal, there was insidious, perhaps understandable, erosion in scientific motivation

—

away from curiosity and concern in favor of fame and fortune. This coincided with a shift from clinical to academic settings as psychoanalytic hegemony yielded slowly to psychopharmacology and neuroscience. Fame became congruent with prolific resumes, citation publications, academic promotion, prizes, and awards. Fortune was fed by industry largesse and emulation of its profit-making procedures; universities filed patents, investigators founded for-profit corporations, and faculty signed contracts to endorse new drugs often with dubious benefits and dangerous side effects. The highly touted "second-generation" drugs were dressed in the emperor's clothes, designed by creative marketing forces and ratified by willing academics.

All this was fueled by gargantuan pharmaceutical profits generated by a rapidly expanding market, itself the product of direct, often misleading, advertising to the public. This was enabled by lax FDA standards and oversight in an era of political deregulation and national corporate greed. Big Pharma profits were directed to infiltrating and influencing scientific organizations, meeting agendas, medical school curriculum, practicing psychiatrists' prescribing habits, and academic psychiatrists' political influence, including leadership of professional organizations. Not to mention lobbying Congress in favor of deregulation.

Corporate dominance and degradation of drug research was facilitated by a change in federal funding priorities from clinical to basic neural sciences and the concurrent closure of NIMH drug research. FDA, industry, and academia clung too long to double-blind placebo-controlled studies as the gold standard for efficacy and safety. Short in numbers and duration but sufficient for statistical significance, this lacked real-life validity and was an absurdly low hurdle for marketing approval. Samples excluded comorbidity or concurrent medications and compelled compliance while fertile women, children, and seniors were seldom included. Only recently has a distinction between efficacy and effectiveness been stressed, but Big Pharma has shunned comparing new patented drugs to cheap generic prototypes and has avoided effectiveness studies. Instead they have designed, implemented, and outsourced their own studies, then coauthored or "bottom-drawered" the results to meet commercial goals. Poster citations sometimes substitute for refereed journals.

—

ACNP did little to oppose these changes; instead, it swam with the tide. Its membership ballooned to include a majority of basic and jointly trained members, accompanied by a dramatic decline in sophisticated clinical researchers and increasing attention to programs devoted or linked to posters on esoteric topics by multiple authors (up to twenty), often with little or no clinical relevance and not subjected to independent review. Ethical guidelines were promulgated, but little was done to enforce them or sanction those who violated them. Members dutifully recited their corporate affiliations, but nobody cared that naming a conflict of interest did not eliminate it.

It is doubtful if the founders of the ACNP would recognize or endorse its current form. But if or how change can occur is highly questionable when foxes are loose in the hen house. But if ever there was a time for fundamental and decisive leadership, it is now. Laissez-faire principles and "bottom up" tinkering are hardly the answer.

Not only does libertarian philosophy shun authority and experience, but it subscribes to Henry Ford's famous epigram that "History is Bunk." What followed that dictum was the Edsel, the biggest design failure in the history of the automotive industry. The ACNP has entered an Edsel era. It will not be bailed out this time by government or industry, although natural forces (which libertarian's prefer) might intervene. Big Pharma has killed the goose that laid the golden eggs by degrading clinical research and making manifestly false claims for its products. Slender profits from generic drugs may trim its sails. Tea Party deficit hawks and Congressional investigative committees may stifle some of the symbiotic greed that currently binds academia to industry.

As a result, slim economic times might shrink the ACNP, shed some fortune seekers and citation hunters, and revive a lost commitment to better, safer, more affordable treatments evaluated by skilled clinicians, free of commercial incentives, and motivated by love of science and their patients.

That is the way it once was. One final maritime metaphor describes the way it is today. The ACNP is like a ship cut from its moorings, adrift on the ocean. It has failed in its two primary purposes: sophisticated, productive, ethical research translated into safe, effective, affordable treatments by creative, relevant basic science. Instead, a core of distinguished and talented clinicians is dwindling and dying, unenlightened by their translational aspirations. Should the ship be salvaged or allowed to sink?

One possibility would be to recommission the vessel as "The American College of Neuroscience" (ACNS) and advocate vigorously for the revival of a Federal Drug Evaluation Program (FDEP). Its contemporary task would be threefold. The first would be to conduct small intensive studies designed to link individual drug response to the genotype and its phenotype using symptom-specific rating scales and avoiding DSM categories of disorders. The second task would be to use this seedbed for the selection of novel compounds to compare with existing generic prototypes in studies of sufficient size, statistical power, and duration to ensure efficacy, safety, generalizability, and economic utility. These studies would be funded, but not managed, by pharmaceutical companies in return for patent rights on genuinely innovative and cost-effective compounds. The third task would follow naturally from the first two; the creation of a new cadre of highly trained and well-paid investigators with lengthy tenure coupled to incentives for productivity and creativity. These scientists would be encouraged to seek academic appointments but forbidden to engage in all industry involvement during or following their federal contracts.

The renamed ACNS would meet regularly with FDEP investigators to discuss potential translational topics carefully chosen by a select panel of distinguished but commercially independent peers. Meetings would be modeled on the early ACNP meetings with limited attendance and leisurely agendas conducive to extended and collegial dialogue. Participation and funding by industry would be encouraged but without involvement in the selection or presentation of topics or compounds.

The currents and tides swirling around the ACNP are symbolic of a tsunami, not a sea change. Proportionate prophylactic action is called for.

—

Big Pharma: A Second Opinion

A thread running through this memoir has been the ubiquitous impact of greed on all aspects of contemporary America. Generic concern was voiced in my prose poem, "Greed: The Deadliest Sin" in "Piece 10: America," also illustrated in that piece by the bit, "Mammon and Modern Medicine." The concern was present, *sub rosa*, during my brief sojourn in the pharmaceutical industry in Piece 11 and expressed more openly during my forty-year involvement with psychopharmacology research in the previous bit, "Sea Change or Tsunami?"

While in the final stages of putting to bed this memoir, I chanced to read *No One Would Listen,* a blow-by-blow account of how Bernie Madoff wreaked havoc during my lifetime on the financial sector with a fifty-billion-dollar Ponzi scheme. In the book, Harry Markopolos documents his repeated but failed attempts to alert the SEC to exert its fraud oversight function. Now a full-time "whistleblower," Markopolos has the following to say about the pharmaceutical industry after he attended a Chamber of Commerce "Summer Bash" sponsored by Millennium Pharmaceuticals:

> I particularly wanted to meet people from the pharmaceutical world, which I discovered was ripe with fraud. As I had learned in my investigations, the health care industry makes Wall Street look honest. It's a two-trillion-dollar-a-year business with no controls and limited auditing. On Wall Street the crooks at least have the decency to try to hide their frauds, but those people cheating Medicare don't even bother doing that. Wall Street is only taking your life savings, but in health care they may be stealing your life. I was surprised to discover how little "care" there is in health care. It's obviously no surprise that the pharmaceutical industry is a completely profit-driven business, but the methods companies devised to earn more of those profits were surprising—and in the case I discovered, illegal.
>
> I've been working on several cases that remain under investigation or under seal, meaning in both cases I can't

discuss them. Truthfully my career aspiration is to prove that a drug with more than a billion dollars in annual sales is actually killing Americans and citizens across the globe, that in the clinical trials the dangers of this drug were revealed, and that the executives knew about the dangers and went ahead and marketed it anyway. I've been working on this case for a few years now without much success, but I hope someday I'll be able to find a key witness to get this case filed with the Department of Justice.

Underlying all this is Big Pharma's strategy of using its profits to pay whatever fines are imposed by regulatory agencies as "the price of doing business."

Learning from Lithium

By the time I graduated from the Maudsley in 1966, my psychiatric training and two-year psychopharmacology fellowship were behind me but, during that time, our discipline had acquired drug treatments for every one of its disorders. Lithium was the first and the last of those treatments to be discovered, bookends for the entire repertoire of effective compounds. It was also the last drug I worked on before I was launched on my career, research that involved me in significant international controversy. For the remainder of my fifty-year career, nothing truly innovative was added to our pharmacopeia despite billions of federal, foundation, and Big Pharma dollars, a disappointing outcome that has brought clinical neuropsychopharmacology almost to a halt.

This qualifies lithium for a closer look, an inquiry that has only seemed appropriate in retrospect, after we were distracted and beguiled by the drug manufacturers' seductive and misleading advertising of "second-generation" drugs.

The irony of this is exquisite; lithium is not a drug but a metallic ion ranked number three in the periodic table, similar to sodium or potassium, and available in pure form under our noses. As such, God holds the patent, a monopoly that discouraged the pharmaceutical industry from investing in or advertising it. Of course, humans had stumbled across lithium early on; it is a ubiquitous element found in clay, many water sources, and rocks (hence *lithia* is Greek for "stone"). The Greeks and Romans are alleged to have advised drinking spring water, presumably high in lithium, for the treatment of mania. Certain areas in Japan and Texas, with water supplies containing lithium, were found to have low suicide rates leading to the suggestion, never implemented, that drinking water might be spiked with lithium just as salt has iodine added to prevent hypothyroidism. Some beers (Lithia) and soda beverages (7Up) included lithium just as, early on, Coca-Cola contained cocaine.

Traditional medicine also used lithium. First, to treat gout (it dissolves uric acid crystals in kidney stones) and then as a salt substitute in the management of hypertension. Unfortunately, lithium accumulates in the body and can cause neurological disorders and congestive heart failure, leading to death in toxic amounts. In 1948, after lithium had caused several deaths, it was banned as a food and drink additive by the FDA.

Paradoxically, the modern history of lithium began in the following year in Australia. As with all the first effective drugs in psychiatry, this was discovered while looking for one thing and finding another (serendipity). The psychiatrist, John Cade, was searching for a toxic metabolite in urine that he believed might cause manic-depressive disorder. In April 1970, after I had been in America for eighteen months, I met and heard John Cade describe his research and discovery at the conference on *Discoveries in Biological Psychiatry* in Baltimore, organized by Frank Ayd and me. His account, published in our book of the same title, reads as follows:

> One can hardly imagine a less propitious year in which to attempt the pharmacological rehabilitation of lithium. That the attempt was made by an unknown psychiatrist, working alone in a small chronic hospital with no research training, primitive techniques and negligible equipment was hardly likely to be compellingly persuasive.

Cade was testing his assumption that a metabolic substance might be responsible for fluctuations in mood in manic-depressive disorder analogous to the changes in mood and behavior due to thyroid hormones in thyrotoxicosis and myxedema. He did this by injecting the urine of patients into the peritoneum of guinea pigs. He found the urine of manic patients was far more toxic, causing seizures and often leading to death of the animal. Cade reasoned that urea was the toxic substance but in order to quantify the effect, he needed to use higher amounts. Because uric acid was relatively insoluble in water, he turned to the most soluble salt available—lithium urate. When this was injected, "after a latent period of about two hours the animals, although fully conscious, became extremely lethargic and unresponsive to stimuli for one to two hours before once again becoming normally timid and active."

Knowing the history of lithium use in humans and already working with manic-depressive patients, Cade decided to see if the effect of the lithium salt on behavior in guinea pigs had any therapeutic effect on mania in humans. He describes what happened when he gave lithium to his first manic patient. "This was a wizened man of 51 who had been in a state of chronic manic excitement for five years. He was amiably restless, dirty, destructive, mischievous and interfering. He had enjoyed pre-eminent nuisance value in a back ward all those years and bid fair to remain there for the rest of his life." By the fifth day of lithium treatment "he was more settled, tidier, less disinhibited and less distractible." Within three weeks, he was transferred to a convalescent ward and after two months of close observation was well enough to go home and return to work. After a few months he stopped taking lithium, relapsed, and was readmitted. Within a month of resuming lithium, he was "completely well and ready to return to home and work."

At the Baltimore Conference, Cade reported equally satisfying results in nine patients with mania. Three out of six patients with schizophrenia showed a reduction in restlessness or excited behavior but all remained psychotic. In three chronically depressed patients, there was no improvement in symptoms. Cade went on to systematically study a series of naturally occurring alkali metals but found nothing with an equivalent therapeutic value. His concluding comment was, "That lithium, a simple inorganic ion, can reverse a major psychiatric reaction must have, quite apart from its substantial therapeutic value, profound theoretical significance in unraveling the mystery of the so-called functional psychoses."

It is worth pausing to underline the immense significance of Cade's research, in part because it is so often overlooked or subsumed by others. First, it is remarkable because it was the very first scientific evidence of a biological cause leading to drug treatment for a major psychiatric disorder, made almost three years before the discovery of chlorpromazine for schizophrenia (May 1952) and eight years before the discovery of imipramine for severe depression (September 1957) and iproniazid, an MAO inhibitor, for "atypical depression" (April 1957). Cade's reference to "the so-called functional psychoses" may have been a tongue-in-cheek reminder of the strong prevailing psychoanalytic belief that these disorders were the result of faulty parenting and could be corrected by psychotherapy.

Secondly, also noteworthy, is the impeccable research strategy by a self-trained scientist working in primitive conditions. Cade's move from findings in animals to testing in humans became the basis for "translational" research strategies, the future paradigm in neuropsychopharmacology.

Third is the precise manner in which Cade established the specificity of his findings; a unique action of lithium compared to other alkali metals and confined to one particular psychiatric disorder, chronic mania.

One might have expected these findings would have ignited worldwide excitement and emulation but the Zeitgeist was not conducive. Chronic mania was a relatively rare disorder, often misdiagnosed as schizophrenia in America where psychoanalysis was the predominant paradigm. In Britain and Europe, the prevailing interest was in classification and diagnosis ("descriptive" psychiatry), while novel treatments were viewed with skepticism, often verging on nihilism. Only in Scandinavia did a few psychiatrists follow the lead of Cade in Australia. In his opening remarks at the Baltimore conference, he states, "The person who has done more to achieve this recognition (of lithium) has been Mogens Schou in Denmark." This was due in part to Schou's personal interest in bipolar disorder among family members and perhaps also because of a new reliable method for measuring lithium levels in the blood which made research safer and more scientific.

—

Schou's contributions and the controversy that ensued came in the mid to late 1960s, after the intervening discovery of drugs for all the other major categories of disorder: schizophrenia, major depression, mania, atypical depression, anxiety, insomnia, and attention deficit disorder. Schou and his colleagues focused on the only remaining major category without an established treatment, bipolar disorder. So lithium became the treatment that both opened and closed an almost twenty-year era separating the first from the latest category of drug treatments, now known as the "mood stabilizers."

A number of factors distinguish the significance of the second from the first of these twin bookends. While the new treatment indication was innovative and much needed, it was not highly original; using lithium to treat the manic component of bipolar disorder followed directly from Cade's unique discovery of its efficacy in chronic mania. What was both unique and controversial was the new concept of "prophylaxis," the alleged ability of lithium to prevent relapses in the long-term management of the disorder. In untreated bipolar disorder, a person often experiences a lifetime of unpredictable relapses or "cycles" of either or both mania and depression (hence the older term "manic-depression"). When Cade first discovered lithium in chronic mania, proving the efficacy and specificity of treatment was simple—a person who had been sick and hospitalized for years and for whom there were no other known treatments suddenly and quickly recovered and remained well. If they stopped lithium, they relapsed but recovered, equally quickly, when it was resumed. This required no statistics to prove, and a small sample or even a single patient was convincing enough!

Proving the efficacy of lithium in preventing unpredictable and highly variable episodes of either or both mania and depression was an altogether more difficult task, especially when there were now antidepressants with which to compare it. It was this situation that confronted Professor Shepherd and me in 1967 when we critically dissected Schou and Baastrup's research and replicated their results with the antidepressant imipramine.

The ensuing controversy ignited passionate and prolonged debate. When research produces equivocal findings, providers fall back on clinical experience, usually their own, to guide them. So lithium gradually established itself while Shepherd and I contented ourselves with having reached the wrong conclusion for all the right reasons.

Over fifteen years later, I received a letter from Michael Shepherd inviting me to write a book review for the journal he edited, *Psychological Medicine*. The book, *The History of Lithium Therapy*, was an uncritical, passionate paean of praise for lithium, "the king of drugs." Here it is:

The Book Review

The reader deserves an honest opinion. If he doesn't deserve it, give it to him anyhow.

—John Ciardi, on the role of reviewers

No human being is constituted to know the truth, the whole truth, and nothing but the truth; and even the best of men must be content with fragments, with partial glimpses, never the full fruition.

—William Osler, MD

The History of Lithium Therapy. By F. N. Johnson. (Pp. 198; illustrated) Macmillan Press: London. 1984

Book review published in *Psychological Medicine*, 1985:

One might hope that those who record history are more objective than those who create it. The fact that the author of *The History of Lithium Therapy* is an academic psychologist may have spared him from the prejudices of his own prescribing habits but, as he confesses in the preface, "I am hardly unbiased in my view of the importance of lithium."

Neil Johnson claims to have authored three previous texts on lithium and dedicates this book to "Nete and Mogens," counts John Cade as his friend, and endorses other enthusiasts who see lithium as the "king of drugs" responsible for the "third revolution in psychiatry."

Let me confess, as reviewer, that I am hardly unbiased myself. The book contains a gallery of portraits among which mine appears somewhat like that of a wanted man who "with Michael Shepherd, labeled lithium prophylaxis a therapeutic myth." Since Professor Shepherd's picture is not included, there is no doubt who the real villain must be. The text does indeed read rather like the script of a B movie with its good guys (for lithium) and bad guys (against it) battling through hyperbole towards an ending that could (and perhaps one day will) be set to music as the advocates of lithium, like the Lone Ranger, ride victorious into the sunset. The script ends on page 136 as follows:

> They may have made mistakes, reached the wrong conclusions, misinterpreted or gone beyond their data, but it was all done in good faith and only with the omniscience of hindsight can we find fault; at the time their ideas were the springs from which new concepts and new theories flowed. Above all, they kept lithium in the mainstream of medical practice so that when the time was ripe and the world was ready, the true nature of lithium could be revealed and understood.

The prologue to this book portends these biases accurately enough to raise hackles on the mildest sceptic. Lithium is being taken, it claims, by one person in every two thousand in most civilized countries (possibly more in Denmark). This is "because depression [sic] is a crippling condition." In a simplistic tour de force Johnson declares that "manic depression" is more accurately called "recurrent endogenous affective disorder." It follows naturally that lithium is singled out for much of the chemical revolution in psychiatry. "At a stroke, the elusive aetherial Freudian psyche was replaced as the primary object of attention in psychiatry by the polyphasic, physico-chemical system called the brain." Lithium "like no other single event, led to psychiatry becoming truly interdisciplinary." Its ubiquitous use "suggests a new basis for classification of psychopathological states." It is so cheap and easy to administer that it will transform health care in underdeveloped countries whose psychiatric services are otherwise "stretched to breaking point."

For the remainder of the book another ten chapters tell the credulous reader how this miracle came to pass. Much of the history is told in the tedious and picayune detail of a high school term paper (supplemented by another fifty pages of notes and references at the end of the book). The early use of lithium in gout, the pseudoscientific rationale to support it, and the struggles of its advocates and detractors underline the current debate with unconscious irony. An early critic took an early enthusiast to task because "too continuous study of one subject led to something like mesmeric dazing and diminished an author's experimental resources."

The persistence of early beliefs in lithium's therapeutic value is attributed by Johnson to "the durability of hypotheses advanced by those regarded as authorities in their field, to the lack of impact of scientific papers upon members of the general medical profession and to the part of advertising by the manufacturers of lithia tablets and lithia water." Later in the book we read how a leading New York psychiatrist recently wrote a popular best-seller about lithium called *Mood Swing* which "sold in excess of one million copies."

Much is made of earlier hints that vague mental symptoms associated with uric acid diathesis might benefit from lithium. Of more compelling interest is that the Danish internist, Carl Lange, published a monograph in 1886, *Concerning Periodic Depression and its Pathogenesis*, which included the use of a lithium-containing mixture for preventative treatment. Subsequent Danish psychiatrists credited Lange for his description of depression but denied his claims for lithium. Foremost among these critics was the father of Mogens Schou. The dramatic irony of this generational disagreement seems strangely appropriate to Hamlet's homeland.

A persistent disappointment in this book is its failure to fulfill a significant historical function of perceiving analogies or probing metaphors. It never asks whether the lessons of history are being learned or lived again. Why is it that the lithium ion has held as much allure for modern chemophilic clinicians as base metal did for the auric alchemists of medieval times?

The modern history of lithium begins in Chapter 3 of this book with a description of John Cade and his discovery of the ion's effects on manic patients. Cade proceeded from the mistaken assumptions that mania was a state of intoxication due to an excess of some normal metabolite excreted in urine to the conclusion that lithium (which he selected since it produces the most soluble salt of uric acid) was effective because it corrected a deficiency of an essential trace element. Sandwiched between these two erroneous assumptions was the astute observation that lithium benefited ten patients with mania that he treated in a Melbourne hospital and subsequently reported in the September (1949) issue of the *Medical Journal of Australia.*

A conflicting view of Cade emerges. Described as a modest man, he also noted that the publication of his discovery coincided with the tenth anniversary of World War II. Although he took lithium himself before giving it to patients, he never revealed that his first patient died of lithium toxicity. He published an account of psychiatric history (*Mending the Mind*) without identifying himself as the discoverer of lithium but became irritated if others described the observation as serendipitous. Perhaps Cade's interpretation of the word was too literal. Horace Walpole's original account of incidental discovery concerned not only its hero (a prince of Serendip) but also a mule blind in one eye. Cade's finding can certainly be attributed not only to curiosity but to his single-minded (even myopic) interest in trace metals and a stubborn persistence in pursuing his simple-minded hypothesis. Time will tell if history concludes (as this version does) that one day John Cade "may well be generally recognized as ranking among the most influential figures of twentieth century psychiatry."

In the spirit of pseudodrama the next chapter is entitled *The Toxicity Panic* and relates the fatalities that occurred when lithium chloride was sold in America as a salt substitute and an understaffed FDA delayed action because of the complacent view that it was a food and not a drug. The subsequent chapter (*Early Confirmations*) relates the impact of these events in Australia, and the use by Noack and Trautner of the new technique of flame spectrophotometry in 1950 to measure lithium levels. This work was largely overlooked, but it set the stage for Mogens Schou and what Johnson calls "the second era of lithium

—

in medicine." This chapter relates Schou's collaboration with others and traces the evolution of the concept of "prophylaxis." It also portrays some personal motives that are helpful in understanding Schou's resistance to placebo-controlled studies and his evangelical belief in lithium. There are apparently a number of instances of manic-depression in Schou's family, including a brother whom he treated with maintenance lithium, producing results that appeared as a "miracle" to the family. It is of special interest that this relative appears to have suffered from recurrent unipolar depression and Schou is reported to have commented: "How *could* I put him or others like him in a clinical trial where he would face the possibility of lithium being withdrawn?"

This experience and attitude may also explain the somewhat sensitive (even paranoid) response to the opposition and criticism which developed towards lithium in the late 1960s. Johnson concludes: "The lithium pioneers could afford to take these difficulties in their stride in the hope that, with time, even those who doubted the efficacy of lithium could not help but eventually be converted."

This blithe pronouncement ushers in a chapter on the *Therapeutic Myth* controversy which is fully recounted, but subtly fails to focus on its central issue. The nub of this debate was the claim that lithium was "prophylactic" in recurrent unipolar disorder (much more prevalent than manic or bipolar disease), despite the absence of an action in acute depression. This expansive and improbable claim was bolstered with the declaration that it would be ethically improper to subject it to controlled prospective evaluation.

The most self-fulfilling aspect of this "history" is that it was written in the year preceding the final publication of the studies that settled the matter. Both the collaborative Medical Research Council trial in the UK (Glen et al. 1984) and the NIMH Study Group project in the USA (Prien et al. 1984) appeared after this book was safely in press. The larger of these studies (Prien et al. 1984) involved over two years' prospective follow-up in one hundred seventeen bipolar and one hundred fifty unipolar patients given lithium, imipramine,

—

the combined drugs, or placebo. Among its conclusions are the following:

(1) Imipramine is preferable to lithium for long-term preventative treatment following recovery from an acute episode of unipolar depression.
(2) For both bipolar and unipolar disease the preventative effects of both lithium and imipramine parallel their effects in acute episodes.
(3) Even when lithium and antidepressants are effective they are not panaceas. Only a quarter to a third of patients with bipolar or unipolar disease were "treatment successes."

Another failure of this book is the absence of any attempt to address this controversy in a broader context. Claims for new cures often stir controversy. Iconoclasts pit against protagonists; young turks challenge established experts. Claims of even the most distinguished scientists must be subject to controlled scrutiny to eliminate bias, especially when objectivity is compromised by clinical and ethical convictions derived from treating family members. Benjamin Rush is not remembered for bloodletting, nor Linus Pauling for megavitamin therapy.

In such controversies questions about judgment are often perceived as ad hominem attacks on integrity through the eyes and egos of the investigators. Some idea of the animus involved in this debate can be felt from the letter written by Cade to Schou after *The Lancet* had reluctantly published the Danish workers' attempt to rebut the questions about prophylaxis with their flawed discontinuation study. Cade complains that *The Lancet* "did not have the decency to produce an editorial annotation acknowledging that you and Poul (Baastrup) had K.O.'d Blackwell and Shepherd in the final round! No matter. Your contention has been proven so convincingly that the whole world must be persuaded."

Following this triumph over controversy, there is a chapter to share the credit for the "spread of lithium therapy" around the world and to recall the names of those "few individuals whose perception to new ideas was above the average, [who] seized upon a promising suggestion and by experiment, astute observation and not a little guesswork and faith, amplified the weak signal into a loud and clear message which others could not ignore."

After this roll call there is a penultimate chapter on developments and crises. The former consist mainly of cataloguing the potential new uses to which any panacea is applied, and the latter is a euphemism for adverse effects. But readers can be reassured: "Each of these crises led to a ripple of unease among those engaged in administering lithium treatment and each left a scar on the reputation of lithium therapy, but the therapy has survived more or less intact."

It is something of a relief to read in a final chapter devoted to the future that it "seems unlikely that dramatic new developments will take place." Perhaps we all deserve a respite from lithium and it really is time for this simple ion to take its place in history. What that place deserves to be is not accurately described in this book. It should probably have parallel status among many other useful psychotropic drugs, none of which is a panacea but all of which may be viewed within the perspective of Sir Aubrey Lewis' (1963) temperate admonition:

> We are not living through a period that marks a new epoch; there is no Galileo or Darwin, no Harvey or Newton in psychiatry and psychology, nor, to put our aspirations on a more realistic plane, have there been discoveries during the past twenty years comparable to those that have signaled the growth of therapeutics in surgery in other fields. Psychiatric advances have been less dramatic and less conclusive. Still, to those who have taken part in them, they have given the satisfaction and excited the hopes out of which enthusiasm is generated.

Who should buy this book? Perhaps those who share the late Nathan Kline's view of lithium as the "Cinderella" of psychopharmacology will want to have this unabridged version of the fairy tale at their fingertips.

—

Nathan Kline

Nathan "Nate" Kline, quoted at the end of the review, was someone with whom I had crossed swords about lithium in the correspondence columns of the *American Journal of Psychiatry*. It was a witty exchange which amused the readers without bruising any egos. In the last couple of years, when I edited two of the ten volumes in *The Oral History of Neuropsychopharmacology*, I elected to dedicate Volume Nine to Nate Kline. Here is my explanation of why I did so:

> This Volume is dedicated to Nathan S. Kline who was both a founding member of the American College of Neuropsychopharmacology and its sixth President (1967). Unfortunately Dr. Kline died at the early age of 67 in 1982 before this history project was initiated. There is nobody who better personifies the pioneering spirit that initiated the field of psychopharmacology. Nate was intensely energetic, creative, curious, challenging, provocative, and entrepreneurial. In 1952, at age 38, he started a research unit at Rockland State Hospital in New York, named the Nathan S. Kline Institute after his death. He initiated the use of reserpine in schizophrenia and then chlorpromazine. Among the first also to use tricyclic antidepressants and MAO inhibitors, his research team recognized the potential link between clinical and biochemical mechanisms. For these accomplishments he twice won the Albert Lasker Award. Nate was a researcher, busy practitioner, publicist, politician, and world traveler. His popular book, *From Sad to Glad*, is still in print and available on Amazon. He published over a hundred scientific articles and is credited with lobbying the Congress to originate Federal funding for psychopharmacology research. For better or worse, the results he obtained at Rockland State Hospital helped to trigger the process of deinstitutionalization for people suffering from severe mental illness.

It is strange how the threads of one's life come to connect otherwise stray bits and pieces. Although Cade and Kline were never involved together with lithium and lived continents apart, no two people better deserve to be singled out as among the earliest and preeminent founders in the field of drug discovery for treatment of mental illness.

A Case Study: Science, Hubris, Nemesis, and Redemption

Long, long before men and women became scientists, the Greek playwrights portrayed the justice meted out toward the overweening pride and ambition of their heroes by the gods' wrath and retribution. Hubris invited nemesis and only rarely was there hope of redemption. Nothing Freud or the analysts added altered this dynamic as the following case study from the twentieth century illustrates:

The Case

Jose Manuel Rodriguez Delgado
(1915-2011)

This biography has an unusual provenance and was not something I might have anticipated writing. Born almost twenty years after Delgado at the beginning of the neuropsychopharmacology era, I was not familiar with his pioneering work in physiology using electrode implants in animals and humans to modify emotion and behavior. It might have crossed my horizon during psychiatric training (1962-1967) at a time when his research began attracting international attention, but I was too immersed in my own animal pharmacology studies to take serious note.

Jose emigrated from Spain to the USA in 1950 and spent twenty years in America before returning to Spain when controversy engulfed his career. Based on his pioneering work at Yale University, he was among the small number of clinical and animal researchers who became founding members of the ACNP in 1961. Although we were fellow members for most of our careers, our paths never crossed; neither of us served on any of the organization's committees or held office nor did he receive any of its awards.

In 2005, at the age of ninety, Delgado was interviewed for the ACNP's Oral History Project (OHP) by Joel Braslow, a psychiatrist and historian but not a member of the organization. The interview is published in Volume 2 (*Neurophysiology*, 201-207). It is relatively brief, and some rather vague answers suggest early cognitive impairment. Additional comments on Delgado's pioneer contributions are provided by the series editor, Tom Ban, in the preface (ibid., xv) and by the volume editor, Max Fink, in the dramatis personae (ibid., xliv). Three of Delgado's key publications in English are cited (ibid., xxii).

Jose Delgado died at the age of ninety-six just three months before December 2011 when the ACNP celebrated its fiftieth anniversary. It was not until nine months later that I received a request to write a six-hundred-word obituary due to some reluctance among members better suited to the task, perhaps attributable to the still-ongoing controversy about Delgado's life's work. I had two months to complete the task. After a brief overview of existing information, I felt convinced that the topic deserved a more exhaustive analysis, both because of the unusual perspective it offers from a historical view of science, but also for an opportunity to offer a much-maligned pioneer some belated redemption.

The Man of Science

Jose Delgado was born on August 8 in Ronda, a province of Malaga in Spain. His father was an ophthalmologist who Jose planned to emulate until he became entranced by the work and writings of Santiago Ramon y Cajal, often considered the "father of neuroscience." Cajal was a Nobel Laureate in 1906 in Physiology and Medicine, together with Golgi, for work on the structure of the nervous system. Captivated by the mysteries of the nervous system, Jose began working as a student in physiology under Juan Negri at the Madrid Medical School. On the first paper listed in his bibliography, he is as second author to J. G. Valdecasas who worked with Severo Ochoa in Negri's lab on glycolysis of heart muscle. It was published in 1933 when Jose was a pretentious eighteen-year-old!

229

Delgado must have formally become a medical student around the outbreak of the Spanish Civil War in 1936 between the elected Republican government (loyalists) and the insurgents led by General Franco, supported by Nazi Germany and Italy. As the fascists gained control, first Ochoa and then Negri fled Spain while Delgado dropped out of his studies to join the Republican side as a medical corpsman. After the fascist victory in 1939, he spent five months in a concentration camp before returning to medical school to complete his MD in 1940, graduating *cum laude*. He then began work immediately as an instructor in physiology, and in 1942 obtained his Doctor of Science, also *cum laude*.

Between 1942 and 1950, Jose resumed his animal research in physiology and received several awards; Countess of Maude's Prize (1944), Roel Prize (1945), and the Ramon y Cajal Prize awarded by the Spanish government (1952). During this period, he published fourteen papers on his primate research in European journals, mostly in his native language. This work primarily involved selective brain ablation and electrical stimulation of various nuclei and regions with implanted electrodes.

At this time, Jose was handicapped by difficulty obtaining primates for his research. In the OHP interview, he tells of traveling to Africa to purchase animals. On the two-week return journey, he bonded to a gorilla and, feeling unable to operate on his "new friend," donated it to the local zoo! Later on, this period in Jose's career would be characterized by his detractors as "under the fascist regime" implying guilt by association with fascist atrocities, while ignoring his service as a corpsman on the Republican side, incarceration in concentration camp after the war, and humanitarian treatment of his animal subjects.

In 1950 Delgado won a two year James Hudson Brown Scholarship to Yale University Medical School and joined the physiology department under John Fulton. Impressed with his work, Fulton appointed him an assistant professor in the department (1953-1955), promoted him to associate professor (1955), and eventually to full professor of both physiology and psychiatry in 1966 at the age of fifty-one. Delgado flourished at Yale; described by a colleague as a "technological wizard," he invented a device he named the "stimoceiver," a small implanted array of electrodes that permitted two-way communications with a fully mobile animal and allowed Delgado to stimulate different regions of the brain, producing changes in behavior and affect.

Delgado's research was a sophisticated and less destructive continuation of Fulton's earlier work. In 1935, Fulton had reported on his experiments demonstrating a dramatic reduction in violent behavior by a chimpanzee following ablation of the prefrontal cortex. This finding was credited with providing the impetus for the Portuguese psychiatrist Moniz to extend the work to humans by performing lobotomies on psychiatric patients, claiming excellent results for which he won the Nobel Prize in 1949.

With this background and working in Fulton's department, Delgado expressed his wish to shun the crude ablation of brain pathways, replacing that with more discrete direct chemical and electrical stimulation of selected areas. Possibly encouraged by Moniz's fame and success, Delgado extended his animal experiments into twenty-five carefully chosen patients with chronic treatment refractory epilepsy and schizophrenia at a Rhode Island asylum and for whom there were no effective treatments available. His groundbreaking paper describing the results was published in 1952. This appeared with the provocative title, "Technique of Intracranial Electrode Placement for Recording and Stimulation and its Possible Therapeutic Effects in Psychotic Patients" (Conf. Neurol. 12, 315-329, 1952).

1952 was the watershed year in neuroscience. At precisely that moment, chlorpromazine was being given to schizophrenic patients for the first time with success that would spawn the neuropsychopharmacology revolution. Delgado positioned himself between the burgeoning disapproval of mutilating surgical lobotomies and the belief that direct electrical or chemical stimulation of specific brain areas was scientifically and clinically superior to oral administration of drugs whose effects on the brain were inevitably mitigated by metabolism in the liver, obstruction from the blood-brain barrier, and uncertain distribution throughout the brain.

Delgado was not entirely alone in these beliefs. His 1952 paper narrowly preempted publication of somewhat similar research in humans by Robert Heath, chairman of neurology and psychiatry at Tulane University.

In a seventeen-year period (1952-1969) Delgado produced 134 scientific publications on his research in cats, monkeys, and patients, both psychotic and nonpsychotic. This work included research on both physiological and chemical stimuli of specific regions in the central nervous system (*Ann. N.Y. Acad. Sci.* 64, 644-666, 1956). In 1959, he reported on cerebral excitability in the monkey after administration of iproniazid, an early MAO inhibitor antidepressant (*EEG. Clin. Neurophysiol,* 11, 396, 1959), and in the early days of the ACNP he published a review titled "Neuropharmacology of Behavior" (*ACNP Bull.* 4:1, 1966).

Nevertheless, the bulk of Delgado's research focused on his special area of expertise in electrical stimulation. In the early days, this tended to focus on discrete emotional and behavioral outcomes in individual animals and, more rarely and selectively, in humans. A retrospective review of Jose's pioneering work at this time by John Horgan in *Scientific American* ("The Forgotten Era of Brain," October 2005) comments, "Delgado limited his human research, however, because the therapeutic benefits of implants were unreliable; results varied widely from patient to patient and could be unpredictable even in the same subject. In fact Delgado recalls turning away more patients than he treated."

It was in the decade from 1960 to 1970 that several events occurred which ushered in the controversy that would end Jose Delgado's career in America. After 1960, some of his research involved work on more global social behaviors, sometimes in colonies of monkeys inviting speculation about mind control in human society. Two particular events in this time period encouraged Delgado to widen the scope of speculation about the possible societal and philosophical implications of his research.

In 1963, during a spell in his native country, Jose performed and filmed an experiment that would bring him international attention. After implanting his "stimoceiver" in the caudate nucleus of a fighting bull at a Cordoba ranch, Jose stood in the bullring. Waving a red cape and facing the charging animal, he brought it to a sudden halt by pressing a handheld transmitter. Two years later, in 1965, the *New York Times* published a front-page story, including a photograph with the headline, "A Matador's Radio Stops a Wired Bull," by John A. Osmundsen. During an interview with the reporter, Jose Delgado speculated about the implications of his research in changing human behavior and society: "Electrical brain stimulation does not simply evoke automatic responses but reactions that become integrated into social behavior according to the individual's own personality or temperament," Dr. Delgado said. A videotape of the bull experiment, narrated by Delgado himself, is still available on YouTube today.

Sometime after 1965, Delgado received an invitation to contribute a book to be published in a series entitled *World Perspectives*. This was the forty-first volume in a series edited by Ruth Nanda Anshen. This remarkable woman lived to be 103, obtained her PhD in philosophy under Alfred North Whitehead, and was an author, editor, and philosopher who established the Seminars on the Nature of Man, named after her at Columbia University. Her proclaimed wish as an editor was to be an "intellectual instigator" of new ideas. To this end, she sought out and edited the works of many of the world's leading scientists and thinkers, encouraging them to speculate on the broader societal and philosophical implications of their own often narrow fields. The goal was to "extrapolate an idea in relation to life." To this end, she had edited the writings of individuals as diverse as Albert Einstein, Paul Tillich, Eric Fromm, Jonas Salk, and Margaret Mead. For each of the many series she edited in her lifetime, she selected an editorial board of the world's leading thinkers.

For *World Perspectives* she chose twelve individuals. To better understand the company Jose Delgado was invited to join, and the impact it may have had on his contribution, I will briefly list them:

- *Sir Kenneth Clark*: One of the best known historians of his generation and writer, producer, and presenter of the BBC TV series *Civilization*.

- *Richard Courant*: An internationally acclaimed mathematician, a German Jew who fled Nazi Germany to become professor at New York University, and founder of the Courant Institute of Mathematics.
- *Werner Heisenberg*: A theoretical physicist of international stature who developed the principle of quantum theory named after him and for which he received the Nobel Prize in1932.
- *Ivan Illich*: An Austrian-born philosopher and internationally acclaimed social critic of medical hegemony in his book *Medical Nemesis*.
- *Konrad Lorenz*: An Austrian zoologist, a founder of modern ethology who discovered the principle of "imprinting" in newborn birds and shared the Nobel Prize in 1973.
- *Robert M. MacIver*: Chancellor of the New School of Social Research at Columbia University and president of the American Sociological Society.
- *Joseph Needham*: A British scientist and historian of Chinese science who was a fellow of the Royal Society, the British Academy, and recipient of the Queens's Companionship of Honor, the only person to hold all three titles.
- *Isador Isaac Rabi*: Received the Nobel Prize for Physics in 1944, honoring his discovery of nuclear magnetic resonance.
- *Sir Sarvepalli Radhakrishnan*: An Indian scholar of comparative religion whose writings reconciled the traditions of East and West. He was president of India after the end of British rule from 1962 till 1967. He was also professor of Eastern Religion and Ethics at Oxford University (1936-1952) and received a knighthood from the king in 1931.
- *Karl Rahner, SJ*: A German Jesuit and one of the most respected theologians of the twentieth century whose ideas influenced the Second Vatican Council.
- *Sir Alexander Sachs*: An American economist, member of the National Policy Committee prior to World War II, he recommended to President Roosevelt that America pursue nuclear research. Knighted by Queen Elizabeth for counsel to the Office of Strategic Services during the war.
- *C. N. Yang*: A Chinese-American physicist who became Albert Einstein Professor of Physics at Stony Brook and founder of the

Institute of Theoretical Physics named after him. He received the Nobel Prize for Physics in 1957.

Finding himself in such distinguished company, it is impossible to know if Jose Delgado was emboldened or seduced but, either way, he chose a thought-provoking, perhaps provocative title for his volume, *Physical Control of the Mind: Toward a Psychocivilized Society.* Nor is it possible to know how much editorial influence was exerted either by the editorial board or the series editor on the title, style, or content. But because this book became the backbone of the controversy that engulfed Jose Delgado, it seemed imperative that I become familiar with what was actually said. So I was able to purchase a used hardback copy from Amazon for only eleven dollars.

What follows is a brief review of the book's structure and content with verbatim quotations to represent Delgado's actual thoughts and ideas:

The editor's introduction to the series contains this statement (ibid., xiv), "The volumes in this series endeavor to demonstrate that only in a society in which awareness of the problems of science exists can its discoveries start great waves of change in human culture."

This ideal finds an echo in Delgado's own acknowledgments; "As T. M. Hesburg, president of Notre Dame University has said, 'Scientists cannot be neutral. We must understand the social responsibility attached to our research and the moral impact it has on the world of men, including ourselves."

The volume begins in Part I with a discussion of "Natural Fate Versus Human Control." Contrary to the reflexive feel of "Physical Control of the Mind" (a.k.a. mind control), this is a nuanced discussion of the caution required in exerting freedom of choice, the need for awareness of outcomes, personal responsibility, and a caution that mankind should pay more attention to development of man himself rather than machines.

The next chapter contrasts our increasing knowledge and control over material resources with our relative ignorance of the functions

—

of the brain and mind. It ends with a quotation from a contemporary psychologist, "Man's greatest problem today is not to understand and exploit his physical environment but to understand and govern his conduct . . . If he is to survive he must proceed to explore himself and to control his own activities . . . If science provides knowledge society will display wisdom" (Beach F. A., "The Perpetuation and Evolution of Biological Science," *Amer. Psychologist*, 21: 943-949, 1966).

The concluding chapter of Part I on "Mental Liberation and Domination" ends with the following:

> The thesis of this book is that we now possess the necessary technology for the experimental investigation of mental activities, and that we have reached a critical turning point in which the mind can be used to influence its own structure, functions and purpose, thereby ensuring both the preservation and advance of civilization.

Part II of the book is a philosophical *tour de force* that explores the well-trod topic of "The Brain and Mind as Functional Entities" followed by "Extra Cerebral Elements of the Mind." Beginning with Aristotle, Plato, and Socrates, it proceeds on to an extended discussion of how mind and emotions develop, the nature-nurture hypothesis and the work of scientists from Freud to Harlow in humans and primates.

Next are back-to-back chapters on "The Mindless, Newborn Brain" and "Sensory Dependence of the Adult Mind" that end with the rather platitudinous statement, "The cerebral mechanisms which allow us to receive, interpret, feel and react, as well as the extra cerebral sources of stimuli, should be investigated experimentally."

Part III titled "Experimental Control of Brain Functions in Behaving Subjects" is essentially a synopsis of Delgado's scientific research in lay terms accompanied by photographs of both animal and human subjects. It deals particularly with systems for punishment and reward in the chapter on "Hell and Heaven within the Brain," followed by a chapter on memory and hallucinatory mechanisms, and finally with inhibitory effects, primarily on aggression.

—

Part IV is "Evaluation of Electrical Control of the Brain." Here is where Delgado gets to grips with the essence of scientific and philosophical concerns raised by his research findings. To do justice to the claims he is alleged to have made, I will quote his written words verbatim as they relate to each specific aspect of the research:

- *Activation of the "Will":* We may conclude that electrical stimulation of the brain (ESB) can activate and influence some of the cerebral mechanisms involved in willful behavior. In this way we are able to investigate the neuronal functions related to the so-called will, and in the near future this experimental approach should permit clarification of such highly controversial subjects as "freedom," "individuality" and "spontaneity" in factual terms rather than in elusive semantic discussions. This possibility of influencing willful activities by electrical means has obvious ethical implications, which will be discussed later. (*World Perspectives,* 184-189)

What Delgado fails to point out is that all the evidence he cites is from animals, consisting of cats, monkeys, and roosters which occasionally appear able to impose some volitional components on ESB induced changes in emotional state or motor activity. For example, isolated roosters stimulated by ESB to become restless would attack other roosters when placed in their presence. This is far removed from his claim that "in the near future" it might be possible to use ESB to influence the highest levels of free will in humans. Jose's hyperbole extrapolates far beyond the limits of his experimental findings, and one can only be grateful that he adds a caveat about the ethical implications of what he is suggesting.

- *Characteristics and Limitations of Brain Control:* The possibility of man's controlling the thoughts of other men has ranked as high in human fantasy as the control over transmutation of metals, the possession of wings, or the power to take a trip to the moon. In the world of science, however, speculation and fantasy cannot replace truth. In spite of its spectacular potential, ESB has practical and theoretical limitations which should be delineated. (ibid, 190)

Here a comment on semantics is appropriate. Although the overall tone is reasonable, Delgado persistently substitutes the word "control" when "stimulation" would be more accurate. Similarly, while admitting the limitations of ESB, he also alleges its "spectacular potential." Note the company in which he places ESB by equating it with mind control.

- *Predictability*: When electrodes are introduced into a cerebral structure and stimulation is applied for the first time, we really cannot predict the quality, localization, or intensity of the evoked effects. We do not even know that a response will appear. The anatomical and functional variability of the brain are factors which limit the predictability of ESB results . . . the location of a desired target requires careful exploration and implantation of only a few contacts may be rather disappointing. Present information about functional mapping in most cerebral areas is still rather incomplete. (ibid, 191)

Note that these modest assertions are made after twenty years of research in multiple species and tend to undermine Jose's earlier hope that electrode placement would be a far more precise and predictable methodology than oral administration of drugs.

- *Functional Monotony*: Electrical stimulation is a non-specific stimulus which always activates a group of neurons in a similar way . . . The responses, therefore, are repeated in a monotonous way, and any variability is related to changes in the stimulated subject. This functional monotony rules out the possibility that an investigator could direct a subject toward a target or induce him, like a robot, to perform any complex task under remote-controlled orders . . . The inherent limitations of ESB make realization of this fantasy very remote . . . Induced performance of more complex acts would be far beyond available methodology. (ibid.,191-192)

This should be reassuring to a reader concerned about mind control but it is curiously discordant with the prior comments about ESB's spectacular potential and possibility of controlling the human will.

- *Skillful Performance*: The acquisition of a new skill is theoretically and practically beyond the possibility of electrical stimulation, but ESB can create the desire to perform certain acts which may be skillful. (ibid., 192)

This is a nuanced statement, but what follows makes it clear that the "certain acts" are confined to those which already exist in the subject's repertoire; what changes is the emotional or volitional climate that encourages them to appear.

- *Individual Stability*: ESB cannot substitute one personality for another because electricity cannot replicate or influence all the innumerable factors that integrate individual identity. Contrary to the stories of science fiction writers, we cannot modify political ideology, past history, or national loyalties by electrical tickling of some secret areas of the brain. (ibid., 193)

Once again, there is a puzzling dissonance between the disparaging tone of "tickling the brain" and Delgado's opening aspiration to modify the highest levels of the human will. These might reasonably be imagined to influence political ideology and national loyalty.

- *Technical Complexity*: Electrical stimulation of the central nervous system requires careful planning, complex methodology, and the skillful collaboration of specialists with knowledge and experience in anatomy, neurophysiology and psychology . . . These elaborate requirements limit the clinical application of cerebral electrodes . . . At the same time, the procedure's complexity acts as a safeguard against possible improper use of ESB by untrained or unethical persons. (ibid., 194)

This is an accurate and honest statement, but it omits to say that in addition to the technical constraints that stand in the way of wider clinical use of ESB is the paucity of compelling evidence of specific or replicable benefits in humans (discussed below).

- *Functions beyond the Control of ESB*: A pattern of behavior which is not in the brain cannot be organized or invented under

—

electrical control . . . Because of its lack of symbolic meaning, electricity could not induce effects comparable to post-hypnotic performances. (ibid., 195)

These statements are reassuring.

- *Medical Applications*: Delgado begins with a general overview of the role of implanted electrodes in medicine which he describes as a "magic window . . . a new method found to impose therapeutic order upon disorderly activity." He notes that "in spite of the tremendous potential . . . The growing acceptance of even experimental surgical interventions in most organs including the human heart is in sharp contrast with the generally cold reception to the implantation of wires in the human brain." He attributes this to, "the persistence of old taboos in scientists as well as in laymen, and to the more logical fear of opening some Pandora's Box." Following this hyperbolic rhetoric, he moves on to discuss specific medical applications.

- *Diagnosis*: Delgado rightly points out that EEG recordings from the surface of the skull have been relatively unhelpful in localizing abnormalities in psychomotor epilepsy due to lesions of the temporal lobe compared to depth electrodes. He concedes that both EEG and depth electrodes have "failed to provide decisive information" in mental disturbances and states, "The absence of significant data must be attributed to the lack of refinement of present methodology." Next, he suggests that the administration of drugs via implanted electrodes may be useful to "test the specific pharmacological sensitivity of a patient thus orienting his medical or postsurgical therapy." He provides no examples or citations in support of this. Finally, he correctly notes the utility of electrical stimuli in the accurate localization of areas for ablation in Parkinson's disease. One can conclude that while implanted electrodes may be useful in dealing with structural lesions of the brain, they have not been shown useful or effective in mental disorders. After twenty years of experimentation, it is perhaps overly optimistic to blame this on defective methodology as opposed to a faulty hypothesis.

- *Therapy.* In addition to the acknowledged use of electrocoagulation of localized areas of the brain in neurological disorders (involuntary movements, intractable pain, and focal epilepsy), Delgado lists a variety of mental conditions for which it has been tried, including anxiety, fear, obsessive-compulsive disorder, and aggressive behavior. Again, he cites no results or research but comments, "Others are more skeptical about the usefulness of depth electrodes and electrocoagulation in treating mental illness." Delgado concludes this section by stating, "Many other possible applications could be explored." He lists what these might be and the appropriate brain location to be stimulated by EBS including a two-way radio communication system. These are anorexia nervosa (feeding centers of the lateral hypothalamus), insomnia (median or caudate nucleus), and "the increase of patient's communication for therapeutic purposes by excitation of the temporal lobe." Earlier, he provides three citations to support the production of "pleasurable sensations by repeated excitation of the septum and other areas" in patients with schizophrenia but makes no comment on the significance of this in the treatment of the disorder. Jose concludes by saying, "The delivery of brain stimulation on demand to correct cerebral dysfunctions represents a new approach to therapeutic feedback. While it is speculative, it is within the realm of possibility according to present knowledge and projected methodology."

Clearly Jose is extrapolating far beyond the bounds of his or any other research, possibly in response to the series editor's desire to "reveal basic new trends in civilization, to interpret the creative forces at work today . . . and to point to the new consciousness which can contribute to a deeper understanding of the interrelation of man and the universe, the individual and society and to the values shared by all people" (back cover). This is a grandiose and burdensome mandate for any scientist to fulfill without risking the mantle of mad scientist!

- *Circumvention of Damaged Sensory Inputs.* Delgado begins by saying, "The miracle of giving light to the blind and sound to the deaf has been made possible by implantation of electrodes, demonstrating the technical possibility of circumventing damaged sensory receptors by direct electrical stimulation." After citing individual case studies in a blind and a deaf individual where the technique was used diagnostically, Delgado concludes by stating, "It is doubtful that refined perceptions comparable to physiological ones can be provided by electronic means, but the perception of sensations—even if crude—when hope had been lost, is certainly encouraging and demands the continuation of research efforts." The contrast between the concluding and opening statements is a striking example of the struggle between a scientist striving to remain objective and an author responding to the humanitarian and philosophical demands of his editor.

• *Brain Viability*: The question of when to terminate life support in an apparently brain dead individual and the limitations of the EEG as a determining factor lead Delgado to speculate on the possible use of electrode implants to "determine the parts of the brain considered essential for the survival of human personality." This novel suggestion has not stood the test of time. The ethical squabbles continue.

• *Ethical Implications*: Delgado begins with a telling admission; "Therapeutic use of electrodes in cases of mental illness must still be considered an experimental phase" (ibid., 209). He moves on to define the characteristics of informed consent for the procedure; "The experimental subject understands all the essential aspects of the study, the types and degrees of risks, the detrimental or beneficial consequences, if any, and the purpose of the research" (ibid., 210). This is in line with the NIH Policies for Protection of Human Subjects issued in 1966. He goes on to a more specific caveat; "Children and adults with mental disturbances cannot give proper consent, and relatives must be consulted. Their decisions, however, are easily influenced by the picture presented by the attending physician, thus increasing his responsibility which preferably should be shared by a group of three or more professional consultants" (ibid., 211). This last suggestion may reflect the NIH proposal to initiate Institutional Review Boards (IRBs) as a mechanism for wider input into ethical decision making. This was not fully implemented until after the National Research Act (1974) promulgated a National Commission for the Protection of Human Subjects (1974-1978) following which DHSS and the FDA provided detailed guidelines (1981). Despite all this, there has been continuing concern about their implementation because, by definition, the IRB's may at times fall prey to their institution's conflicts of interest in order to obtain research funding. After expressing these constructive and ethical constraints on the therapeutic use of implanted electrodes, Delgado goes on to propose a loophole that meets his philosophical agenda. "There is one aspect of human research which is usually overlooked: the existence of a moral and social duty to advance scientific knowledge and to improve the welfare of mankind" (ibid., 211). He continues, "Subjects with implanted electrodes provide a good example, because . . . this type of research may provide data of exceptional value available only from man without any risks or even demands on the patient's time and attention" (ibid., 211-212). Note that Jose had inadvertently replaced "subject" with "patient."

- *Electrical Stimulation of the Psyche*: Here Delgado begins an attempt to justify his not-yet-fully-revealed philosophical objective. He first lists the anticipated objections to mind control via ESB: "The prospect of any degree of physical control of the mind provokes a variety of objections: theological objections because it affects free will, moral objections because it affects individual responsibility, ethical objections because it may block self-defense mechanisms, philosophical objections because it threatens personal identity" (ibid., 214). The next sentence begins, "These objections, however, are debatable. A prohibition of scientific advance is obviously naïve and unrealistic." He considers that "the role of electrical stimulation of the brain" is to "add a new factor to the constellation of behavioral determinants" (ibid., 215).

- *"Toward a Psychocivilized Society"*: This, Part V of his book, is where Delgado finally unveils his philosophical intent. The purpose is development of "a future psychocivilized human being; a less cruel, happier and better man" (ibid., 232). This is a startlingly grandiose idea; to accomplish what two millennia of admittedly flawed religion has failed to accomplish. And this alteration in normal human behavior is to occur using the same technique that has failed to remediate the brain's malfunctions and about which the scientist in Delgado has expressed many realistic reservations and constraints. The justification for this intrusion into normal human behavior is that "the concept of individuals as self-sufficient and independent entities is based on false premises" (ibid., 232). Later on, Jose expands on the concept of external control of normal human behavior. "To discuss whether human behavior can or should be controlled is naïve and misleading. We should discuss what kind of controls are ethical, considering the efficiency and mechanisms of existing procedures and the desirable degree of these and other controls in the future" (ibid., 249). He lists the available techniques for accomplishing control into two groups; modifications in neurophysiological activity (chemical and physical agents, including EBS) and positive or negative social reinforcements (including hypnosis, sensory deprivation, conditioning, and brainwashing) (ibid., 249). To be fair to Delgado, he does attempt to present a benevolent view of what he is proposing:

> The phrase "control of human behavior" is emotionally loaded, in part because of its threat to the "inviolability of the ego" and in part because of unpleasant associations with dictatorships, brainwashing and selfish exploitation of man. Well known novels like Huxley's *Brave New World*, Orwell's *1984* and Condon's *The Manchurian Candidate* are exposés of utopian societies with obedient, soma drugged, satisfied individuals whose activities are planned by the master minds of the ruling council." (ibid., 247)

Jose's response is to stress that his "orientation should not be identified with authoritarian control. To the contrary, awareness of our own needs and attitudes is our most effective instrument for maintaining our own integrity and control of our own reactions . . . Awareness is a major element in defense against external manipulation" (ibid., 254-255). Mankind's motto should no longer be "Know Thyself" but "Construct Thyself" (ibid., 244).

The irony of all this is that the subtlety and ambiguity of Delgado's presentation of his often-conflicting scientific and philosophical goals would be to place his book in the same category as the novels from which he sought to distinguish himself. But unlike the authors of fiction, he would be held to account personally and vilified as a consequence.

Here it is important to underline the fact that Delgado's view of "mind control" was as a benevolent and elective mechanism to improve human behavior. It is justifiable to suggest that this grew out of his early adult experiences with the evils of fascism which deprived him of his mentor, terminated his medical and neurophysiology training, and, as a medical corpsman for the side opposing fascism, probably exposed him to its evils, ending with his incarceration in a concentration camp.

Hubris

It is the certainty that they possess the truth that makes men cruel.

—Anatole France

Hubris is an occupational hazard for the scientist, an overflow from the natural seedbed of belief and enthusiasm essential to support the energy and enjoyment needed in the pursuit of discovery and the "eureka" moment. What triggers the growth of hubris from a natural sentiment to excessive pride and how that manifests itself is less obvious. Clearly, at some point, there is a loss of objectivity essential to good science with a resort to hyperbole about personal accomplishments, both resulting in exaggeration of results beyond the limits of the data.

Factors that enable the evolution of hubris include the fame and fortune essential to a successful scientific career; fame to support academic stature and promotion, fortune to fund research and sometimes for personal gain. Also included are public adulation and iconic-named awards, not least the Nobel. Certainly the scientific and public Zeitgeist can contribute an environment of expectation to help seduce a susceptible or unwary scientist.

In her preface to the series *World Perspectives* and Jose Delgado's volume, *Physical Control of the Mind*, Ruth Anshen states, "Our authors are aware that the sin of hubris may be avoided by showing that the creative process itself is not a free activity if by free we mean arbitrary or unrelated to cosmic law." There is an ironic lack of awareness in this rather obscure statement—of failure to see that placing her authors in the company of intellectual and international giants and offering them a world stage might unleash the hubris she views as avoidable, inviting the cosmic law the Greeks named "nemesis." Whether Jose's philosophical beliefs were predetermined or influenced by being in such company remains unclear.

Jose Delgado grew up in the footsteps of his Spanish idol and role model, the Nobel Laureate Santiago Cahal, and may well have viewed himself as the natural successor to his Portuguese predecessor and Nobel Laureate Egas Moniz, himself influenced by John Fulton, who then became Jose's mentor and role model. This was a distinguished lineage. Jose's own discoveries and scientific contributions followed on the heels of the birth of modern neuroscience and peaked in the years preceding the Decade of the Brain. Scientific expectations and public adulation were high, both fed by the drama and publicity surrounding the bull experiment. While this might fairly be viewed as self-aggrandizement, placing oneself at personal risk to prove a point was almost a right of scientific passage ever since William Harvey inoculated himself with syphilis (and wrestled with a bear that Queen Elizabeth the First gave him).

Delgado was almost alone in his field and had preempted his major rival, Bob Heath at Tulane, in electrical brain stimulation. This was in 1952, when the future of neuroscience was still an uncertain footrace between physiology and neurochemistry, between electrodes and drugs. During his twenty years in America, Delgado moved rapidly up the academic ladder to the rank of full professor in both physiology and psychiatry, succeeding Fulton as head of research in physiology. During this time period (1950-1970) he accumulated two hundred scientific publications, and became a fellow of the New York Academy of Sciences and a Guggenheim fellow. He was the Salmon lecturer at the New York Academy of Sciences in 1968 and discussed the topics addressed in his book.

This was all heady stuff, enough to sustain and inflate anyone's ego. But itemizing the risk factors for hubris does not amount to an indictment. Probably the best indicator would be Delgado's book. Its title alone is evocative, but the contents do not quite live up to what it claims. Speaking as a scientist, Jose is relatively modest and stays quite close to his data; it is only as philosopher that he waxes grandiose. But philosophy, in its original meaning, has mostly to do with theories, not facts; "the study of the fundamental nature of knowledge, reality, and existence" (OED). In this regard, the author did what was asked and expected of him. This does not rise to hubris but what may do so is that Delgado clearly linked this philosophizing to the results of his own research in an extravagant manner.

This raises the question of whether what happened next can be construed as a just, divinely ordained comeuppance or something that had a more complex etiology.

Nemesis

Vaulting ambition that o'er leaps itself

—Shakespeare in *Macbeth* (Act 1, scene 7)

To whatever it was due, something looking like nemesis was not long delayed; in the early 1970s, the scientific, political and social Zeitgeists all began to turn against the subject of brain electrodes. In the world of neuroscience, it was impossible to not notice that chemistry was outstripping physics. Neuropsychopharmacology had reached its apogee: the success of new drugs for every category of mental disorder, the drama of deinstitutionalization, the explosive growth of Big Pharma with the largesse it showered on academics, clinicians, advocacy groups, and scientific organizations, including the ACNP and, most importantly the Nobel Laureate award to Jules Axelrod and colleagues in 1970 for work on the catecholamine hypothesis of depression.

All of these events stole the spotlight away from Delgado. Although he had been a founding member of the ACNP from 1961, he became something of an anomaly, a neuroscientist whose major interest was in physiology and electricity, not neurochemistry or drugs. In the timing and trajectory of his career, he suffered the same fate as those most interested in ECT.

To make matters worse, Delgado had collaborated with two Harvard researchers, Vernon Mark and Frank Ervin, who published their book on *Violence and the Brain* in June 1970 in which they suggested brain surgery or ESB might be used to quell violence among inner-city blacks. Matters were made worse, attracting public attention, because one of Ervin's students, Michael Crichton, had published his best seller, *The Terminal Man,* about a bionic experiment gone wrong based on research by Ervin, Mark, and Delgado (Delgado et al., *J. Nerv. Ment. Dis.* 147, 329-240, 1968).

Guilt also came by association—in 1972, Bob Heath at Tulane University published a controversial article describing an EBS experiment in which he attempted to change the sexual orientation of a gay man by stimulating the caudate nucleus while the man was having sexual intercourse with a female prostitute.

The most effective and persistent opposition to EBS and all forms of psychosurgery, often lumped together, came from within psychiatry by Peter Breggin. A one-time Scientologist (from 1972 to 1974) and an avowed humanist and libertarian, he is identified by some as "The Conscience of Psychiatry" and the "Ralph Nader" of our discipline. He has conducted lifelong and effective crusades against psychiatric medication, brain surgery, and ECT, publishing books such as *Toxic Psychiatry, Talking Back to Prozac,* and *Talking Back to Ritalin.* He is an advocate for psychosocial treatments above medical or biological interventions and the iatrogenic harm he believes these cause.

Breggin has an immaculate academic background in psychiatry; a graduate of Harvard (with honors), he trained at Massachusetts Mental Health Center and the State University of New York before a two-year appointment at NIMH and has held academic appointments at Johns Hopkins University, and George Mason University. Like many zealots for causes, he is also a polarizing figure with both the public and profession; his vehement opinions are cited frequently in the media and are eloquently expressed in a plethora of articles and books. In 1971, he founded the International Study of Psychiatry and Psychology, a nonprofit organization devoted to furthering his causes. This has included lobbying Congress in opposition to federal funding of the treatments he opposes, including psychosurgery in 1972.

Breggin has been an expert witness in trials that involve harm to patients but not a dispassionate one. In 2005, the Philadelphia County Court of Common Pleas disallowed his testimony on the grounds it failed to meet legal standards for scientific rigor and that it critiqued a treatment, not because it was counter to acceptable standards of care, but instead conflicted with Breggin's personal ideology about what treatment standards ought to be.

In an editorial in the *Duquesne Law Review* (Vol. 13, p. 841-862) that critiques psychosurgery, Breggin describes Delgado's book as "the most totalitarian document in the psychosocial literature." He goes on to say:

> He [Delgado] attacks the concepts of free will and personal freedom . . . he declared man wholly unfree and called for experimentation to facilitate his control through physical means. He literally wanted our children educated in their early school years to turn them on to psychiatric neurosurgical technology as a panacea for human anguish and conflict.

Here, verbatim, is exactly what Delgado wrote about education:

> What I am proposing is a modification of the curriculum to introduce the discipline of "psychogenesis." Its purpose would be to teach factual scientific material about cerebral mechanisms, to increase the student's awareness of his own mental and behavioral activity and to show him how to use his intelligence to decide which behavioral determinants to accept and which to reject. The present orientation of courses in psychology and sociology should be adapted and expanded to this plan. (ibid., 261-262)

In essence, what Delgado is suggesting is that neuroscience should be added to psychosocial factors in the curriculum in order to broaden a child's awareness and choices in later life. For Breggin to turn this reasonable and nuanced suggestion into the "infliction of neuropsychological techniques as a panacea for human anguish and conflict" is selective quotation driven by personal opinion and paranoid thinking, wrapped in political rhetoric.

Breggin also uses selective quotes from Delgado's philosophical discussion of the relative role of personal and social factors in shaping behavior to accuse him of joining others doing research on EBS, who "impose their ideas upon individual human beings . . . by words and deeds alike these psychosurgeons have assaulted political liberty and personal freedom."

In sequence with the shifting scientific Zeitgeist was a similar swing in political and public sentiment. This had roots going back to World War II when the public enemy number one was communism, which reached its peak in the early to mid-1950s, instigated by the rhetoric and witch hunting of Senator Joe McCarthy and fueled by defeat in the Korean and Vietnam Wars. Sometime in the early 1950s, the CIA initiated a large-scale operation to explore chemical and electrical methods of altering and controlling behavior that might be useful in covert operations. This continued into the late 1960s when Richard Helms served from 1966 to 1973 as director of the CIA under Presidents Johnson and Nixon. Codenamed MK-ULTRA, this effort channeled millions of dollars into the research coffers of one hundred forty-nine projects distributed among forty-four colleges or universities, fifteen research institutions, several pharmaceutical companies, twelve hospitals, and three prisons.

Some public concern and awareness of these events must have begun circulating in the early 1970s because in 1973 Richard Helms ordered all CIA documents pertaining to the experiments be destroyed. The following year, *The New York Times* published an exposé instigating public outrage and Congressional hearings. Naturally enough the destruction of the relevant CIA documents fed public paranoia and fueled attempts to identify the scientists who might have been involved. In 1977, some saved documents surfaced, and others were declassified under the

Freedom of Information Act in 2001. In much of this material, names and places had been redacted. Successive Congressional hearings have followed these paper trails. The end result has been an Internet flooded with Web sites authored by conspiracy theorists and victimologists that have continued for forty years and are still active today.

Searching these websites for truth and accuracy is akin to looking for needles in haystacks. Instead, one finds innuendo, misinformation, guilt by association, and outright falsehoods. Jose Delgado does not fare well in these Aegean stables; his name is inevitably linked to his 1969 book and its provocative title, *Physical Control of the Mind*, since it provides a fertile source for out-of-context misrepresentations so ably demonstrated by Breggin.

An example from a Web site devoted to Quotations on Technology of Mass Mind Control (www.rense.com) lists alleged statements by Delgado in a "1974 Congressional testimony." By this time, Delgado had returned to Spain, and the statements were made in 1972 by Breggin (a Scientologist at the time) as part of his attempt to block further brain research by the Harvard group. That testimony consisted of a compilation of quotations from advocates of lobotomy and fabricated statements attributed to Delgado including, "We need a program of psychosurgery for political control of our society," "Someday armies and generals will be controlled by electric stimulating of the brain," "Man does not have the right to develop his own mind," and "Everyone who deviates from the norm can be surgically mutilated." The Web site that propagates this travesty of truth couples these quotations with another from Hermann Goering, Nazi Reich marshall.

Over a quarter century after Breggin's intemperate testimony to Congress incited such unjust public and political condemnation of Delgado, a book, *Ethics of Psychiatry* (ed. R. B. Edwards, Prometheus Books, 1997), included a chapter on *Psychosurgery* (by Jean Isaac and Virginia Armat) with a section titled "Breggin Mounts His Campaign" (ibid., 370-374). This is a detailed critique of the unscrupulous means by which Breggin acquired his information and manipulated it to his ideological intentions. The authors state, "Breggin's 'research' paper on psychosurgery which was entered into the Congressional Record in February 1972 and his testimony in congressional hearings (chaired by Senator Edward Kennedy) early in 1973 relied far more on hysteria than on science." In a more general condemnation of Breggin's ethical behavior, they later say, "Breggin was no more to be tied down by clinical realities than by scientific evidence; like his mentor Thomas Szaz, he offered rhetorical arguments and denunciation by analogy. From then on, Breggin's attacks on other forms of treatment would consist primarily of equating them with the long discarded lobotomy. All limbic system surgery was lobotomy. ECT was another type of lobotomy and treatment with neuroleptic drugs, chemical lobotomy." This adequately describes Breggin's indiscriminate ideological agenda.

Another accurate appraisal of this campaign of disinformation in the context of Delgado's career is contained in a *Scientific American* article by John Horgan. He relates the following: "Strangers started accusing Delgado of having secretly implanted stimoceivers in their brains. One woman who made this claim sued Delgado and Yale University for one million dollars, although he had never met her."

In early 2001, two reporters from the magazine *Cabinet* visited the eighty-five-year-old Delgado and his American wife at their home in Madrid (*Psychocivilization and its Discontents, Cabinet*, No. 2, Spring 2001). In the article, they cite the same Web site misquotations attributed to Delgado in 1974, but at the time the article was published, a late retraction appears in the references:

> Since publishing this article it has come to our attention that Delgado did not in fact testify to Congress on that date. The quote in question was actually a compilation of statements from Delgado's various publications *which are accurately cited* (italics added) by Dr. Peter R. Breggin in *The Return of Lobotomy and Psychosurgery*. It was this article that was presented to Congress on 24 February 1972.

The source of this retraction is not given, but note that while it corrects the attribution, it upholds the accuracy of Breggin's allegations and almost certainly came from him.

The authors' published interview with Delgado includes the following statements he made at the time. "We know too little about the brain. It is much too complicated to be controlled. We never knew which parts of the brain we were stimulating with the stimoceiver." Later on, he says, "It is impossible to decode the brain's language. We can obviously manipulate different forms of electrical activity but what does it prove?"

The questions raised on these Web sites about Delgado's possible involvement in CIA covert research is also dubious and vague, perhaps in part because of the destroyed and redacted material. Delgado did acknowledge receiving some support from the navy and air force research arms and he did publish one article on *Control of Behavior by Electronic Stimulation of the Brain* (*Naval Research Review*, May 1-7, 1959). Delgado denied any connection with the CIA, but conspiracy theorists suggest that the army and navy research arms served as a conduit for funding.

Other distinguished psychiatrists are identified with somewhat more credibility. They include Jolyon West, director of the Neuropsychiatry Institute at the University of California, Los Angeles, who is alleged to have worked on Sub-project 95 involved with experiments to induce posthypnotic suggestion and erase memories. West was an acknowledged expert on cults, torture, brainwashing, and mind control, and was also alleged to have top-secret clearance.

Another distinguished psychiatrist named was the Canadian Ewen Cameron, whose involvement in CIA research was acknowledged and widely criticized, including "depatterning" experiments in Sub-project 68. Cameron served as the president of the Canadian, American, and World Psychiatric Associations.

I mention these two individuals not to discredit them but only to draw attention to the discrepancy between how their likely involvement in CIA research escaped the level of professional criticism and ostracism leveled at Delgado, whose own involvement was never clearly established. Following Cameron's death, the Canadian Medical Association journal published an obituary that was a paean of praise for his scientific accomplishments and benign personality—someone with "an abiding interest in promoting the social wellbeing of the entire community."

The Rest of the Story

On the cusp between the sixth and seventh decades of the twentieth century, Jose Delgado must have felt like a man alone in a leaky rowboat facing the onset of the "perfect storm."

In 1969, he was placed on the world stage by an editor-philosopher who invited him to extrapolate the accomplishments from his innovative and groundbreaking research on EBS in an attempt to illuminate its relevance to the future of humanity. Seduced by this mandate, he inflated the modest research findings into a grandiose philosophical vision intended to demonstrate its relevance to the future of humanity, toward what he called a benignly framed "psychocivilized society."

Unfortunately the timing, tone, and title of his volume could not have been worse or more provocative. In the world of science and psychiatry, it aroused the skillful rhetoric of a libertarian ideologue and fellow psychiatrist who was lobbying Congress to eliminate all funding for this kind of brain research and which coincidentally stirred public outrage.

In the public and political domain, this contributed to an upsurge of anger toward covert CIA research on aspects of mind control by drugs and electricity that involved some of the country's academic and psychiatric institutions.

Caught in these cross-currents and the changing Zeitgeist, Delgado was subjected to intense and disproportionate disapproval and ostracism at a time when he was almost certainly aware that EBS had run its course, had very little else to offer, and no likelihood of being funded in the future.

He was providentially rescued from this existential predicament by an invitation to return to Spain and participate in the development of a new school of medicine in Madrid. In 1971, he accepted the position as chairman of physiological science at the Autonomous Medical School of Madrid with the promise of support and facilities equal to those at Yale. Here he found safe harbor but retained his post at Yale until 1974, at which time Jose and his wife left America and returned to reside in Madrid. Delgado had lived in America for twenty-four years, from 1950 at age thirty-five until 1974, at age fifty-nine.

Delgado continued to publish at a prolific rate in both English and Spanish in a wide variety of American and European journals. In Spain, he continued his work on electrical cerebral stimulation in animals and extended his research into the influence of magnetic fields on cerebral function. Throughout this period, he also continued to expound his philosophical ideas about brain-mind-behavior relationships. His books and articles on such topics increased in proportion to his scientific output in later years, including titles such as *The Purpose of Human Life*, *Neurobiology of Values*, *Biological Unity of Brain and Mind*, and *The Neurological Basis of Modern Humanism*.

Jose Delgado's total scientific and philosophical output included over five hundred publications, a majority written after he returned to Spain. Altogether, he authored six textbooks, the last of which was titled *Happiness (La Felicidad)* which went through fourteen Spanish editions and remained on the top ten bestseller list for over a year in 1989. His bibliography on file with ACNP concludes in 2000 when Jose was eighty-five years old. In that year, he had four publications, including his last in English titled "Neural Imprinting of Human Values" (*Int. J. Psychophysiology*, 35, 237-246, 2000).

In the last few years of his life, Jose and his wife returned to America and lived quietly in San Diego where he died at the age of ninety-six; I was unable to find any obituary that recorded the life and death of this productive scientist and remarkable human being.

Redemption?

The title is posed as a question partly because redemption may be of little value postmortem except perhaps to disciples and family members. But, more importantly, not all the facts are at hand. Jose Delgado's career deserves the full-time services of a talented, unbiased biographer with the time and resources to pursue many unanswered questions. This would be a service to the history of science. His story could be of inestimable value as an object lesson to young scientists in our field about the pitfalls and hazards of a scientific career, including the danger of mingling philosophy with research.

What I was able to discover in the eight weeks I was given to write an obituary only served to whet my appetite in the search for truth due to the inescapable feeling that an injustice had been done to this man. The Greek playwrights were stingy in their allocation of redemption, but here maybe is someone deserving of that benediction.

The Obituary

Just prior to this book going to press, I submitted the preceding 10,000-plus-word biography to the ACNP together with a 1,200-word obituary—twice the suggested word length. In agreement with my basic thesis and the need for a redemptive tone, we negotiated a small reduction to 1,000 words without altering the content, which will appear in print before the book is published.

13. Psychosomatic Medicine

Two West: An Island in the Analytic Ocean

Mental tensions, frustrations, insecurity, aimlessness are among the most damaging stressors and psychosomatic studies have shown how often they cause migraine headaches, peptic ulcers, heart attacks, hypertension, mental disease, suicide, or just hopeless unhappiness.

—Hans Selye

At first, my one day a week at the University of Cincinnati was devoted to teaching psychiatric residents about the new psychotropic drugs. This was an uphill battle; I was the token biological psychiatrist in a totally psychoanalytic department, similar to the majority of academic programs in America and quite unlike those in Europe, although Austria was Freud's homeland. Most of the trainees were in analysis with a faculty member; at best, medication was regarded as an adjunct to facilitate psychotherapy, and any undue interest in drugs was interpreted by their supervisors as a defense to escape from verbal intimacy with the patient.

Matters were made worse when, about this time, the national medical examiners decided to allow graduating medical students to enter psychiatric training without any intervening experience in medicine or surgery. Margaret Mead, the distinguished anthropologist, was a visiting

257

professor who expressed her disapproval of this. Her experience, like mine, told how closely body and mind were intertwined.

Fortunately teaching is always a two-way street; as I taught residents psychopharmacology they opened my mind to the emotional nuances of mental illness. I became more "psychologically minded" as they learned to value the benefits of medication, scientific rigor, and careful diagnosis.

When I joined the department full-time, the chairman, who had written a book on psychiatry in family practice, was wise enough to put me in charge of the psychosomatic inpatient unit, 2 West, at Cincinnati General Hospital. The assignment did not sit well with the entire faculty, some of whom warned residents that a rotation under my direction would "ruin their career." This advice provoked me to challenge one leading psychoanalyst to a public debate. Some of the best and most inquiring minds among the residents elected to join me, and three went on to become chairmen of leading academic departments.

The psychosomatic unit had a distinguished past under the direction of George Engel, an internist who was psychoanalytically trained and internationally recognized for broadening the narrow focus of medicine with a "biopsychosocial" model that emphasized the integration of its three components in understanding illness and disease. When I took over as the junior faculty member, Engel's views were superimposed on those of Hans Selye, quoted at the beginning of this piece. Selye was Hungarian at birth in 1907, graduated as a doctor of medicine and chemistry in Prague at age twenty-two, and emigrated to the United States in 1931 and Canada in 1936. An endocrinologist, Selye coined the term "stress," studying its effects on the psyche and soma in animals and humans, producing a prodigious body of knowledge in seventeen hundred publications and seven popular books before his death in 1982.

The stress model of psychosomatic disease was modified by the psychoanalysts in their customary manner—by attempting to link personality traits in selected individuals to specific medical diagnoses. For example, they speculated that peptic ulcer was due to "unmet dependency needs" and hypertension to "stifled aggression." Such stereotypes, drawn from a few, highly selected individuals were largely mythic, a fact that became painfully obvious when peptic ulcer was shown to be a bacterial infection caused by Helicobacter.

But, in 1970, the views of Selye, Engel, and the analysts were dominant and popular with both faculty and residents. When I joined 2 West, the head nurse, Kathie Eilers, was assisted by a creative and talented psychologist, Susan Wooley, whose father pioneered the first heart-lung machine. This began a collaboration that lasted five years, spawning a new and different way of thinking about psychosomatic disorders.

Our theoretical framework evolved from the work of a social scientist, David Mechanic, at the University of Wisconsin in Madison and turned the view of psychosomatic medicine on its head. Instead of looking for specific character flaws in individual diseases, it focused on the behaviors that psychosomatic patients displayed in common, independent of diagnosis. It examined and defined the wood rather than the trees.

This view was popular with the nursing staff who daily witnessed the common behaviors among groups of patients on an inpatient ward, which physicians or therapists, treating single patients for short periods in outpatient offices, missed or overlooked. This approach made an important distinction between a person's "disease" (physical symptoms and signs) and their "illness" (how the disease was experienced and responded to behaviorally).

This difference is easily recognizable; take a hundred people with the common cold and the same rate of runny nose. Some stay home to be cared for by a loved one, others go to work and give it to everybody else. At the severe end of the disease spectrum, consider the sudden onset of crushing chest pain. Some people walk up and down stairs to make sure it's real; others call the life squad immediately. A week later, in intensive care, some people are demanding to go home while others are reluctant to get out of bed.

What accounts for these individual differences? Another psychologist, Howard Leventhal, developed a "Health Beliefs Model" to explain the way in which response to the signs and symptoms of disease can differ from one person to another, depending on a host of variables, including their upbringing, life stress and experiences, mood states, social support, attitudes, and beliefs.

Based on these two models, applied to our inpatient experience, we defined "illness behavior" in psychosomatic patients as characterized by "disability disproportionate to detectable disease" and set out to identify and describe its characteristics. It is this discrepancy between detectable disease and patient behavior that drives some doctors to despair. Unable to make a diagnosis or produce a cure, they resort to rejection and labeling such people as "hypochondriacs" or "crocks." Unfortunately, "illness behavior" is often an "eye of the beholder" diagnosis. Some physicians are unempathic or constitutionally inclined to prefer patients who are stoical and uncomplaining. Some settings are conducive to a dismissive response such as prisons, the army, or doctors, often in primary care, operating under unreasonable time constraints.

It was incumbent on us to not only define illness behavior but to evolve a convincing explanation for its cause and its management. Identifying the outward manifestations of illness behavior does not identify the cause (or etiology, as it is called in medicine) any more than pain or a fever reveal an underlying source leading to correct treatment. For example, fever may be due to a virus or a bacteria, but only the second responds to antibiotics.

So we need to know why a person is behaving sick. A helpful, indeed essential, axiom is that "Nobody behaves sick if they know how to behave healthy." There are two basic reasons a person may adopt a sick instead of a healthy role, and both are usually present but in varying degrees. First, the person is trapped in an existential predicament where they are unable to meet the demands and expectations of a healthy role. They lack the necessary skills or fear failure and are trapped in a situation from which they cannot escape. Perhaps they have been promoted beyond their ability and have a harsh boss. Maybe they are overwhelmed by parenting, lack the skills, and have an abusive, demanding spouse. There are an infinite number of such situations often concealed by shame and secrecy. The way out is often blocked by low self-esteem, depression, lack of energy, social phobias, or a learning disability. So illness becomes a safe harbor or a shield. This first set of variables is called "avoidance behavior" by cognitive-behavioral psychologists or "primary gain" by psychoanalysts.

The second set of forces to be reckoned with is the factors that reward or reinforce the sick role. This is called "positive reinforcement" by psychologists and "secondary gain" by psychoanalysts. It includes monetary incentives (litigation, entitlement programs, and compensation—awarded or sought after) and, more commonly, sympathy, caretaking, help, or status as a "special" or complex patient.

Almost always, both these sets of factors coexist in a push-pull combination of primary and secondary gain. Treatment follows logically, increasing a person's capacity for healthy behavior and decreasing or removing the rewards for illness behavior. This is much more easily said than done. It requires time, sophistication, empathy, and a competent knowledge about both mind and body. The model demands many different points of attack. It must begin with a thorough physical evaluation and review of medical records, which reassures the patient their concerns are taken seriously. If there are existing or impending financial rewards, treatment is unlikely to succeed, and this needs to be frankly discussed with the patient.

Family and caretakers need to be involved and agree to encourage the patient's increasing attempts at independence while reducing or removing their own oversolicitous caretaking. Many have their own unmet needs to care for others. Physical rehabilitation is often called for and patients are encouraged to set their own goals. It is reasonable to suggest that talking about pain or disability often makes it worse. Workplace accommodations may be necessary.

Existing physical and emotional problems must be adequately but conservatively treated, especially comorbid psychiatric disorders which are seldom openly acknowledged. The commonest form of illness behavior is a chronic pain disorder in which nine out of ten patients have depression, manifested by poor motivation, lack of energy and pessimism—all barriers to rehabilitation.

—

We studied this treatment approach and its successful outcomes for over two years and published our results in a leading medical journal, but it is seldom used today. We had the luxury of extended inpatient stays and reasonable insurance coverage in the days before managed care. By definition, people with psychosomatic disorders have "preexisting conditions," high deductibles, and expensive co-pays. Those who complain of pain often end up addicted to analgesics.

Some things have changed and some stay the same. "Psychosomatic medicine" is now a term seldom used, largely replaced by "behavioral medicine." In 1975, the head nurse on 2W and I were married and we still are, thirty-six years later!

Name Changes

When I use a word it means just what I choose it to mean—neither more nor less.

—Lewis Carroll in *Through the Looking Glass*

What names we call those who treat mental illness is a moveable feast, depending on the available tools of the trade, which segment of that population we serve, and the stigma that sticks to our field like super glue. Here is a brief history:

In the nineteenth century, when the only treatment for serious mental illness was institutionalization out of town in a rural setting, psychiatrists were known as "alienists." The name was derived from the Latin *alienare:* "to deprive of reason," and later from the French *aliene,* for "insane." It was not a flattering appellation because of an association with the word alien, also derived from a French word, *alienus:* "unflattering, distasteful, or being from another country or world." The stigma attached to mental illness inclined the uninformed to assume the second meaning.

The real life of an alienist in the late nineteenth century is portrayed in Caleb Carr's classical novel of that name, published in 1994. The name was still in vogue in 1923 when Arthur Conan Doyle published a Sherlock

Holmes short story (not one of his best) called "The Adventures of the Creeping Man" in which the main character's bizarre behaviors are believed by Holmes and Watson to be "a case for an alienist."

Our field's preferred name was coined early but not fully adopted until much later. In 1808, the German physician, Johann Christian Reil, derived the composite title "psychiatrist" from three Greek words—*psyche*: "mind or soul," *iasthai*: "heal," and *iatrico*: "medical." When the first effective biological and psychological treatments appeared in the mid-1930s, our discipline became more strongly associated with medicine, and the title psychiatrist prevailed over alienist. In its archaic meaning, "alienist" remains today as the title used to describe a physician who is accepted by the law courts as an expert in adjudicating mental competence.

In the 1970s, my own area of special interest, the boundary between psychiatry and medicine, underwent a name change. Originally called "psychosomatic medicine," this was the almost exclusive domain of physicians seeking to couple psychoanalytic theories with selected medical disorders, a hegemony facilitated by the fact that only physicians could become analysts.

The disorders falling under this rubric included hypertension, peptic ulcer, asthma, ulcerative colitis, chronic severe pain, migraine, chronic fatigue, hypochondriasis, and the like. It soon became clear that psychoanalytic principles alone were inadequate to explain the cause, treatment, and outcome of these conditions. Broader cognitive-behavioral and social theories and interventions began to intrude, and their success opened the door to involvement by health psychologists, social scientists, nurse practitioners, and others.

The new title was behavioral medicine. At first, it coexisted alongside psychosomatic medicine but eventually new therapies, societies, and journals developed, which espoused a multidisciplinary approach and welcomed different disciplines as members. A strong believer in these principles, I joined the new Society of Behavioral Medicine and eventually became a board member. I even agreed to run as a straw man candidate for president, happily accepting my inevitable defeat by someone with better research credentials and name recognition.

—

In the summer of 1989, I presented a paper at the annual meeting, entitled "What is Behavioral Medicine?" The text that follows in slightly modified form provides a picture of the forces operating in this new area betwixt medicine, psychiatry, many other disciplines and fields of inquiry.

Published in *Medical Encounter*, Vol. 6, No. 2, Summer 1989:

> Over a decade has passed since Behavioral Medicine became a recognized term.
>
> Behavioral Medicine was born in the complex Zeitgeist of the 60s and early 70s. There was great disenchantment with the limitations of medical technology, particularly in the management of chronic diseases and a wide-spread egalitarianism manifested in civil rights, consumerism, and active public participation in health care. Within medicine, Engel proposed the biopsychosocial model, holistic medicine appeared, and health psychology emerged. Psychosomatic medicine began to shift its emphasis from a preoccupation with personality types and autonomic function to a broader concept incorporating endocrine and immune systems and illness behavior. Other major perturbations took place. Almost forty new medical schools mushroomed, most of them espousing the significance of behavioral science and the humanities as they sought to escape the ivory tower for the community. New areas of scientific interest were created. Analgesic abuse and the medicalization of distress spawned the chronic pain management movement. The word "compliance" was coined as prescribing became no longer the unique prerogative of physicians but a domain of concern to pharmacists, nurses, psychologists, and, of course, patients. Learning theory escaped its Clockwork Orange image to adopt sophisticated techniques that change perceptions as well as behaviors.
>
> The only point to this catalogue is to illustrate that part of understanding who we are today is to recognize our mixed parentage and uncertain origins. In our search for

credibility, we may wish to trade egalitarianism for elitism and we may even feel tempted to claim we are something we are not (a discipline, a specialty, a field?). On the other hand, not everybody is going to be willing to acknowledge us or admit our independence. What right does a group made up predominantly of non-physicians have to use the term "medicine" in its title? Isn't Behavioral Medicine health psychology by a different name?

Let us now examine the parts of Behavioral Medicine that have been described in other papers and their reliability in establishing the identity of the whole.

The Bibliography of Behavioral Medicine

Colleagues have analyzed the content of two Behavioral Medicine journals. Unfortunately, the best of Behavioral Medicine may not be found between the covers of just two journals that happen to bear its name. To begin with, eminent researchers in this area are as ambitious as any others and likely therefore to place their best work in the more prestigious journals with wider circulations. Even the two journals analyzed are changing their formats; *Annals of Behavioral Medicine* has just recently become peer reviewed and is seeking more research oriented papers, while the *Journal of Behavioral Medicine*'s contents are increasingly empirical.

Clinical Work and the Tools of the Trade

In analyzing what we actually do, it is clear that those who work under a Behavioral Medicine banner do so in a multimodal and multidisciplinary manner, often within a matrix organization. Our tools are a smorgasbord ranging from sophisticated technology, such as biofeedback, to equally sophisticated but totally cognitive strategies. Behavioral Medicine programs tend to spring up like weeds where the soil is fertile but is not fenced off inside rigid boundaries. Such programs need to have their mission and resources defined, but not by which

—

265

discipline is in charge. Probably the best example of the way in which concept overrules discipline and leadership can be disparate is in chronic pain programs. Around the United States they exist in departments and have directors who are psychiatrists, psychologists, anesthetists, neurologists, or rehabilitation medicine physicians. Almost all operate from a common conceptualization with similar programs but are sponsored by different disciplines.

A final point is that the clinical arena is dictated not only by the quality of the soil and an absence of fences but also by the availability of fertilizer. Our medical students have wryly added Axis 6—the insurance payer—to DSM-III as a major determinant of treatment choice. Unfortunately the treatments we purvey are often not covered services.

Relationship to Public Health

Others have demonstrated very well the relevance of the Behavioral Medicine model in the specific public health domain of AIDS research and prevention. They observe that Behavioral Medicine is a concept, concerned with the relationship between health and behavior. It is not a discipline or domain or even a field. Understanding this distinction is vital as the Society of Behavioral Medicine struggles with the issues of credentialing and accreditation. These belong within their disciplines. While we can and should help others define excellence in research and clinical work, to attempt credentialing within Behavioral Medicine is inappropriate and could imperil our organization. To define criteria within disciplines and across modalities would become a nightmare. As soon as there are credentials to bestow, there will be turf to defend.

The Conceptual Nature of Behavioral Medicine

Precisely because Behavioral Medicine is multidisciplinary and multimodal, it is tempting to seek or espouse models or theories. Otherwise we run the risk of appearing to become tinkerers or "jacks of all trades and masters of none." In an arena of such diversity (and uncertainty), structure can easily serve to bind anxiety. There is nothing intrinsically wrong with models, and the illness behavior model is my personal favorite. However, remember their limitations. Illness behavior, for example, can be an elusive construct. The major instrument to define it is neither particularly valid nor reliable and seems to reflect the old-fashioned concept of neuroticism as much as anything else. In a small piece of unpublished work, a colleague and I asked the treatment team on our renal dialysis unit to evaluate the illness behavior of about thirty patients, all very well known to the staff. Despite careful training in the concept, there was little correlation among team members: Illness behavior was in the eye of the beholder. My warning is that in defining Behavioral Medicine it is safest to stick with the simple concept and to regard models as helpful but disposable adjuncts to our functioning.

The conclusion after examining these four "parts" of Behavioral Medicine is that they are not all equally valid and that, as always, the sum is more than the parts.

There are still issues to be resolved. Behavioral Medicine's representation should continue to broaden and remain strongly multidisciplinary. We should eschew accreditation and credentialing for fear that it will create barriers and turf. Above all, we must remember that our allegiance is to a concept and not to the development of a new discipline.

I have two highly pragmatic litmus tests of my own that help me to ally with Behavioral Medicine. When I attend our annual conference, I am struck by the quality and diversity of the presentations and posters. I understand ninety percent of them and enjoy eighty percent. By contrast, when I attend the American College of Neuropsychopharmacology annual conference, of which I am also a Fellow, I understand thirty percent and enjoy ten percent.

—

Secondly, I remember a series of articles in a popular weekly publication which invited Second World War generals to describe the characteristics of an ideal general. An astute critic noted that each general described himself. So when you attend the annual meeting of the Society of Behavioral Medicine and someone asks you to define Behavioral Medicine, look around. You will see people who are wedded to a concept more than a discipline, who may be psychologists, physicians, nurses, or some other health care professionals, who are knowledgeable and scientific but pragmatic. There are no snake oil vendors. Most of all, you will find that you are surrounded by people who are collegial, friendly, involved, and energetic. They are not concerned about turf or control, but if someone asks them to take charge they know how to do an excellent job.

Behavioral medicine can be defined by its people and the quality programs they create. Defined as a discipline it will dwindle, credentialed to death.

As this specific new field became established, the term "behavioral medicine" began to be used in a generic sense as a synonym covering the entire field of psychiatry. It now describes academic departments, health care systems, clinics, and insurance agencies dealing with mental illness that formerly flew under the flag of psychiatry. As with so much in our modern culture, economics was a major driving force.

Psychotropic medications can now be prescribed by nurse practitioners and are used increasingly by well-trained physicians in primary care and other specialties. Big Pharma has done its best to expand these markets and the indications for drug usage. Therapy is now provided at lower cost and often equally well by social workers, psychologists, nurses, counselors, and case managers.

As this field has expanded, the role of psychiatrists has contracted and diminished. The full consequences of this are unclear for the welfare of the patients and our discipline. Many patients now have therapy in one clinic and are prescribed medications elsewhere with little or no communication between providers and undetermined consequences. Psychiatrists resent their role as "pill pushers" and don't do a particularly good job in the role. Many mourn the loss of their ability to do therapy as well as their declining incomes.

Behavioral medicine in its original and specific form is also undergoing stress from economic forces. While research still seems to flourish, clinical programs find it difficult to obtain insurance support for multidisciplinary teams that attempt to modify complex behaviors, employing time-consuming, intensive, and multiple interventions that are difficult to prove effective or sustained.

The surviving programs often focus on management of chronic pain and some have become enmeshed with pharmaceutical companies that market expensive and addictive drugs, a relationship increasingly under the scrutiny of Congressional committees and regulatory agencies.

If what Lewis Carroll said in fiction applies to real life, as it seems to, we can look forward to more name changes in the future. I hope my discipline survives, whatever banner it flies beneath.

Yes and No

In 1989, over twenty years ago, I was invited to contribute a chapter on "Chronic Pain" for a leading textbook of psychiatry. I decided that a good way to bring home how this form of "illness behavior" develops would be to present the history of an imagined (not real) fellow physician. Here is the story of Bob Townsend told again in the *Wisconsin Medical Journal*, 1987.

Published in *Wisconsin Medical Journal*, November 1987: Vol. 86:

Some people suffer more than they should; their disabilities lie beyond the realm of detectable disease. By the time a person reaches our Pain Management Program they are at the bottom of a slow imperceptible slide into illness and are trapped somewhere between failure or fear of leading a healthy life and the seductive rewards of staying sick. It can happen to almost anybody.

Bob Townsend was one week short of his 56th birthday when he had his first heart attack. A busy internist with a large affluent suburban practice, he had just returned home from the office at 8:00 o'clock in the evening when the pain developed. Bob had always been a minor hypochondriac who worried about his heart in medical school, but this time he knew for certain what it was. He asked his wife, Jenny, to drive him to the nearby hospital, was admitted to the intensive care unit, and hooked up to a monitor less than an hour after the pain began. For the next two weeks his course and recovery remained predictably benign; he was a model patient and nobody expected problems. A month later Bob was still at home and had not yet begun to talk of returning to work. Jenny had got used to having him around; she even enjoyed the chance to cosset him. There hadn't been much of that in the busy times while Bob was building his practice; he was always responding to the needs of his patients while she was caring for the kids. As a nurse she had lots of nurturance to bestow and in the past she had sometimes resented the way that patients always came first. Besides, Bob had never been comfortable with closeness; he pulled away from her and usually found some excuse to escape to his study or the office. Now that the kids were gone and she had Bob to herself, Jenny was in no hurry to see it end; after all he had earned the respite and insurance was no problem. Bob's accountant had insisted that he take out excellent disability coverage if only because there was no one to see the patients when he was sick.

—

Bob was surprised himself when he realized how much he liked to have Jenny pamper him a little. There hadn't been a lot of that in his own life; his father had been a busy remote businessman who had died after a heart attack when Bob was ten years old and his mother had devoted herself to cooking, cleaning, clothing the kids, and getting them to school on time. There had been a lot of duty and obligation but not much hugging or kissing. One reason Bob had gone into medicine was to care for others in ways that he missed for himself. Perhaps it really was his turn now; anyway he certainly wasn't ready to confront a return to the treadmill he had just stepped off. As Bob's reputation had grown so had his practice and the demands that it placed on him.

Six weeks after his heart attack Bob had a second episode of chest pain. It was crushing, and Bob thought he was having another heart attack; this time Jenny was away and he was alone. He felt terrified but managed to find some Demerol in a desk drawer. Half an hour after taking it the pain was almost gone, and when Jenny returned, he refused to let her take him back to the hospital. Twice in the next three days the pain came again, and he dealt with it the same way before reluctantly returning to his cardiologist. The expert was puzzled; there was no objective evidence of reinfarction and yet the pain was not typical of angina. There were a lot of tests, all equivocal or normal. Both Bob and Jenny noticed the change that crept over him; he became morose or irritable and slept poorly. They had attempted gentle sex a few times but now Bob was either not interested or incapable. He pushed Jenny away when she came close. At the same time she noticed that he expected her to care for him more; he even let her help him get dressed.

To start with, Bob had continued to read the medical journals; now they went unopened. If he thought about work it was to complain that he would never be able to live up to the expectations of his former patients. The void that existed remained empty; Bob had been too busy for hobbies or close friendships. A few colleagues stopped by but quickly went away; Bob was preoccupied with his puzzling pain and they had little else to talk about. Jenny was also worried that Bob dwelt endlessly on his pain. He seemed to pick up and amplify any new sensations, ruminating about their significance and seeking Jenny's reassurance. Bob also depended more and more upon Demerol; he insisted that nitroglycerin didn't work and that ordinary analgesics were not enough.

Six months after his heart attack Jenny discussed her concerns with Bob's cardiologist. At his insistence they visited a famous clinic in a nearby city. The workup was thorough but the results inconclusive; the official diagnosis was "atypical chest pain," and the only new recommendation was that he might consider discussing the relationship between stress and pain with a psychiatrist. Bob was furious; how dare they suggest it was all in his head and anyway there wasn't any stress—only boredom and anger. Jenny was inclined to agree with him; they returned home disgruntled. Bob's heart hurt all the harder and Jenny was now doubly determined to protect and care for her husband.

Another year of hospitals, tests, and Demerol passed before Bob sought the Pain Clinic's help to unravel his predicament. Our labels and explanations seemed to make sense of his suffering. Chronic pain syndrome, gate control mechanisms, serotonergic pathways, and multiple systems theory appealed to his intellect without attacking his integrity.

We began a gradual process of physical rehabilitation that restored Bob's stamina and self-confidence; simultaneously he relinquished his dependency on Demerol with the help of a tapered pain cocktail and low doses of an antidepressant. In the program Bob mastered distraction procedures and relaxation techniques while Jenny learned to reward his successes and ignore his failures. Some months later when Bob was ready to return to work and had learned to trust us, he began to talk about separating his personal needs from his practice. Painfully, Bob acquired his most valuable new skill; how to say yes to his wife and no to his patients.

It Only Hurts When I Cry

This short story was published in the *Wisconsin Medical Journal* in January 1987, Vol. 86. It is a real patient with the name and some details changed.

Lucinda did not look like a clown. She was short, skinny, and sad. At her outpatient evaluation the staff was preoccupied with Lucinda's many pains, wheezy chest, and ailing heart. Her hobbies hardly seemed significant.

After she was admitted to the pain unit, Lucinda's cardiac condition was stable, her pain was chronic, and she remained sad. Lucinda grudgingly agreed there was nothing fatal or malignant that caused her suffering, yet she was unable to give up her aches or their audience until she glimpsed solace elsewhere.

Lucinda's slow progress ended abruptly soon after she told us that four generations of her family were clowns, including men and women, from grandparents to grandchildren. Each clown created his/her own unique face; either White (the provocative French mime), Auguste (the boisterous German bully), or Tramp (a downtrodden American bum). Lucinda was too old to be Mime and too slender to be Tramp. She chose Auguste, a jovial extrovert who jostled the other clowns.

One day Lucinda brought her clown regalia to the hospital and painted on her face to entertain the other pain patients. It was a metamorphosis as dramatic as caterpillar to butterfly. Lucinda's crescent lips curved upwards into a smile that spread as far as the crow's feet around her eyes. As she went into a routine Lucinda shed her limp, her shoulders lifted, and her voice lost its weary timbre.

—

Once clowns are attired they adopt an etiquette. Profanity, smoking, and drinking are forbidden. If children rush up to tweak their bulbous nose or tread on their oversized feet, clowns are enjoined to banter back. Irritability and anger are outlawed. Lucinda played the role to such perfection that her aches were no longer obvious. Nobody knew for sure if they still existed. Talking about pain makes it worse, so in social situations staff and patients are instructed not to inquire. But at morning rounds, when we wear our white coats, we are allowed to ask. Lucinda told us that the pain was hardly present when she clowned. She sounded surprised, although it was something she had noticed years before but had ignored. Instead, the worse the pain the less she had performed, so that even the clowns in her "ally" left her alone.

Once Lucinda learned she could control the pain everything else came quickly. She mastered biofeedback, reached her exercise quotas, and slept soundly. When we asked her later what helped the most, she talked about learning to be assertive with her family and no longer letting the kids take advantage. She learned to set limits on their demands and to get her own needs met without needing to suffer or be sick.

Our time on the pain unit ran out together. My monthly stint as attending physician was over the day Lucinda was discharged. At morning rounds the patients sit in the day room waiting for us to see each of them in turn. As I looked up I saw Lucinda in the wings, ready to walk on stage. She smiled and sat down. The rehearsal was over and the performance was about to begin. I asked her how she would make it in the real world without greasepaint. Lucinda laughed and said she thought she could; "now that I can be a clown without letting the kids walk all over me."

Light Touch

This short prose poem was published in the "Ad Libitum" section of the *Annals of Internal Medicine*, Vol. 105; No. 5, 1986. It illustrates the subtlety of the pain experience.

Tickle is a curiously dilute form of pain; it travels the same path through the body to the brain. Both sensations are enhanced by the presence of another person. Biologically it makes perfect sense. Suffering and pleasure were meant to be shared, nourished by comfort or communication. Talking amplifies pain, inviting solace. Tickling is for two. When nobody is there, the sensations diminish or disappear.

In my practice I often see chronic pain. Intractable but benign, it ruins life rather than ending it. I witness its contortions and attend to its sighs. Seduced by its symptoms, I become the significant other. Only when we can discover some new pleasure in a patient's life am I emancipated from charts as thick and heavy as tombstones. Often we cannot. Bad thoughts, scant sleep, and poor coping collude with the pain. To break the circle I am sometimes tempted to prescribe. Drugs named antidepressants block rumination, induce sleep, and restore coping. When that happens I wield my pen lightly. It feels like a feather.

—

Dactylic Doctor

Published in *Off Hours, The Physician's Guide to Leisure and Finance*, Vol. 2, No. 3, 1986:

> Rickety rackety
> Doctor O'Flaherty
> Treats patients called crocks
> Willing to pay.
>
> Hypochondriacal
> And in love with their doc
> The pain they complain of
> Won't go away.

—Barry Blackwell, 1986

14. MEDICAL EDUCATION

Education is a method whereby one acquires a higher grade of prejudice.

—Lawrence J. Peter (1918-1988)

Education's purpose is to replace an empty mind with an open one.

—Malcolm Forbes (1918-1990)

A Lifetime Perspective

These two quotations from contemporary wise men convey polar opposites, yet both are correct. Medical education steers a dangerous course between Scylla and Charybdis as students are molded into a profession with all its mores and prejudices while simultaneously force-fed facts, like a goose being prepared to become foie gras.

This paradox presents a problem for medical educators; how to be a mentor and role model for the idealized physician who is nurturing and knowledgeable enough to both care for and cure patients (Marcus Welby, not Dr. House).

This *Medical Education* piece covers my career as educator from naïve neophyte to seasoned skeptic in stages that span thirty-two years within a fifty-seven-year time period from medical student in 1954 to retired physician in 2011.

–

The six bits encapsulate that experience. First is an essay written for *Pharos,* the journal of the *Alpha Omega Alpha* Medical Student Honor Society. It was published in 1977, shortly after I became the founding chair of psychiatry at Wright State University in Dayton, Ohio. It paints a broad-brush view of the problems I hoped to address by helping to design an innovative curriculum to train a new breed of humanistic, community-oriented family doctors willing to work in underserved rural areas.

Next is a short essay, "Dream Doctor," describing a dream I had the night before I gave a talk to the charter class of medical students at Wright State about "Being a Physician." It encapsulates the stress and anxiety associated with adopting the physician role and was published in the *Archives of Internal Medicine.*

"Medical Education and Modest Expectations" is an editorial summarizing the lessons learned from the Wright State experience and published in *General Hospital Psychiatry.*

Next is the unpublished text of a talk to the graduating class of psychiatric residents at Wright State in 2010, thirty years after the first class of medical students graduated and long after the start of a psychiatric residency program. By this time, the medical school had abandoned its original goals for a more traditional model.

The last two bits, a short essay and a poem, illustrate how pragmatism and metaphor can link psychiatry to medicine for educational purposes. "Primary Care Psychiatry" also teaches how our field evolves. In 1983, the patient received psychiatric advice when today he would be prescribed Viagra, a form of treatment much closer to his own expectations.

As you read these bits, you will note some repetition but it is not redundant. Some things are worth saying over in hopes they are remembered. Today, we hear the same plea to train and recruit more primary care physicians in underserved areas but there is a continuing failure to address the root causes of our inability to do so.

Old Stresses and New Directions

Published in *The Pharos* of *Alpha Omega Alpha*, January 1977, Vol. 40, No. 1:

Despite rigorous medical school admission procedures, designed to select the brightest and best qualified applicants, the demands of medical education tax the coping capacity of most students, and overwhelm a few. About forty percent of students experience significant stress, and eight percent drop out. Half of those who experience stress seek help, two-thirds of these have symptoms of anxiety or depression, and a third report interpersonal or sexual difficulties. In a class of two hundred, two or three students may have a psychotic break.

The educational process that produces these stresses is equally open to question. During the past decade, two major concerns have surfaced. The amount of information to be transmitted has increased dramatically. Medical knowledge now has a half-life of five years, and it is predicted that three quarters of the knowledge useful to a practicing physician will have to be acquired through continuing medical education. Secondly, imparting of this information within the Flexner tradition has created physicians who have come to regard themselves as technical specialists and who have been segregated from the needs of people and communities. This process has produced a social and political backlash, with a demand for more emphasis in medical education on producing physicians interested in primary care in community settings.

Given these facts, let us first examine the current system to see how it imposes stress and molds its educational end product, and, second, examine the changes proposed in the newer medical schools, to see how they are likely to impact on the problems of student stress and the educational process.

Old Stresses

Joan Priestley, a journalist who entered medical school in the fall of 1974, has written eloquently about her experiences, and I shall quote her in some detail. She begins as follows:

> There they were, 201 excited and anxious people, mostly white and mostly male, nervously fingering their introductory packets, listening to the deans saying that now they were part of a special community. The import of what I was actually doing with my life by entering medical school never really struck home until I walked in the door that first day of class. I approached medical school from an essentially fear-based perspective, fraught with overwhelming awe for the seemingly superhuman intellect and endurance necessary to become a physician. And, of course, the counterpart to that was the continuously gnawing doubt and fear that I lacked those traits and would not make it through.

Recently, members of the graduating class at Southern Illinois University completed an unpublished review of their experiences in medical school entitled "Going through the Change." They found the commonest and major sources of concern by far to be information overload, performance anxiety, and problematic relationships with the faculty. While these may be identical in any graduate program, social and personal expectations accentuate them in medicine. "Saving lives" implies the need to know it all and to apply it perfectly. Priestley writes:

> Throughout our entire daily education, we examine and describe the human body, its physical components, processes and malfunctions. Hopefully, this narrow focus will give us the background and insight necessary to exercise control over peoples' desires to take medication, to reproduce or abort children, to understand their sexuality, to cling to life, or willfully terminate their existence. No other professional school makes even a pretense of training students for such awesome and complete power over people's lives.

—

But before reaching this goal, the student must assimilate a vast knowledge, one expanding exponentially; one that cannot even be acquired until a new vocabulary of more than 13,000 words has been mastered. He also has a discomforting awareness that the art of applying this information is not found between hard covers. So students turn to the faculty for an allocation of learning priorities and for physician role models. Such expectations are easily frustrated and can manifest themselves (sometimes appropriately) in concerns about unfair grading procedures, ineffectual teachers, irrelevant lecture topics, or the arbitrary application of faculty power over student affairs.

In the area of personal stress it is useful to recall Sigmund Freud's aphorism that all human behavior is governed by the seeking of gratification and the avoidance of conflict. During training, the medical student is exposed to meager rewards and considerable conflict. At an age when most other humans are independent and wage earning, the medical student must subordinate these personal gratifications for professional growth. The demands of a crowded curriculum and the responsibilities of patient care can restrict even normal outlets. Nine out of ten students report that they date less in their first year, and a quarter lose a steady relationship soon after beginning their training. There is an abrupt decline in the number of concerts, plays and movies students attend. Joan Priestley paints the same picture:

> This school is not just a series of lectures and homework; it is a rite of passage we endure together. We have immersed ourselves in an environment which is not only new, but alien, and we are somehow persevering to survive the constant drain of nonstop studying and weariness and trauma and lack of sleep and lack of sex and loneliness and tears and spaciness and unexpressed frustration and anxiety ridden tensions.

The third to a half of students who are already married may begin to experience alienation within their existing relationships; in the process of gaining credentials to help others, they may withdraw from their own significant relationships. As one expert has noted, "Professional development is a big pain in the ass, especially if you are only a relative of the person participating in the program." About half of married

—

students report that school imposes strains on their relationship by reducing time spent with the spouse. The total impact of these stresses on the students' outlook can be profound. Priestley observed the following:

> As students, we become "adjusted," inured and, finally, oblivious to the overwhelming impact of our situation. It IS possible to retain one's humanity and capacity to enjoy life while in medical school, but it requires conscious effort and vigilance. I had spent the four months pretty much continually blitzed, while feeling that the school presented NO creative channels for facing, dealing with, and discharging the extreme stresses it placed on us. Those of us who are both innately creative and energetic, as well as blessed with an eidetic memory, slide by intact. The rest of us have to make severe trade-offs in terms of relationships, time, and energy. I found that my humanity and capacity for playfulness were ebbing away. It did not seem possible to go through medical school without surrendering one's compassion, humanity and human feelings.

This decline in extrinsic rewards and support systems coincides with an increase in conflicts of a very personal nature. The student begins to deal with the most intimate aspects of the patient's life, from performing vaginal examinations to hearing private confessions. He has a beginning awareness of the conflict imposed by the patient's desire for a friend and society's demand (codified in law) that the physician bear final responsibility for health care. These burdens are imposed within a context of uncertainty that can only be resolved by the experience and judgment that a student, by definition, does not yet possess.

Joan Priestley observes:

> I succumb now and then to the ego-inflating lure of feeling "special," and have become more arrogant and aggressive, less patient and tolerant, when dealing with "lay people." Why should I have to wait in lines or waste hours doing

housekeeping, when there are already such severe demands on my time?

The feeling of being special probably begins with the accolade of selection from among the many who apply for admission to medical school. This process is further reinforced within the curriculum by what Priestley calls "subtle programming":

> There is a lot of subtle programming which comes along with our daily instruction, and it exerts tremendous pressure to be calm, clinical, dispassionately adult—and totally detached from our bodies and feelings. Our lecturers calmly discussed babies with ghastly deformities in terms of "this interesting case," as though speaking about a block of wood.

> Our experiences as medical students are subtly conditioning us to become cerebral and unfeeling to the point of brutal insensitivity. The acronyms—SLE, EMG, PMN, PNS—which cover anything from anatomical features to devastating diseases. The obscure language certainly exerts a strong influence to retreat into clinical detachment to flatten and avoid our feelings. Such verbiage helps us to forget that we're not gods; we don't know all there is to know about body malfunctions; our many medical terms simply contribute to the overblown image we ascribe to doctors.

Some students' capacity to cope during training is further weakened by the loss of social support systems. The majority of students report that they have inadequate nonmedical contacts in the community (fewer than five nonmedical acquaintances). This deprivation is felt most by single students and by women but becomes more marked as time progresses, so that by the end of the third year two-thirds of all students consider that medical training has significantly hindered the development of relationships outside medical school. The divorce between future physician and the community begins early in the educational process and is reinforced by the nature of the experience itself. Priestley comments:

Truly there IS a very real wall which separates doctors from "lay people," and that wall is the medical school experience. No other educational program entails learning such mountains of typed handouts; no other classes have lecturers constantly parading around in white coats. That's all reserved for us.

Already in our careers, we know unconsciously that we have had experiences which will be shared by only a tiny fraction of the population. How many people around town can truthfully say, "I got up at 8:00 a.m. today—to saw a human head in two; to hold a human heart in my hand; to do a glucose tolerance test; to pick apart a dead man's genitals?" There is a definite, buried feeling that we are somehow special, set apart, and standing above the rest of the world because of these extraordinary experiences.

Then there are also stresses imposed by professional identification and the rites of passage from student to specialist. Not every student finds the role models that encourage adoption of a professional identify. Particular problems may be encountered by minority students, who experience difficulty in adopting the value systems and attitudes of a profession that remains predominantly male, white, affluent, and conservative. The significance of finding appropriate role models in medical school is often stressed but seldom explained. Priestley's observations are relevant:

More importantly, I had made peace, somehow, with the discomforting fact that we can NEVER learn all there is to know, or even all that we're taught in class. It cannot be done, no matter how superhuman we pretend to be, or how much self-flagellation we impose. But we CAN learn enough to become competent doctors and certainly enough to pass our exams here.

The role model may be a straw at which the drowning student clutches. "Who I will be like" becomes more important than "what I need to know."

Finally, one must ask what all this stress and information overload does for the educational process itself. What it did to Joan Priestley is described as follows:

> It used to freak me out to see people sleep in class. That represented the epitome of the martyr syndrome—to be dead tired, yet still drag one's aching body to class, only to fall asleep there. Now I feel that snoozing is a great way to mark time through a dull lecture.

> Last year I was traumatized whenever I missed a class, since I always took copious notes. Now, however, the story is quite different. It's actually hard to convince myself to go to ANY lectures, since the teachers are only reading their eight-page handouts to us, and the Phi Chi scribes take far better notes than I do.

Taken all together, these reflections reveal how the process of medical education acts powerfully to shape attitudes in the developing physician. Chosen to be different, discouraged from doubt, segregated by special rituals, encouraged to control, and overwhelmed by detail that discourages contemplation, the student is shaped into an end product that is as discordant with vanishing personal ideals as it is with emerging social expectations. In the past decade, political and social discontent with this end product has been expressed as a felt need for physicians with a more humanistic concern in comprehensive and continuing care coupled with a willingness to deliver it in the context of people's personal environment rather than in segregated centers of academic excellence.

New Directions

These social and political forces have encouraged the development of a number of new medical schools whose stated goal is to train primary-care physicians to work in rural communities. The newer developments in these schools have fallen into three categories: attempts to select a different type of student, design of new curricula, and the increase of community influences on the education process.

—

285

A student who applied recently to one of these new schools told the interviewer that the cab driver who drove from the airport had accurately depicted the kind of student the school was recruiting and had suggested appropriate answers to interview questions. Like every other medical school, this one believed that one answer to providing a new type of physician is to select a different kind of student. In the past, abundant attempts to correlate admission criteria with subsequent performance have failed but the belief persists that given enough skill or the correct tests, it can still be done. Nobody has seriously considered the alternative hypothesis that the type of individual chosen is relatively unimportant because the molding and role modeling of medical education is strong enough to shape or destroy almost anybody. About the only consistent finding in the literature is that medical students tend to be more "obsessive-compulsive," a character trait correlated with "adjustment" to the educational process. Since compulsives are good at making lists, delaying gratification, and planning ahead, this would be predicted; but compulsives also tend to like collecting things (sometimes called research), retaining control, and avoiding close emotional involvements—behaviors that are particularly antithetical to the humanistic physician. It may be that selection procedures that favor compulsives (and most do, since we value what we are like ourselves) are sounder bases for educational survival rather than for eventual practice.

Attempts at curriculum change have addressed both process and content. Social pressure for more physicians has created changes that conflict with good educational process. Around the country, medical schools have made Faustian deals with the federal government, in which bricks and mortar were traded for more medical student bodies. As a result, class size has risen to the point where it has become almost impossible to implement what has been learned about ways to improve teaching and learning. The medical school should be an *adult* educational experience. This means involvement, feedback, interpersonal recall, and small group process. Not only are these the best ways to impart knowledge, but possibly the only way in which to influence attitudes. To accomplish this with classes of over two hundred requires more faculty, not more buildings. Some of the immediate additional teaching effort could come by diverting manpower away from residency training and back into medical student education. New schools have an opportunity to develop medical student programs first, only adding residency training if and when it is consistent with and supportive to the major mission of the school. In the past, part of the current manpower crisis was contributed to by pouring postwar federal support into large residency programs. In medical education, the tail began to wag the dog. Another interference with the process of medical education was an attempt to reduce curriculum from four to three years. The schools that have attempted to cram a quart into a pint pot have found the pace too frenetic and are reverting to the older pattern. Another attempt to reduce information overload and facilitate self-education is to cut the core curriculum. At the newest medical school (Wright State University), contact with faculty can occur for only twenty hours each week in the first two years. Each quarter lasts only eight weeks, allowing two weeks for either remediation or selective experience. The third-year clerkship is followed by a fourth year that is entirely elective. These attempts to create a more relaxed tempo, and to encourage self-learning, also carry risks. They demand effort in planning self-instructional methods; they divorce students from faculty, perhaps to the detriment of role modeling. As the process develops, paradoxes become apparent; departmental chairmen, who are required to cut their courses in half, tend to discard the more subtle, functional, or integrative aspects of medicine in favor of the basic. This means that most faculty-student contact is expended on the simplest materials, leaving students to educate themselves in the complexities.

The demand for humanitarian primary-care physicians has led also to changes in curriculum content. Founded on the Jesuitical concept of early conversion, more and more behavioral science has been crammed into the first two years. There is little consensus about what should be taught, how much, or by whom; early on, psychiatry abandoned the field to psychology, and now both disciplines are being usurped by departments of medical sociology. Each has repeated the error of its predecessors in attempting to establish its prestige with a heavy emphasis on scientific content but little demonstration of utility. Attitudes are not learned in segregated sections of the curriculum, but only after constant repetition in relevant situations. Another

—

287

contemporary curriculum catchword is integration; disciplines have given way to systems, and faculty have been "bused" from basic science faculties to neural science programs. Integration is not necessarily collaboration. Another possible way to minimize this difficulty is to retain a traditional disciplinary approach with the addition of vertical special interest committees designed to insure proper representation of areas that require integration, such as geriatrics, genetics, cancer, and sexuality. This approach can be further facilitated if time in the first two years is devoted to correlation sessions in which patients are chosen who allow the integration of basic and clinical issues with social and psychological dimensions.

It would be quite fair to wonder whether all these curriculum changes are as misdirected as our attempts at student selection. Tampering with the curriculum could be like looking through the wrong end of a telescope. Nothing that appears in the curriculum is as powerful as what happens in the clinic. When students are seduced by hard-nosed clinical role models, they quickly lose the humanitarian instincts that survive the ordeal of medical education. If this is true, then it may help to locate medical schools in the community rather than sequester them in ivory tower university hospitals, but the only total solution is one that addresses its attention to influencing the role models themselves. This effect could be had by abandoning conventional clinical rotations in order to meld clerkships into an extended six-month correlative experience during the third year. Psychiatrists, family practitioners, other physicians could work together on common problems in medical practice to serve as role models for a humanitarian approach to the total patient. The possibility that role models are the major influence in medical education is not popular or even acceptable; it smacks of the apprenticeship that Flexner derided when he recommended the scientific model for medical education, a shift that has brought us to our current discontent. But Hippocrates knew the virtue of role models, and his oath exhorts physicians to a lifetime of teaching through example.

Much cynicism is openly expressed concerning the problems of medical education and the predicted failure of current attempts to modify the process. Both faculty and students become acutely aware that they have enrolled in an educational experiment that must be

—

conducted not just to satisfy their personal goals, but to meet external criteria applied by accrediting agencies and National Board examiners. The benefits of change are subtle, remote, and often immeasurable. Those who participate in such experiments must face an added stress created by the dilemma of being unique but conforming to existing standards.

Dream Doctor

Published in *Archives of Internal Medicine*, Vol. 144, April 1984:

I was both flattered and worried when asked to address the freshman medical students in their introductory course on *Being a Physician*. Medical students are looking for certainty, are inclined toward the dramatic, and are in training to take control, whereas psychiatrists are beguiled by ambiguity, shun emergencies, and train others to gain control of themselves.

Anxiety about the talk worked on my unconscious, and shortly before I was to deliver my address, I had a dream. In the dream, I was treating a woman newly admitted to the hospital with a bleeding disorder. I decided to set up an infusion, but was uncertain which drug to use. The ward copy of *Physician's Desk Reference* was missing, so I was forced to continue a fruitless search elsewhere. When I returned to the patient's bedside, still in doubt, I found that the intern had started the infusion. As I approached the bed, the patient began to bleed profusely from around the infusion needle. The flow of blood grew rapidly from a trickle to a deluge. I grabbed at the sheets and bedclothes in a futile attempt to staunch the bleeding, and at the same time was aware of the beseeching eyes of the intern, the recriminatory eyes of the nurse, and the terrified eyes of the patient. Then I awoke.

The dream encapsulated the unique stresses of the physician's role: the necessity to make decisions in ambiguous situations, to take control in emergencies, to be responsible for finding a cure. I decided to use the material of the dream in my talk, presenting it as a case that had actually occurred.

—

The themes of the talk went well but the students pressed hard for facts: "Who was the woman? What was the disease? Did she die?" I deflected their quest for facts by interpreting it as a defense against anxieties aroused concerning their roles as future physicians.

When the talk was over, their questions stimulated my own associations. The scene that surfaced was of Guy's Hospital, London, where, twenty years earlier, I had been an intern to a professor of surgery. A particular patient came to mind. Because her case was so striking, an account had been published, which was available to refresh my memory.

She was a 42-year-old woman who had noticed a lump in her breast while bathing and had been admitted for emergency biopsy. The medical student estimated her hemoglobin level to be eighty percent. An inner quadrant, hard, pinkish-gray tumor was found, on frozen section, to have large numbers of round cells consistent with anaplastic carcinoma. The breast was removed. As the patient was leaving surgery, the pathology laboratory phoned to say that the peripheral blood smear showed acute paramyeloblastic leukemia with thrombocytopenia. We began an anxious watch for uncontrolled hemorrhage from the wound and her menstrual period, which started several days later. She required several pints of blood as her hemoglobin level fell relentlessly. Fourteen days after operation and a month to the day after noticing the lump in her breast, she died. An autopsy disclosed undiagnosed leukemic deposits throughout the internal organs.

Feelings of remorse and anxiety were reawakened by this memory. The inflicting of unnecessary suffering and the occurrence of uncontrollable hemorrhage were components of both this experience and the dream. Unlike the patient in my dream, however, the real patient had been doomed from the outset. I could not account for the acute sense of frustrated therapeutic hopes that had characterized my dream.

The most painful material is buried the deepest! A second memory surfaced. Through a series of coincidences, I had admitted my mother

—

290

to our unit for emergency surgery. Things went poorly, and she slipped into a coma. I had signed off the case, but late one afternoon while I was doing rounds, the chief resident asked me to run a sample to the pathology laboratory. Carrying a tube of my mother's blood, feeling hopeful and responsible, I arrived as the laboratory was closing. I was too late; the technician refused the sample. A few days later, my mother died without regaining consciousness.

Once again I discovered, painfully, that teaching is learning. The students' relentless search for fact had led to my recollections. Next time I gave the talk it would be as a doctor with experiences that were rooted not in dreams, but in reality.

Pale as the Sheet that Shrouds Her

Disease has smudged the mirror
of her too familiar face.

Perched in a sterile dome,
audience to a white ballet
I view the butchery and eavesdrop
while they pluck her womb
and snip it from her tangled gut.

My crimson origins glisten
in a stainless dish.

Apprentice, I learn the trickery.
A deft mechanic ties the bleeders,
debates the baseball scores,
teases the scrub nurses, chides the residents,
teaches the students. Left and right brain
doing different chores. In sleep, when
the halves embrace, the surgeon dreams.

It doesn't work for me. Dreamless,
awake, I watch and weep.

—

291

Afterwards, in Recovery, she bleeds.
First a trickle, then a deluge.
Loitering outside her cubicle
the intern hands me a warm tube.
If the lab can find some absent factor
her blood may clot and stop. But
I arrive too late. A weary technician,
eager for home, won't cooperate.

Rage contracts in me, pushing memory
deep into dreamtime.

—Barry Blackwell, date unknown

Medical Education and Modest Expectations

Published in *General Hospital Psychiatry*, 1985:

From the Hippocratic ideal to the Marcus Welby image, the social stereotype of the physician is of one who is always available, constantly kind, and unerringly wise. How to best educate physicians to fulfill this exacting role is an old and difficult problem. Neither society nor the profession has been modest in their expectations of meeting these ideals.

Medical educators have voiced their concerns for over fifty years. In an address to Harvard medical students in 1927, Francis Peabody, a distinguished internist, complained that " . . . young graduates have been taught a great deal about the mechanism of disease but very little about the practice of medicine—or to put it bluntly, they are too scientific and do not know how to take care of patients." In 1978, George Engle, another distinguished internist, proposed a new biopsychosocial model of medicine and commented:

Medical education has grown increasingly proficient in conveying to physicians sophisticated scientific knowledge and technical skills about the body and its aberrations. Yet

—

at the same time it has failed to give corresponding attention to the scientific understanding of human behavior and the social and psychological aspects of illness and patient care.

In the fifty years between these almost identical admonitions, the faculty and curriculum of medical schools have expanded prodigiously: the amount of time devoted to teaching the behavioral sciences and psychiatry has increased from 26 to 362 hours during the 4-year interval between admission and graduation. The extent of experimentation can be gauged from the observation that 43 different disciplines or departments are engaged in teaching these topics and that as many as 7 different programs collaborate in some schools.

The fact that these concerns persist and the pluralism of attempts to address them indicate the absence of an ideal answer. If anything, modern medical terminology has further eroded this possibility. The competent generalist has given way to the highly trained subspecialist and the art of practice has been eclipsed by the science. Doctors have clustered around city medical centers and shunned rural communities. As the technical competence of the profession has increased, its availability and humanity have been called into question.

The failure to modify this problem and increasing awareness of its existence suggested the need for a more radical approach. Beginning with the Kennedy administration a wave of "new and developing" medical schools began to open. By 1978 over thirty had appeared. Many were community based—less expensive to build and less elite in image, they were to attract a new breed of student and faculty dedicated to producing primary care practitioners with a humanistic bent who would be willing to work in rural settings.

At the tail end of this experiment I became the founding chair of psychiatry in one of these new schools. Many of the faculty were eager to experiment with the curriculum and the admissions committee was flexible and innovative in accepting a wide variety of applicants: the charter class included a helicopter pilot, a housewife, a classics major, and a black physical therapist. Still, there are shortcomings to selection as a way of seeking change in medical practice. Interviews are

—

poor at predicting future performance; the goals of the school were widely published and most applicants were well briefed by the cab driver on the way from the airport to the admissions committee. The motives that attract people into medicine sometimes carry their own seeds of destruction. Early deprivation may breed a compensatory need to nurture that manifests with an intensity that can seduce an admissions committee. Yet the same deprivation may foster poor coping strategies and impairment later in the face of practice and its stresses.

The dedicated student also appeals to admissions committees. Studies show that medical students do indeed tend to be compulsive, and this trait is correlated with "adjustment" to the educational process. Because compulsives are good at making lists, delaying gratification, and planning ahead, this would be predicted; yet compulsives also tend to like retaining control and avoiding close emotional involvements—behaviors that are partially antithetical to the humanistic physician. It may be the selection procedures that favor compulsives are sounder bases for educational survival rather than for eventual practice.

Medical school offers the student a lot that breeds arrogance and stunts humanity. The rites of passage are enticing but the curriculum is a meat grinder. From the start students feel part of a special community. They are awed by stories of the superhuman intellect and endurance needed to survive. Few, if any, are allowed to flunk out but forty percent will experience significant stress and a few will become psychotic. The students begin to intrude into the most intimate aspect of other peoples' lives. They perform vaginal examinations, touch bodies, and hear confessions. Students learn a language that will segregate them from others; over 13,000 new words must be assimilated and acronyms abound. PMS, ECG, BUN, and CNS are sign posts to insensitivity that transcribe people into "interesting cases." Former "straight A" students find themselves struggling. Nine out of ten students begin to date less, and half those that are married report alienation from their spouses. There is an abrupt decline in the number of concerts, plays, and movies that students attend. As they begin to sever their friendships and support systems, this adds to the stress but simultaneously segregates them from the public. Feeling special becomes part of surviving.

How to temper this process and sustain the sensitivity of the person who became the student is an unanswered question. Most of the new schools added ethics and humanities programs and some made innovative experiments that had to struggle hard to compete in an already overloaded curriculum whose graduates still had to prove themselves in traditional tests set to measure the standards of traditional schools.

Others have documented, tongue in cheek, the difficulties of designing a "benign behavioral science" course. The fate of one such experiment with which I was involved can probably serve as a stereotype for others. The concerns that are voiced about medical practice and the biomedical model originate from the time when Christian orthodoxy permitted dissection of the human body provided that a strict segregation was preserved between the physician's province of the body and the church's domain of the mind and spirit. This dichotomy fostered an attitude in which life is stripped of its social and psychologic complexity and reduced to a technology reliant on physical phenomena. In medical school, this dualistic approach is fostered by the psychologic defenses that students mobilize to cope with the stress of exposure to the dead body. We designed an experience to heighten the students' awareness of this situation and its relevance to future practice. Faculty from the departments of anatomy, pathology, psychiatry, and humanities met with students on the first day of class to discuss their feelings and formally share in the introduction to the cadaver. That evening the students wrote a fictional biography of the cadaver and next day shared this and the experience of their first dissection with the faculty.

This experience in humanizing the student-cadaver encounter was originally popular but failed to survive for reasons that are intrinsic to the problems of changing medical education. In order to create a summer break for students, the task of dissecting the entire

—

human body was condensed from two semesters to one. Some of the founding faculty who designed the class left and were replaced by more skeptical faculty who had not shared in the planning. The class size expanded and contained fewer idealists and more younger traditional students. After three years the polarization between staff and students was such that the experiment was dropped. Philosophy confronted logistics and lost. The paradox is that the very scientific advances that create the need for humanism simultaneously crowd it out of the curriculum. Our failure was symbolized when a student who participated in this experiment cut the penis off a cadaver and flashed it on campus.

We may be looking at this problem through the wrong end of the telescope. The greatest anxieties of medicine come in practice and not in the preparation for it. Our own study of residents in training found that the main stresses of adopting the physician role are acting in unexpected emergencies, dealing with ambiguous situations, and making decisions without adequate data. The strategies that residents adopt to cope with their anxieties include appearing more certain than they feel, assuming absolute control in emergencies, and adopting a set approach to complicated problems. Thus, the essential tasks of the physician role arouse anxieties and coping strategies that may initiate a process of alienation from the patient. They breed an arrogance, a certainty, and an insensitivity that provoke inevitable responses in the patient. Some patients adopt a passive dependence, others react angrily to this paternalism, and only a few are able to meet the physician's needs for information or control in an effectively assertive way.

This basic dynamic of the physician-patient encounter needs to be more clearly enunciated and better understood. Physicians often discover it themselves when they relax after years in practice and find that their encounters are enhanced if they are able to share their own and their patients' beliefs and uncertainties. The arrogance that becomes a reflex to deal with life-threatening emergencies during hospital training mellows with time and tempo of office practice to become an occasional and necessary tool for taking control in ambiguous situations.

—

The degree to which this process of humanization can be accelerated is questionable. Attempts to do so in pregraduate training occur at a time when they are least relevant and they compete poorly in an overcrowded curriculum. During internship and residency the goals of humanism are subordinate to the more pressing tasks of role adoption.

There is no Holy Grail; like Canute I have learned that the tides of medical education cannot be turned. If changes come about as a result of the new medical schools it will be because they flooded the marketplace with physicians. The laws of supply and demand are operating to fill the less popular, least paid, and unpopulated places. Those who practice there will find the limited degree to which education abbreviates experience and the greater extent to which time tempers science with the art of medicine.

In return for more modest expectations about what medical education can accomplish, the profession may feel less frustrated, the public less disappointed, and individual practitioners less prone to impairment.

A Fifteen-Minute Ed Check

(All you should know to be a good psychiatrist)

In 2010, I received an unexpected but intriguing invitation to be the commencement speaker at the graduation ceremony for psychiatric residents at Wright State University in Dayton, Ohio. This was thirty years after I had been founding chair of the department. Particularly exciting was that the current chair had been a resident in Cincinnati when I was a faculty member. The satire behind the title of my talk, *A Fifteen-Minute Ed Check*, derives from a widely expressed concern that today's psychiatrists are little more than "pill pushers" poorly trained in psychological understanding and psychodynamic principles. This is the mirror image of how it was when I arrived in America. So I was delighted to learn that the Wright State psychiatry program was nationally known and respected for having shunned this false dichotomy by developing innovative ways to train psychiatrists with sophisticated biopsychosocial knowledge and talents.

—

If the medical school no longer aspired to turn out humanistic primary care physicians, I would gladly settle for the right kind of psychiatrist. So I began my talk . . .

Wright State University School of Medicine was one of over thirty "new and developing" medical schools initiated during the Kennedy administration intended to train a breed of humanistic primary care doctors willing to work in rural settings. I will return to this theme at the end of my talk.

You and I are at opposite ends of a career and the learning curve that enlightens it. Despite all the carping about medicine today, limitless choices and learning opportunities lie ahead of you. I will soon morph from a "shrink" into a "shrunk," but during fifty years I spent time as an army sergeant sanitary engineer, a field ambulance reserve army major, a psychopharmacologist, a family practitioner, director of research for a pharmaceutical company, head of a psychosomatic unit, chair of two academic departments, consultant to Blue Cross, medical director of a small managed-care company, a lay student in a Catholic seminary (after I gave up medicine but not sex), and, finally, after I discovered I am spiritually handicapped, a return to medicine as the only psychiatrist in a women's prison looking after over a hundred inmates with mental illness.

Every step along that way I taught, learned, and published papers with coauthors that included medical students, psychiatric and medical residents, pharmacists, pharmacologists, pharmaceutical reps, psychologists, epidemiologists, consumers, nurses, and internists. Medical education, even at its best, is replete with redundancy, but patients and colleagues always teach. Learning is lifelong.

So during this fifteen-minute "ed check," half will be devoted to caring for yourself and half to caring for patients. Seven minutes for each.

Know and Own Yourself

I own an odd upbringing and an unusual personality. I have taken the MMPI twice in my lifetime and failed both times. In 1938, at age four,

—

my parents took me to India and settled in Calcutta where I developed amebic dysentery. After I recovered on a diet of apples and bananas, they sent me to a "safe" school in Darjeeling, close to Mount Everest. When World War II broke out, we were stranded, and I spent from age five till eighteen in all-male boarding schools in India and England. So I developed my brain and body in an intensely competitive environment that encouraged independence and accomplishment but lacked nurturing or feminine role models, stifling emotion and sensitizing me to abandonment.

British psychiatry largely shuns psychoanalysis and discourages introspection. But when I came to America and Cincinnati at age thirty-four, I was the token biological psychiatrist in a strongly psychoanalytic department. I absorbed its insights through my pores and married a psychologically minded wife, head nurse on the psychosomatic unit. I wasn't cured but did learn to capitalize on my strengths and cope with my deficits. Chance and common sense are cheaper and sometimes quicker than a formal psychoanalysis.

Choosing Your Life Partner

If this advice comes late, be comforted. There is a small literature on physician lifestyle and traditional medical marriages to which I have contributed. Divorce rates in physician marriages tend to be lower than the population norm, and although spouses complain of the burdens, four out of five consider their marriages to be happy and say they would marry the same person again. Attitudes and behaviors have improved since William Osler wrote, in *The Student's Life*, "What about the wife and babies if you have them? Leave them! Heavy are your responsibilities to yourself, to the profession and to the public. Your wife will be glad to bear her share of the sacrifices you make." Things were even worse in earlier times. William Harvey's wife, Ann, had to put up with her husband inoculating himself with syphilis and then treating it with mercury. He also practiced wrestling with a bull Queen Elizabeth I had given him and purchased two leopards as pets.

My own contemporary advice is shaped by a two-trial learning curve: a first marriage that lasted seventeen years and produced three children and a second that has lasted thirty-four years and produced a single son, about to become a physician. Based on these experiences, I suggest you choose a life partner who is psychologically minded, who is at least or more intelligent than you are, and who has a strong sense of humor. Above all, do not choose a real or metaphorical patient.

Cultivate Equanimity

Sir William Osler's more enlightened comment was that equanimity is the mark of a good physician. This is the capacity to stay calm in adversity, a characteristic that leads to sound decisions and soothes a nervous patient's angst. This is how President Obama confronts the Tea Party! If, like me, you have inherited a hysterical gene, you may need personal or professional help learning to think before you speak or act.

Care for Yourself

The old medical school axiom states, "You don't care for others unless you care for yourself." It is true. Capitalize on your compulsive traits. You wouldn't have got this far if you didn't have them. Make plans and lists. Schedule time outs for family, friends, hobbies, and leisure activities. I played vigorous rugby until age thirty-four, cook exotic meals, cultivate a large yard, and write short stories and poetry. Gardening has the added advantage that, unlike children, if you don't like what grows, you can pull it out and throw it away!

There are two ways not to care for yourself: an unbridled urge to save the needy and the excessive desire to make money.

Many medical students, me included, say, "I always knew I wanted to be a doctor." This is self-affirming; ambitious parents love it, and it may impress an unsophisticated admissions committee. But it is often the fruit of a poisoned tree. Banished to boarding school and fearful of abandonment, I loved to "treat" my mother's bunions with colored paint ("medicine"). Like many attracted to the "caring" professions, I was motivated to care for others in ways I lacked myself. As Talbott's long-term follow-up research has shown, such medical students are at risk to neglect their own needs and burn out, leading to drug or alcohol

—

abuse and dysfunctional marriages. The cure is to titrate your empathy against reasonable boundaries.

Making money as a motivation has its own pitfalls. You may be protected by your choice of our specialty, which is not procedure-oriented but it is time-intensive. Many of the patients I have treated throughout a long career have been indigent inner-city folks, sometimes homeless, lacking health insurance and, now, incarcerated. But I always saw them as a faculty member or salaried employee. Needing to make money by billing fee-for-service can create a conflict of interest that stifles empathy toward the poor, uninsured, the ungrateful, or the "no shows." The contemporary, but misnamed, "not-for-profit" health care industry has adopted the motto, "No margin, no mission," making my kind of naïve altruism difficult to sustain. The health care corporation that took over our inner-city hospital in Milwaukee closed most of its psychiatric services, including the academic and residency programs. So be smart in choosing a job. Look carefully at the revenue sources and the conditions you work under, including whether you will be subjected to "productivity ratios." The dean who recruited me from Wright State to the University of Wisconsin assured me that economic support for the academic program was as "secure as Fort Knox." It wasn't!

Caring for Others

Patients as Persons

I always consider it a compliment when a patient says, "You don't seem like a psychiatrist." This usually means not fitting the cultural stereotype of a "blank screen" but always treating people as persons first. As a nearly retired, aging citizen, I am now often on the patient side of the medical encounter. Specialists I consult often see me as a problem to be fixed, not a unique individual. I have become an arthritic, ataxic crock. If I have a name, it is Mr. Blackwell. Not doctor, not professor, not scientist, not poet, author, gardener, husband, father, spouse, or good cook. And, most of all, not Barry.

It is alarming how often our own discipline still refers to people as diagnoses. "Schizophrenics" or "eating disorders." Time is never so

—

short, even in a despised "med check," that you cannot see the person first. What I learned during my time in family practice is that brief sessions are compensated for by being cumulative and sequential. I once wrote an article for JAMA titled "Primary Care Psychiatry," which became the cover of the Japanese version of the journal! Even when time is short, particularly if it is short, be certain to inquire and write down details of a person's day-to-day life. You cannot measure norepinephrine, serotonin, or dopamine levels, only a person's thoughts, feelings, or behaviors manifested via life changes and events.

A Grand Rounds topic: "When does a boundary become a barrier?"

"Compliance" and the Therapeutic Alliance

After a two-year fellowship working with rats and cats on the pharmacology of the MAOI and cheese interaction, I realized I was too clumsy to be a lab scientist, and I was less interested in how drugs worked than in why people did or did not take them.

I wrote my first article on "Compliance" for the *New England Journal of Medicine* in 1973, and the last book of my career, over twenty years later, was titled *Treatment Compliance and the Therapeutic Alliance*. The subtle but profound shift from compliance to alliance is relevant to the whole of clinical practice. Both patients and doctors exaggerate how much of what is prescribed is consumed. The reason is simple: miscommunication and misunderstanding. Doctors are trained in knowledge, certainty, and advice giving. They seldom inquire about the patient's attitudes, beliefs, expectations, and experiences about what may be wrong or what might help before they prescribe. As a result, half the expected pill taking fails to occur. So ask, listen, negotiate, and agree before treating.

Nature and Nurture

Never underestimate the significance of the patient's genes. Adolf Meyer taught the importance of detailed family histories to determine the influence of both nature and nurture. As a dog owner who has not been psychoanalyzed, I incline toward the belief that nature often

—

trumps nurture. Puppies are separated from their litter long before most behaviors can be modeled. But sheep dogs will herd guests at a cocktail party, Labradors swim in your pool, bird dogs bark at helicopters, and hounds slip their collar to follow a scent. Many of the complex behaviors we attribute to personality are as genetically determined as are the disorders for which we prescribe drugs. Just ask your patients.

Illness and Disease

When I took over George Engel's former psychosomatic unit in Cincinnati, I collaborated with two talented cognitive-behavioral psychologists to develop a novel approach. We abandoned the traditional attempts to link specific physical disorders with particular personality profiles. This was before the discovery that peptic ulcer disease was caused by Helicobacter, not by unmet dependency needs.

We described a generic syndrome we called "Illness Behavior," defined as disability disproportionate to detectable disease. To make this determination requires acceptance of the fact that someday everybody dies of something and that the attribution "disproportionate" can only be made after the most thorough physical evaluation for any biomedical disorder. This is an essential ingredient to what follows because it establishes in the patient's mind that their somatic preoccupations and concerns are not being dismissed or lightly labeled as hysterical, malingering, or spurious. Once this is accomplished, the underlying concept becomes, "Nobody behaves sick if they can behave healthy."

This generous axiom can be understood in psychodynamic or behavioral terms. What determines a person's illness or response to physical disease is contingent on what they seek to avoid (primary gain or avoidance learning) and what they find supportive or rewarding (secondary gain or positive reinforcement). By this push-and-pull dynamic, people avoid insoluble existential predicaments which they lack the skills or temperament to deal with, and they are lured or seduced into sick roles that are comfortable or comforting. Insight or understanding does not always or readily result in behavior change. which may require multiple interventions at the family, individual, or workplace level.

—

Summary

In fifteen minutes, I have defined four ways in which you can care for yourself and four ways to care for others. They are:

Know and own yourself, choose a life partner well, cultivate equanimity, and care for yourself.

Approach patients as persons, achieve a therapeutic alliance, explore nature and nurture, and undertake a biopsychosocial evaluation of disease and illness using both psychodynamic and behavioral concepts.

The Wright State Experience in "Humanistic" Medicine

Wright State School of Medicine was born in 1974, during a decade when over thirty new schools were founded, of which Ohio added three more.

The impetus was a societal demand for more "humanistic" primary care physicians that peaked three decades after the end of World War II. It was created by tension between the advances in medicine and the evolution of various "rights" movements (civil, feminist, gay, and patients'). In those thirty years, medicine mutated from comfort care with panaceas and placebos to advances in technology that made it more complex, expensive, invasive, and impersonal.

But this concern was not new. In 1927, Francis Peabody, a distinguished internist, noted that "young graduates are too scientific and do not know how to care for patients." Fifty years later, in 1978, George Engel, an equally distinguished internist, analytically trained in Cincinnati, echoed the same sentiments, "Medical education has grown increasingly proficient in conveying to physicians sophisticated scientific knowledge and technical skills about the body and its aberrations. Yet, at the same time, it has failed to give corresponding attention to the scientific and psychological aspects of illness and patient care."

As a disciple of Engle, I inherited his psychosomatic unit in Cincinnati and practiced the biopsychosocial model he espoused. I welcomed the challenge of developing an innovative curriculum to accomplish the mission of training humanistic physicians in a new medical school.

The dean established a "Medicine in Society" program staffed by an ethicist and a sociologist with which psychiatry shared curriculum time for what normally passed as Behavioral Science. I recruited a vice chair who was a psychoanalyst and a director of medical student education who was a cognitive behavioral psychologist.

We designed and later published articles on two interdisciplinary projects. One was with faculty from the English department which used selected literature dealing with physicians and patients with the goal of encouraging students to "read between the lines" on the psychological and emotional themes of the medical encounter. The second was called "The Student-Cadaver Encounter" planned by faculty in Anatomy, Pathology, Psychiatry, and Medicine in Society." Students were "introduced" to their cadaver and asked to write a fictional account about the person they were to dissect. Content analysis showed they mostly described themselves.

Later we discovered these kinds of projects were not exactly new. In 1979, a colleague and I conducted a mail survey of behavioral science teaching in American medical schools (published in the *American Journal of Psychiatry*). In the fifty years between Peabody's and Engel's concerns, the amount of curriculum time devoted to behavioral science and psychiatry increased from twenty-six to 362 hours over the four years of medical school. Forty-three different disciplines or departments were involved and up to seven different programs collaborated in some schools.

If the amount of effort is proportional to the difficulty of a task, it will not surprise you to learn that at WSU we failed to accomplish our mission. In 1985, I published an editorial in *General Hospital Psychiatry* titled "Medical Education and Modest Expectations," which analyzed the sources of failure, none of which were unique to WSU but are generic to medicine.

Here is a quote from that editorial: "The degree to which this process of humanization can be accelerated is questionable. Attempts to do

—

so in pregraduate training compete poorly in a curriculum increasingly burdened with expanding scientific knowledge. During internship and residency the goals of humanism are subordinate to the more pressing tasks of role adoption."

The editorial concludes with the following thought: "Education can only abbreviate experience to a very limited degree. Instead it is time in practice that tempers science with the art of medicine."

Which brings us back full circle to the earlier part of my talk: there are things you will learn in practice that build on the excellent foundations laid in this residency program. So keep your eyes, ears, minds, and hearts open. What may be described in fifteen minutes can take a lifetime to acquire!

Primary Care Psychiatry

Published in *Journal of the American Medical Association*, August 1983, Volume 250:

> The next patient was late. I leafed through our primary care clinic's chart. The referral slip said "impotence, psychotic?" The workup was thorough: no diabetes, no neurological signs, and a normal review of systems. But after that the resident's notes betrayed his frustration: "Impossible to interview; maintains a monologue with vague delusional statements and demands for meds."
>
> When Joe showed up in the psychiatry clinic I was surprised. Half our referrals from primary care don't come; perhaps they feel accused of inventing or imagining their ailments. As I left my office to greet him, Joe was delivering a sermon in the waiting area on some aspect of his religious convictions. A four-square physique and a name full of c's, y's, and z's suggested a home on the Southside. That is a culture with strong values and clear-cut beliefs. Few psychiatrists work there, and their offices, like adult bookstores, have front and

back entrances. If my stereotype was accurate, plain talk would clearly be in order; psychological jargon would not. Looking me in the eye, Joe launched into his monologue. He had suffered from epilepsy all his life and had borne the stigma with fortitude until he retired from the brewery five years ago. Deprived of the dignity of work, Joe had bolstered his manhood with an affair that quickly ended in remorse and a return to the religiosity that consorted with his seizures. After a period of conscious-stricken prayer, God and two fellow helpers had appeared at the foot of Joe's bed to tell him that his suffering would cease if he agreed to lead a better life. When Joe believed that his part of this bargain was fulfilled, the seizures stopped and he no longer needed anticonvulsants. Two years ago the unearthly trio reappeared, promising him continued good health in return for continued good behavior. Joe had complied.

But now he was 70, and his wife was dying in a nursing home. He had just moved from their old home into an apartment with a woman friend who wanted more than companionship. Joe was pushing hard to prove himself and find some comfort, but his body wasn't cooperating. He felt inadequate and a trifle guilty.

Joe had taken certain practical steps to solve his new problem. He visited a urologist who examined him, found nothing wrong, and declined Joe's request that he prescribe testosterone (or anything else). Later, after taking all the vitamins and potency aids he could buy in a health food store, but to no avail, Joe had turned to the Primary Care Clinic. And now, psychiatry.

At this point I interrupted him with a question (time was passing)—what did he want of me? Joe didn't answer the question because he was very deaf. Again I interrupted, this time shouting my question. He answered, "Testosterone," either by needle (he pointed to his rear end), or under the tongue (he opened his mouth). Unable to communicate with

—

307

him verbally, I wrote out my recommendations, numbering them as follows:

1. The urologist said you don't need testosterone. I agree.
2. Your problem will go away when

    (a) You stop trying so hard.
    (b) You are less worried.

3. Try prayer. It worked before.

Joe took the pad but looked puzzled. "I don't have any glasses."

The end of our consultation had arrived and the next patient was waiting. Throwing caution and confidentiality to the winds, I shouted my advice into his ear. Joe listened carefully, became thoughtful, and then nodded.

Reading the nonverbal signs that our interview was over, Joe held out his hand and thanked me kindly, saying he would be back for further advice when he needed it. Later, as I struggled to code our encounter for billing purposes, I had the comforting thought that if psychiatry does become extinct (as some predict), I might enjoy being a primary care practitioner again.

Psychosurgery

Published in *Off Hours*, Vol. 2, No. 1, January 1986:

(For a medical student learning psychiatry who hopes to become a surgeon.)

> Our eyes engage.
>
> Clenched lids
> can't staunch
> the flow of tears

—

I operate on her awake
with questions that cut
pauses that retract
            for her sake

We arrive
back where it began
        Her black ailing mom
                    . . . alive
        Her white unwed dad
                    . . . dead
When she was five
When purebred peers
nicknamed her
                    Honky

Now I see
the pale skin
the muddled genes
the almost afro hair

Now her despair
makes sense
Bereft
she wants to die

Waiting
to ask her white dad
why he left her here
half black
                    Alone

Quickly, I close.
Sadness
has spread too far

                    —Barry Blackwell, 1986

15. Compliance

To Take or Not to Take: That Is the Question

Keep a watch also on the faults of the patients, which often make them lie about taking things prescribed.

—Hippocrates

Of all the "nondrug" factors that influence treatment outcome, none is as important, or more often overlooked, than when the drug is not taken at all or not in the manner intended.

Neglect of this topic is curious; ever since Eve ate the forbidden fruit, it has been obvious people sometimes fail to follow directions. Although Hippocrates, the "father of medicine," warned of this, it was largely ignored and the word "compliance" did not appear in the medical literature until 1975 when it replaced the term "medical dropout."

Several factors explain the late interest in this important topic. First, although Hippocrates laid the blame on the patient, research has shown that physicians seriously underestimate the size of the problem with their own patients. Secondly, when most drugs were panaceas or placebos; not taking them hardly mattered and failed to alter the course of the disease. It was not until the midtwentieth century and the discovery of modern pharmaceuticals, including antibiotics, analgesics, steroids, and psychotropic drugs, that failure to take medication became a life-and-death

–

310

matter. Thirdly, the arrival of modern medicines contributed to the "patient's rights" movement and the demand for a more active role in treatment decisions. Lastly, added impetus was due to the involvement of additional disciplines in the prescribing process, including pharmacists, psychologists, optometrists, and nurse practitioners.

My interest in the topic of compliance originated in the midst of this ferment. I published my first article on it in 1972 and the following year was invited to submit a second, titled "Drug Therapy: Patient Compliance," to the *New England Journal of Medicine*. Shortly after that, I participated and presented papers at the first two (and only) International Conferences on Compliance at McMaster University in 1974 and 1977. These jumpstarted research in the field with which I remained involved for a quarter century, culminating in editing a book, *Treatment Compliance and the Therapeutic Alliance,* in 1997, at the end of my career.

In that quarter century (1972-1997) over 12,000 articles were published, involving fifty different conditions of which pediatrics, psychiatry, and several chronic disorders were involved, including asthma, diabetes, glaucoma, and hypertension. Seat belts and smoking cessation were latecomers in the field.

Despite the volume of research, quality and consensus were lacking. Compliance is not an easy subject to study because the problem tends to disappear under scrutiny, and covert observations without the patient's knowledge raise ethical concerns. Consequently, over half the studies failed to yield any conclusions.

The positive results were kaleidoscopic and varied, often involving attitudes and beliefs that are both difficult to measure reliably or to influence predictably. Nevertheless, some generalizations did emerge; the extent of noncompliance (complete or partial) involved about a quarter of inpatients and half of outpatients. Factors associated with good compliance are when patient expectations of treatment are met, if they are satisfied or supervised, and if the disease is serious and the patient feels susceptible. Involved family members, friends, or care providers often make a positive contribution.

—

Poor compliance is associated with chronic diseases and prolonged treatment, regimens that require lifestyle change, asymptomatic diseases (glaucoma, hypertension, and diabetes), complicated regimens, significant side effects, stress, isolation, and alcoholism.

Most of my writing and teaching about compliance was conceptual and based on reviews of the research literature, but at Wright State School of Medicine (1974-1980), I designed and supervised a study with three medical students as coauthors who monitored and measured their own compliance over an extended time period and published the results and conclusions in the *Journal of Medical Education*. I also supervised a study with two pharmacy graduate students interested in doing a doctoral thesis on patients with hypertension, comparing the effects of compliance counseling, use of a plastic pill container, and both interventions in combination. Counseling improved clinic attendance, the container improved pill taking, and the combination produced the most significant improvement in blood pressure. The results were published in the *American Journal of Hospital Pharmacy*. Plastic pillboxes have since become an almost ubiquitous component in the management of chronic conditions, particularly in the elderly.

One amusing sidelight in the compliance field has been attempts to find a more congenial word to describe the problem. "Compliance" attracted disfavor early on because it conjured up images of serfdom and submissiveness. Attempts to replace it that failed included "drug defaulter," "adherence," and other terms, which led one author to make the tongue-in-cheek comment that "adherence seems too sticky, fidelity has too many connotations, and maintenance suggests a repair crew." So the majority of scientific publications continue to use "compliance," a one-sided word that describes a complex dyadic collaboration.

The Therapeutic Alliance

The semantics of the compliance problem is resolved when it is viewed as a treatment alliance between two individuals who need to negotiate and reconcile their differing roles, knowledge, attitudes, beliefs, and goals.

Doctors are trained to portray knowledge, certainty, and confidence. They are often quick to inform and slow to inquire. Patients, on the other hand, are often anxious, intimidated, or subdued during the encounter and reluctant to be assertive.

Consider the following interaction between myself and a patient:

Randolph was a thirty-year-old former intravenous drug user newly diagnosed as positive for HIV. During his first admission to hospital for medical treatment, the nurses noted he was suspicious and depressed. As an outpatient, he had rejected offers of medication or grudgingly accepted, but never taken it. On this admission, his urine was positive for cocaine.

When I was asked to consult and visited him on the ward, he freely admitted to using cocaine to counter his feelings of "disgust," but he agreed that after a brief euphoric interlude, he quickly lapsed back into feeling suspicious and disgusted. Our conversation continued with a more detailed analysis of why Randolph used cocaine, what it did for him, and how he thought it worked. Based on his experience, he agreed cocaine could alter his mood and behavior, but at some cost and only temporarily.

When I asked if he would consider an alternative in the form of prescribed medication, he wanted more information about what that meant. I explained that, unlike cocaine, medication worked slowly but that the effects lasted much longer if he continued to take it. He should not expect the immediate "high" but a more gradual improvement with less suspicion and disgust. As a bonus, he would no longer crave cocaine. Was he interested in doing this experiment?

Randolph agreed it was worth a try. After discharge, he came to our homeless clinic and was started on an antidepressant with a low dose of an antipsychotic medication after a careful explanation of possible side effects. He was asked to repeat his understanding of the regimen and given a typed sheet of what to do, when to come back, and who to call if he needed advice.

—

Two weeks later, Randolph returned to the clinic; he was pleased and surprised to report that he was feeling much less disgusted with life. He was sleeping soundly at a nearby shelter, and his urine was clean. I congratulated him, asked if he had any questions or concerns, checked his understanding of the regimen, and made another appointment.

Blind Insight

Shrinks think their illusions
Oughta offer solutions,
When often they don't.

Taking a horse
To the water
Won't make it drink.

—Barry Blackwell, 2004

16. MILWAUKEE

The Place

A Great Place on a Great Lake

—City motto

I have lived over a third of my life and half of my career in Milwaukee, misleadingly characterized in the media as a "beer and brats" city. Originally the home of seven Native American tribes and situated on the shores of Lake Michigan, its name, in dialect, means "gathering place by the water." It began as a small trading post, founded by a French Canadian, which became home to immigrants fleeing the 1848 revolution in Germany and Austria. Other nationalities from Europe followed, including those from Italy, Poland, Ireland, France, Serbia, and Russia, joined later by Mexicans and the Hmong. This patchwork multi-ethnic quilt is reflected in the summer music festivals for which the city is famous.

In the century from 1840 to 1940, the population exploded from 1,700 to 587,000, peaked at 741,000 in 1960, and dwindled to 594,000 in 2010 due largely to the loss of much of the brewing and light manufacturing industry.

Milwaukee has seventeen universities and colleges, with the highest per capita student population in North America, but it also ranks as amongst the most racially segregated cities with an above-average crime rate. Fortunately, it also has a vibrant cultural life with excellent theater, opera, orchestra, ballet, public museums, and architecture, including the stunning Calatrava Art Institute.

Early Days

Kathie, Adam, and I moved from Dayton to Milwaukee in 1980 after the charter class of medical students graduated. It was already clear (see Piece 14: Medical Education) that the goal of producing primary care physicians for underserved areas would fail. Selecting a surgeon as founding dean did not help, especially an aggressive and ambitious individual whose primary goal was to create the post of vice president for health affairs and take over the school of nursing. The feminist faculty, my wife, Kathie, among them, was proud and protective of its professional independence, a position I openly supported and which ultimately led to resigning my chair in the school of medicine.

Although the birthplace of the Wright brothers and aviation, Dayton was an undistinguished and dwindling city, halfway between Columbus and Cincinnati. So I was glad to be recruited by the University of Wisconsin School of Medicine in Madison to participate in a new venture, the obverse of the Wright State experiment. This well-established medical school was seeking to create an urban campus in Milwaukee, the largest city in Wisconsin, to provide teaching access to a medically underserved inner-city patient population with a high incidence of chronic and severe medical disorders. Mount Sinai, the downtown Jewish hospital, was facing an urban flight to the suburbs and having problems filling its beds. Perhaps an academic affiliation with a well-credentialed faculty might stem the tide and attract better-insured patients. Attempts to broker such a deal with the local medical school (the Medical College of Wisconsin, formerly Marquette) failed; the Jesuits and Jews were still at odds!

Instead, this became a "marriage of convenience" between Madison and Mount Sinai; the hospital would gain prestige and paying patients, the medical school would have access to pathology for teaching with space and support for faculty salaries, paid from hospital revenue. So in the summer of 1980, I was attracted to this scenario. During my recruitment, I quizzed the dean about the economic integrity of the deal and was assured it was "as safe as Fort Knox."

In hindsight, the timing was terrible and the assurances worthless. The costs of health care and insurance were increasing exponentially and, on the horizon, the government and insurance industry were about to address "overutilization" of inpatient services. Medicare and Medicaid introduced statistical norms for length of hospital stays by diagnosis (the DRG), while the insurance industry introduced "managed care" with which hospital stays had to be "preauthorized" and monitored for appropriateness, duration of stay, and outcome. Not surprisingly, the hospital census of beds filled declined and revenue dwindled.

Traditionally each faculty member received a guaranteed percentage of total salary (the "base") from the university or, in this case, the hospital's revenue. This was meant to cover teaching, research, and administration. In addition, each faculty member also generated income from their own practice which was fed into the university practice plan for two purposes: as "overhead" to pay for life insurance, health care premiums, and retirement plans, and, secondly, to pay a negotiated salary "supplement."

As hospital revenue declined, so did its ability to fund the faculty members' base salary. When the medical school also pleaded poverty, the only way for faculty to maintain their total negotiated income was to earn more money from practice, reducing time spent on teaching and research. While faculty unhappily made this adjustment, hospitals were having an even harder time making ends meet.

In 1980, there were five inner-city hospitals but, over the next decade, bankruptcies, closures, and mergers took place. The Lutheran Hospital merged with the Catholic Deaconess Hospital to become Good Samaritan. Then Good Samaritan (Lutheran-Catholic) merged with Mount Sinai (Jewish) to become Sinai-Samaritan. When this occurred, the psychiatry department moved its offices to the Samaritan campus.

These interdenominational mergers created culture clashes difficult to manage, and by 1990 and within two years, a new dynamic was emerging.

—

The surviving institutions coalesced into three major "not-for-profit" health care corporations, the largest and most aggressive of which was named Aurora. Inevitably, Aurora acquired Sinai-Samaritan and renamed it Aurora-Sinai. It was now the only remaining inner-city hospital, still the Milwaukee campus of the Madison medical school, but now bearing the entire burden of the inner-city indigent and Medicaid population. Good for teaching, bad for revenue.

Faculty were now exposed to a new breed of aggressive hospital administrator, armed with novel mottos learned in business school: "No Margin, No Mission" and "Every Bucket Must Carry Its Own Water." The meaning was clear; make a profit or else, and nobody is going to bail you out, even a more affluent institution in the same corporation.

The writing was on the wall: specialties like psychiatry and primary care, based on personal care and not on remunerative technical procedures, were doomed. The dean fled back to Madison, and within two years, Aurora pulled the plug on the psychiatry department and its residency training program. Internal Medicine and Family Practice lasted a little longer until Aurora issued an edict that faculty were no longer to treat underfunded Medicaid patients. Those who refused were asked to resign or fired. Those who submitted became "Aurora Doctors" but no longer faculty; there was no one to teach and no patients to teach on. But the former chair of family medicine is now the CEO of Aurora and doubtless a millionaire.

No Margin, No Mission

Published in *Journal of the American Medical Association*, May 18, 1994, Vol. 271:

> For psychiatric educators like myself who direct a consultation-liaison service, the integration of mind and body has always presented a clinical and pedagogic challenge that is being accentuated by the changing economic environment and recent influx of managed care.

—

When I first came to work in our urban teaching hospital thirteen years ago in 1980, the inner city was served by five hospitals; four have since merged or gone bankrupt, and ours is the only one remaining. As each of the others closed, it passed on its population of uninsured, underfunded Medicaid and Medicare patients. The state of Wisconsin took two actions that unwittingly made matters worse for our impoverished institution. It deregulated hospital construction, inviting an influx of three for-profit psychiatric hospitals, siphoning patients with indemnity insurance to the suburbs. This simultaneously reduced the number of people receiving integrated care in my hospital and increased its economic plight by limiting cost shifting. Second, the state obtained a federal waiver from the Medicaid freedom-of-choice stipulation and placed the city's entire welfare population of mothers and children into health maintenance organizations (HMOs). The capitation for these patients was below that for commercial patients in the same HMOs, although they had more complex and costly conditions.

Many of these patients customarily received care in our hospital, and I and my academic colleagues lobbied to continue to provide it. But by the mid-1980s hospital administrators had learned the lessons of survival and the language of the business schools with such slogans as "No margin, no mission" and "Every bucket must carry its own water." Hospitals and HMOs began to barter with each other, ratcheting down fees and divesting themselves of expensive Medicaid subpopulations to low-cost providers. Recently our hospital sold its entire HMO population to a national organization, which divested the mental health capitation to its "behavioral health" subsidiary. They in turn kept the commercial patients but subcapitated the Medicaid population to yet another agency unaffiliated with our institution. The sickest and poorest of our patients and those most in need of integrated care could no longer obtain my services in the same hospital where my colleagues care for their medical needs.

Clearly this is not what Congress intended when it mandated that Medicaid patients should obtain both their medical and psychiatric care in general hospitals.

Recently I was asked to offer a consultation on a man with acute postsurgical delirium whose HMO had "subcapitated" its mental health services to another provider outside my hospital. I called the HMO's phone line to request prior authorization. First I was asked questions that could only be answered if my consultation had already been performed, and then the patient was offered an outpatient appointment. Finally, when I explained the patient was pulling out his intravenous lines and needed immediate attention my inquisitor asked, "What is delirium?" Such "little battles" sometimes yield grudging approval; others end in delay or denial, necessitating a lengthy appeal that is often not responded to.

As managed competition looms, some of its obvious implications need closer scrutiny. Few people, myself included, doubt the need to control mental health costs. Vague end points, diagnostic ambiguity, and elastic interventions create considerable "moral hazard" which can readily jeopardize a capitated system. Some element of management is inevitable. In HMOs, primary care practitioners have traditionally served as gatekeepers to specialty care. However, presumably because they are considered ill equipped to do so in psychiatry, it has now become traditional for HMOs to separate the capitation for medical services from that of mental health and substance abuse. Access to care for patients is limited and approved by telephone through inexperienced and medically untrained case managers. This system is often referred to as a "carve-out." This appropriate surgical metaphor is softened by adding the prefix "behavioral health." Management of this "behavioral health carve-out" is spawning a new national industry.

But there is a tradition to the use of the word *behavioral* in medicine that is associated with the application of

—

psychological principles to medical practice (as promoted by the Society of Behavioral Medicine, to which I belong). The new usage of the term *behavioral* has become a synonym for all psychiatric services. Paradoxically, "behavioral health carve-out" describes the segregation of psychiatric from medical services—the polar opposite of the integrated intention of the original use of the term *behavioral*.

This is not only antithetical to the "biopsychosocial" treatment model that educators like myself espouse, but it has paradoxical insurance implications. A frequent argument to support provision of mental health services is that they produce a reciprocal reduction in costs of general medical care (the so-called offset). I cannot see how this is facilitated by dividing the patient's care into separate domains. In my experience, once the capitation is split, "health maintenance" occurs in name only. Neither side willingly accepts fiscal responsibility for primary or secondary preventative programs, such as smoking cessation, weight control, and pain management.

Of broader concern is the question of access of the general population to mental health services. A majority of contemporary mental health care is provided by the primary care sector. Can this population be willingly diverted to the specialty mental health sector? If so, people with psychosomatic complaints are likely to be seen by the least expensive mental health providers and will be doubly deprived of physician contact.

Businesses and corporations are preparing to negotiate with health care cooperatives. As prudent purchasers, I advise them to consider quality outcomes, consumer satisfaction, and capturing the cost offset as factors in any decision about whether to "carve-out" psychiatric and substance abuse services. Choosing this option may well incur the potential hidden costs of economic mind-body dualism.

—

In community hospitals like mine, psychiatric educators who confront managed competition must prepare to have their philosophical assumptions and populations they serve compromised and eroded. Clinical revenue to support faculty positions may dwindle and physician role models who teach mind-body medicine to students and residents will be endangered. As educators we are learning a hard lesson: no margin, no mission.

During this health care holocaust, lasting over twenty years and leading eventually to "Obamacare," I was able to create a new Department of Psychiatry and training program only to watch it collapse. Unlike the animals, mankind is the only creature able to anticipate its own death, but, fortunately, unable to predict the more immediate future. So following my installation as the first chair of psychiatry at the Milwaukee Clinical Campus, I set about recruiting a faculty and then designing and implementing a residency training program.

This necessitated developing a curriculum and clinical rotations to cover all aspects of the specialty and then obtaining accreditation. We accomplished this at the first attempt and set about recruiting medical students interested in psychiatry. This was a difficult task; psychiatry is at the lower end of the physician income and prestige scale, but it attracts foreign graduates eager to gain a foothold in America; some are very bright, but there can be problems understanding and adapting to the beliefs, attitudes, and mores of a new culture that slow the educational process and role adaptation.

Adaptation to the Physician Role

My background in family practice and medical education, as well as experiences in psychosomatic medicine, earned me a joint appointment as professor of medicine and as a consultant on the medical wards as well as the chronic pain program run by Neurology. Exposure to residents in training was a natural continuation from teaching medical students and stimulated further interest in how individuals adapted to the exacting role of becoming a physician. That interest was also responsive to a thought-provoking editorial by Norman Cousins in a leading medical journal in which he identified the internship as, "The weakest link in the entire chain of medical education," and posed the question of whether it was a legitimate preparation for practice or a "hazardous form of hazing." This concern was amplified by an awareness of the increased risk of suicide among interns and residents.

Together with my senior faculty psychologist and the chief medical resident, we designed a study to identify the key variables in adaptation to the physician role during residency. Based on our own experiences and the literature, we developed a sixty-item questionnaire to measure attitudes, stressors, and coping strategies during residency training. It was mailed to all 1,098 residents in Wisconsin in 1982, endorsed by a letter from the chief resident in each program.

A total of two hundred residents responded (18 percent). This is a low response rate that constrains the reliability of our conclusions although they have face validity (they seem sensible). The results were published in the journal *General Hospital Psychiatry* and summarized in the following abstract:

Successful role adoption (making difficult decisions, displaying leadership, dealing with uncertainty, being responsible for patient care) is the primary task of residency, balanced by an increasing stress in maintaining social support systems in family and peer groups. Work factors that accentuate the tension between these two aspects create the most stress. The degree to which role adoption is accomplished, the stress imposed, and coping strategies employed differed significantly with gender, specialty, and program type.

There were important differences between men and women; women had a greater expectation that the program would provide social support; when lacking, it was more of a stressor for women that increased with time, including when program demands prevented them from fulfilling obligations to family and significant others. Women also reported more stress from being on call and irregular hours. Although stress is lower to begin with in men, they also reported an increase in these stresses as training progressed. Men were more comfortable assuming control

—

in emergency situations and less troubled dealing with patients who doubted them as doctors.

Surgical residents reported less stress dealing with complex problems, unexpected emergencies, irregular hours, and being on call. They also expressed less belief in social support systems and more belief that hard work is part of training. Trainees in affiliated rather than medical school programs adapted more readily to the physician role, reported less stress in coping, and were less inclined to believe their education was the program's responsibility.

As academics age, "publish or perish" pressures modify both output and content. There is a diminution in creative and original research; the great English physician, Sir William Osler, noted the "comparative uselessness of men above forty years of age." But there is often a compensatory increase in reviews, book chapters, and editorials. Perhaps even books, although that effort is usually lacking any financial rewards. In my case, the topics reflected a continuing interest in patient compliance, chronic pain management, illness behavior, primary care, and antidepressants.

Nonetheless, a changing environment offered new interests and challenges. Early on, this involved the problems of homelessness and mental illness.

Homelessness

Living on the streets without a roof over one's head is not new in America. It echoes the "boom or bust" cycles in our economy, magnified by a host of secondary influences: the Civil War, the Great Depression, and lesser recessions amplified by fluctuations in low-income housing stock, gaping holes in the federal "safety net" enlarged by changing politics, inadequate community services for people with mental illness or substance abuse, an epidemic of AIDS, unemployed veterans from the latest war, and surges of "not in my backyard" public sentiment.

In 1980, when I moved from Dayton to Milwaukee, homelessness was again on the rise. We were entering a recession, President Reagan was "trimming" the welfare rolls, "gentrification" of the inner city was under way, more Vietnam War veterans were jobless, and outpatient mental health services were squeezed by managed care protocols and health care corporations with the mantra, "No margin, no mission." Nobody deserved what they couldn't afford. If you were homeless, that was not much.

The main purpose in establishing a Milwaukee campus was to enlarge student access to the wide spectrum of urban health care and its problems. Milwaukee already had an enviable reputation for meal sites and shelters serving the homeless backed by local churches or hospitals and staffed by volunteer citizens and professionals. Soon after I joined the campus, I volunteered as the first psychiatrist at Saint Ben's Health Care Clinic and meal site, a short walk from my office at Mount Sinai Hospital in downtown Milwaukee. I became familiar with the problems of homelessness at a time when Congress had turned its back on the problem while a series of studies by the Institute of Medicine and others were reporting the reciprocal relationship between physical disease, mental illness, AIDS, poverty, and homelessness.

Alerted by these reports, in 1983 the Robert Wood Johnson and Pew Foundations funded a four-year demonstration project on homelessness to be implemented in nineteen cities selected from the fifty-one largest urban areas in America. The project was administered by a National Advisory Committee which included five city mayors, chaired by Henry Maier, mayor of Milwaukee. In 1985, twenty-five million dollars were awarded to nineteen of the forty-five cities that submitted applications. Milwaukee was included, and I became involved. The data was collected over a two-year period from 1985 to 1987 and included 63,000 homeless clients seen in seventeen of the cities. (Two were omitted due to incompatible data categories.)

The results of the study provided the first national database on the prevalence and problems associated with homelessness. They were published in a book, *Under the Safety Net* (Norton, 1990), coedited by Philip W. Brickner, et al. I was invited by the editor to coordinate and write the chapter on *Psychiatric and Mental Health Services*. This was a collaborative effort among six contributors representing coworkers,

—

clients, and patients in four cities; Albuquerque, Baltimore, Milwaukee, and San Francisco.

The following are selected quotations from the text of that chapter chosen for lay readers.

Under the Safety Net

One may reasonably expect that at some time or other the conscience of the community will awake and admonish it that the poor man has just as much right to help for his mind . . . The task will then arise for us to adapt our techniques to the new conditions. Possibly we may often be able to achieve something if we combine aid to the mind with material support.

—Sigmund Freud, address to the Fifth International Psychoanalytic Conference, Budapest, 1918

Why are the Mentally Ill Homeless?

Homelessness is multiply determined, contributed to by both socioeconomic and clinical factors. The former includes societal problems such as increasing poverty, reduced availability of low-income housing, and lack of affordable health care that are not unique to the mentally ill but that may affect them as a vulnerable population. Some socioeconomic factors have a more specific impact upon the mentally ill; they include stringent eligibility rules or long waits for disability benefits and neighborhood resistance to group homes. (Not in my back yard; the NIMBY syndrome.)

Particular to the mentally ill have been several effects of deinstitutionalization. Its impact has been debated, but in one state hospital thirty-five percent of patients released became homeless within three months. However, by no means have all the mentally ill among the homeless been institutionalized, and some have had no contact with the mental health system.

—

Widespread closure of mental hospital beds led to a reduction of the hospitals' capacity to provide asylum to the disabled, with both good and bad connotations. At the same time, the provision of adequate community support has been limited by the failure of community mental health centers to attend to the needs of the chronic population, by failure to shift resources from institutions into the community, by failure to develop new support programs, and by absence of attention to linkages between agencies. The need for, but the lack of, community residential facilities has been clearly defined.

From a clinical viewpoint it is possible to see how individuals with psychiatric illnesses might have difficulties obtaining support when both societal and medical resources are inadequate and poorly integrated. As a population they display poor social skills, thinking and judgment clouded by psychosis or substance abuse, behaviors that often appear bizarre, and impulses that may be poorly controlled. Not only do these difficulties diminish the capability to garner scarce resources, but they also invite discrimination and stereotyping.

Finally, the plight of the homeless who are mentally ill has been unwittingly worsened in some states by commitment laws that discourage involuntary treatment until violence is imminent or has occurred. It is easier to arrest those who behave bizarrely than to get them into psychiatric care. Coupled with the lack of mental health services, this has contributed to criminalization of the chronic mentally ill. In Albuquerque, New Mexico, a survey comparing the mentally ill homeless with other homeless individuals found that the mentally ill homeless had more often been in jail (80 vs. 64 percent) or had been the victims of crime (77 vs. 58 percent).

Whatever difficulties mental illness imposes or compounds, its presence is neither a necessary nor a sufficient cause for homelessness. Many homeless persons are not mentally ill, and only a minority of the mentally ill are homeless.

—

The process of becoming homeless involves disconnection from family or friends. Not surprisingly, a common characteristic commented on by those who work with homeless individuals is the problem of alienation or difficulty with affiliation evident in interpersonal relationships and in relationships with social agencies. This problem is contributed to by an overwhelmed social service system which often exposes the homeless to frustrating and dehumanizing experiences, by stigmatization and the social circumstances of homelessness, by psychiatric illness, and perhaps by psychological difficulties based on earlier developmental trauma.

Homeless persons are often easy to identify because of their poverty, the fact they frequently must carry all their possessions with them, and because of the difficulty they face in maintaining personal hygiene as the result of the lack of facilities. This high visibility and this low socioeconomic position isolate them and invite discrimination or stigmatization, manifested by their being banned from public places or simply objectified and ignored by the public and passersby.

Homeless persons are vulnerable to the dangers of crime and victimization. They often express fears of being beaten, attacked, robbed, or raped. This leads them to be careful of whom they talk to or where they stay. In some cities women prefer shelters to hotels because of the crime rate and isolation in the latter. Even in the relatively safe environment of a stable San Francisco shelter, women who have seen each other for months or even years avoid speaking to one another.

Although not peculiar to those who are mentally ill, an inability to affiliate is sometimes a component or product of psychiatric disorders. Psychotic conditions complicate family dynamics in the community, and certain personality types, such as borderline, antisocial, paranoid, or schizoid, occur relatively frequently among the homeless and are characterized by difficulties with attachment. Substance abuse often results in loss of affiliative supports through family rifts and unemployment. In Detroit, seventy percent of those who were homeless on admission to a state hospital had become so at a time of family breakup, rejection, or crisis.

Problems of affiliation among the homeless may have a developmental origin in some cases. One study of the early experiences of homeless men found a high frequency of separation and delinquency during childhood. A case control comparison among women found that those who became homeless had been physically abused eight times more often than housed women (forty-two vs. five percent). Another survey found that eighteen percent of homeless women in Albuquerque had histories of sexual abuse.

Case Examples of Homeless Individuals

Mike H. was referred to the outreach team by a waitress from a coffee shop on the outskirts of the city. When he was first seen, his appearance was rough and dirty, his clothes were disheveled, and he emitted a foul body odor. Mike explained that he had been on the streets for almost twelve years and that he was trapped there by evil spirits and demons that made up the "masonry of the universe." They kept him from leaving the boundaries of a four-block area within which he slept in a sleeping bag on the steps of a local church.

The outreach team visited Mike two or three times weekly, taking food and candy, often buying him coffee. They sat with him on the sidewalk, listening, offering advice, and coaxing him to venture in the van outside his area. On one occasion a team member shared the food Mike had retrieved from a dumpster. Little by little over many months the team members gained his trust; he became more comfortable with them and seemed to look forward to their visits.

—

The team's next step was to obtain Social Security benefits. A field representative met Mike in the coffee shop and completed the paper work. Next the team found a psychiatrist willing to conduct an evaluation outside his office. Attracted by the possibility of obtaining income, Mike agreed, and they met on a downtown street corner within Mike's "safe zone." The psychiatrist confirmed a diagnosis of paranoid schizophrenia. Among other things Mike told him: "I see eyeballs and stuff; heads and eyeballs just hanging there. Spirits tell me the bodies are controlled by computers, just sad soul-destroying things. The bodies are pre-engineered."

As Mike's trust in the team grew, he ventured outside the boundaries of his domain and agreed to accept a community support program as his payee after Social Security was awarded. Once in the program, he agreed to take medication, and he is now stabilized and living in housing. The street outreach team continues to see Mike weekly and finds that he has now made other friends whom he visits regularly.

Bill W. is a 37-year-old white male first contacted by the outreach team during a hot summer when he was living on a park bench because this was "his job." He wore a heavy coat and soiled clothes, was starving and dehydrated. After daily contact with an outreach staff had provided him with food and fluid for six weeks, Bill agreed to be seen at the county medical complex, where he was found to have active tuberculosis involving his spine, an organic confusional state of uncertain etiology, and schizophrenia. When his medical workup was complete, Bill was discharged back to the streets, still confused and psychotic with a complex regimen of antituberculous and antipsychotic medication. On his first night he returned to an emergency room complaining he had suffered a stroke and was admitted to a psychiatric unit. After two weeks Bill was still confused but less psychotic and was discharged into the care of the outreach team to be transported to a shelter. While the team was filling his prescriptions at a pharmacy, he wandered away and was

—

lost for six weeks. During this time he was seen repeatedly in the emergency room but diagnosed as "malingering" and sent away. The emergency room was not aware of his inpatient admission and failed to notify the outreach team of his visits. Finally Bill appeared at the community support program. He was agitated and crawling around the floor. The mental health outreach nurse accompanied him to the mental health center, where he was readmitted. The inpatient staff kept him for a brief stay and was preparing to discharge him again to a shelter when the psychiatrist for the homeless intervened. On the basis of information from the outreach team, the emergency rooms, the psychiatric nurse, and the inpatient unit, the psychiatrist insisted on and obtained placement in a long-term residential facility, where Bill's complex medical and psychiatric condition could be properly care for in a protected environment.

Betty W. is a 38-year-old black woman with chronic paranoid schizophrenia who often traveled between cities in the state, living on the streets and in shelters. Her delusions made her distrustful of even the most dedicated caseworkers and clinicians. One day she collapsed on the library steps with a pulmonary embolus. In intensive care she refused all treatment, accused the staff of being demons injecting her with "ground-up black babies," and was placed in restraints to prevent her from ripping out her intravenous tubes. The psychiatrist working with the homeless knew of her admission and consulted on her care, participating in an emergency guardianship hearing. He recommended the use of intravenous psychotropic medication, along with anticoagulants, and this resulted in the gradual disappearance of Betty's psychotic thinking and delusional system. Before discharge, contact was made by the psychiatrist with her caseworker at the shelter where the psychiatrist also worked. This ensured continued treatment, and the change in mental status and behavior was remarkable to everyone who had previously known Betty on the streets.

Amy P. was 65 years old and had lived at a small women's shelter for nearly a year. She was generally mute and could be found cradling and crouched over a doll she kept with her at all times. She occasionally smiled but refused all attempts of psychiatric or social service intervention. One evening, while she was waiting in line for her bed at the shelter, she fainted and was taken to the General Hospital, where it was found she had a cardiac condition which was easily controlled with medication. During her medical stay she received a psychiatric consultation. With the help of psychiatric medication she agreed to be discharged into a geriatric halfway house and later to a co-op living situation. She continues to carry her doll with her, but she has a home and small community within the mental health residential system, and her quality of life is much improved.

Ron T. is a 22-year-old white male who had been homeless for two years and was his own payee for Social Security disability benefits with a diagnosis of chronic undifferentiated schizophrenia. He first came to the attention of the psychiatric nurse for the homeless when he was seen in the emergency room complaining of a rash and was found to have the worst case of body lice the experienced physician had seen in twenty years. Ron denied psychiatric problems of any kind and claimed to have "plenty of money." He knew that he had Social Security checks but could not remember where. When transferred to a psychiatric unit because he was floridly psychotic, he was found to have fourteen hundred dollars in cash in his pockets. The nurse and psychiatrist for the homeless recommended that Ron be placed in the community support program, which would also assume payeeship for the Social Security benefits. After three weeks' treatment Ron was no longer psychotic. He was accompanied from the hospital by the psychiatric nurse for the homeless, who introduced him to the community support program staff member. They helped Ron collect his Social Security checks from the post office and gave him new clothes, arranged housing at a room-and-board facility, and set up a daily monitoring schedule to supervise his medication and dispense spending money. Several months later Ron is planning to move into an efficiency apartment to cook and care for himself. He believes the medication helps and states, "I was in terrible shape before. I couldn't even find a place to live."

Conclusion and Summary

In the implementation of mental health care for the homeless, a number of innovative programs have evolved to meet the needs of persons hitherto poorly served by traditional psychiatric services.

This system of care deals with a group of patients who often have multiple problems, contributed to by social and economic deprivation, the manifestations of both medical and mental illness, and difficulties in affiliation with other individuals, families, and health care agencies.

A central feature of the care provided is the way in which both personnel and programs attempt to promote attachment to services that are designed for easy access, to be well integrated and attuned to meet the entire hierarchy of human and health care needs. This is accomplished by nurturant, patient, and persistent nonmental health workers who use case management and networking methods. They are supported by mental health professionals who aim to provide on-site availability, in-service education, and linkage to the whole spectrum of specialized psychiatric services. Viewed within a historical and policy perspective, these new programs are part of a reform cycle that is focused on caring and community support rather than prevention of mental illness.

The implementation of this system of care remains far from ideal. Better coordination could occur with correctional services and between mental health and substance abuse providers. Education of both the police and the public should be enhanced. Cooperative relationships with teaching institutions and training programs for different mental health disciplines are in their infancy.

Finally, the relationship of these new health care for the homeless programs with traditional psychiatric services needs to be defined. Ultimately the older established community programs might themselves implement effective mental health care for the homeless but only if they can assimilate and apply the lessons that have been learned.

The RWJ/Pew Demonstration Project had important outcomes; it aroused public interest and concern and stimulated political involvement. Congress passed the Stewart B. McKinney Homeless Assistance Act, which was signed into law by President Reagan in July 1987. In 1987 and 1989, Congress appropriated seventy-five million dollars for health care services and established an Interagency Council on Homelessness that coordinated six federal agencies and the fifteen programs that provided shelter, housing, and other services to the homeless population. McKinney was a moderate Republican elected to the U.S. House in 1970. The act was named after him following his death from the complications of AIDS, the first U.S. congressman to die from the disease.

These events laid the groundwork for my subsequent sabbatical and appointment to NIMH in Washington, D.C., as the staff director to a national advisory committee in support of the Federal Interagency Council.

Inside the NIMH

Published in *Wisconsin Psychiatrist*, Winter 1992:

An academic invited to spend time at the NIMH might well feel like a holy man asked to visit Mecca.

My sabbatical was overdue. Seven years had stretched past ten, and I felt burned out by the warfare of urban psychiatry. Our new residency training program had just become fully accredited. My experience working among homeless people had made me a candidate for the position of Staff Director to an about-to-be-appointed federal Interagency Task Force on Homelessness and Severe Mental Illness. Not surprisingly, when invited to fill this position, I said yes. In October 1990 I began to commute twice weekly to Washington, D.C., while the bureaucracy ironed out details of an Interagency Personnel Agreement (IPA) which allows the federal government to hire talent at prices above what they can normally afford (the sponsoring university pays the balance). In December I moved to the capital to begin a planned eighteen-month stint while my wife and twelve-year-old son remained behind in Milwaukee.

The political impetus to form a Task Force arose out of a report to Congress on the effects of deinstitutionalization and concerns raised in the House of Representatives. These forces coalesced in May 1990. The decision to focus on severe mental illness rather than on homelessness in general probably resulted from a covert coalition between a right wing desire to clean up the streets and a left wing concern to care for the most seriously disadvantaged. The creation of a task force by Secretaries Sullivan (HHS) and Kemp (HUD) took the initiative away from the Congress and placed it politically (and more safely) within the executive branch of government.

Representation on the Task Force mirrored that of the existing Interagency Council on Homelessness (part of the McKinney legislation in 1987) and reflected a well-recognized need for coordination between HUD, HCFA, SSA, the Department of Labor, the White House, the Veterans Administration, and NIMH.

Who should chair such a task force was less clear. The decision that this be the director of NIMH was in conflict with the HUD opinion that homelessness was primarily a housing problem and the fact that their representative to

—

the Task Force was an assistant secretary who outranked the director of NIMH in the federal hierarchy.

This tension laid the basis for a contentious first meeting with open confrontation that was resolved when the then director of NIMH quit his position a week later to return to his home university. The Deputy Director who replaced him was a career bureaucrat, eager to become the first psychologist to head NIMH, who went to great lengths to avoid conflict and sought consensus among the more powerful members of the Task Force.

However laudable the intention and composition of this Task Force, its purpose was hampered from the start by major political constraints. Its charter required the appointment of a national advisory committee. There was lengthy rumination about how to select sixteen individuals who could represent every form of expertise and also reflect ethnic, geographic, and gender diversity.

More arduous still was the problem of how to keep the balance of power in federal hands so as to protect against intemperate advocacy interests and potential minority reports. The appointment process proved to be so protracted that the problem solved itself. It took six months for the process to be completed during which time the federal representatives had met frequently enough to determine direction. This left less than nine months for the advisory committee to respond and for a final report to be written.

It was during this interval, prior to the appointment of the advisory committee, that I served as Staff Director while the Task Force attempted to define the scope of the problem and the appropriate issues to address. I was located at the NIMH in the Office of Programs on Homelessness and Severe Mental Illness, one of two programs directly attached to the Director's office (the other is AIDS).

The NIMH is in Maryland, northwest of Washington, outside the District but inside the beltway. It is housed in a vast white glass and steel rectangular building. Its functional and minimalist architecture conceals endless windowless corridors opening onto crowded cubicles. Parking is hopelessly inadequate. Newcomers must car pool or scramble for lots adjacent to local shops. I was lucky to find space behind a nearby Chinese laundry at fifty dollars a month.

That was the *good* news; the bad news was that I had no office, telephone, or secretary. For three months I squatted in temporary space, moving from one location to another. After two months a telephone line was installed. Its number, 0000, seemed symbolic—I was beginning to feel like the biggest zero at the Institute.

Meanwhile, we worked our way through several temporary secretaries with semiliterate skills. This threadbare infrastructure and support system is reflective both of inadequate federal salary scales and an administration preoccupied with outside political appearances but neglectful of morale and organizational issues under its roof. Looking good is an obsession. What another agency, a senator, or congressman *might think* is preemptive. All of it supported by bureaucratic procedures of Byzantine dimensions and an organizational style characterized by malignant compulsivity.

All outside correspondence from significant sources becomes "controlled," passing through weeks of review while answers are sanitized. The smallest matters are repeatedly scrutinized; plans are made and remade, doing and undoing in a search for safe perfection. The interaction between this political paranoia, bureaucratic system, and inadequate infrastructure is stultifying.

One of my tasks as Staff Director was to prepare speaking points and minutes for meetings. A memo that had taken my temporary secretary an hour to type was returned with dozens of picayune corrections. Frustrated, I protested the need to distinguish style from substance. "The trouble," I was told, "is that you write like an Englishman."

Another of my tasks was to develop background papers on significant issues relevant to homelessness and severe mental illness. One of the areas identified was legal and civil rights, obviously a sensitive and politically charged topic involving state commitment laws. At first we planned a conference with experts inside and outside NIMH. Concerned about controversy, we canceled it. Next we searched for an outside expert who could be relied upon not to upset the various advocacy groups. Nobody seemed safe so I undertook a discrete telephone survey of alleged experts most of whom didn't want to commit themselves by telephone on complicated and contentious topics. Finally, frustrated, I wrote a position paper on my own. Nobody commented.

This seemed a signal to me of futility and I decided to return to Milwaukee where I felt more needed and useful. My departure less than halfway through the projected sabbatical coincided with the first meeting between the Task Force and the Advisory Committee. Its report is due to be issued early in 1992. I await it with interest. Buried in the mandate is a massive paradox of major political proportions; how to address the needs of a vulnerable minority without tackling the prohibitively expensive social and political issues that affect the entire homeless population.

This current cycle of homelessness is the third in our history: the first following the Civil War, the next during the Great Depression, and ours beginning with the Reagan Administration. Social programs simply cannot be funded forever out of "growth." Recession, a tax-mean public, the frenzied feeding of special interest groups, a federal-state shell game, an inefficient bureaucracy, and lack of political leadership are all a part of the problem. I am skeptical of

—

the extent to which they will be addressed in the year of a presidential election.

Finally, I discovered that outsiders do not fare well at an elite organization preoccupied with its institutional narcissism. In the first six months I was at the NIMH, I received not a single social invitation to share lunch or dinner or to enter someone else's home. Coupled with the fact that I was separated from family and living alone, the social isolation was devastating.

Toward the end of my stay, when my distress was obvious and my loyalty was in question, kindred spirits began to make cautious overtures, eager to share their own frustrations. Over lunches out of the building I learned more about why the NIMH is not a happy place. In years past, people remembered an intellectual Camelot with freedom of inquiry and open debate. The Institute was concerned not only with research but with education and service. In recent times, the leadership had emphasized research but interest in education has virtually vanished. Service is equated with research demonstration projects. This agenda has been associated with a loss of any sense of autonomy and freedom of inquiry. Raising funds, competing for budgets, and designing research projects are preemptive. The national oversight function of service and education has become a sinecure, submerged by the philosophy of the new federalism. Those who remain and remember the old days are often trapped in civil service straitjackets, waiting for retirement or hoping for a change in administration.

I was fortunate to be able to escape but am left wondering to what extent I was undone by my own naiveté and narcissism. Tact and diplomacy were never my long suit. For me the underdog comes before the organization. First Amendment rights mean more to me than the government they protect us from. With hindsight, perhaps an accurate job description or an honest interview could have deterred me from making this trip to Mecca. Yet there are good things to remember—the

—

friends I did make (mostly the "little people" and those from the less "powerful" agencies), an insider's look at government, and a respite from the health care holocaust.

Two months after I returned to Milwaukee, the mail brought an impressive document. It was the "Administrator's Award for Meritorious Achievement" signed by the director of NIMH and the administrator of ADAMHA. A band-aid for my wounded narcissism? A bid to buy my silence? Or just a nice touch? Who will ever know? But perhaps a friend summed it up best when she noted, "Experience is what you get when you don't get what you want."

AIDS

Published in *Psychiatric Times*, February 1986:

An immigrant
it came an alien
without a name
creeping in at the
coasts like other cultural
quirks.
Cerebrus with different
heads it changed its faces
while it spread.
In the East
it was *Kaposis sarcoma*
on the West
it was *Pneumocystis carini*
purple skin blebs
on the outside
white webs of lung
fungus on the inside
opportunistic
organisms
that borrowed the
body.

Not much was known
when it was named
*Acquired Immune
Deficiency Syndrome*
Acquired from whom?
Whatever it was
it wasn't emancipated
liberated or even
affirmative.
Only gay men were
picked.

But then
the phallus is a great
inoculator.
Men are the spreaders
inserters, intruders
of the venereal world.
Women are the vessels,
lesbians give each other
nothing (unless it's love.)

The lepers of Sodom
suffered slowly
eroded by organisms
their life style invited.
Cryptococcus, hepatitis
mononucleosis,
amebiasis, herpes,
toxoplasmosis
    wasting flesh
    burning fevers
    bloody stools
    strangled breath
behind barriers
behind masks
beyond antibiotics
    staying alive was awful;
    None did.

Scientists scurried
to find a cause
scraping frugal support
from a penny pinching
President Reagan
whose moral majority
had read Revelations
and knew Apocalypse

when they saw it.
Soon scientists
discovered gays with
Aids differed from
those without.
More partners and
poppers, more
rimming and fisting,
more trips to bath
houses.
Evangelists and
epidemiologists
agreed;
promiscuous sex was a
risk factor.
What you reap depends
on how you sow the seed.
The vagina is a paved
passage to the ovum
but the rectum
is an absorbent entry
of fragile mucosa, an
orifice where doctors
put drugs
or force feed prisoners;
a portal where semen
might seep into the flow of
blood.

Something new was
about.
Oscar Wilde, Plato,
Michelangelo
were all immune.
Now something
invisible suppressed
the T4 cells which
assist B lymphocytes,
quell infection.
Virologists,
immunologists
venereologists
quibbled,
vying in a quest
to find the cause.

was it
    the poppers that
    open sphincters
    and prolong
    orgasm?
was it
    something like
    a male tampon
    leaking toxic
    pathogens?
was it
    a mutant virus
    embracing the
    double helix like
    mistletoe on oak?
was it
    an animal disease
    that skipped
    the biologic fence
    to man?

was it
   antigenic overload
   induced by all the
   other organisms?
it was
   the epidemiologists
   living like Fellini
   characters in gay
   bars and bath
   houses who ferreted
   out the cause.
The clue was the cases
that came in clusters
linked by a Typhoid
Mary,
spreading the disease in
silence in the baths;
in the dark
no one saw his spots.
One lonely traveling
salesman fucked
two hundred and fifty
fellow gays each year
in the several years
before he sickened.
So in the end
promiscuity was a
statistical artifact.
True, viruses do
prosper at parties
but a single stoic
who goes to work
can give the common
cold to a factory

full of friends.
All it takes is
one bad hit.

The people from Haiti
fetched migrant hopes
and non-naturalized
germs by boat.
In Miami the germs
multiplied.
Abetted by Aids
Toxoplasmosis gondii
grasped an opportunity
of getting to the brain.
Officials found names
for conditions buried
nameless or unknown
back home in Haiti.
Disease and
discrimination
spread together.
Blacks with French
accents became tame
targets for interpreters
muffled behind masks.
Trapped between
new home prejudice
and old home
persecution
sexual preference
was hardly a subject
for honest talk.

Nobody was going
to say they were gay.

Instead blame rested
on ritual or voodoo.
The inquisitors saw
reality refracted like an
object underwater.
In Haiti gay is taboo
but married men
called massisi
do rent their bodies
to the tourist trade.
Fighting poverty
they protect their wives
from pregnancy
by anal intercourse
infecting them instead.
In Haiti Aids
spread to women.

Next it was needles
proving there was
a front door
to the body.
Addicts in shooting
galleries shared
syringes,
poking dull pricks
into thick veins,
breaking immune
defenses until a time
came when the
blameless were afflicted.
Hemophilia is a disease
of men who bleed
spread by women
on an X chromosome

that penetrates male
soma only when
coupled to an
impotent Y.
To stay alive
for twenty extra years
each bleeder needs
an annual clotting
factor contribution
of two hundred
thousand donors.
Blood banks were not
insured against addicts
or infected gays
who sold their plasma
for quick cash
to buy another hit
or fix.
The national blood
supply became a
tainted well;
a woman with a
hysterectomy,
a man with heart
surgery, a baby with
jaundice were
transfused to death.

Now a ninety-year-old
nun and an impeccable
grandma began a new
category.
"No known risk
factor" appeared.
It spread fear

faster than a virus.
Not that the virus
was slow growing.
Sponsored by an
open society it saw
its openings.
Gays with Aids
loved bisexuals,
Bis with Aids
loved heterosexuals,
Bis and straights
loved their wives,
wives with Aids gave
birth to babies.
Babies were loved by
uncles who were
junkies
aunts who were street
walkers
mothers who were
easy lays.
The virus multiplied
in a culture medium
of nutrient juices
a slum gullion
of sweat, saliva,
blood, semen
and colostrum
freely shared;
stirred and fermented
by love.

Hysteria and science
illness and morals
co-mingled.
It was costly to linger.
One hundred grand
a month or more

for intensive care
that nobody paid.
Insurance companies
said Aids
was self inflicted
(or had pre-existed)
Government agencies
said Aids
was not a research
priority
(nor even a Medicaid
category)
Inside intensive care
gays and junkies
lasted long enough
to go bankrupt.
Outside intensive care
landlords evicted
tenants, teachers
excluded kids,
preachers preached
damnation,
gays screeched
genocide;
then all at once
intensive care came
cheap;
the innocent were
infected.

It took four years
to trap and microscope
to letter and number
the virus
HLT/III.
People said
better knowing than
not,

better truth than hope,
better but
it was a sneaky virus
lurking inside the cell
stalking an unsure host
leaving spoor in the
blood that could be
spotted years before
it broke cover.
People said
better knowing than
not,
better truth than hope,
better but
an arrow or a bullet
are quicker than
a slow snare
or waiting wounded.
   Instead
people said
better hope than truth,
better not than
knowing
if tests suggest
you have pre-Aids
or maybe Aids
or maybe not.

Soon the world was
infected spread from
the hot hub of Africa
by French speaking
connections from
the old Congo to Haiti,
from Haiti to
New York when

Papa Doc died
and Port au Prince
became a paradise
for gays.
Some said it was
a mutant monkey virus
evolved to man;
a second genesis
divine revenge
for the slave trade.
Inside America
Aids spread to every
State became federal
and fully emancipated.
The numbers are now
fifteen thousand
give or take a few.

Everyone is waiting
for a vaccine
in a foot race
between virus and
science.
Everyone is waiting,
practicing virus control
by chastity and
monogamy.
Everyone is waiting
redefining old values
and discriminating.

Barry Blackwell,
February 1986

Wearing a White Coat

Published in *General Hospital Psychiatry*, 1993:

The white coat is an emblem of medical authority. Wearing a white coat poses special questions for psychiatrists, particularly those of us who work in consultation-liaison and hospital settings.

I first became aware of the ambivalence attached to this article of clothing thirty years ago at the Institute of Psychiatry in London. As a new resident in psychiatry without either a Ph.D. or board certification in internal medicine I was relegated to the "B" stream at the rural Bethlem Hospital. Out in the country everyone was comfortable wearing street clothes. But later, when I was promoted to the "A" stream at the Maudsley Hospital in town, I joined Professor Sir Aubrey Lewis' team and was expected to wear a white coat. This seemed to be a symbol of academic rigor not merited by lesser mortals.

After I migrated to America I was recruited by Maurice Levine to become the token psychopharmacologist in Cincinnati's psychoanalytic stronghold. Nobody, not even I, wore a white coat. White coats seemed to hang better on the European disciples of Kraepelin and Greisinger than on the American followers of Freud and Jung. Of course, all this was historical and subject to change. At some point Freud, the neurologist, discarded his white coat to become the less formally attired psychotherapist. I don't know whether or not George Engel (an internist and an analyst), who ran the psychosomatic unit in the 1940s that I inherited in the 1970s, wore a white coat.

Psychiatrists between these times invested themselves in demedicalizing our discipline. The internship had been temporarily abolished but, astonishingly, I witnessed anthropologist Margaret Mead (as a visiting professor in Cincinnati) castigate Maurice Levine for allowing psychiatric residents to ignore medical history-taking. This was hard on a man who had written the seminal text, *Psychotherapy in Medical Practice*. On his deathbed with terminal leukemia, Maury wrote me one of his famous memos promising that when he recovered we would chair together an exciting new conference integrating psychodynamic with biological approaches. Maury died and I left. His ardent disciples preserved the status quo and it was some time before the first white coat appeared in that department.

Over the next decade, I served as an administrator and occasional teacher; the only white coat I wore was as a visiting professor at the Cleveland Clinic. My hosts presented me with a well-starched, full-length coat, embroidered with my name as a memento. It still hangs in my hall closet, gathering dust.

So much for the past. Now psychiatry is hell-bent on remedicalizing. White coats are on the rise. Axis III notwithstanding, we psychiatrists have our very own organic disorders, not just syndromes (and ICD 9, the medical classification, be damned).

As for myself, I am again heading a consultation service with a multidisciplinary team staffed by an internal medicine resident, psychiatry resident, psychology intern, and psychology faculty member. Shortly after a change in rotation, I noticed that our new psychiatry resident was wearing a white coat. One of the first consultations she tackled involved an irascible older woman who was refusing to cooperate with the medical and nursing staff. The resident had made a credible attempt to obtain a detailed psychiatric history but had been rebuffed. The team wondered if the white coat and her traditional attempt to be "physicianly" had colluded in the patient's rejection of what she perceived as one more attempt at authoritarian control.

The team talked about the white coat as a sartorial Rorschach test, eliciting positive and negative transferences. In a recent editorial, Feinstein reminds us about "white coat hypertension"

—

345

and the fact that the presence of a correctly attired physician is a strong inducement to temporary treatment compliance, just as visiting the dentist elicits a "toothbrush effect."

The psychiatry resident, who had completed a year of internal medicine, felt that the white coat was a valuable transitional object between disciplines. She had already performed her own personal research using an ABA design (coat on, coat off, coat on). An intubated patient in the ICU had refused to respond to her without the coat but did so the next day when she wore it. The resident noted a similar response from staff, who seemed more willing to spontaneously share information if she was in uniform rather than out of it. At morning report she felt better accepted as a team member and more likely to get a referral. Pharmaceutical representatives were generous with samples when confronted with a white coat and even waived the need for her signature.

Perhaps because our resident was female, she also noted that her white coat kept her warm, protected her clothes from hospital debris, and had pockets that held objects for which she might otherwise need a handbag.

Next, I quizzed the medical resident. He always came to rounds fully attired, regarding his white coat as an "important piece of equipment," though he took a flexible approach. He recalled working with a demented and confused elderly patient and deliberately removing his white coat so as to blend in with the family who were attempting to calm their relative's irrational fear of hospital staff. On a pediatric rotation he had worn a white coat emblazoned with a Mickey Mouse.

Lastly, our psychology colleagues reported no desire to wear a medical uniform (although many would like to admit patients and some wish to prescribe). They agreed with the need for a professional demeanor—psychology has outlived its 60s flirtation with love beads and long hair. But a white coat was an unwelcome mantle of authority that could induce reaction, dampen dialogue, stifle autonomy, and discourage mutuality. In dyadic communication, white coats induce white noise.

The team's conclusion was that white coats are not for everybody or for all occasions. Who wears one is determined by personal history as well as by present circumstance. I cast off my white coat long ago. To wear one now would feel like false advertising—a promise to the patient of physicianly skills I may no longer possess.

So my advice to the residents who work on our consultation service about whether to wear a white coat or not is simple: "If it feels right, if the coat fits, wear it."

My Conversion Experience

When I returned from my spell at NIMH and my aborted sabbatical in 1991, my career in Milwaukee was already past the midpoint (1980-1998). I was in bad shape psychologically, almost certainly depressed, distressed about my marriage and the nine months apart from Kathie and Adam. It was a time of spiritual crisis. On my bookshelf was a leather bound edition of William James's classic book, *Varieties of Religious Experience*. Based on lectures James gave at Edinburgh in Scotland in 1901 and 1902, this Harvard professor of medicine and psychology spoke and wrote about how individuals, facing what seemed an insurmountable conflict might "find and maintain happiness" in religion. The book has been reprinted thirty-six times and remains in print after over a century. In it, James elaborates on the "conversion experience" and its common expression in all the world's religions. Unknown and unread by me at the time, instinct guided me in the right direction.

Soon after my return, I made a pilgrimage to the magnificent church (now a basilica) at Holy Hill, a few miles north of Milwaukee. It stands, high on a hill, overlooking the surrounding forest, a place to which people flock in fall to admire the changing colors. But now it was November, with frost on the ground and a deep chill in the air. I took with me a loaf of bread, water, a Bible, and writing materials. Alone in a small room, in an empty retreat house below the church, I stayed for two days and nights reading, meditating, and praying.

For several days, since writing this, I have felt unable, or unwilling, to say more about that experience. But it was profound and life-changing, influencing my beliefs and behaviors for the next fifteen years, initiating a spiritual quest described in "Piece 18: Spiritual Pilgrimage." This reluctance may well be due to knowing the eventual outcome of the search and questioning the authenticity of my conversion experience. As James remarks, "Conversion can wane, but so can love." Leaving the reader with that enigma, we can return to events of the next eight years, leading to my retirement in 1998.

Conversion had immediate practical consequences. I began a dialogue with Father Tom, the priest at Kathie's church, which led to becoming a member of the parish, filing for an annulment from my former marriage, and, eventually, wedding Kathie in a Catholic ceremony. (See "Piece 21: Marriage.")

Archdiocese Affairs

This also led to a wider involvement in the affairs of the archdiocese. The archaic procedure of annulment familiarized me with canon law and the local tribunal that administered it through lawyer-priests. After my own annulment was approved by Rome, I was invited to become a consultant to the Tribunal in Milwaukee concerning the emotional validity of an applicant's claim their marriage was "nonsacramental" and therefore eligible for annulment. This required me to review and comment on each spouse's deposition and those of witnesses, but without face-to-face contact—a troubling omission I dealt with by clearly identifying its limitations in my reports.

The only serious problem that occurred was when a disgruntled and very narcissistic physician, with powerful contacts in Rome, threatened my life after the tribunal rejected his annulment. I was shown his photograph and advised to avoid contact!

—

My work with the tribunal led to an appointment as member of a mental health advisory committee chaired by the auxiliary bishop which determined, monitored, and authorized psychiatric treatment for the victims of sexual abuse by clergy.

This took place in the early days before the full national scope and size of the problem became clear. It was also before our liberal archbishop was "outed" by a former adult gay lover seeking to extort hush money and at a time when the auxiliary bishop was accused in legal proceedings of keeping a secret coded diary of sexual allegations against clergy that he declined to reveal.

I liked and respected both of these men and, to a limited degree, interacted with them socially. The auxiliary bishop involved me in two projects of a somewhat sensitive nature. The convicted serial and cannibalistic killer, Jeffrey Dahmer, underwent a religious conversion in prison and was baptized prior to his own murder by a fellow inmate. Until his death, he was visited by and corresponded with a Catholic nun. I was asked to review these letters and offer an opinion on whether they should be archived or destroyed. The content was extraordinarily mundane, devoid of any forensic or psychiatric interest, and my advice was to destroy them.

The second assignment was to conduct an on-site review of a lay youth minister employed by a suburban parish that had a strong charismatic element in its church membership. This man planned an overnight retreat for the youth and acquiesced to their request to include a charismatic prayer service to involve "speaking in tongues and being slain in the spirit." He did this without seeking approval of the parents or the priest. One of the young women, in psychiatric treatment for an eating disorder, became hysterical during the ritual and demanded to return home. During the drive back, she insisted on stopping at the priest's residence to make a confession in the early hours of the morning, after which the youth minister dropped her off at home—to be greeted by upset and angry parents, one of whom was a prominent fund raiser for the archdiocese. I was asked to provide a written report with recommendations for disciplinary action. I did so, including suggestions for clarification of the church's regulations and oversight of charismatic prayer in youthful and vulnerable individuals. I never heard the outcome.

This work was "pro bono" but the auxiliary bishop presented me with two beautiful volumes of *Aboriginal Australian Art*. He struck me and others as being a deeply spiritual person; someone in whose presence one automatically felt calm and at ease.

Both the bishop and archbishop are retired, their careers sadly tainted by the sexual scandal and its fallout. Each had been a strong candidate for preferment within the hierarchy earlier, during Vatican II, but had fallen out of favor with an increasingly conservative magisterium. Their careers, like my own, were shaped to a degree by social change beyond anticipation.

Community Affairs

As my time in Milwaukee proceeded, I also became more involved in community activities. Academics, like business leaders, are targets for invitations to join not-for-profit boards in their areas of interest or expertise. Deans and vice chancellors expect this pro bono activity as one way of raising the visibility and influence of their domain. Apart from the Bhore Foundation (See *Jay Bhore* in Piece 3: India), I became involved in two such boards, both related to mental health services and both of which I ended up chairing.

The first was Health Care for the Homeless, a 501(c)3 organization responsible for the distribution and oversight of state, federal, and foundation support for meal sites, shelters, and case management services. Not-for-profit boards experience difficulties intrinsic to their structure and mission. Often there is tension between a full-time salaried executive director and a board expected to provide advice and direction without undue interference in day-to-day operations. This is a balancing act with boundaries that not everyone is equipped to manage. As chair of the board, I experienced this tension in two ways. The executive director expected annual increases in pay but had never been subjected to a proper performance evaluation. She independently obtained a consulting firm's opinion, based on national statistical norms, that she deserved a large annual increase. At the same time, she passively but persistently obstructed attempts to implement an objective review of her performance.

Secondly, this kind of impasse can have an adverse influence on board members. Some feel compelled to take sides, and others question why they should spend time in a hostile environment they are not paid to put up with. In my instance, both outcomes were in play: some members voted with their feet, stayed home, or declined to do the subcommittee work needed to gather data, while others took sides. It was not an atmosphere I was willing to tolerate or had the patience and political skills to resolve. Eventually I quit, and the executive director got her raise.

The other not-for-profit organization was entirely new and innovative. In the 1960s, state mental hospitals were emptying out onto the streets and discharged patients were becoming homeless or repeatedly readmitted due to absence of community resources. A group of patients in New York banded together and found funding to pay for a building where they organized themselves into a self-supporting daytime community and named it the Fountain House. A major objective was to help each other find part or full-time work. The idea caught on and spread literally around the country and then the globe in major metropolitan communities, funded from philanthropic sources and state funds.

Eventually the idea found its way to Milwaukee and was adopted by a coalition of not-for-profit agencies already engaged in mental health advocacy and support. They found a suitable building downtown and recruited an energetic and passionate social worker (with a doctoral degree) as executive director. The Mental Health Association (MHA) assumed a leadership role; a brand-new Fountain House was formed and named the Grand Avenue Club (GAC).

I became a founding member of the charter GAC board and then its chair. The main purpose was twofold: first to create a "work ordered day" with skills training, and then to seek and obtain local businesses

—

willing to hire people with mental illness and pay them a living wage in return for a guarantee that individuals would be supported by GAC and replaced if unable to work. The whole enterprise was managed, to the extent possible, by the members themselves, supported by volunteers and a small paid staff.

The board was made up of members with mental illness sitting alongside community and business leaders. It was congenial, energetic, and fully cooperative with the executive director who had excellent administrative and leadership skills.

The first difficulty that occurred was significant but hard to resolve. The lead organization (MHA) was accustomed to professional leadership and retaining top-down control in a manner inconsistent with the GAC model of self-sufficiency and empowerment. This was both a fiscal issue over ownership and control of space but, more fundamentally, a philosophical and psychological difference about the capacity of people with mental illness to manage and govern their own affairs.

These differences quickly became divisive and acrimonious, threatening the alliance of mental health not-for-profits. Outside consultants were recruited to mediate the dispute and set up a series of negotiating sessions in which I played a key role on behalf of autonomy for the GAC and severance of ties with the MHA. This view eventually prevailed and the GAC has become, under the leadership of the original executive director, one of the largest and most vibrant and successful Fountain House communities in America (perhaps worldwide).

After some years, GAC moved to one of the most architecturally admired buildings downtown with more space and amenities. Each year the club hosts an annual awards program to honor the corporations and business organizations that provide employment to members. Perhaps its most valuable but subtle contribution is a decline in the stigma of mental illness and the public attitudes that create a barrier to productive employment.

Travel and Teaching

Another enjoyable and rewarding aspect of academic life is the ability to travel and teach. During the years in Milwaukee, these two "perks" came together in a novel way. As medicine and psychiatry became more complex, licensing boards began to require physicians to stay up-to-date with annual quotas for continuing medical education (CME). This spawned a new industry; it did not take Yankee ingenuity long to realize that an educational tax deduction could be creatively coupled with a vacation. All that was required was an academic teacher with a repertoire of daily lectures willing to trade them for a free vacation, spouse included.

This was how Kathie and I came to visit Egypt, Russia, Australia, and New Zealand, places we might otherwise never have seen. A bonus was meeting colleagues from around the country and visiting psychiatric facilities in other nations. We saw an open-air unit in Australia for psychotic aboriginal patients unused to living inside buildings and a Russian institution at a time the Soviets were accused of placing dissidents into mental hospitals. We were in Russia when Chernobyl blew up and had to be Geiger-counted on our return. In Egypt, we slept within sight of the pyramids, and in New Zealand, I ate sheep's kidneys for breakfast, something I learned to love when meat was rationed in World War II. (Kathie abstained!)

For more about domestic travel, see "Piece 28: Travel."

End Games

Back in the office during the early to mid-1990s the economic and political situation continued to deteriorate. Public and professional outrage toward managed care had escalated. People were enraged that access to specialists was blocked by "gatekeepers" or needed "prior authorization." Worse still, it might be a "preexisting condition," in which case you were on your own, perhaps facing bankruptcy.

—

Psychiatrists bemoaned their role as "pill-pushers" and the loss of income and increased patient load they faced when condemned to "fifteen-minute med-checks." Patients wanted to talk, but psychiatrists were not paid to listen, and psychotherapy was outsourced to less expensive providers (social workers or psychologists). The temperature was raised when the leadership of the American Psychiatric Association weighed in, became vociferous, and condemned colleagues who were benevolent toward the new trends.

I was numbered among these renegades, having made my opinions known in public debates and editorials or opinion pieces in our state newsletter (the *Wisconsin Psychiatrist*). While I disliked or disapproved of many of the tactics and strategies adopted by managed care, my support was based on philosophical and pragmatic principles.

My core belief, based in part on my experience as a young psychiatrist and family doctor in England, is that health care is a basic human necessity that must be provided by the government because it cannot be equitably or cost-effectively managed by market forces or commercial competition. The reason is simple: nobody wants to die, so everybody wants the best available medical care, irrespective of cost. This is true even if you believe in heaven and hope to go there. Even so, nobody is in a hurry.

Health care is not like clothes or a car where people settle for what they can afford: a suit or blue jeans, a Ford or a Lexus. We know this is true because the largest share of Medicare is spent on the last six months of life, usually to no avail. Nobody buys a BMW on their deathbed. But bankruptcy due to terminal illness is increasing.

At a pragmatic level, affordable care for everybody means nobody can have everything; rationing and choice, guided by "best practices," are inevitable. Again, the facts are certain: in America's unregulated marketplace, we spend more of our GDP on health care for worse results than any other civilized nation. This is not because the rest of the world is "socialist" but because they are fair-minded and cost-conscious.

The cynical political claim that "we have the best care in the world" is true only for the millionaires who can afford it or for people who believe that an early death is a just penalty for poverty.

Believing these things, I set about doing my best to gather data on the issues and educate others by my writings. With our chief psychologist, we studied the impact of case review on the quantity of care provided (does rationing reduce care? It didn't) and published the results in the *American Journal of Psychiatry*. With my vice chairman, we published an article on "The Educational Implications of Managed Mental Health Care," published in *Hospital and Community Psychiatry*.

In the *Wisconsin Psychiatrist*, I gave vent to opinions as well as data in several articles and editorials. (See the following bits.) These efforts brought more blame than praise. At professional meetings, I began to hear hints of ethical concerns, at first personal, later directed to creating a "code of ethics" for psychiatrists working in managed care. I responded to this with the editorial on *Personal and Situational Ethics*. In the end, nothing changed.

These educational and research efforts coincided with the waning stages of my career. In 1994, I stepped down as chair, handed the department over to my vice chair but remained on the faculty for another two years, bolstering my practice income by working as a consultant to Blue Cross and Blue Shield.

Once it became clear that the fate of the academic program was sealed and that closure was economically and politically inevitable, I resigned and accepted a position as medical director of a small managed care company in Milwaukee for the same salary I earned as a department chair. There I tried to practice what I preached as a fair-minded adjudicator of the quantity and quality of care provide to the patients by my colleagues.

I did this for two years without having to face a lynch mob, before taking down my shingle in 1998 at age sixty-four.

—

Managed Care Is Here to Stay—Let's Deal Constructively with It

Published in *Wisconsin Psychiatrist*, Summer 1996:

It is difficult to see how our profession's "credibility and dignity" are enhanced by the demagoguery and demonization of managed care that have gripped our new leadership (*Psychiatric News*, June 7, 1996). Now that National Health Insurance is moribund, managed care is the political reality we must deal with. It is not a cast-in-concrete monolith but an evolving concept that has progressed beyond its early errors which included limitations to access, rationing by inconvenience, and insufficient attention to quality.

Consider the following statements which can fairly be made about contemporary managed care:

- Managed care is responsible for containing health care costs after decades of inflation brought about by unbridled subspecialization, including interminable psychotherapy. Both the employers and the government are delighted with this restraint. Equally pleased are many taxpayers (like those in Oregon) who are tired of subsidizing rising entitlements.
- Managed care has developed ways of defining levels of care and medical necessity for treatment which have provided much needed objectivity that the Federal Diagnosis Related Groups (DRG) system was unable to offer our specialty.
- Managed care has encouraged ways to integrate the continuum of care so as to offer people the least restrictive, most economical level of care. This stretches limited (often "mandated") benefits further.
- All of the above have almost eliminated the excesses of the for-profit private hospitals which led to corruption, criminal lawsuits against providers, and public denigration of our profession.

- Managed care provides the tools most likely to make a reality of insurance parity between medical and mental illnesses.
- Managed care organizations are now credentialed, accredited, and held accountable in ways that the private practice of outpatient psychiatry has never offered or experienced.

Our APA leadership's attack on managed care is coupled with implications that our specialty is aloof to entrepreneurship or economic self-interest and is speaking unselfishly on behalf of the impoverished and downtrodden.

Consider the following statements that can fairly be made about our profession:

- Most psychiatrists are in the top ten percent of the social strata which is growing richer while the poor get poorer.
- Psychiatrists bill 15 times the minimum wage for a 15-minute med check.
- Only a minority of psychiatrists are willing to treat Medicaid patients.
- Compared to the general public, psychiatrists have been almost immune from downsizing and "re-engineering."
- Most psychiatrists drive expensive cars, take overseas vacations, eat out often, and live in wealthy neighborhoods.

So why have we, the APA membership, elected this leadership and why do we applaud it so vociferously?

Just as race horses are bred for speed, physicians are bred to be in control. Remember the internship, the ER and the ICU with their role reinforcement for autonomous decision-making in ambiguous life-threatening situations? But physicians lost

—

357

control of health care because they were unable or unwilling to control costs.

It does not take a rocket scientist (or psychoanalyst) to speculate that the ire and angst beneath our leadership's rhetoric and hyperbole is a displacement of anxiety about our profession's future role in the medical market place. But surely there is a more constructive way to deal with this than to project it onto managed care and minimize it by spurious self-aggrandizement?

We will regain control of our destiny when we learn to master capitation and risk management and when we are willing to accept that rationing of resources is our own responsibility. Once this happens we will be in a position as individual providers or as groups to negotiate directly with the people who pay for health care.

Anatomy of a Med Check

Published in *Wisconsin Psychiatrist*, Fall 1996:

> *There has to be something to talk about other than medicines.*
> *You're treated like a "thing" by a technician.*
> *In the door, out the door, because the clock's ticking.*
> *People shouldn't be giving medicines unless they know the person.*
> *There are two types of psychiatrists—the talking one and*
> *the one that does refills—we feel shortchanged.*
> *All they ask real quick is how are you doing—by the time I leave*
> *I remember all kinds of things.*

As part of my responsibility to chair the Wisconsin Psychiatric Association's committee on liaison with consumer agencies, I recently completed seven-hour-long focus sessions with consumers who represented all the major advocacy groups in Milwaukee. The quotations above are a few selected statements which express a widely felt area of dissatisfaction.

—

It appears that consumers are not happy with the med check. Even the term is dismissive.

But what is a med check? What distinguishes a good from a bad med check? Although I have been a teacher for thirty years and have a major interest in "compliance," I have never seen this issue addressed. More importantly, I have not asked myself these questions and I cannot remember teaching a resident the necessary skills.

At the most basic level, a med check is fifteen minutes of a psychiatrist's time billed at more than fifteen times the minimum wage. Do we give value for money? Some psychiatrists seem to feel that such a short time is inherently useless. While fifteen minutes is a lot less than our customary fifty minute hour, it is all that most primary care providers have for an office visit. It is about the average time I spend with the dozen or so people I meet every Thursday evening in our Health Care for Homeless Clinic. As in primary care, our knowledge of each other is sequential and cumulative (three hours of acquaintanceship annually, on average).

Seeing a lot of people in a short time is a stress on anyone's memory. I always refresh my recall from personal details recorded in the chart so that this visit is linked to the previous one. I make a point of reading the chart and then going myself to the waiting room to greet the patient by name. As we sit down, I ask, "How did your daughter's wedding go?" "How was your vacation?" "Has your leg healed up?" "Did you finish painting the kitchen?"

From these specific questions I move to the more general issue of how life is proceeding: job, marriage, children, leisure? Any new or unusual events? Once I learn these things, I already have a good idea of what the medication is or is not doing. So now I ask more directly—after all this *is* a *med check*. There are several medication issues to touch on but the amount of time devoted to each varies with the phase of treatment. Early on I focus on knowledge of the medicine, its name, dosage, regimen, and the likely duration of treatment. I emphasize the delayed onset until improvement takes place and the common side effects that occur immediately. I advise the patient about the concurrent use of alcohol, what to do if a dose is forgotten, and explore how best to tailor the treatment to their lifestyle. In the case of mood stabilizers, I explain about target plasma levels.

Next I pay particular attention to compliance, taking care to make confession or forgetfulness easy to admit. The final assessment is about the extent to which a person's quality of life is improved by taking medicines. I try to interpret drug action in terms of everyday events. Does it improve enjoyment, benefit sleep, diminish voices, decrease energy, impair sexual function, or cause weight gain? My final brief inquiry is about any contacts with other therapists or physicians. This is to encourage collaboration as well as to avoid splitting. It makes me aware of whatever psychosocial issues or difficulties are being addressed and alerts me to any possible need for communication with the primary care practitioners who may be prescribing medication that can interact.

Conceptually, I distinguish three components to this approach. First, I establish a personal relationship. Second, medication is offered as a way to maximize the quality of life, and, lastly, its use is integrated with other psychosocial or medical interventions.

If psychiatrists agreed on the ingredients of a med check, it would facilitate training, measurement, modification, and improvement. The false dichotomy between talking and prescribing might disappear. Communicating these goals to consumers would create realistic expectations about what can be done in fifteen minutes and satisfaction with our encounters might be improved. A name change might help. How about "Continuous Integrated Medication Management?" Sounds better than "Med Check."

Personal and Situational Ethics

Published in *Wisconsin Psychiatrist,* 1996:

Next to having a patient commit suicide, there is probably no more personally disturbing event than being accused either of malpractice or an ethical violation. In my work as a Managed Care Medical Director, the task of credential reviews makes me aware of how many colleagues have endured malpractice suits—the majority of which are dismissed or settled for trivial amounts, but only after several years of distressing legal maneuvers. I had been fortunate to avoid this, until I was exposed to allegations of ethical impropriety related to my present professional role.

No formal or specific complaints emerged and the concern shifted from a personal to a situational one with a request that the WPA consider a code of ethics for physicians who work as Medical Directors in managed care organizations.

Because I felt responsible in some unidentified way, I began to reflect about the topic of personal and situational ethics. Over the course of almost forty years as a psychiatrist, I have worked in a variety of professional roles.

As a resident involved in the discovery of the "cheese reaction," I spent two years doing animal research. This included cats housed in cages around the walls of the crowded World War II Nissen hut where we conducted our experiments. But the animals were not selected for dissection and death at random. The more friendly and extroverted became informal pets. Eventually I took one home for my children—a large tiger-striped male they named "Moppet" who lived out his life in domestic luxury.

I also did research on patients—but not until I had taken an MAO inhibitor and eaten cheese myself to no avail. Reasoning (incorrectly) that there must be something unique about

—

patients (instead of cheese), I obtained informed consent from a middle-aged woman (and her husband) and then I provoked a hypertensive crisis in the patient. Later on I performed a two-week-long series of experiments on another patient who volunteered to be admitted to our Metabolic Unit after she had experienced a hypertensive crisis, provoked by Marmite (a yeast extract). Although the experiments and amounts of tyramine were carefully controlled and she suffered no harm, several months later the patient committed suicide. An autopsy revealed a subarachnoid hemorrhage—perhaps she used the knowledge gained in my study to kill herself.

After I completed my residency training in psychiatry, I went into family practice for a year. By today's standards I was not well trained. I recall a man in his prime, the father of several children who came to see me with calf pain that I misdiagnosed. Days later he died a painful death of pulmonary embolism in his wife's arms. I recall the home visit I made to comfort her and the guilt I felt.

When I migrated to America in 1968 it was to work as the Director of Psychotropic Drug Research for the pharmaceutical company that had marketed Thalidomide a few months previously. Several employees had been charged and convicted of concealing adverse information. As a result the corporation was managed by attorneys whose watchdog functions stifled all creativity and risk taking. During the development of a new antidepressant, I gave the drug for the first time to human volunteers—prisoners in the Cincinnati workhouse who exchanged the primitive conditions of a crowded cell for the comfort of a research unit. I presented data from these studies at national meetings—one of which was held in Montana where participants were given certificates as "honorary inmates" of the State penitentiary.

Much of my later life was in academia, but that, too, was not an ethical safe haven. I have loosed residents on the public who should never have been graduated (one of them murdered his wife—the social worker on our psychosomatic unit). Patients I treated have killed themselves and I was surprised subsequently when reading my own records to realize I should have known better.

One patient with acute excited catatonia died while I was injecting intravenous Haloperidol (not an FDA indication). I conducted a class experiment with placebo on medical students, which the Chairman of Pharmacology felt was "unethical," but which *The Lancet* published without question.

This could be an endless litany colored by each person's job description. I have never been the Medical Director of a large State or County institution, but how do they handle allegations by advocacy groups that patients are deprived of their civil liberties? What do they do when a minority provider group claims that it was discriminated against in a bid for a clinical contract, despite what appeared to be an impartial review process?

The attempt to define ethical guidelines that fit each and every clinical role is fraught with difficulties. Standards may vary from one situation to another and we seldom understand enough about the specifics of each job. Standards also change over time and with the psychosocial Zeitgeist. There used to be psychoanalysts who married their patients just as psychopharmacologists did research on prisoners. Even with the existence of guidelines there is no guarantee of probity. During my time in Wisconsin two WPA presidents have been accused of sexual violations and one served time in prison for pedophilia.

The point of this essay is not that ethical parameters do not exist or should not be applied. It is that we not waste time trying to define an ethics for every occupational or professional role. Individuals should be held accountable both for their own ethics and the ethical allegations they

—

lodge against others. Too often these are unspecific and arise in a context where they may be a displacement of economic or political motivations.

The constitution of the WPA provides for an Ethics Committee where peers can lodge individual allegations about each other. All that is required is that they be specific and detailed enough to be subject to corroboration and scrutiny. There is no need to diffuse this powerful mechanism or confuse it with the contemporary witch hunt against managed care.

Checks, Balances, Backlash and Blame

Published in *Wisconsin Psychiatrist*, Fall 1997:

Managed care may be mostly driven by money but there is more on the minds of most Americans. Independence, equity, and quality are all significant social values. As a nation of immigrants, many of whom were refugees from authoritarian regimes, autonomy is a pre-eminent American ideal. Not surprisingly, we rejected government run health care and opted for a free market system—only to find our independence infringed upon in unanticipated ways by gatekeepers and case managers. The consumer's access to specialists is impeded and the providers' control over clinical decisions has been eroded. As a result we are gripped by a "false nostalgia" for fee for service and the search for a Marcus Welby who never was.

It is possible for provider groups and academic departments to regain control of their destiny, but only if they transform themselves into managed care organizations equipped with the information systems and case management tools required to handle a capitated full risk population.

David Mechanic, a social psychologist (formerly from UW Madison), recently described the professional and public response to managed care in an editorial published in JAMA. Professional outrage at gag

—

rules and network exclusions coupled with press-fueled public anger over "atrocity incidents" have resulted in legislation, litigation, and regulation. Adding political to commercial micro management may be poor public policy, but when rationing health care becomes explicit, so does the ease of assigning blame. Mechanic draws an analogy between the scapegoating of managed care in America and the way the British government is pilloried for the failure of its single payer system to afford all things for all people.

Commenting on the heterogeneity of managed care and the disparate conclusions about clinical outcomes in different populations, Mechanic states:

> The fact remains that whatever real problems exist in some managed care organizations and for some difficult to treat subgroups, managed care offers a feasible way of providing competent care while maintaining reasonably comprehensive coverage at a price purchasers are willing to pay.

Americans are apparently committed to incremental change—if this feels like slow torture it may be preferable to the apocalyptic alteration that occurred when the British government made all doctors civil servants on my fourteenth birthday.

Also part of the American experience is the patchwork quilt of state-by-state experimentation. My personal favorite is Oregon because its health plan pinpoints the tension between what the public wants and what people are willing to pay. The July issue of *Psychiatric Services* describes the origin and principles of the Oregon plan in detail. After extensive town hall debate and community input, the legislature, led by a physician who was senate president, developed a list of disorders prioritized on the basis of treatability and the burden each imposed on the person's quality of life. Out of 745 diagnoses the state pays for treatment according to its tax revenue. Currently conditions above 578 are eligible, including all the major "biochemical" psychiatric disorders. Hypochondriasis, conversion disorder, and antisocial personality fall below the cutoff and are not covered.

—

Most of America has yet to achieve such a pragmatic and philosophically appealing system. Elsewhere equity is obstructed by economic anomalies. There are too many uninsured citizens (especially schoolchildren) and too many unmanaged Cadillac indemnity plans (especially schoolteachers). There are too many managed care companies with stockholders making large profits and too many well-heeled physicians looking to purchase shares.

As the pendulum swings, American style, we note the checks and balances provoked by the backlash and blame. Some are wise, others are shortsighted.

A Common Sense Approach to Dissociative Identity Disorder

Published in *Wisconsin Psychiatrist*, Winter 1997:

> Therapists and managed care organizations are both in a bind when it comes to the treatment of Dissociative Identity Disorder (DID) (a.k.a. multiple personality disorder (MPD). There is no controlled research and there are no authoritative published guidelines. Experts are split into opposing camps. On the one hand are believers in "alter integration" and on the other are those concerned with the "false memory syndrome." Lawsuits are filed on behalf of patients made worse or family members falsely accused, brought by attorneys on contingency fees suing therapists for malpractice if they continue to treat, and abandonment if they don't.
>
> History suggests how we got to this sorry state of affairs. In 1906 the American psychiatrist, Morton Prince, wrote his book, *The Dissociation of a Personality*. He noted that his patient, Miss Beauchamp, "was very susceptible to suggestion, for it was easy to make her believe that a medical percussion hammer was a rabbit or a dog." Earlier he observed, "All of these phenomena were produced while Miss Beauchamp was in the waking state . . . no resort was made to hypnosis." In the following year, 1907, the French neurologist, Janet,

—

published a book on *The Major Symptoms of Hysteria*. By now there were about twenty cases of MPD in the literature and Janet astutely commented, "For some reason, I don't know why, it is in America that the greatest number of remarkable cases have appeared." He made two pertinent observations about therapists involved in this work; they have a "kind of mystic admiration for the subject, an exaggerated seeking after surprising and supernormal phenomena." He goes on to state, "Whatever precautions one may take, the ideas of the observer in the end influence the somnambulism of the subject and give it an artificial complication."

By 1970 there were still fewer than 100 cases in the literature, but by 1980 the number exceeded 200 and by 1990 it had ballooned to 6,000 or more—the vast majority in America.

Why the syndrome escalated and why it remained predominately an American phenomenon are unanswered questions. Our credulity, concern for victims, cultural fascination with the bizarre, faith in psychoanalysis, and access to therapy may all have contributed. The publication of books like *The Three Faces of Eve*, *Sybil*, and *The Courage to Heal* created public interest and a climate of acceptability for heroic therapeutic efforts.

The demographics, natural history, and diagnostic features of DID are fairly well agreed upon. The modal patient is female, Caucasian, in her late 30's, and well educated. A majority have been in treatment for an average of seven years before diagnosis. The symptoms are "kaleidoscopic," including anxiety, affective, somatoform, and psychotic features. Symptoms of PTSD, eating disorder, and substance abuse are common. The prevalence is uncertain, varying from estimates of three percent in the general population to fifteen percent of psychiatric inpatients (the majority unrecognized).

The possible etiology is often assumed to be prolonged childhood physical and/or sexual abuse, in which dissociation

—

is a defense maneuver and often serves the purpose of enacting an internalized approach to the overwhelming stress. There is also evidence that not every case has such a history and that abuse occurs equally or more often in some other Axis I and Axis II disorders. Genetic and other vulnerability factors (including the capacity to dissociate) must also play a role. Why the problem declares itself in the second or third decade is also unclear, but may relate to developing trust in therapy or the emergence of environmental triggers, such as an abusive spousal relationship or offspring at an age that recall the patient's own childhood.

Two principle treatment strategies are derived from psychoanalytic theory. The first involves recovery of memory, recreation of the trauma, and attempts at reconciliation, including confrontation with perpetrators. The second involves attempts to identify separate "alters" and then to integrate them, if necessary using hypnosis.

In 1993 the International Society for the Study of Multiple Personality and Dissociation surveyed more than 2,000 members to establish community norms of treatment. Mean length of treatment was almost four years, averaging two sessions a week at the cost of $14,000, but occasionally exceeding $100,000. Over a third of patients were self-pay and in ten percent of cases the therapist provided services pro bono. Only one percent were paid for by HMOs. Almost all patients were in the kind of psychotherapy described above and two-thirds were being hypnotized.

There has been virtually no published work in refereed journals that describes the success of these approaches, which have become increasingly discredited culminating in a PBS Frontline exposé entitled *The Search for Satan*. This documented the extravagant and uncorroborated claims of ritual satanic abuse and the extraordinary lengths to which a few therapists have gone to treat these unfortunate people.

To understand how this occurred requires a close look at the dynamics involved and the distortions that can occur in the therapeutic relationship. It may be true that a majority of patients with DID were subjected to rejection, abandonment, and even abuse or denigration in earlier childhood. Memories of such events are probably stirred up by concurrent triggers in the second or third decade. But why do these events give rise to iatrogenic complications during therapy?

I think it is a mistake to accuse therapists of implanting or actively encouraging this. All that is needed is a sympathetic listener, unwilling to ask critical questions for fear of rejecting the patient. The rest derives from the patient's desperate need for a nurturing parental figure. The transformation of early rejection into contemporary satanic ritual abuse and the search for perpetrators to confront stem from potent psychological demands. They satisfy primitive narcissistic needs for unusual suffering, they seek to denigrate the alleged abuser, they meet the cultural Zeitgeist for identification with the victim, and they provide an exotic appeal to the interest, sympathy, and narcissism of the "wounded healer" within some therapists. Under these circumstances it is only too easy for dissociation to become "an excuse from living" and therapy to provide the sole source of ego gratification. This is reflected in the extraordinary efforts that some therapists are willing to expend and the extent to which they can come to share the patient's beliefs with a "folie a deux" intensity.

In thirty years as a psychiatrist, I cared for only one patient with DID, but did so for more than ten years. This highly intelligent woman began to show signs of dissociation after about two years of outpatient psychotherapy. When she complained of dissociative episodes during a medication check, I notified her therapist. Her care was transferred within the agency to another (male) therapist for hypnotic alter integration work. The patient's condition deteriorated dramatically requiring several hospital admissions. The patient revealed that she and the therapist had signed a book contract and he was video taping her sessions to demonstrate the alters and regression. The therapist was disciplined for boundary violations and the therapy was radically revised to discourage dissociation and directed more toward developing insight into situations that provoked regression and building social skills for dealing more effectively with them. When I closed my practice five years later, we discussed these alternative approaches and the patient expressed her profound gratitude for the path we had taken.

Since joining a managed care company I have been involved indirectly in the management of another half dozen or so patients with DID and have been surprised to discover the extent of therapists' continuing commitment to alter integration work and the beliefs that accompany it. Patients are admitted to hospitals on Halloween to protect them from satanic perpetrators who program them via phone call. The police are not informed because "they are part of the cult" and (in one case) an attempt to obtain a second opinion was countered by the claim that a prominent Wisconsin psychiatrist was a cult member.

Because of polarization in the field, it is often difficult to obtain an independent evaluation when the patient insists on seeing only "an expert." At times the patient foils a referral because the new therapist reminds one of her alters of a former perpetrator. Meanwhile, the cost of therapy escalates alarmingly, occasionally consuming up to a quarter of a million dollars in care.

In the absence of scientifically acceptable information, what does common sense dictate as the preferred way of managing DID? I offer the following suggestions:

1. Transference can be intense and highly seductive. Therapists need to restrain any fascination for the bizarre, titrate their own needs to nurture, exhibit a benevolent

—

skepticism, set firm limits, and maintain a sense of their own personal boundaries.

2.   Belief in the reality of a patient's childhood traumas should not mean the uncritical acceptance of contemporary allegations of satanic abuse. A caring, concerned approach is not incompatible with gentle skepticism and a search for collateral confirmation.

3.   In the majority of (perhaps all) cases it is best to deal with dissociation as an unhelpful childhood defense that can be overcome by understanding its triggers and finding more appropriate adult ways to deal with them. This may involve cognitive behavioral work, social skills training, stress management, or couples therapy. Pharmacologic management is never primary, but can sometimes help reduce distressing symptoms or dissociative tendencies.

4.   Alter integration work should probably be attempted only in those very rare instances, when the patient has a strong observing ego, is willing to have one alter assume executive control, and is able to contract for safety so that every environmental upset is not converted into a reason for hospitalization. Therapists who attempt this approach should be certain that they have the necessary skills and that the patient understands the risks of unbridled regression and alter proliferation. Finally, they should be able to afford lengthy treatment.

Taking Down My Shingle

Published in *Wisconsin Psychiatrist*, Spring 1998:

In my sixty-fourth year I have decided to take down my shingle before I die with my boots on. I'm in good company. Despite an aging population, the majority of Americans retire before they become eligible for Medicare. If genes

—

were determinants I'd already be long retired. My father, who started life driving a horse-drawn delivery wagon, quit his job as a highly successful business executive at age sixty-two. He turned his back on the tea trade after more than thirty-five years and played golf or fished till he died ten years later—sitting in his favorite armchair, smoking a cigar and sipping scotch.

But, like old soldiers, doctors seem to have a hard time letting go. Ours is a seductive, even addictive, profession. Often we need to care for others in ways we lacked ourselves. Growing up in an all-male boarding school from age five, some of my earliest memories were wanting to be a doctor—an interest that was heavily endorsed by my mother, who allowed me to "treat" her bunions with colored water.

Medical school in mid-century Britain was a light-hearted affair. I spent more time on the rugby field and in local pubs than in lecture halls or on hospital wards. Even so, I knew I wanted to be a psychiatrist before I qualified—helped perhaps by reaction formation to the emotional sterility and stiff upper lip of an English public school.

Once I became an intern, I practiced my profession with a passion. As a resident at Europe's premier academic training institute and as part of a hierarchical medical establishment, it was "publish or perish." By the time I completed residency I had twenty-five articles in major scientific journals. Writing and research as sources of gratification became insatiable. If my output fell below five papers annually I feared that this would be "the year the world forgot me." My accumulated paper count reached 200 before I realized I would perish however much I published.

With hindsight, I figure that less than ten percent of my writing was worthwhile and maybe only one percent memorable. Science teaches humility. Medline memory goes back only three years and even original discoveries soon become secondary citations. The Sixth Edition of the *Textbook of Comprehensive Psychiatry* credits the discovery of the cheese reaction to the "American psychiatrist Barry Blackwell (1907-)." Although of a different nationality and not yet dead, I certainly should be retired now that I'm ninety!

Whatever the individual rewards of work, its generic gratifications are to earn a livelihood and feel wanted. I am fulfilled in both domains. If I leave any legacy, it is in the students I have mentored and patients who were comforted.

During forty years my jobs have included family practitioner, pharmaceutical company researcher, token psychopharmacologist in a leading psychoanalytic department, director of a psychosomatic unit, founding chair in two medical schools (one brand new, the other traditional), staff person to a federal task force on homelessness, and medical director of a managed care company.

While not extravagantly wealthy I realized recently that I had become an "appliance employee," working not for a living but to purchase the next new household gadget.

I have enjoyed teaching (medical students, residents of assorted disciplines, psychology interns, pharmacists, and chaplains), doing research (animal and human), administration (not for profit and for profit), and treating patients (from folks who were homeless to the Cadillac trade). But I no longer am driven to do any of these things. Perhaps my self-esteem has gone up with the stock market, bankrupting the narcissistic motivation to work. Age has created insidious decrements in my memory, concentration, tolerance, and persistence (not Alzheimer's, I hope). The thresholds are lower and the margins slimmer even as my waistline expands. Those who don't alter their expectations to match these subtle changes fall easy victim to depression.

—

That's not for me. My defenses tend toward the manic. Recently, I converted to Catholicism, fell in love with my wife (again), and feel more intrigued by the spiritual than the psychological world. When people say, "What will do you do when you retire?" I'm inclined to answer, "Nothing." This is truly every compulsive's dream but I realize it will create a vacuum into which new interests can expand. There are several books I'd like to write (but probably won't), and a black Labrador named Stanley who needs a lot of walking. Since my spouse still works, I'll also be a househusband and can practice my crude brand of fix-it—superglue, hammer, Drano, and concrete. As a retirement gift, the family has added a vacuum cleaner to my repertoire.

Are there any regrets? Certainly not my move to America—this melting pot of entrepreneurs and idealists—a country appreciated more by us immigrants than by its second generation citizens. Perhaps I could have aspired to more ambitious goals professionally or politically but, while I possessed the energy and intellect, I lacked the tact or temperament.

Some things I will not miss. The phone ringing at night, our professional hubris (the public call it "M-Deity"), and the rhetoric about managed care. The townsfolk of Salem created witches with about the same ease that today's providers translate economic self-interest into ethical imaginings.

I will miss writing these essays and editorials. Believe it or not, whether you feel relieved or not, this is my final column. I've shed my M.D. and moved on. May your own career come to as comfortable and complete a close as mine.

17. The Bread And Butter Of Psychiatry

Words are a form of action, capable of influencing change.

—Ingrid Bengis

As I look back over my career, my writings, and this memoir, something is missing. Seeking to emulate Mark Twain by hitting the high spots, I have overlooked the every day—eager to portray the glamorous and omitting the mundane.

When I assemble the pieces, I see something missing in the jigsaw of my life. It is not cheese, research, foreign travel, managed care, pharmacology, publications, or even teaching and mentoring. It is the people I hoped to help, those suffering from mental illness or trapped in existential predicaments.

While I prescribed modern medicines, the essential ingredient to whatever success ensued was clothed in talk. Not always an hour long but sometimes brief and sequential; in my office, at a bedside, on the streets, in the clinic, or a prison.

During my life, the wheel of psychiatry has turned full circle. First, it was all therapy, then mostly medicines, now we mingle chemistry with words, dabbling in psyche and soma.

—

But prescribing is not understanding; sometimes the damage is too deep to repair or we lack the tools or skill to fix it. Here are some bits of that missing piece of the puzzle:

Open File

Henry is a Harvard man. Even his suffering is dignified. He is the only patient I have who sits in my chair facing the clock. After he learned the protocol of therapy, Henry would stand up promptly at ten minutes to the hour and make his parting comment.

Our meetings have agendas like those he once presided over as a partner in the city's oldest advertising agency. Henry manages the minutes subliminally to cover each week's concerns. His genteel humor and subtle manipulations keep me amused and on my mettle, so we enjoy our encounters though we never openly agree on their purpose.

The suffering started eight years before, when blood vessels that supplied part of Henry's brain began to silt up. The flow ceased to one eye and to the muscles of his larynx, shutting off his vision and stifling his voice. Months of medicine and surgery restored the senses but not the confidence with which he once saw and spoke. So Henry retired punctually at age sixty-five to excel at leisure.

The day Henry went home from hospital, he slept in a separate bed in a different room for the first time in forty-two years. Henry's wife, Harriet, devoted her energy to good causes and raising funds as she had once done to good mothering and raising children. Henry played golf and painted as he had once competed and created. Nothing was shared but his headaches; Harriet dealt with them dutifully.

Henry was certain the headaches had a hidden cause that would kill him. The best doctors had probed, diagnosed, and prescribed, only to prove the reality of a symptom they could not cure. My view was different. Henry suffered from Harriet. I could not get him to say this, to ask for what was lacking or to name the awfulness inside his head. Once or

—

twice, when I shared with him how others might view his predicament, tears welled up but never words.

Henry's best skill as an ad man had been writing copy. I asked him to put what he could not say onto paper. He brought back sheets of lined school paper filled with tidy sentences. I invited him to read them so as to catch the inflections and intonations that went with the words. Henry's soft modulated voice, tanned, open-necked face, and carefully creased clothes gave the appearance of an elderly film star reading his script. He sounded mildly surprised as he spoke his own thoughts aloud:

> Like the air we breathe and the food we eat, intimacy and affection—sharing all things—are prerequisites to life itself. No man is an island. I have a real hunger to share, to share experiences—emotional, intellectual, and physical. Sharing of emotional experiences can be a source of solace or an enhancement of joy. Sharing intellectual experiences increases understanding and immeasurably increases the pleasure of discovery. Sharing a physical experience doubles the pleasure and the knowledge that one is giving his partner the same satisfaction.

There are three pages of these notes in Henry's file. He continued:

> I often think how Harriet and I could improve our relationship in doing just a few simple things together. The lonely time of day, the time of going to bed, could be made into a time of growing intimacy by providing us with one bedroom, instead of two, with twin beds to insure proper rest. A dialogue summing up the events of the day, showing that we really share our lives, could grow into erstwhile intimacy and perhaps even affection. When I come down for breakfast in the morning I have to restrain myself. I am impelled to throw my arms around Harriet, to embrace her and kiss her. I refrain. I know she doesn't like it. Maybe she could grow to like it.

—

Reflecting on his own predicament, Henry suggested a solution:

> I have often hinted, or perhaps actually proposed, a cruise or trip to Europe or the Far East as a happy and perhaps interesting opportunity to get away from our own separate interests and be alone with each other. I haven't actually put it that way. Perhaps I should. Harriet has shown no interest in such a trip.

There is a break in the notes before they end with a paragraph written in different ink. As he reads them, Henry's tone becomes brisk; the sadness fades away:

> We've just returned from five days in Canada and I have re-read the notes I wrote last week. The list itself and the generalities that introduced it are trivialities. The assignment itself begs the question. Why the headaches? The answer that we've prematurely arrived at and with which I do not agree, makes Harriet the heavy in this dreary drama. Let's look further—we haven't ruled out the organic or biochemical.

When Henry stopped reading, there was a long pause. A door had been opened and slammed shut. Finally, I began where he left off with an inventory of the investigations and treatments imposed on Henry by experts in clinics around the country. Every nerve ending and muscle fiber in his head, every blood vessel and crease in his brain had been probed or visualized. He had tried or taken biofeedback, acupuncture, relaxation, meditation, hypnosis, as well as many of the drugs thought to modulate the chemicals that mediate pain and pleasure. Nothing worked. The headaches were worse.

"Why not explore another avenue? If there were more sharing might there be less suffering?" I asked. Henry shifted in his seat and folded his arms tightly to his chest. With a resigned smile and shrug, he politely assented, "What have I got to lose except these damned headaches?" We retraced our path. Now that the words were written down, could they be spoken? Henry would try but didn't sound hopeful. Several sessions later, we reviewed the lack of success; Henry's manner forbade an open assault while Harriet evaded him with community ventures using her desk as a buffer to shelter behind.

I suggested a couples session, and it was several weeks before Harriet could fit it into her schedule.

When they came, they arrived in separate cars. Harriet wore a tailored suit and spoke in matter-of-fact tones; she sat apart from Henry on the couch while I occupied my own chair. After fifteen minutes of polite chat, I asked some pointed questions. Henry remained quiet and Harriet brushed them aside. With Henry's permission, I read aloud his essay; watching Harriet's face tighten and her eyes slip away. As I finished reading, Harriet looked at her watch, then at the clock, but said nothing. Henry stood up and left the office to fetch a cup of coffee. I forget what else was said, but my notes in Henry's file for that session say, "Some progress; she seemed relieved at the nonsexual nature of his needs." I left it open for her to come back.

She never did, but something happened outside of my office. The next week, Henry told me that Harriet had begun to talk about taking a cruise. They picked the Greek Islands, and Henry worked on an itinerary. As plans progressed, his headaches became worse. Harriet was too busy getting ready to leave to talk about the trip. Henry used sly strategies; he littered her desk and night table with brochures and prompted his friends to talk about their own cruises. Still, it was frustrating and painful, so when Henry heard of a new treatment for headaches, he began to take large amounts of a drug that altered blood flow through the vessels to his scalp.

It made him feel terrible; he complained bitterly to Harriet at breakfast. Next day, Henry noticed a file card in the jumble of papers on Harriet's desk. It was dated, and written on it in her precise lettering were his own exact words from the day before. "My headaches are worse; I feel terrible; I don't want to do anything."

We talked about what it might mean. Did she keep a file; for what purpose? So that posterity would know she paid proper attention? Henry asked Harriet. Flustered, she said it was meant to remind him to tell the doctor if he called.

—

Next day, the desktop was tidied, but the card was still there. Unfiled.

In our session last week, Henry remembered more. His headaches had been so bad during that week that he had refused three times to accompany Harriet to the symphony, the ballet, and a neighborhood meeting. She had gone alone.

Next week, Henry and Harriet leave together for the Greek Islands. He has promised to call me soon after they return.

The file is open.

For Sale

He was rummaging through some papers on his desk, waiting for Sophie, when she marched briskly through the open door and plumped herself down on the sofa. She had on a silver fox-fur cape topped by a scarlet beret that matched her lipstick. Before he could close the door or sit down himself, she announced emphatically, "I'm a whore."

He paused a second or so before inviting her in a deliberately neutral tone to "say some more."

She did. "It's disgusting, don't you think, for a seventy-five-year-old woman to be going with two eighty-year-old men at the same time?"

"Two?" he asked innocently, knowing about Max from earlier sessions. Sophie had taken up with Max soon after her last husband died. He balanced her checkbook, chauffeured her to the grocery store, and snored next to her at the movies. Early in therapy, when she began the antidepressants, she had complained her orgasms were inhibited. After the dose was lowered, she said no more. Twice, he tried to stop the drug, but each time, the grayness descended, and all of her pleasures dwindled.

Taking her therapist's knowledge of Max for granted, Sophie told him about the second man in her life. It was an old flame, rekindled. "His name's Sid. He asked me to marry him in 1929, but I told him no because I wanted to work. Sid said I could work, and he'd quit but then the Depression came. We both had to find jobs. Now he lives in Cincinnati, and his wife's in a nursing home with Alzheimer's or something. She doesn't even know his name." Sophie paused to reflect on this and then added, "I'm glad all three of my husbands died suddenly."

Ignoring this digression, he prompted Sophie to say more about Sid. In the past month, Sid had become ardent, driving his Lincoln Mercury fifty miles to Dayton several times a week and often arriving unannounced. Like a timid teenager from sixty years earlier, Sophie strove to keep her two suitors apart. This caution of hers eased a nagging concern that his chemical tinkering might have tipped Sophie from sadness into an erotic mania of insatiable urges and unchecked impulses. She told him that Sid was chairman of the board in a large paper corporation. Like each of her husbands, and like Sophie herself, Sid was successful and self-made. Once Sophie was over the depression and had regained her purpose, she was a match for anyone. Sophie played demonic bridge, entertained lavishly, and insisted on credit for the senior citizens' courses she enrolled in at the university. When an instructor at the YMCA questioned her wisdom in joining an aerobics class, she produced a certificate from her internist to prove she was in shape.

As her therapist, he wasn't sure what Sophie needed from him now. She surely wasn't having doubts about the wisdom of sex after seventy. For Sophie, sex simply wasn't sinful. It was a practical matter. Earlier in therapy, she told him of how she had been driving to a party with her first fiancé when she realized they hardly knew each other. Sophie ordered him to turn the car around and take her to bed. That must have been the man she married instead of Sid.

Nor did Sophie seem to need any help with strategy. He recalled the courting of her third husband, a distinguished professor in the English department at the university. They had met soon after he became a widower. Instantly smitten, the professor declared his interest but coupled it with the intention to remain in mourning for a year. Sophie was sympathetic. She understood the need for the delay but saw no reason to deny themselves sex. They were married two months later.

—

Often in therapy, there were doubts about what his patients wanted. Only a few had wild psychoses or aberrant chemistry that taxed his training. More often, like Sophie, they came for advice, absolution, or an opportunity to iron out an ambivalence or two. He met all these needs like a bartender sworn to secrecy, a minister without a collar, or a friend whose only obligation was to listen and nod. When he was down on himself, he complained to his wife that all he ever did was to sell solace and that it had as little to do with doctoring as work in a massage parlor had to do with a degree in physical therapy.

His mind drifted back to Sophie sitting on the sofa, and his own thoughts merged with her predicament. An image crystalized in his mind. After all these years of living with three husbands, she must feel like an empty house, up for sale. He shared the metaphor with Sophie, wondering what she would make of it. Sophie stayed silent a long time. A sheen of sorrow spread across her eyes. When he saw the tears glisten, he asked how she felt.

"Used up. But it's true I'm available. So what do I have to offer?"

"Offer?" he echoed, wondering if Sophie saw in herself only what she thought the world would see. A widow turned seventy proffering sex?

The thought was mirrored in his own mind. A doctor turned therapist prescribing drugs? He knew that danger well. It was both the product and the producer of sad thoughts, spiraling down to depression.

When Sophie answered, it affirmed his fear that she was dwelling on the dark side.

"My daughters will think it's disgusting. At my age."

Intuitively he sidestepped her statement. Instead, he used the time that was left to gently remind Sophie of the things she did so well and the companionship she had to offer.

At the end of the hour, he asked, according to ritual, if she needed another prescription. Sophie said no, not this time. When she left, she seemed calmer than when she came.

—

Child's Play

Published in *Psychiatric Times*, 1986:

Sally was just short of her twenty-eighth birthday and was surprised to find that she still enjoyed messing about with the doll house. It was a four-bedroomed frame house, more pretentious in its prime than any that had been lived in by the dozens of kids who played with it over the years. Well used and homely, the house stood against one cream coated wall of Sally's dog-eared office. Littered about the room were toys in different stages of dissolution, victims of child abuse. A wooden truck with three wheels angled itself against her desk. A rag doll with one eye winked from the book shelf, its arm looped around her textbook of child psychiatry in an affectionate cuddle.

Sally's second thoughts were to understand why she was enjoying herself. Introspection had become a reflex now that she was embarked on her own analysis. So she let her mind loose to ramble through its associations. It had been difficult to keep the child inside herself alive in the meat grinder of medical school. Friendship had been postponed, hobbies were mothballed, and fun became a rare commodity. After graduation an exacting internship had often placed her in emergency or ambiguous roles, forcing Sally to play parent to her patients by assuming control or exhibiting a calm certainty she seldom felt.

The past two years of psychiatric residency had been a welcome respite with time for introspection and permission to rediscover her fantasies and whims. Now that she was working with kids on her child psychiatry rotation, Sally felt more fortunate still. Delayed gratification was part of becoming a doctor; there were two more years of training yet and perhaps another two beyond that to pay off her debts before she could begin planning to have a child of her own. She would be thirty-two at the start line, almost twenty years

—

after her biology made motherhood possible. Even then there would be problems: finding the right partner and coping with the disruption to her career.

Sally stopped arranging furniture in the doll house and sighed. Perhaps she should settle for child psychiatry. It meant another two years of fellowship but the vicarious pleasure of other people's kids might be a hedge against her own uncertainties. It was something she liked and could do easily; child's play she mused, smiling at the unconscious pun and telling herself to talk about that with her therapist.

The door opened and Sally jumped to her feet, self-conscious lest the nurses find her playing by herself on the floor. They must have knocked and gone away because the only person there was Luke. Shrimpy, sad, and seven years old. Anybody less like the intrepid Luke Skywalker would be hard to find, she thought. Then Sally remembered the reason his parents had named him Luke. They were evangelists with high hopes but a narrow view of nature.

Luke was not like the placid Christ child they read so much about in their Bibles. His infant excesses and greedy demands seemed to them like original sin. Starved for love they could not give, and unresponsive to discipline that meant nothing to his needs, baby Luke had rebelled. His parents saw the mark of Cain in their offspring and made it their mission to subjugate him.

Sally learned of what had followed from the caseworkers in protective services who had taken Luke into custody. She hardly wanted to remember because the images that were invoked only interfered with what needed to happen between the two of them. The fading bruises on Luke's body and the fear in his eyes were reminder enough.

"What would you like to do today?" she asked, reaching out to touch Luke's arm.

—

384

"Nuthin'," he whispered, jerking his arm away.

"There's a house; we could play with that," Sally suggested, omitting the word doll because he was a boy.

Luke stood his ground silently and remained close to the open door.

Sally shut it, then sat on the floor next to the doll house. Luke watched. She pushed several wooden boxes towards him, each containing small painted figures to place in the doll house.

"Choose a set and let's pretend," she invited.

Luke eyed the boxes suspiciously. One contained a traditional family group including parents, a brother and sister, a dog and a cat. Another was a medical team with a doctor (male of course), a nurse (female naturally) and patients of various kinds. The third was a Superman set, complete with Superman himself; his arch enemy, Luther; his girlfriend, Lois; and assorted cops or villains. Luke stared at the boxes for a long time while Sally said nothing, fearful of provoking some reflex resistance.

After a while Sally reached for the family set. "How about this one?" she asked.

"I hate it," Luke spat back, "besides we don't have a dog."

"Well, what about the doctor and the nurse?" Sally continued hopefully.

"They can't do nuthin'," he countered, "they're dumb."

But soon after Luke said this he sat on the floor, a fraction closer to Sally. She waited silently for another five minutes.

"Have you ever wished you could be Superman?" she asked.

—

Sally was watching his face closely and thought she saw the wrinkles ease and the eyes admit interest. But it was momentary. Then his skin tightened again and his face closed as he answered.

"Kids can't fly; I'd only crash."

"But let's pretend," Sally persisted. "Who would you most like to be?"

His reply surprised her. "Luther," he muttered. None of the children she had treated in the first two months of her child psychiatry rotation had ever wanted to be the villain.

"O.K," she said, handing him the wooden figure. "What would you like to do now?"

For a moment it was touch and go as Luke's need to share secrets with somebody safe overcame his ingrained mistrust. He pushed the wooden figure of Luther towards the doll house, placed him face down on the floor of the smallest room and pulled its door tightly shut. Next, he picked up the remaining cops, villains, and Superman, placing them shoulder to shoulder in front of the closed door.

"What's going to happen now?" Sally inquired, genuinely curious.

Luke paused and sensed he could speak. "They ain't ever going to let him out. Luther is bad. They won't give him food. Only water, sometimes with salt in. If Luther cries they hit him. He wants to die."

For a long time there was silence. Luke stared at the doll house while Sally fought to control her feelings so she could think more clearly. Finally she asked, "Isn't there anybody who can rescue him?"

Luke's answer came quickly. "Luther don't want to get away. He's bad; he needs to be punished."

Sally groped for her reply. It was more intuitive than thoughtful. "Is there anyone who could help Luther feel better?"

Luke glanced up, then looked quickly away. "Everyone's against him; there's nobody left."

Sally noticed the forgotten female figure in the wooden box. She picked it up and held Lois out toward him.

"Look, here's a psychiatrist. They talk to people. Do you think she could help Luther?"

For the first time Luke looked Sally full in the face. "Maybe. I guess so. If she's nice." Then he looked away again. Sally leaned forward to touch Luke's shoulder. This time he didn't flinch. They stood up and she walked with him toward the door, her arm around his skinny shoulders. "Let's try. Will you come and talk to me next week?"

Luke nodded and she ushered him gently from the office. As the door shut behind him Sally realized she had ended the session early. She sat at the desk, put her head on her arms and wept, hoping she would feel better before the nurses sent the next child in to play.

Reflections

Published in *Psychiatric Annals*, 1984:

The people we treat are mirrors to our own mortality, the images refracted by our readiness to perceive them. Sometimes the other person is a fellow physician and then the reality and its reflections are often distorted.

—

A few months after I became Chief of Psychiatry at Lutheran, I received a call from the Medical Director at Children's Hospital. Would I see a pediatrician who was depressed . . . the staff were concerned about poor work performance and long absences . . . the physician had agreed to see me . . .

In my office Paul was certainly dejected; but behind a hangdog appearance was an appealing and childlike charm. His gentle manner and quiet voice put children at ease; he had a reputation for rapport with the most disturbed kids and cared for more than his share of those with intractable or incurable diseases.

Paul took control. "I know I'm depressed but this time I haven't been able to get on top of it. Should I start taking that new antidepressant? It has fewer side effects and the others always make me constipated."

Encounters with physician patients often begin this way; we are trained to take charge, diagnose, and treat. Paul was holding in check the underlying feelings of embarrassment and helplessness at being in my office. He was also telling me that he had a biochemical disorder and that drugs were the best solution. I sidestepped by asking him to tell me more about himself and the events that led up to this visit.

The story traced a familiar path. Paul's skill with the sickest children led to many referrals from colleagues and requests for consultation from house staff. He felt unable to say no and was quickly seduced by his own success, the affection of the children, the gratitude of the parents, and the approval of his colleagues. As work expanded he took less and less time for respite or refreshment; neglect of his wife and own son had made them angry and him guilty so he now immersed himself even more in work to escape the tension at home. The strain had taken its toll. He was sleeping poorly, waking tired, and coping poorly with daily routines and decision

—

388

making. "I've become a lousy doctor and I'm not able to give the children what they need."

I felt quite confident that Paul would respond rapidly and in the usual way to antidepressants and supportive counseling. As we met weekly over the next month, we tried to better understand events contributing to his depression.

Paul was a large and ungainly man. He looked cramped and uncomfortable on the sofa in my office as he traced his early upbringing. He described his mother as "probably schizophrenic"; she drank heavily, was unpredictable and often verbally as well as physically abusive. She ignored his two sisters and focused her unpleasant attentions on Paul. His mild and ineffectual father provided neither a buffer nor a role model. Paul grew up insecure and with little self-confidence. The seeds of future depression were sown along with a fear of sharing these feelings with others. The only redeeming feature of Paul's early upbringing was his intelligence. His mother called him a "genius" and Paul learned to play on her better side by studying hard and bringing home good grades. His own stifled longings to be loved and held changed gradually into a desire to give to others what he lacked himself. As soon as the wish to become a doctor was announced it elicited more longed-for attention. Family routines were adjusted to accommodate his ambitions, and for the first time Paul began to feel special. Medical school had not been easy. Despite his native intelligence, Paul's psychological need to be a physician was so intense that success became a source of extreme anxiety and tests were a torture. He somehow scraped through the pre-clinical years and began to flourish with patient contact.

After graduating, Paul was drawn naturally to pediatrics. An intuitive understanding of children's fears and needs grew out of his own early years. He was highly regarded, especially by the nursing staff who observed and appreciated his calming

—

influence and clinical skills. Outside of his work Paul had few interests. He listened to jazz and enjoyed acting as a member of the local repertory group. Paul had a talent for assuming roles that contrasted with the rest of his restricted life but even this ceased after he met Cynthia. She was a second-year nursing student. One year after they met they married; within six months she was pregnant and never went back to complete her degree after their son, David, was born. Paul described Cynthia: "She was so quiet and understanding; I felt I could protect her and that she would be a good mother. She was very patient and I don't ever remember seeing her angry." The contrast to Paul's mother was clear and the reasons he valued Cynthia's nurturant, calm qualities were obvious. Their eager entry into parenthood was partly ordained by Paul's determination to repair his past.

Paul regularly visited my office during the several weeks it took to obtain this information. He seemed to benefit from the medication and from sharing his feelings. There were a few side effects which he alleviated by adjusting his own dosage and regimen. Six weeks later, he was feeling so much better that we extended the time between visits. There seemed little unusual or remarkable about this episode of depression or its response to treatment, so I was not unduly concerned when Paul called to cancel his next appointment because he had flu and the one after that because he was busy.

Three days after the second missed appointment, I received another phone call from Paul's Medical Director. Paul's performance at work had deteriorated seriously; he seemed over sedated and incapacitated. It had been necessary to temporarily suspend him from duty. In my office next morning, Paul was untidy and disheveled. He blamed his worsening mood on the approaching anniversary of his father's death and admitted to medicating himself with sedatives because of insomnia and nightmares. He had also increased the daytime dose of antidepressants. He stated that "the people at work probably think I am abusing drugs" but insisted that he was taking no more than the amounts we had discussed.

We agreed that Paul should be hospitalized. He preferred to be admitted locally (even though he was known to our staff) because he wanted to stay close to Cynthia and David. Having Paul in the hospital would allow us to better assess his possible drug dependency and provide an opportunity to involve his family.

Paul was admitted the next morning. A dramatic emotional, physical, and social disintegration ensued. I had decided to withhold all medication to obtain a clearer view of Paul's mental and physical status. A few days later (after a visit home) a routine drug screen was strongly positive for benzodiazepines and analgesics. The plasma levels were far above therapeutic amounts. Confronted with this, Paul equivocated; he admitted to low dose occasional drug use, argued about plasma half-lives, and implied a laboratory error. But confirmatory evidence of impairment and drug dependency came from other sources, impossible to refute.

The information at the hospital (from several sources) was that Paul had been very effective when he joined the staff ten years before. Five years ago, he began to miss days off work, and to change appointments with patients frequently. Clinical situations others would have dealt with easily became major problems. Two years ago, following an injury to his leg, he had periods of frantic activity followed by four to five days of complete letdown and several days off work. He spent considerable time with drug company representatives and took home large numbers of samples. In the last six months, there had been memory lapses when Paul would claim to have dictated notes that did not exist.

Cynthia's account of events at home was equally revealing. She sat in my office, tears running down her face, clutching and slowly shredding a tissue in her hands. Her manner vacillated between a pathetic helplessness and angry remorse. "When I first knew him he seemed so confident but it was only a cover. Soon after we married I knew he was taking drugs to cope with work. It was so important for him to do well, but he wasn't able to say no . . ." Early on Paul had taken amphetamines; the habit had begun in medical school and continued until the state licensing board had clamped down on stimulant use. For the past five years Paul had used analgesics and benzodiazepines to blunt his performance anxiety but without providing the artificial energy and zest he needed to meet his self-imposed demands. Cynthia had found drug samples hidden in the house, but when she begged him to throw out the pills he flew into rages. On two occasions he physically abused her and afterward drove her to an emergency room in a neighboring city. Once he went berserk, tore apart the house, and injured himself. Cynthia's sadness turned to anger; "This last week while he has been away has been the calmest I can remember; David has stopped having nightmares and I haven't had to take anything to sleep myself. I honestly don't know if we want him back . . ."

Paul's problem had been concealed by his own shame, his colleagues' loyalty, the family's fear and my own clinical naiveté. The manner of unmasking was doubly damaging. He was deprived of drugs that had kept the self-doubts and insecurity at bay and he felt demeaned by the discovery. His depression became profound but clinically confusing; he refused to eat or dress. He lay in bed and quickly lost weight. At times he was confused and delusional. Paul's physical condition deteriorated dramatically. There were several episodes of paroxysmal heartbeat with evidence of previous myocardial damage and moderate hypertension. Liver function tests were abnormal, suggesting damage secondary to prolonged drug abuse, and a CAT scan showed cortical atrophy (possibly related to long-standing drug and alcohol abuse). Despite this, psychological testing showed no intellectual deterioration and his intelligence was in the high superior range.

Paul remained hospitalized for over three months. His depression showed only moderate improvement on maximum dosages of each of the major antidepressants. He refused to consider the excellent programs available for rehabilitation of impaired physicians, citing his reluctance to be away from Cynthia (who would be unable to care for David) as well as poor insurance coverage. He had meager disability insurance and almost no savings. For most of his career Paul had worked as a salaried employee of a corporation and had lived up to his income.

Time ran out in our acute, short-stay unit and the alternatives seemed barren. Several couples and family sessions broke down in bickering or ended in silence. Children's Hospital was willing to have Paul back on a trial basis and contingent on participation in an impaired physicians' program. But he could not function with even minimum clinical competence. Nor could Paul afford a lengthy stay in a private hospital. As a last alternative Paul agreed to go to a neighboring VA hospital; a second opinion had suggested he might recover some motivation and self-respect in a less structured environment where he was not known.

Our final session before the transfer was bleak. To some degree Paul gave me his confidence but I had been unable to replace the chemical supports that had bolstered his past. At rare moments he reverted to an old self when challenged or stimulated; at other times there was a staged quality to his depression as if it were a part he acted. We were both relieved to separate; if he returned we would try again.

Three months later Paul's psychiatrist told me that he was ready for discharge and shortly afterward Paul came to see me during a visit home. As we chatted Paul smiled more than I had seen before. He seemed tentative but was taking some initiative in planning for his return. He had enrolled in the impaired physicians' program where he would be subjected to random urine checks. We agreed to meet weekly and to hold joint sessions with Cynthia monthly. There was to be

—

open communication with the Medical Director at Children's to monitor his return to work. Paul was now taking quite heavy doses of an antidepressant and major tranquilizers and seemed as convinced as ever that he could not function without chemical support.

Within a month Paul was having serious difficulty. He presented a zombie-like appearance and reported extreme difficulty at work where he was only responsible for two or three outpatients. He was reluctant to initiate any social contact for fear of being unable to sustain a conversation. He felt self-conscious and tongue-tied, and had great difficulty concentrating. A progressive behavioral program to extend his activity and restore his confidence failed at the first step. At home he became totally dependent on Cynthia and was doing little else but watching television. Several phone calls confirmed this bleak picture. At work it had been necessary to transfer care of his patients to another pediatrician; at home Cynthia felt trapped, frustrated, and angry at the complete role reversal in their relationship. The impaired physicians' program reported Paul to be distant, remote, and difficult to engage. Paul was one of the less than ten percent of physicians they could not reach for help. His urine remained clear of addictive drugs but there were marked Parkinsonian symptoms with a shuffling gait and paucity of motor movement due to the high doses of medication he was taking.

Paul's inner world had become a ceaseless roundabout of painful thoughts which foretold failure and forestalled action. He had slipped back to that time in his life when nothing he could attempt was good enough or worthwhile. But now he was bereft of the inner regard and external rewards that came from medical practice. The drugs he had taken secretly to sustain his defenses were now part of his public and private shame.

There seemed no alternative but to readmit Paul although there was little left to offer but a respite. Perhaps the massive amounts of benzodiazepines Paul had consumed (equivalent

—

to over 100 mg of diazepam daily for several years) had permanently altered his brain chemistry to a degree where only the addictive drugs could be of benefit. A hastening physical deterioration seemed to lend credence to this idea. Within a few days Paul had a severe episode of paroxysmal tachycardia during which his blood pressure and pulse were unrecordable. The medical residents on call administered diazepam and within ten minutes Paul had recovered. For the rest of his treatment Paul remained on the drug but it never restored his emotional or intellectual ability to function.

Paul's general physical condition was appalling; his appearance had aged more than ten years and he had Parkinsonian symptoms with hand tremors and a shuffling gait which persisted when drugs were withdrawn. The medications to remedy this worsened his depression and he lay immobile and silent in bed for much of the day. Yet another opinion suggested that Paul be transferred to a different hospital for electroshock therapy. When we parted I squeezed his hand and got back the glimmer of a smile.

Six weeks and ten treatments later Paul was out of the hospital and back in my office. My notes from that visit read, "Better than I have seen him, wearing a suit and contemplating a comeback." Later in this session Paul confided how at times he considered suicide but had rejected the idea as a poor example for his son. My notes comment, "Still, there is a realistic risk . . . but not much to be done."

The time of recovery is always one of risk as the inertia of depression lifts but the realities that provoked it remain. In Paul's case the reality worsened. The corporation voted to terminate his contract and health insurance ended with it. Paul's few assets were tax deferred and inaccessible. Cynthia was struggling to maintain a budget and considering a return to work but had no skills to sell and did not trust Paul to provide the child care. The house was on the market and they were selling their few antiques. Paul had filed for disability but there were clauses disbarring drug addiction and long delays in adjudication. The disability would need to be total and permanent so to obtain it would require Paul to relinquish medical practice.

Paul shared this darkening scene at our weekly sessions to which he now came by cab; his car was sold and Cynthia had never learned to drive.

Paul felt Cynthia had no respect and little liking left for him.

His simple and softly spoken summary of these events was, "Loss, loss, loss."

At our last meeting Paul shared a small piece of good news; the insurance company had agreed to pay and the house could be saved. The family would be provided for.

Next week the weather was terrible. Paul called to tell my secretary he was unable to get a cab and she reminded him of his appointment the following week.

Two days later Paul killed himself. He left no note, only a message. When Cynthia called to break the news, she asked if I had told Paul he should not come back because I had nothing left to offer.

I went to Paul's funeral and I was surprised to find so many gathered to mourn the death of a man who seemed so friendless in life. Later those closest to Paul invited me to share his wake and I learned about the man I had never met. A nurse who knew him well read this poem:

A giant and an orphan child he was—
    Our paradoxic friend.
Bare head that almost touched the sky,
Big feet that tangled in the muddled nap of life,
He swayed between the mighty and the lame—
Our friend of times gone by.

—

Unto his friends he bared his soul,
And reading theirs he loved and angered with a mighty roar.
He played, made mischief, war and peace
With not politeness, colleagues' grace
But with the psyche's vibrant core.

Yet the child within was battered, naked, and without a home.
For many years it bore the body of the man
    and tried to be both son and father to his guest
    sang Blues full throated, played the frantic drum,
    chased twisting fugue that tumbles here and there across itself.
The fugue will find its home, its rest.
The boy could not.

His frame began to fail beneath the giant's weight,
    his bones began to break and fold,
The food once thrown the orphan boy
    built flesh too frail for giant's hold.

The fight went on for many a year.
The giant left.
The boy walked on alone
    until at last he could no more.
Nor more be carried by his friends—
For that withheld in dawn of time
    could not be taken by a soul long gone.

An so he took his body,
Paradoxic friend.
And as so oft in times now past
He seeks one last forgiveness—
And bids we let him go.

               —Paul's Friend, Name Unknown

Our Fathers

Published in *Wisconsin Psychiatrist*, Winter 1994:

> *"The poets and philosophers before me have discovered*
> *the unconscious; I have discovered the scientific method*
> *with which the unconscious can be studied."*
> FREUD. Father of Psychotherapy

> *"Many forms of insanity are unquestionably the*
> *external manifestations of the effects upon the brain*
> *substance of poisons fermented within the body."*
> THUDICHUM. Father of Neurochemistry

She wakes me up in early morning doubt.
Crazed eyes and alien name: Luz Medino.
Both fuel the need in me to know about
her persona, gene pool, Puerto Rico.

Sour culture and unruly cells enslave
her brain in bitter juice. It can't go free
slumped sad inside its melancholy cave,
bound by its own unravelled chemistry.

The day they cut her breast away she wept.
Her hardwood face dissolved in acid tears.
Except for dream-infested nights she kept
slammed shut that angry door to all her fears.

She doesn't rage against her fate. So sure
she is a devil who deserves to die
that words or drugs have not produced a cure
and Freud or Thudichum can't tell me why.

—Barry Blackwell, 1994

An Everyday Nameless Fear

A nice thing about psychiatry is it can take you into strange territory, for example elevators. As this next poem suggests, they are an upwardly mobile metaphor for everyday life.

At a first visit, we often ask our patients, "Do you have any phobias or irrational fears?" Fear of elevators is common among the 530 named phobias to date, mostly given Latin or Greek names by learned physicians (Wikipedia).

People with phobias will do anything to avoid triggering them (avoidance behavior). If you live in a city, you may be lucky with snakes (ophidiophobia) or chickens (alektorophobia), and even if you fear riding in cars (amaxophobia), you can always walk or take the bus or subway. But try avoiding elevators in a metropolis. Most lawyers, accountants, and wealthy medical specialists (seldom psychiatrists) like to live like vultures where they can look down on you.

As is often the case in medicine, the cure can be worse than the disease; jump in, push the button, and stay there until your heart, pulse rate, sweating, breathlessness, and terror subside (flooding). Be assured they will, but you may not believe it, and anyone else in the elevator may hate it or catch what you have.

Strangest of all, elevator phobia has no name and not even psychiatrists have been able to find one, although they may make money treating it. When they submit their bills to an insurance company, they must hide behind "claustrophobia," a generic term for "closed spaces" that does no justice to being trapped in a mobile, potentially lethal, metal casket. If I was a Greek or Latin scholar, I'd find a way to translate "Black Hole of Calcutta." Neither Hippocrates nor Michelangelo dreamt of elevators; the British knew how to build a lethal dungeon, but Isaac Newton missed the hint when the apple dropped.

After this, you may decide not to read the poem and, instead, turn the page.

—

Elevators are . . .

Elevators are elusive,
Up or down, open and shut
But not when you want one.

Elevators are toxic
To Type A temperaments;
Eager to arrive early.

Elevators are oral,
Engulfing us all
Behind closed doors.

Elevators are obedient
To you. No one else's
Finger push will do.

Elevators are intimate
Like one night stands,
Too transient to wait.

Elevators are rejecting,
Emptying everyone
Out on the floor.

Elevators are faulty;
Steel vaults for bodies,
Buried in basements.

—Barry Blackwell, April 2010

Rebirthing

There are many ways
To integrate and mend
A cracked persona.

Celebrate your assets,
Befriend the defects,
Meld psyche with soma.

Think and feel in synergy,
Reframe old wounds,
Unlock trapped energy.

Search for and choose
A grounding vision,
An angel in the rock.

Then walk the talk,
Shun the victim game,
Cease blaming others.

Nourish second chances,
Seek smiling faces
That nurture you anew.

Psyche and soul flourish
When faith and grace
Reunite the whole.

—Barry Blackwell, July 2000

Doctor's Holiday

Christmas was coming. There was nothing he could do about that. Frozen waves rimmed the lake and steam rose from its surface like a witch's cauldron. The secretaries and staff baked cookies and brought them daily to his office, an edible advent calendar. There were peanuts stuck together with chocolate, candied fruit suspended in flour, and rum essence in round balls. Everyone ate them in uneager anticipation of more to come.

Presents were wrapped and unwrapped. Only a few of the doctor's patients brought gifts. Third-party insurance had muffled their gratitude. Besides, if you read the papers about health care costs or lived next door to a doctor and his Mercedes, wishing one a Merry Christmas and a prosperous New Year was difficult to do. One of his patients, Stefan, lived downtown in a rooming house, untroubled by envy or newspaper editorials. He was a survivor of four winters in Auschwitz who spent life in America evading imaginary Nazi persecutors. Stefan came monthly for medication that helped him sleep and cleared his mind of alien ideas. Last month, he had showed everyone in the office a slip of official U.S. Secret Service notepaper that had scribbled on it, "Leave Stefan alone; he is one of us." Stefan pestered people but was well-known and tolerated about town. At the office, the doctor's secretaries indulged Stefan and, after a while, when they gently reminded him they had work to do, he would leave, feeling content. A week before Christmas, he came to his appointment with a brown paper bag. From it, Stefan took four oranges, giving one to each secretary and another to his doctor, who carried it proudly home to show his wife and eat after supper. It was an immaculate orange with no pips. Next morning, he asked his secretary if she had enjoyed hers, but she had thrown it away.

The doctor's mind was filled with images of Snow White and her rosy red apple when he was interrupted by Frank's phone call. It was good news. Frank's attorney had called to set the hearing date for his industrial compensation case. Frank had been waiting impatiently to sue the insurance company for his suffering from the foot he had injured at work. They had ended his support after retraining him for a job that didn't exist and then ceased paying his medical bills when a consultant they hired alleged Frank was malingering. At his last visit, Frank had wondered where the money would come from for Christmas presents; he was torn between the indignity of accepting toys from Goodwill and the misery of witnessing his six-year-old son's empty stocking. Frank's mother had offered to pay for the family to go home to Alabama for the holidays, but he had turned that down to be around in case his attorney called. Now there seemed enough hope to tide them over Christmas, and the phone call came to an end without Frank making his usual request for more Valium.

Christmas worked its way into the lives of all the patients who came to the doctor's office that week, old and new. Julie was seeing him for the first time, seeking help for the pain and bewilderment of a broken marriage. Her daughter had just arrived for Julie's share of joint custody. She came bringing her first menstrual period and decked out with the gold jewelry her father had given her for Christmas. Julie, who had spent weeks choosing the ring her daughter had always wanted now felt like taking it back. Helping her sift through these feelings, he recognized again the lines of the old prayer—the courage to change, the serenity to accept, and the wisdom to know the difference. Most of what he did was prodding his patients toward those insights.

Sometimes the doctor mixed in a little medicine, mostly for those few people he saw with true melancholia. Gerald was like that, mired in a gray, joyless fog that tinted his whole life. He was a resident in radiology, one of those doctors who was only comfortable with the images of people. The gulf between Gerald's needs and his ability to get them met was wide and painful. Three mothers had died and disappointed him, the first as he entered adolescence. Gerald planned to spend this Christmas with her family, who were farm folks. He was surprised when his father didn't seem to care, but at the age of thirty, Gerald still felt guilty about not going home. After talking it over, they had upped the dose of his antidepressant and discussed which drug to try in the New Year if this one didn't work.

There were no patients booked on the last afternoon before the holiday, and the doctor planned to clear his desk. As always, it was a struggle to empty the in-tray after noon. He had to push his mind to make even the smallest decisions, so he welcomed the interruption when the phone rang, and it was Frank again. The voice was so soft, he strained to hear it. There was a pleading and an urgent quality. Two days before, Frank had gone to meet the school bus on his son's last day in kindergarten. The boy ran into the street under the wheels of an oncoming truck as Frank watched from his own parked car. Frank was calling from the intensive care unit at the university medical center where the boy was still comatose and on a respirator. Frank wanted two things: a prescription for something to help with sleep and prayers for the son's recovery. The doctor called in the prescription and mumbled his way past the second request.

That evening, after work, was the first Christmas Eve that the doctor and his family had ever spent in their own home. His wife's parents had become snowbirds and gone south, so the family focus had shifted to his place. This year, they had cut down their own Christmas tree. It was eight feet tall and fitted easily under the high ceiling of their old home. He watched the lights blinking on the tree and then set about starting a fire while he waited for his wife to return after collecting their five-year-old, Elliot, from school. The artificial log burned with blue and green flames as it kindled the real wood and warmed the empty stockings hanging from the mantle. Last night, Elliot had left his Christmas wish list on the hearth with cookies and milk for Santa's elves. His not-so-modest requests were for a third kitten, cross-country skis, and a playground of his own. This morning, they had read the reply that two cats per house was all there were to go around, and playgrounds were too big to deliver down chimneys. Skis were a possibility as Santa planned a snowy winter. Elliot seemed satisfied, although in the weeks before Christmas he asked skeptical questions as older friends suggested that Santa was Dad in disguise. So his wife had rented a Santa suit and recruited a neighbor to drop by later that evening in the hope of buying another year of innocence.

It must have worked because on Christmas morning, after opening his presents, Elliot went outside on his own to see if Santa had dropped off a playground in the front yard. Afterward, the three of them attended Mass together, walking to the church on the corner of the street despite the bitter cold. Inside, the nave was cozy with Christmas worshippers packed together in rows beneath a scarlet-and-gilt ceiling supported by tall marble columns. The people who prayed here had a lot to thank God for. Feeling guilty, he put a ten-dollar bill in the collection plate, puzzled at how many regular parishioners ignored it. His wife explained afterward that they made their deductible year-end contributions earlier in discreet envelopes. When it came time for the sign of peace, he thought the folks in the next pew scanned him curiously before offering their hands to shake. His wife joined the communion queue; Elliot complained that he felt hungry and wanted some of the magic bread. Waiting for her to return, the doctor remembered Frank's son briefly and hoped that the thought would pass for a prayer. After the service, they led Elliot to admire the crib, but this year he was not impressed and soon tugged them away, eager to return to his new toys.

After they arrived back home, the family began to gather. He put the turkey in the oven and methodically prepared the trimmings and vegetables. He had learned the rituals and recipes from his mother, not because she taught him but because he had observed them often. When it came time, he supposed the same traditions would be transmitted by his grown children who watched him work at the stove and sink. It was English fare; stuffing that smelled of lemon and sage, bread sauce flavored with onion and cloves, thick brown gravy, chopped carrots and turnips, and dried peas that gave everyone gas for days and which triggered family jokes as traditional as the food.

This year they were ten at table, not including the newborn baby their friends had brought. She had jet-black hair and according to her mother (who was breastfeeding) already possessed two teeth. They bundled her from person to person in communal enjoyment of her tightly screwed-up eyes, red puffy cheeks, and pursed lips. It was her first and his forty-ninth Christmas.

After dinner, they sat around the fire in mellow content, gossiping and telling tales about those who were not with them this year. The evening ran on toward its end with only one interruption. Frank's mother called to say that, worn out by the bedside vigil, he was morose and inconsolable. The doctors had declared his son to be brain dead. Frank believed them, but his wife and family, born-again Christians, had begun a twenty-four-hour prayer vigil. Frank did not attend. He no longer believed in miracles and only wanted to know why and why now. Early on Christmas morning, Frank's cousin, with troubles of her own, had ended them by blowing out her brains with a shotgun. The family was fearful Frank would do the same and worried because he had pains in his chest. As the doctor listened, he said nothing. It was on the edge of belief and beyond sympathy. Finally, he told her to take Frank to the hospital and called the duty doctor to have him admitted. As usual at Christmastime, the ward was almost full, and there was only one bed left.

When he returned people were shuffling about and readying themselves to go home. Nobody asked him about the call. Incurious, cheerful, and content, they were full of food and ready for bed. They parted, kissing and hugging briefly before stepping into the frigid air. He and his wife put the dirty glasses in the dishwasher, turned off the lights, and went upstairs. The sheets were cold, and as he lay awake, waiting for their bodies to warm the bed, he tried to recall Christmases from his own childhood but couldn't. His memory had always been poor, or perhaps there was some other reason. It didn't seem to matter much. The years that were left numbered less than those he had forgotten. He reached out to wrap himself around his wife and, cuddling her to the curve of his body, quickly fell asleep.

Morning Coffee

This cafeteria is a collecting place,
A dingy museum of hope and cigarette butts,
But the man at the next table
Has made up his mind.

His hands on the table
Are cuddling a coffee cup;
His chest props up his chin
And his eyes are curtain-closed.

As he dozes the day away
The sloping shoulders say
He is a veteran of living,
With no victories to celebrate.

A few shrugged off memories
Warn him that
Yesterday was depression, tomorrow doubt.
Only today may be safe.

So he snoozes between sips
Between caffeine and Thorazine
Living from moment to moment,
From molecule to molecule.

If you knew enough it would be
That he made the right choice
To stop and not go on
To stay and not retreat.

Later, eyes open, he says hello.
But nobody notices or nods.
Now he knows the comfort
Of not existing . . .

—Barry Blackwell, circa 1995

Tranquility

Published in *Wisconsin Medical Journal*, September 1986: Vol. 85:

It was a balmy day with warm sand and calm waves lapping along the lakeshore. When I teach people to relax, I use these images to graft over the anxious turmoil of their lives. I tucked the thought away. I was here for a respite.

Leaving the beach for the swings, I took five-year-old Adam and his pal, Christopher, with me. Together we ambled across a wide grassy meadow, its edges in shadow where pine trees grew and picnic tables sat. In the far corner, a couple half-faced each other. The man was playing a harmonica with earnest, expert zest; the woman was strumming a guitar and singing, not in perfect pitch but with a pleasing cadence. Some teen-agers strolling past paused to applaud, but were ignored. The couple was doing this for themselves.

Coming closer, I recognized Rosie and Robert. Shortly after I arrived in town, Rosie sought me out, describing herself as a schizophrenic whom nobody would care for. The diagnosis was doubtful but her ostracism was not. Rosie functioned quite well between episodes of wild psychosis which were triggered by unwise intimacies. In over twenty years she had passed many times through the revolving doors that open unwilling hospitals to inhospitable communities. Now she was barred from inpatient units unable to cure her and shunned by psychiatrists unwilling to treat her for the pittance that Medicare sometimes paid. But Rosie was streetwise and a survivor. She found an agency social worker who understood the metaphor of psychosis and an academic psychiatrist able to afford a "good teaching case." Hilary interpreted Rosie's struggle with the alien environment and I prescribed "pills" to buffer her against it.

Rosie never treated me as more than her medicine man; she came for tranquilizers, not advice. The major tranquilizer she took with a wise reluctance. The brain is a fine-tuned but well-protected organ. The doses of drugs that penetrate its barriers often do damage when they mistake receptors that modify behavior for others that modulate movement. The rhythmic writhing of her lips and tongue testified to that. The minor tranquilizers Rosie took with alacrity. Aimed at the limbic lobes, they brought a rapid respite for which she would con me into giving her more with stories of lost scripts and stolen purses.

We struck a bargain. In return for the drugs she liked, she took the ones I thought she needed. A balance was achieved, between us and within her brain. It was not total tranquility but it was not turmoil and her tongue was still.

Over the past year, Rosie had come to each of our offices with Robert. He was an older man and a professional musician who served as someone between a friend and a father. The money they made playing the sidewalks and smaller cafes supplemented Rosie's occasional earnings as an organ tuner. Hilary saw them as a couple and helped them titrate their intimacy. She charged them two dollars and each paid half. On medication visits Robert waited politely outside my office and the State paid.

Nothing of this prepared me to recognize Rosie and Robert as two people making music in the park. As the distance between us closed, I became aware of my swim shorts, unshaven face and the two noisy ragamuffins in tow. There was still time to turn away, so I did, unsure of whether I was protecting Rosie's integrity or my dignity.

A few days later, I passed Rosie and Robert entertaining on the sidewalk outside the Summerfest grounds. I hid in the crowd and hurried past.

Shortly after this second sighting, Rosie missed her monthly appointment but called to make another. She sounded cheerful and calm, but priorities had changed. She needed my medications less than the money she and Robert were making among the crowds. For Rosie, it looked like this might be her first tranquil summer.

18. Spiritual Pilgrimage

The Seminary

It is never too late to be what you might have been.

—George Elliott

My task is really not to change myself but to become familiar with who I am.

—Maureen Cook

When I told people I was retiring, I quickly became weary of the inevitable response, "What are you going to do now?" I didn't have a clue and felt inclined to say, "Nothing." Like all compulsives, I imagined there was relief in letting go, and I was certainly determined to quit medicine. If it was true that "nature abhors a vacuum," all I had to do was to wait. My conversion and deepening involvement with the church probably shaped the outcome.

Early in adult life, a blend of hubris and atheism made me look down on those who espoused religious or spiritual convictions. I viewed them as self-deluded folks, lacking intellectual vigor or easily misled. As a young psychiatrist, I seldom inquired about a patient's faith life.

By the time I retired, I was wiser; I envied those who claimed a spiritual side and wondered what I might be missing.

As the century drew to a close, I decided to seek an answer to that question. St. Francis Seminary was a short distance from the archdiocese headquarters I was already familiar with, looking toward Lake Michigan and nestled in several acres of woodland. It offered a variety of educational opportunities for laity in addition to priestly vocations. I was ready to give up medicine but not sex! Two of these were master's degrees; one in Pastoral Studies (MAPS), and a more rigorous and traditional Masters of Divinity (MDiv).

But first there were hurdles to cross: two interviews with former graduates to assess my capability and suitability for the seminary, next an essay for the dean describing my purpose, and finally an interview with a psychologist to screen out the emotionally troubled or immature, including potential pedophiles.

I was accepted and enrolled in the easier of the two programs, MAPS, but was required to take prerequisite courses in 101 Philosophy and Religion. Classes were small and intimate, usually six to twelve individuals including seminarians (all male) and lay students like me (mostly women seeking second careers as educators or lay administrators in local parishes coping with the priest shortage).

Faculty were outstanding and the academic standards demanding, including oral and written exams at the end of each course. Essays had to be formatted and footnoted to meet precise requirements. In class, I took meticulous notes and condensed them onto four-by-six-inch index cards, which I kept on my person to memorize. Competitive as ever, I was determined to maintain an A average, not an insignificant goal alongside seminarians forty years my junior.

As important, if not more so, was the social environment and sense of community. St. Francis is approached through an avenue of tall trees, arching protectively over a long driveway leading to a statue of St. Francis and the entranceway. Inside, the hushed corridors led to a solemn chapel; the wall behind its altar adorned with a large crimson and gold painting of Jesus as rabbi and teacher. The students, seminarians, and faculty mingled over meals at common tables in the refectory, worshipped together in the chapel and shared in a rich variety of extracurricular lectures and seminars.

—

I became immersed in all these activities, was elected to the student council, and helped lobby for more attention to women's issues on campus, a plea the Catholic Church was not yet ready to hear. In class, I asked the probing questions many were reticent to raise and received open and honest answers. A sense of the depth and quality of disputation is illustrated in a term paper I wrote for the course on "Catholic Faith and Doctrine." (See "Creed Term Paper" in this piece.)

In addition to classroom dialogue, the faculty kept office hours for private discourse and queries. As an added door to my inner self, I sought a spiritual director whom I met with monthly in the comfort of her sister house, adjacent to the seminary.

I kept my workload to a modest six to eight credit hours each week and, other than domestic chores, had only one additional commitment. The year I retired, the governor of Wisconsin appointed me to the State Mental Health Council for an initial three-year term, followed by a second term during which I served as chair. This was a pragmatic counterpoint to my spiritual quest but also an opportunity for "good works."

Wisconsin is well-known for a commitment to innovative mental health policies; it pioneered the case management model of community care in the mid-1960s in an effort to unite fragmented agencies or services and prevent the recurrent hospitalization of those with severe and recurrent mental illness. During the time I served on the council, the state made a major commitment to another Wisconsin innovation, the so-called "Procovery" movement. This sought to empower people with mental illness to capitalize on their intellectual, emotional, and spiritual strengths in order to play a larger role in their own rehabilitation even when full recovery or cure was unattainable. (See "Faith in Recovery" in "Piece 19: Three Good Deeds.") Funds were allocated to support this concept at the community level, and several leaders in the movement were appointed to the council.

The existence of State Mental Health Councils was mandated by the federal government as part of the legislation covering "block grants" that channeled millions of dollars annually into each state's coffers. The council's purpose was to ensure citizen oversight of the distribution and appropriate use of the funds at the community level. Compliance with this mandate was overseen by the NIMH. This requirement was honored in the breech; I knew from my time at the NIMH that the state council reports were filed in a closet and seldom or never read.

The dynamics of this arrangement created an inevitable conflict between the governor who appointed the council members (on the advice of the state mental health bureaucracy) and some members of the council (myself included) who felt that empowerment ought to include the right of persons with mental illness to nominate their own representatives. At stake was control over millions of dollars. This predicament and the tension it generated was not too dissimilar to that between salaried leadership of not-for-profits and volunteer lay members who are legally responsible for board actions and fiscal integrity.

Matters came to a head when time came to vote for a new council member. One chosen by the bureau and approved by the governor and another supported by me and the Procovery advocates. Paper ballots were distributed, collected, and counted by the staff member to the council. The result was announced: the officially preferred candidate won by a single vote. I requested the ballots, recounted them and discovered a "mistake." The reverse was true; the Procovery candidate had won. Hurt and wounded by the conflict and subsequent debate, she declined to serve, and I subsequently resigned. My spiritual search had not made me a better or more tolerant board chair.

Back at the seminary, tensions were also developing. The liberal archbishop had reached retirement age, and his mandated letter of resignation was accepted by a pope moving in a more conservative direction. Meanwhile, the archdiocese was struggling to cope with the pedophile scandal and its financial fallout. The new conservative archbishop was confronting the likelihood of bankruptcy, the need to sell property, and refigure which programs and facilities would survive. Part of the hierarchy's response to the shame and chaos was a return to more rigid and traditional liturgical practices, including a reversion to its paternalistic and misogynist roots. Both the seminarians and the lay students picked up the scent.

—

Once again, my inclinations were toward the losing side. St. Francis has a magnificent bell tower looking out on the lake and reached by an elevator that lets you out into a cozy, intimate space ideal for small group meetings. The group I belonged to gathered here weekly to discuss spiritual matters, made up entirely of women. Our final get-together was a celebration of the Eucharist complete with wine and wafers, led by a member with the frustrated Vatican II desire to be ordained. It was a defiant act, worthy of excommunication, that I found exhilarating.

The last lecture series I attended was on "Feminist Theology" taught by a woman theologian from Marquette University. It was spurned by the seminarians, fearful of the archbishop's displeasure, so I was the only man among twenty women!

During the slow progress to accumulate enough credits to graduate, I came to terms with my puny spirituality. Intellectually I was still a "straight A" student, but I recognized I was spiritually handicapped and afflicted with the Pelagian heresy. Pelagius was a British monk (AD 354-420) who migrated to Rome where he taught and lectured in public about the merit of "good works" and free will while denying Augustine's doctrine of "original sin." At first, he was praised by Augustine for his asceticism and for being a "saintly man" but eventually was declared a heretic at the Council of Carthage (AD 418) and banished from Rome. Some theologians believe Pelagius was closer to Jesus's moral teachings and that Augustine's sexual mores may have laid the groundwork for Catholic misogyny.

By the time I accumulated enough credits to begin work on a thesis, I had also become involved with several Catholic parishes, helping them develop a ministry for people and family members dealing with mental illness. As a retired psychiatrist and Mental Health Council member, I was sometimes invited to talk to congregations on psychiatric disorders and their treatment. This led to friendships with those involved and to the beginning of what later became known as the "Faith in Recovery" program. (See "Faith in Recovery" in "Piece 19: Three Good Deeds.")

In the late stages of my days in the seminary, I also became aware of the mental health services offered by Catholic Charities for people with little or no mental health insurance benefits and began to explore the possibility of becoming the first psychiatrist to work in their clinics.

This confluence of events led to the realization that I already had the requisite medical degree to answer a compelling call to resume providing mental health services to those in need, and it would be all right to abandon the quest for a theological credential that had served its purpose but which I neither needed nor merited.

Choosing and Changing Churches

He was of the faith in that the church he currently did not attend was Catholic.

—Kingsley Amis

Greater love hath no man than he attend the Episcopal Church with his wife.

—Lyndon B. Johnson

If Christ returned today, would He recognize Christianity?

—Popular Saying

Most people achieve their faith affiliation in one of two ways: following in their parent's footsteps or aligning with a spouse. According to the Jesuits, masters of indoctrination, the earlier the choice, the more likely it is to remain permanent, cemented by the rituals of baptism, confirmation, and liturgy. The Jewish faith is also strengthened by strong links to its culture and unique ritual observances.

People may also change their faith affiliation at varying times for different reasons. Perhaps the most common is late adolescence or early adulthood, when the timely tasks of individuation and emancipation loosen the bonds of childhood and parenting. Later in life, conversion, waning spirituality, or growing dissatisfaction with the tenets of a particular faith may dictate these decisions.

Sometime around 2005, Kathie and I decided to quit the Catholic Church. Kathie was a "cradle Catholic" from birth and a member of our parish council, while I was a member for fifteen years following my late-life conversion and our third (and white) wedding, blessed by the Church. Both of us attended Mass weekly, and I was active in parish affairs as a lector and confirmation mentor for kids, including our son, Adam. In the archdiocese, I continued my work with Catholic Charities as a consultant to Bishop Sklba and member of his mental health committee, approving and monitoring treatment for victims of pedophilia. Earlier I had served as a member of the marriage annulment tribunal, after my own was granted.

Kathie and I had shared and individual concerns leading to our decision to leave the Church. At the parish level, Kathie was disillusioned by the autocratic handling of routine matters and passive acceptance of changes in liturgy imposed by the hierarchy. My own dwindling faith life contributed.

Above and beyond personal considerations was a shared realization that Rome was moving relentlessly backward in a conservative direction, undoing the advances of Vatican II. Despite the worldwide spread of democratic principles and female emancipation, the Catholic hierarchy remained rooted in rigid authoritarianism and undiminished misogyny. The doctrinal virtue of *sensus fidelium* (truth sensed by the body of the faithful) was negated as the bishops strove to lock the pedophile crisis in the closet and clung to the archaic dogma that male celibacy bestowed God-given moral and spiritual superiority on their gender.

These trends were prelude to changes about to take place in Milwaukee, which would have implications both for our personal faith lives and the future of Catholicism in America. In 2002, Timothy Dolan was appointed archbishop of Milwaukee on the retirement of the liberal and well-loved Archbishop Rembert Weakland, former head of the international Benedictine order, a star during Vatican II but now out of favor with conservative Rome.

Weakland's retirement was marred by the revelation of an earlier midlife affair with a gay graduate student, and Dolan's arrival was soon followed by the unfolding of Milwaukee's own pedophile crisis, when over 8,000 allegations of incidents were made against one hundred priest perpetrators, leading eventually to bankruptcy. Despite having to shoulder this burden, Dolan's already promising career continued to blossom.

Now aged sixty-two, Dolan has become a model for the refurbished image of the hierarchy and a priest on the fast track. Just before the turn of the century, he served as the liaison between Rome and the American dioceses as well as the rector of the American College in Rome, a seedbed for aspiring priests selected to move up the hierarchy. In 2009, Dolan left Milwaukee to become archbishop of New York; in 2010, he was elected president of the U.S. Conference of Bishops, and in 2012, he was created a cardinal. Press coverage during this period describes him as "big, earthy, and frequently funny," "ebullient," "charismatic," "a genial conservative," and "a gifted politician."

For almost two hundred years, professional observers of the Catholic hierarchy have indulged in identifying and naming "papabile" (one who might become Pope). Timothy Dolan is the first American to achieve this status, an accolade proven to have a fifty percent predictive accuracy.

When Dolan first arrived in Milwaukee, I was toward the tail end of my time in the seminary. One morning I drove there to give a lecture to future deacons and nondegree students on professional and sexual boundaries. Uncharacteristically late, I found the parking lot almost full and chose a spot close to the archbishop's residence (hardly a palace). Guilty that I might have infringed a secular parking boundary, I scanned the area. Walking rapidly toward me was an impressively large and determined-looking man with a ruddy complexion I assumed must be a parking lot attendant. Coming to an abrupt halt, he stuck out his hand in greeting; "Hello, I'm Timothy, who are you?" Only then did I notice the Roman collar and purple shirt front partly concealed by his topcoat. We exchanged genial but brief pleasantries before I sped away to give my lecture. This encounter fits the description of "Hail fellow, well met," consistent with the public and press portrayals of the man who may become the first American pope.

—

When Kathie and I decided to leave the Catholic Church in 2005, we informed our parish priest and both bishops (Dolan and Sklba) of our decision. We invited our priest to dinner and wrote a letter to the bishops. The priest, who knew us best, was supportive and understanding. A highly intelligent and well-educated man, author of several books and multilingual, he had previously led us on a tour of the Holy Land. He clearly had his own doubts and concerns about the hierarchy and might have been happier as an order priest.

Auxiliary Bishop Sklba, a previous confidante of the retired archbishop, in his customary sensitive and spiritual manner, reached out to us and offered to discuss our concerns. Archbishop Dolan sent us a Christmas card with the message; "Dear Kathie and Barry, Good luck in your search for the perfect church. My church welcomes sinners, that's why I'm so comfortable here."

We knew the first sentence was true; the second felt dismissive and patronizing. So we sought for the most compatible and comfortable church we could find. Ironically this led us to the Episcopal branch of the Church of England that I had dutifully attended from ages eleven to eighteen. It has preserved most of the Roman liturgy and rituals but with a more enlightened dogma, including a role for women pastors. Nevertheless, it is mired in a fractious dispute over homosexuality and holy office.

When I look back on my brief acquaintance with Timothy Dolan, I am reminded of Ronald Reagan, a conservative I liked but for whom I would never vote. I admire Dolan's persona but not his theology.

Late Harvest

Published in *Theatre of the Mind*. Noble House. circa 1999:

> Prayer is a want
> God plants at birth,
> But unmet needs,
> A drought of love
> Force weeds to grow:
>
> —

Our haste to speak,
Our introspection,
Our must control,
Our self perfection,
Our lack of trust:

These faults that nip
The buds of faith
Yield no crops; just
Silence between
God and us.

Despite these doubts,
We will keep vigil.
Divine seeds sprout—
What god has sown
He means to reap.

—Barry Blackwell, 1999

On Devotion

Standing in front of St. Francis Seminary is a statue of its patron saint—St. Francis de Sales.

On the day I arrived for my first class, a member of the student council gave each of us a copy of the Saint's *Introduction to the Devout Life*. With it was a note: "Hoping you will find in the writings of our patron inspiration and encouragement as you pursue your formation program in church ministry."

Eager for help in my almost perpetually dry prayer life, I began to read the volume at once, hoping for tips or strategies on how to pray better.

Instead, I found something else. I realized I was reading a love story.

For the first time I saw that faith was not enough. Because faith is a deliberate leap into the unknown, we try to make it safe by intellectual effort. We seek the testimony of saints and the wizardry of contemplative prayer. We choose a moral compass, study the wisdom of the philosophers, and calculate the odds between purpose and chaos in the universe.

But it is not enough; it's not love. It's not devotion.

My difficulty was in loving, not in believing.

I already knew this about myself in the psychological realm but had never applied it to my spiritual life. Growing up from age five in all-male boarding schools, I had a stunted capacity for love or trust and a dread of being abandoned. Love was such a risk for me that I never used the word until I was past forty and began to learn that there was more to intimacy than sex.

Blessed with a wonderful wife, love blossomed late in my life. It had grown alongside faith, following my conversion at fifty-seven years of age.

Suddenly I saw a different purpose to the Incarnation. Not only redemption and salvation but also Jesus as God's gift of love to the world. I saw the resurrection less as a promise of the afterlife and more as an assurance of a perpetual loving presence.

This was a transforming insight. It is a lot easier to pray to someone you trust and love than to a stranger who might abandon you on a whim, at a moment's notice.

Of course, my prayer life will continue to fluctuate. Love ebbs and flows; doubts and thoughts intrude. God may be busy elsewhere. But the foundation has shifted. It is now set on solid ground.

In the Vestibule

This poem was written during a seminar on the relationship between our profile on the Meyers Briggs Personality Inventory and prayer life or meditation.

Thanks, but no thanks!
How come you created me this way,
An INTJ?
We "skeptics and atheists"
Who wait outside the gate?

You made me in your image
Yet we can't communicate?
I try but . . .
Chores preempt prayer,
Rumination ruins contemplation.

But wait, I dimly see . . .
The threads of God's diversity,
Woven in the tapestry of life.
I owe it to myself to use
The gifts bestowed on me.

I *can* find a way to pray . . .

Discern reality, not dreams,
Make work wait,
Plan quiet times,
Meditate on solid themes.

Slowly, the gate opens
Just wide enough
To see my shadow side
Can this be true . . .
Your grace at work in me?

—Barry Blackwell, July 2000

Faith

Our ancestors evolved
At a high price.
Bigger brains knew and counted
The sources of sustenance,
Flesh, water, grain.
Then gained prescience,
A certainty of death.

Cave dwellers
Imagined higher powers,
Placating them with sacrifice,
Their price for peace of mind;
Quelling grief and angst
About famine, drought,
Meager supplies
And brief lives.

Greeks, Romans, and Hindus
Sought certainty in life,
And afterlife beyond,
From pantheons of deities
With human, animal
Or hybrid forms,
Whose lives and fate
They thought to emulate.

The Trinity came late,
God's son a sacrifice.
The entry fee
At heaven's gate
To all eternity:
Belief, without uncertainty.
That mythic truth
Called Faith.

—Barry Blackwell, November, 2009

Works

Some do good
Because of God
And some because they should.

Some do bad
Because of God
And some because they could.

What matters most
Is what you do
And not because of who.

—Barry Blackwell, October 2009

Without Doubt: Beyond Reason

Is faith a truth,
God's planted seed,
Or psychic fruit
Of human need?

Some seek facts
And reason to believe,
Others find conviction
Easier to achieve.

Works don't find
The key to heaven's gate,
Unbelievers, good or kind
Are doomed to wait.

When in doubt
Skeptics are rejected,
Those without
More readily accepted.

—Barry Blackwell, November 2009

Joint Declaration*—Truth Revealed!

One half millennia late
Rancorous debate is done,
Heresy repealed,
Their schism healed.

Devout believers, even sinners,
Get to heaven.
Doubters, doing good, go to hell,
Unforgiven.

*After five hundred years,
the Catholic and Lutheran faiths found common ground.

—Barry Blackwell, Christmas 2002

It's As If . . .

For mankind to survive
Our primal thirst for sin and war
Takes more than the Torah
Or a single sect.

It's *as if* . . .
Everything Jesus said is true.
Only a universal creed
Of loving deeds
Will do.

It's *as if* . . .
Baptism did not create
An easy believer.
Culture and training
Made me a skeptic, doubter.

It's *as if* . . .
Christ's divinity, the resurrection,
The Trinity, Immaculate Conception,
Perpetual virginity.
All feed my incredulity.

It's *as if* . . .
I want to emulate
His Sermon on the Mount
Without faith, despite doubt.
But deeds alone don't count.

Do you wonder why
I try to live
The Jesus myth
As if it's true?

—Barry Blackwell, Christmas 2002

Seminary Cemetery

Next to the seminary are several acres of woodland, speckled with daffodils in spring. In the center of this small wood is a neglected cemetery, last resting place of nuns and priests who served their maker a century or so ago.

Two hundred eighty-one women
In consecrated ground.
Lined like Veterans,
Named and dated
Under humble concrete headstones.
All born and dead,
Unemancipated,
Between Two Councils.

Men are in short supply,
Scattered sparsely about,
Each lying alone
Beneath marble monuments
And etched eulogies.
Their proud tombstones fractured
Or toppled over
By teenage gangs.

Looking on, God wonders
Why She gave them genders.

—Barry Blackwell, April 2000

Question in Feminist Theology Class

"Does a Then and Now analogy
Allow a He and She theology?"

Early Councils dictated dogma
Leaving naught to chance.
Today's debate embraces metaphor
And celebrates nuance.

The past taught uniformity,
Negating every heresy.
The present sought inclusivity
Creating more diversity.

Patriarchy defines a heavenly faith
For Christendom from birth.
Matriarchy aligns its path toward
God's Kingdom here on Earth.

—Barry Blackwell, 2004

Creed Term Paper

Catholic Faith and Doctrine

BY THE POWER OF THE HOLY SPIRIT, HE WAS BORN OF THE VIRGIN MARY AND BECAME MAN

Submitted by Barry Blackwell

Fall Semester 1999

INTRODUCTION

Creeds, like sacred scripture, evolved from an oral to a written tradition. From the fundamental faith beliefs spoken of by the earliest Christians, to what the first Church fathers independently asserted in their letters, to a consensus of faith painstakingly hammered out at Church councils and modified in the early centuries as wisdom confronted heresy.

As we examine the doctrine of the Holy Spirit and the virgin birth three themes will emerge. First, its earliest oral origins remain speculative, obscure from historical analysis, and therefore controversial. Second, the doctrine became central to the early Church's struggle to understand the full meaning of the Incarnation and to define the balance between Christ's divinity and humanity. And thirdly, the doctrine acquired a powerful secondary significance in Mariology.

Perhaps the most striking aspect to this portion of the Nicene Creed is its early formulation and unquestioning acceptance throughout most of Church history. This may seem surprising given two facts. First, like the resurrection, the virgin birth is biologically implausible, and second, the supporting Biblical attestation is slender. As such, the doctrine has been the natural topic of fresh scrutiny in the second half of the twentieth century as the magisterium has endorsed critical Biblical exegesis. In his seminal 1973 text, *The Virginal Conception and the Bodily Resurrection*, Raymond Brown notes that the Church's unquestioning unanimity on the topic of the virgin birth is "cracking in many places."

Not surprisingly, there is considerable tension when such a core and long-cherished doctrine is opened up to new scrutiny. Even reasoned analysis can provoke reflexive accusations of infidelity—if not heresy.

In 1988, a scholarly article by Edward Barrett in the *Bible Review* drew more letters to the editor than any other paper ever published. Only two out of twenty-seven felt it had merit. Daley reports a similar experience after preaching a sermon on the topic to a university audience. Probably the most outstanding example of how contentious an issue this can become was when the moderator of the Church of Scotland preached a "middle of the road" Christmas sermon on the virgin birth in 1993.

It provoked a letter to the national press signed by one hundred ten Presbyterian ministers deploring the skepticism and divisive nature of the comments.

With all these introductory thoughts in mind, we will now venture forth to seek a fuller understanding of what the Nicene Creed conveys to Catholics about the Holy Spirit and the virgin birth.

ORIGINS OF THE DOCTRINE

Matthew 1:18-25 (excerpted):

> Mary was betrothed to Joseph, but before they lived together, she was found with child through the Holy Spirit. Joseph her husband since he was a righteous man, yet unwilling to expose her to shame, decided to divorce her quietly. Such was his intention when, behold, the angel of the Lord appeared to him in a dream and said, "Joseph, son of David, do not be afraid to take Mary your wife into your home. For it is through the Holy Spirit that this child is conceived in her." All this took place to fulfill what the Lord had said through the prophet: "Behold, the virgin shall be with child and bear a son, and they shall call him Emmanuel." When Joseph awoke, he did as the angel commanded him and took his wife into his home. He had no relations with her until she bore a son, and he named him Jesus.

Luke 1:26-35 (excerpted):

> The angel Gabriel was sent from God to a town of Galilee called Nazareth to a virgin betrothed to a man named Joseph, of the house of David, and the virgin's name was Mary. Then the angel said to her, "Do not be afraid, Mary, for you have found favor with God. Behold, you will conceive in your womb and bear a son, and you shall name him Jesus." But Mary said to the angel, "How can this be, since I have no relations with a man?" And the angel said to her in reply, "The Holy Spirit will come upon you, and the power of the

Most High will overshadow you. Therefore the child to be
born will be called holy, the Son of God."

EVOLUTION OF THE DOCTRINE

This section provides a recapitulation of the historical development of
the doctrine from its first written exposition in the Gospels of Matthew
and Luke to its final form in the Nicene Creed and its subsequent fate
throughout Church history up to Vatican II.

The two synoptic gospels that mention the virgin birth were probably
written around AD 80-90. Matthew's almost certainly originated from
Antioch where he was active in the church at that time.

St. Ignatius, the third bishop of Antioch and Peter's successor, was taken
to Rome where he was martyred around AD 110. On the sea voyage,
Ignatius wrote a letter to the Smyraens, the purpose of which was to
denounce the Docetist heresy that Jesus's humanity was an illusion. In
it, Ignatius congratulates the local church on its belief that Jesus was
"God's son by the will and power of God, truly born of a virgin."

Kelly notes that Justin Martyr, writing around AD 150 states, "We say
that the Word who is the first offspring of God was begotten without
carnal intercourse."

Until the middle of the second century, the focus was on the virgin birth
rather than on the conception by the Holy Spirit. This evolved in the
second half of the century when Irenaeus (AD 102-202) in his work
Against Heresies provides the first balanced viewpoint of Jesus's both divine
and human nature and gives a sophisticated analysis of the Incarnation.

Writing a little later, Tertullian (AD 150-240) elaborates the same themes
borrowing from such apocryphal sources as the Protoevangelium of
James.

The role of the Holy Spirit was further elaborated in this time period
by Gnostic apocryphal sources such as the Sibylline Oracles and the
Ascension of Isaiah.

By AD 200, the twin themes of divine conception and human virginal birth were well-developed and used theologically to sustain Christ's dual nature.

Probably the first creedal assertion of the doctrine was in the Old Roman Creed believed to have taken shape in the Pontificate of Pope Victor (AD 189-AD 199). Written in Greek, it contains the words, "who was born from the Holy Spirit and the Virgin Mary."

In the third and early fourth centuries, controversies and heresies continued to rage between the two extremes of Christ's divinity only (docetism) and less than the divine (Arianism). In AD 325, the Emperor Constantinople convened a council of over three hundred bishops to establish correct doctrine. Perhaps because Arianism was predominant at the time—Arius was an Alexandrian priest who died in AD 336—the text of the first version of the Nicene Creed reads: "who because of our salvation came down and became incarnate, becoming man." It omits to mention the Virgin Mary. This was corrected over fifty years later at the Council of Constantinople (AD 381) in which a "fuller statement of faith" was made using the words, "who because of our salvation came down from heaven and was incarnate from the Holy Spirit and the Virgin Mary and became man." This revised Creed kept its attribution to Nicea.

Thus, the historical lineage of the doctrine of the virgin birth is clearly outlined from the time of Matthew's and Luke's Gospels at the end of the first century to the amended Nicene Creed at the end of the fourth century.

The Creed's wording remained unaltered throughout the rest of Church history and proved adequate to sustain the theology of Christ's dual nature. There would continue to be further challenges in the form of fifth century Nestorianism and eighth-century Adoptionism, but the magisterium needed no further authority to rebut them than already existed.

Apart from its central significance in the act of incarnation, the doctrine of the virgin birth has assumed considerable meaning in other areas of Catholic faith, including asceticism, celibacy, and Mariology. These extrascriptural and noncreedal accretions will be discussed later but are noted here because of the degree to which they have contributed to an unquestioning acceptance of this aspect of the Creed throughout most of Church history, until the present.

The virgin birth has never been critically reviewed by any council since Nicea and consequently never declared infallible, though many may consider it so. As Brown notes, "It is an unexamined doctrine, taken for granted."

THE DOCTRINE CRITICALLY EXAMINED

In this section, we will deal with three points of view. A personal analysis built on fairly traditional exegetical material, a brief overview of other contemporary viewpoints, and the broader Catholic faith perspective.

A Personal Viewpoint

Fruitful exegesis requires knowledge of an author's audience and culture to facilitate insights into whatever influences and agendas might color the text. This process is imaginative and informed.

Our time is the final quarter of the first century. The place is Antioch in Syria, on the banks of the Orontes River. Founded almost four hundred years earlier, it is a cosmopolitan city with a large established Jewish colony and a recent influx of Greek-speaking Christians who have fled from persecution in Jerusalem after its destruction by the Romans. The population is a melting pot of Hellenistic, Jewish, and Christian sects. It was here that Peter was the Christian community's first bishop and it was the city where Paul and Barnabas proselytized and from which Paul set sail on his missions to the gentiles. In Antioch, Peter and Paul disputed whether Jewish law should be imposed on gentile converts and the word "Christian" was first used to describe them.

Matthew is assumed to have written his Gospel at Antioch around or shortly after AD 80. Luke probably wrote his at or around the same time in Greece, but as Paul's companion he was certainly familiar with events in Antioch. By the time both Gospels were written, Peter and Paul were dead. Jews, Gentiles, Christians and pagans were competing to define their beliefs. Mark's Gospel, written a little earlier, was available. For Christians, it was a time of crisis in church identity and moral leadership. Matthew, an elder of the church, felt the need to "retrieve the tradition" in order to heighten the dignity, power, and authority of Jesus at a time when hostile Jewish and pagan influences were circulating disparaging rumors of his illegitimacy.

The Antioch Church as a whole was engaged in "apologetic, polemic, and proselytizing activity" among both Jews and Gentiles.

This is the cultural and historical background against which we need to examine the birth narratives in Matthew and Luke. Mark had chosen to ignore all details of Jesus's life before the adult ministry. Whether he felt this was irrelevant, obscure, or embarrassing is not known. But in the context of all the questions being asked and the rumors spread about Jesus in the Antioch community, Mark's account could no longer be considered fully adequate.

The two birth narratives are so different they cannot be derived from the earlier common source "Q," which both authors borrowed from extensively in the rest of their Gospels. Clearly they were not from Mark, although both Matthew and Luke appropriated and modified parts of his text. Each account is so differently embellished, they were not simply copying from each other.

In fact, the two narratives have only two points in common: Mary was a virgin when she conceived, and there was divine intervention announced by an angel. On even these two issues, there is disagreement. In Matthew, Mary is already several months pregnant, and the angel speaks to Joseph. In Luke, the angel announces Mary's impending pregnancy directly to her.

Why would both authors, familiar with events in Antioch around AD 75, include an account of a divinely ordained virginal birth but do it in such different ways?

—

There were at least three forces at play. First, Mark's Gospel was inadequate, incomplete, and stressed Jesus's humanity.

Secondly, the questions around Jesus's divinity and humanity may have already begun to circulate and required a response. Only thirty years later, John's Gospel would set forth a Hellenistic, high Christology that would offer such a mystical explanation of Jesus's origins from the Logos that it would set the stage for Gnosticism and docetism. Antioch was an environment filled with ideas stemming from Peter who had known Jesus both in life and after death, and Paul, a supreme pragmatist who had seen Jesus speaking from heaven. The intellectual and faith environment was one that would encourage a belief in both divinity and humanity. This would be the role that the Church at Antioch would play in later years in finding the middle ground between Gnostic and Arian heresies. Even before John's Gospel was written, Ignatius of Antioch was defending Jesus's dual nature against the Ebionites, who claimed his exclusive humanity and the docetists who denied it.

Thirdly, an answer was called for concerning the rumors of illegitimacy. In her book, *The Illegitimacy of Jesus*, Jane Schaberg examines this issue in great depth, including her exegesis of canonical, apochryphal, rabbinical, and Greek sources. These include Celsus's claim in *True Discourse* (AD 178) that Mary was seduced or raped by a Roman soldier, together with Origen's emphatic rebuttal in *Contra Celsus* (AD 246). Schaberg's conclusions are twofold: there was a strong and early Jewish and pagan tradition concerning the possibility of Jesus's illegitimacy and an equally profound early Christian response to stifle or overlook the possibility.

When we examine the secondary embellishment each author adds to the virgin birth, this conclusion seems possible. Matthew, writing to a Jewish audience, does two things. The genealogy he presents is strikingly unusual by the inclusion of four First Testament women all of whom had either illegitimate children or illicit sexual liaisons. All became Jewish heroines whose concupiscence was later redeemed. Secondly, Matthews's account acknowledges Joseph's concern about paternity and makes him the focus of the angel's visitation. This would appeal to Jewish sensitivities around the betrothal. A wife's virginity was a Jewish man's birthright that not even God would revoke. Joseph must give his concurrence.

—

Luke, writing for a Greek audience, feels no need to pander to Jewish mores but plays to the Hellenistic mythology of a planned union between deity and human. In this account, the angel speaks directly to Mary, announcing the honor thrust upon her.

Consciously or not, both Matthew and Luke probably invoked this theme of a divine role in the parentage of famous humans. This idea can be traced to other world religions (Buddha, Krishna), in Greco-Roman myths (Perseus, Romulus), Egyptian history (the pharaohs), and Hellenism (Plato, Alexander the Great).

The two synoptic Gospels apart, what does the rest of Scripture say about the virgin birth? Only a little.

Most scholars assert that the First Testament is totally silent and that Matthew's quotation from Isaiah (7:14) which predicts that "the virgin will conceive" is a translation error, taken out of context with no predictive relevance or intent. There are stories in both testaments about God intervening in the process of procreation—Abraham and Sarah, Elizabeth and Zechariah—but these are not close parallels to the virgin birth.

We have discussed the other two Gospels in the earlier critique of Matthew and Luke. But what about Paul? Galatians 4:4 states, "God sent forth His son, born of a woman, born under the law." This statement merely affirms Jesus's humanity without any mention of virginity or divine intervention.

1 Timothy 1:4 denounces "myths and genealogies which promote speculation, rather than training in faith." The authorship is uncertain, but the statement was probably written twenty or so years before Matthew or Luke. It may indicate some impatience among Paul's circle with the controversy brewing in Antioch around Jesus's illegitimacy.

Finally, it is worth noting that Ignatius was the only late first—and early second-century Church father to mention the virgin birth.

In spite of the paucity of collateral material to support the birth narratives, many scholars warn against the "argument from silence"

–

435

when considering a time period in which there is so much lost written material and about which relatively little is known for certain.

Other Contemporary Viewpoints

Most of the above material is consistent with mainstream exegesis. There are, of course, more divergent treatments of the texts on the virgin birth.

First, and most noteworthy, is the Jesus Seminar. Meeting in Santa Rosa, California, in 1994, this roving band of skeptical scholars cast their colored beads in a twenty-four to one vote against the historical accuracy of the virgin birth. However, in an act of unaccustomed timidity, they declined to vote on removing the Holy Spirit as a potential father of Christ. Apparently the group was influenced by discrepancies between canonical and apocryphal sources. Their conclusion was quickly criticized as a "rehash of old canards" by "pebble-based" researchers.

The Oxford scholar, Wainright, is credited by Bostock with constructing a theory that John the Baptist and Jesus were both fathered by Zechariah based on Luke's report that Mary lived in his house for three months after she went to visit Elizabeth—long enough to establish pregnancy.

According to Jaki, Muslims who are familiar with the Christian Bible accept Jesus as a great prophet but reject the birth narratives in part because of a pervasive cultural chauvinism that brands women as tainted with sin. The same author attributes a somewhat similar view to Orthodox Judaism and notes that "as soon as the doctrine of the Virgin Birth was publicly preached no more Jews were converted."

The feminist interpretation of the virgin birth is well-developed and scholarly. Schaberg quotes Emily Dickinson to express her conclusion that Matthew and Luke "told the truth but told it slant." She contends that the possibility of Jesus's illegitimacy was stifled by the author's "androcentric" perspective and desire to quell a Jewish slander. If this had not happened, a different kind of theology might have emerged:

—

> When the (unintended) aspect of independence in the virgin symbol is freed from the patriarchal setting then the "Virgin Mother" can be heard to say something about female autonomy within the context of sexual, parental, and creative relationships. This approach would not completely deny that the Church has been correct in affirming a virginal conception, but it would initiate a new state in the complex historical development of the belief.

This seems to be a "what if" position. If one temporarily suspends judgment about the truth of the doctrine, it allows us to apply a feminist approach to our faith life. The author's objective seems to be to cast enough doubt on the doctrine to allow this to happen without taking a firm position on the doctrine itself.

Finally, there is one more position toward the birth narratives taken by the German New Testament scholar Gerd Lüdemann. This is a bold "slash and burn" approach which concludes that the virgin birth is a falsification of history. Lüdemann accuses Brown and other scholars of creating doubt but being too cowardly to accept the consequences of their own conclusions. He has made the same point with regard to the Creed which he claims is often critically examined, found wanting, but never changed.

The principle focus of Lüdemann's attack is not so much the divinity of Christ (which the book leaves unexplored) but the evils of Mariology. "It is therefore time to lift the virgin veil which—woven from a mixture of dogmatics, piety, and fantasy—has lain over the figure of Mary."

This statement ushers in our next consideration of the doctrine of the virgin birth.

The Catholic Faith Context

One might suppose that a creedal doctrine should stand on its own without needing to discuss extracreedal or nonscriptural accretions. But this particular doctrine has developed profound implications for

—

Catholic faith far beyond our exegesis to date. It became the origin and symbol of asceticism, celibacy, and the sinlessness of Christ and of Marian devotion.

In *Catholicism*, McBrien asserts that no theological and doctrinal presentation of Catholicism can claim to be comprehensive if it left out the Virgin Mary. In Marthaler's book on the Creed, the entire section on the virgin birth is devoted exclusively to Mariology. The Annunciation scene in Luke's Gospel is the most widely quoted religious theme in the Bible.

These developments are quite distinct from the forces that brought the original doctrine into being. They began in the middle of the second century with the Protoevangelium of James and were further elaborated in the third century as the doctrine of triple virginity. Mary was a virgin when she conceived, remained so despite the birth process, and preserved this status throughout her lifetime.

Augustine (AD 354-430) was a natural early champion. Devoted to his own mother and disgusted by his personal concupiscence, Mary was the only person (including all the saints) who could be declared free from sin. It was as a result of his birth from Mary that Jesus himself had no original sin. Since Augustine equated original sin with concupiscence, the virgin also became a symbol for asceticism and celibacy. As Campenhausen notes, "The Virgin Birth in its sanctity works as a counterpart of natural sexual activity, and Mary the Virgin Mother then appears as the prototype of purity and chastity, the object of admiration."

When Nestorius publicly challenged Mary's title as "Mother of God" he was ruled against at the Council of Ephesus (AD 431). This provided a strong impetus to Marian devotion.

An all-male hierarchy created a felt psychological need for a gentler female person to act as mediator. By the medieval period, Mary was known as "Spiritual Mother" and "Queen of Heaven." The rosary had become the "poor person's Psalter." As early as 1480, the feast of the Immaculate Conception was celebrated, although it did not become doctrine until Pius IX in 1954. As recently as 1950, Pius XII announced the new doctrine of Bodily Assumption and declared it infallible. Mary became the subject of innumerable visions and revelations around the world. In November 1964, Pope Paul VI referred explicitly to Mary as "mother of the Church."

Although there has been a decline in Marian devotion since Vatican II, both feminism and liberation theology have co-opted their own interpretations of Mary to represent their chosen points of view.

The fact that this devotion is so peculiarly Catholic and relatively devoid of scriptural support makes Mariology a perceived obstacle to ecumenical reconciliation. It is also one reason why scholarly attempts to question the virgin birth meet such vehement and widespread rejection.

A CONTEMPORARY SYNTHESIS

Intellectual skepticism about the virgin birth is not new.

Martin Luther considered it offered three miracles: "The first that God became man; the second that a virgin was a mother; and third that the heart of man should believe this."

At the time of the American Revolution, Thomas Paine noted that only Mary and Joseph knew the truth and that they had not written or spoken about it. He concluded, "It is hearsay upon hearsay, and I do not choose to rest my belief on such evidence."

As this review has shown, cautious skepticism among scholars is normative. Most post-Vatican II theologians conclude that it is impossible to establish the historicity of the virgin birth. Many are content to let the matter rest there. They seem inclined to view the doctrine as a "theologumen"—something Catholics need to believe but theologians cannot prove. This sounds a bit like a theological white lie!

A few scholars, like the feminists and liberation theologians, raise enough doubt to have the doctrine meet their own dogmatic needs.

–

Only the Jesus Seminar and Gerd Lüdemann conclude the Creed is in error. Even the Jesus Seminar stopped short of denying the Incarnation, leaving Lüdemann alone to suggest that the Creed be amended.

Whatever theologians may conclude, the majority of Catholics view this article of the Creed and its accretions with a profound reverence that goes far beyond scriptural support. This seems remarkable in a skeptical era when many no longer believe in miracles. While intellectuals struggle to define reason, the faithful say the rosary! While theologians strain at swallowing a gnat, the congregation ingests an elephant! For many, the psychology that underpins faith appears far stronger than the intellect that explores reason.

The fundamental question to be asked of this doctrine is whether Matthew and Luke's birth narratives add anything to Christology that cannot be more readily (but less beautifully) understood?

Can we accept the reality of the Incarnation and allow it to remain a mystery without demanding an explanation? Do we need to explore the way in which God intervened in sexual mechanisms?

As about to be twenty-first century humans, we know a lot more concerning procreation than our Biblical ancestors. Modern genetics has removed all doubt about how God creates humans. We can reconstruct the genome and clone new beings. There is even a sect in Canada, the Roelians, whose 40,000 members consider cloning for eternity a central mandate of their religion.

Soon enough, we will know which chromosomes convey what behaviors. Theoretically, we could design a sinless human being. If we wished to play God and reenact the Incarnation would we choose Dorothy Day or Mother Teresa to carry the infant to birth? Would virginity matter?

Berry recently reviewed genetic speculation in the journal of *Science and Christian Belief*. Among other possibilities discussed was parthenogenesis, a process by which animal species reproduce without sexual union. After concluding this cannot occur in humans and considering all the other possibilities of genetic engineering, the author concludes that the real issue is the Incarnation and that the virgin birth is best considered as a "secondary miracle."

This view, which coincides with my own, was more fully explored by Thomas. He concluded that the conception of Jesus signals God's new creation—a fact more important than its mechanisms. It should be recognized, of course, that this resolution, like that of John's Gospel, carries the risk of Gnosticism if taken too far. But Catholics today far better understand the doctrine of Jesus's dual nature and are less likely to be pulled to extremes.

On the threshold of a new millennium, we might well ask, "what will be the future of this doctrine?" The Catholic Church does not surgically correct its creeds. But might we imagine that the virgin birth could become a vestigial doctrine? Not via new scriptural analysis, but as our ethical and moral development evolves and our psychological needs shift.

Once we can move beyond the virginity of Mary, we may lose the subliminal notion that the Y chromosome came from God but the X from a human. The more destructive aspects of Catholic patriarchy might dwindle and gender neutrality become a reality.

Will we need to be less preoccupied with Mary's chastity if we come to view sex as capable of being sacramental in relationships, not just concupiscent? If this happens, celibacy may become construed as a choice, beneficial but not essential to priesthood.

Should these events come to pass, the ecumenical door will swing more widely open.

In all of this, we must remember that it is not only reason that informs faith but our innermost psychological needs. And these change with time.

I conclude by quoting a few lines by T. S. Elliot from the poem "Little Gidding":

—

You are not here to verify,
Instruct yourself or inform curiosity
Or carry report. You are here to kneel.

Interactions with the Divine

February 10, 2000

This short essay, written twelve years ago, illustrates the intellectual contortions involved in my vain attempts to find a spiritual life. This included several years at the seminary where the essay was penned in response to a class reading assignment on "Knowing God" (see reference below). This synchronized in an odd way with a poem on the same topic I had written six months previously and also anticipated themes that arose in monthly meetings with my spiritual director.

While reading Chapter 9 of Gill, a light bulb went on in my head. Like Archimedes, I was tempted to exclaim, "Eureka!" as water overflowed the bathtub of my brain.

Chapter 9 is not blessed with two asterisks in the syllabus, so what I write is not for credit. But the intellectual insight is important to my spiritual formation and invites my pen to paper.

Each time I meet my spiritual director she asks, "And where has God been in your life this month?" Although I am getting used to the question, my initial reaction is to flinch and feel guilty. I am called upon to discover, recollect (even invent?) some divine revelatory intrusion into my everyday experience. Usually, not surprisingly, there is none.

Being kind and wise, my spiritual director reassures me that my attempts to make a "leap of faith" (Gill, p. 122) are not all that enters into the equation. God may choose not to intervene. We all have dry spells. So we move on to my prayer life; am I "having a conversation with God?" That too is difficult. I'm weighed down with the psychological baggage of a well-trained physician. A busy intellect, strong control impulses, and an oversized ego. All are impediments to dialogue with the divine.

—

Now listen again to Gill: "Individual commitment and will are to be distinguished from a mutual, interactive and relational response to the divine" (Gill, p. 121). "Religious awareness is mediated in and through our interaction within and among the social or community dimension of our existence" (Gill, p. 124). Most importantly, "Both *seeking* and *finding* are relational activities, for it is only through interaction that the religious dimension is experienced" (Gill, p. 123). I have italicized those two words in the previous sentence because they are the same words used in the title to a poem I wrote more than six months ago. Here it is:

Seek and Find

Man may find God
In anxious prayer
Or maybe not.

Man may find God
In tedious work
Or maybe not.

Man may find God
In glorious nature
Or maybe not.

Man may find God
In pious churches
Or maybe not.

Man may find God
In joyous play
Or maybe not.

Man may find God
In obvious places
Or maybe not.

—

God will find man
Somewhere he searches
And never not.

—Barry Blackwell, circa 2001

The poem voices some subliminal sentiments aroused by my spiritual director's gentle probing. Note also that it relies on paradox (Gill, p. 134). The last stanza unties the paradox. Would the poem be better without it? "Utterances that express both sides of these couplets lose their insightfulness when resolved by too much theological footwork" (ibid., 134). Intellect cannot fill a spiritual void. But surely, searching for a deity implies doubt about its very existence, doubt which the final stanza rejects. But based on what? Wishful thinking?

Still, talk about synchronicity! The poem written six months beforehand resonates with a class in seminary that immediately preceded a meeting with my spiritual director, each raising the same unanswerable questions.

Recently the axis has shifted. I have been experimenting with centering prayer—a form that seeks to obliterate the self. But I tend to nod off. Instead, it might be well to find a better way to acquaint myself with my divine dialogical partner, perhaps "the word made flesh?" (ibid.,127) In our session yesterday, my spiritual director ended by suggesting that I might concentrate more on reading the daily scripture. Another idea based on tacit awareness of my predicament? I'm sure she would agree with Gill (Chapters 10 and 11) that prayer is a form of language, and that all language is, inevitably, reciprocal, and interactive but with less risk of falling asleep.

Today the search continues. Now I feel as if I am looking for an oasis in the desert, still seeking the raw material for a real "Eureka!" moment to replenish the bathtub of my brain!

Reference: Gill, J. H.; *On Knowing God.* Westminster Press, Philadelphia, 1981.

Prayer of Petition

For;

Blind Portrait Painters,
Crippled Alpine Climbers,
Deaf Opera Divas,
Faith-Filled Doubters.

Lord have mercy;

Grant us what
We each have not.

We pray to the Lord;

But are we heard?

—Barry Blackwell, 2003

Judgment Day

People of faith who believe in an afterlife defer judgment until they meet their maker, while skeptics weigh life in the balance when still on earth and aboveground. I suppose priests who are exposed pedophiles sacrifice both eternity and existential peace of mind, provided they truly believe. How can they?

My own balance sheet between belief and disbelief derives from an atheistic upbringing in an agnostic culture, a life's work as a physician, four years attending a Catholic seminary, three years working for Catholic Charities, my experiences with Faith in Recovery, and my recent response to the pedophile crisis and its sequelae.

My career reinforced my upbringing in the era between medical interventions based largely on faith to the application of scientific methods that distinguish treatment effects from placebo response and

445

spontaneous recovery. Both my medical and psychiatric training rejected the mythic claims of snake oil vendors and psychoanalysis in favor of rigorous double-blind studies and sophisticated statistical standards of proof that distinguish between placebo and active treatment.

Nonetheless, unexpected outcomes and flawed conclusions occurred, creating room for doubt. Sans science, Hippocrates opined that "cheese was a bad article of food," and applying scientific methods, I was mistaken that "prophylactic lithium was a myth" for treating bipolar depression.

So a late-life spiritual journey of inquiry began with the seminary, supported by a kindly spiritual director. I learned more than I came to believe, bumping up against a spiritual handicap and the limits of logic and philosophical speculation even as I admired minds as bright or brighter than mine that were also capable of faith.

But my experiences with Catholic Charities, Faith in Recovery, and the pedophile crisis tilt the scale toward doubt, skepticism, and disbelief. Now my judgment falls firmly on the side of reason over faith. At the same time, I recognize and accept my spiritual shortcomings while recognizing that people I admire might differ.

As I write this, a friend, physician, and former neighbor, now at Saint John's, is in our nursing home eager for "God to call him home." I am sad he may not find the welcome he expects, but I say nothing to dampen his hopes.

The Curate's Egg: Today*

Don't ask and don't tell,
Pedophilia is the way
God has paved to hell.

—Barry Blackwell, December 2009

*This phrase was coined in a cartoon published in November 1895 in the British satirical magazine *Punch*. A curate is having breakfast with his bishop and is served a rotten egg. When the bishop expresses concern, the curate replies, "Oh no, my Lord, I assure you! Parts of it are excellent!" The cartoon was titled "True Humility" but instead became incorporated into the English language to describe a bad situation that is falsely portrayed as partly good.

As the haiku states, this theme has contemporary relevance, reflecting the protective silence of the Church hierarchy in covering up the scandal and their subsequent efforts to project something "good" about the Catholic faith by reversing Vatican II, reinforcing ecclesial authority and reintroducing archaic liturgy. The priest turns his back on the congregation, women are purged from the altar, a celibate all-male priesthood is reaffirmed, and the door is slammed shut on a female priesthood. Once more the *sensus fidelium*, the voice of the people, is muted.

Immoral Theology

Two millennia of all-male morality
Have soured sex, confessed it to death,
Condemning untold souls to purgatory.
The celibate Magisterium wed power,
Mating it with authority.

Forbidden impulses, fear of lust,
Shame and disgust were suppressed,
Hid in Pandora's Box.
Theologians second guessed divine intent.
Nature, not faulty reason, was invoked;
Truth revealed in Moral Manuals,
With sex concealed in Latin texts.

Now the lid is cracked; secrets let loose,
The guardians of our faith defiled.
The contents they concealed, spilled,
Their pedophilia revealed.
When morals fail and lust prevails
Sensus Fidelium might teach the Magisterium
A sexual truth or two.

—Barry Blackwell, April 2002

Moral Hazards

Religions' top claim,
The one that makes me mad is,
We're good, you are bad.

God's main gift to them
Is redemption, after which
They can sin again.

—Barry Blackwell, April 2012

This is a haiku doublet in which the two stanzas, both haikus, reflect a common theme. I will make the immodest claim, probably false, that I invented this variation on the ancient poetic form. Perhaps the di-haiku!

Its theme is a by-product of witnessing the Republican Party run-up to the 2012 presidential election. Having survived eleven presidential elections during my life in America, I believe religion intruded itself in an unprecedented way in this election.

The reasons were paradoxical, as was the manner. It was prelude to a climactic clash between Sermon on the Mount "socialist ideals," alleged to be big government coddling the poor, needy, or feckless, and American "exceptionalism," rooted in commercial profit-making enterprises and "trickle-down economics."

In the Bible, Christ's moral vision is pitted against Mammon. But today, in 2012, we had a moral "Tea Party" right wing in cahoots with big business, led by a Mormon bishop who was a multimillionaire.

The campaign was characterized by obscene financial expenditures from anonymous "Super-Pacs" running entirely negative (uncharitable) ads and politicians making claims independently evaluated as varying mostly between partly true to outright falsehoods. Some might say money, slander, and lies!

A second theme, inevitably introduced in this warlike climate, was the relationship between the ideals expressed in the Republic's Constitution, religious freedom, and morality in government. Beneath the rhetoric and hyperbole, it was hard to tell whether government was infringing on religious rights or religion was imposing its morality on government. The wise concluded that neither had the right to do either to the other.

Polls showed that a majority of Republicans thought the president was a Muslim, all evidence to the contrary. Most Democrats believed the Republican candidate had lost his moral compass, expressing chameleon-like beliefs in a desperate desire to become president.

One thing was clear and certain: the American public was wedded to the deistic assumption of religious moral superiority and would never tolerate an atheist as president, even if he or she had the guts to run. The poem chooses to differ; some of my best and most moral friends are atheists.

Not My Will but Thine

If when we merge in prayer
One voice is heard
Only echoes
Of my own emerge.

But if from deep within
My mind discerns
God speaking out
New thoughts can enter in.

—Barry Blackwell, circa 2002

I or We?

Our brains are wired
For altruism or desire,
Layer on layer of
Options, decisions,
From cortex to limbic lobe.
Orchestrating a symphony
Of character and persona,
Generosity or greed,
Compassion or cruelty,
Love or lust,
Trust or deceit; will it be
I or we?

Religion claims
The moral ground,
Names choice, conscience.
What if survival of the fittest
Prevails instead?
That doing good is best
For human kind?
Without divine intervention
Without the imposition of
Crusades and Inquisitions
Or more "just" wars.
No deity, only we
I and thee?

Wolves don't laugh or weep;
Yet species evolve
When law and love best tooth and claw.
Then if genocide, holocaust, homicide,
Guilt, failure and despair
Invoke a "higher power,"
Answers come not from Holy writ
But in genetic code.
Pathways emit their spiritual gifts
Of hope, compassion, love and trust.
So brain and faith agree;
The future lies
Not with I, but we.

—Barry Blackwell, March 2009

19. GOOD DEEDS

No good deed goes unpunished.

—Origin uncertain . . . perhaps Clare Boothe Luce

Fail I alone, in words and deeds? Why, all men strive and who succeeds?

—Robert Browning

Actions are the seed of fate; deeds grow into destiny.

—Harry S. Truman

"Good works" to religious folks are "good deeds" to the public. The church views them categorically; they are never enough for salvation. As the above three quotes illustrate, public opinion is more nuanced; the bishops might complain they are relativistic—variable interpretations imposed by fallible humans on a moral absolute. Of course, it is easier to measure the outcome of our deeds in this world than wait for judgment in the next!

I was involved in several attempted "good deeds" which illustrate the possible outcomes; one was punished, the second was a failure, the third was an attempt to plant seeds that might grow to success, and the fourth had mixed results. Here is how they happened:

Catholic Charities

Sometimes give your services for nothing.

—Hippocrates

Once upon a time, a long time ago, doctors treated the poor and their colleagues for free. Now they seldom do the former and almost never the latter. My youngest son, who graduated *magna cum laude* in politics, philosophy, and economics, could not imagine how that degree could sustain his love of lobsters or satisfy the need for a life of good deeds. So he switched to medicine. A married man with a young son, he discovered that neither the medical school nor its faculty offered health care coverage, so he enrolled in the state insurance program for the poor and was given a bonus of food stamps. (See "Mammon and Modern Medicine" in "Piece 10: America.")

Soon after I retired, and my son began his premed studies at our local university, I learned through my church activities that Catholic Charities had four clinics in the Milwaukee region staffed by psychology or social work therapists but with no psychiatrist. Many patients must have been taking psychotropic medications prescribed by family practitioners or those few psychiatrists willing to accept Medicaid. This is not ideal care. Communication between patients, therapists, and prescribers working in the same environment pays dividends in improved compliance and better outcomes.

So I volunteered to become involved and waited in vain for a response, despite repeated reminders. Professions are competitive and reluctant to collaborate, and bureaucrats procrastinate because decisions incur risk. After two years or more, I insisted on an answer or threatened to withdraw. I was invited to meet their staff during a summer retreat and was quizzed about my attitudes, beliefs, practice style, and relationships with other disciplines.

They were interested; I offered to staff all four clinics on a regular basis for less than a third of my former salary and to absorb the time and cost of weekly travel (over one hundred miles). If the church was

—

453

unable to collect insurance or fees to cover my salary, I would accept a lower rate. The clinics had a sliding fee scale of as little as five dollars a visit for those without insurance. It soon became clear that the church's accounting capabilities were too chaotic to calculate the balance of cash flow to costs, so our arrangement remained in place throughout my tenure.

It felt good to be back in the saddle in a situation I enjoyed.

The people I served were often impoverished minorities in dire financial straits, uninsured, or unable to find a psychiatrist willing to accept Medicaid. There were two problems. First, between a third and a half of the patients failed to show up for their appointments—not unusual in a population where finding a babysitter or a ride to the clinic was problematic. It was not unusual for a young single mother and her child to sit in my office while the child played with toys and I engaged the mother. This was an opportunity to observe their interactions; earlier, in family practice, I had learned that a common presentation of depression in young mothers is, "I am irritable with my kids and feel guilty afterwards."

A second problem was that the availability of a "free" psychiatrist, willing to prescribe, attracted a kind of client to the clinics that therapists were unused to treating. Armed with a hammer, people seek nails. Therapists were trained to do hour-long therapy with patients who were insightful, verbally adept, and eager to come regularly to talk over their problems and issues. For a while, I felt this might sabotage my involvement but was grateful to discover that the ability to share our opinions and titrate the interaction of medication and therapy was mutually satisfying, although this was not something for which insurance paid.

The therapists were interesting people and most were excellent at their jobs. One social worker spent her days off cleaning other peoples' houses; she made more money per hour, and the work satisfied her compulsive personality!

For those patients with no insurance or unable to pay for medication, I was able to provide free samples or help enroll them in drug assistance programs provided by the pharmaceutical companies, a positive feature of the industry.

I was also fortunate to have a boss who was supportive and knowledgeable; it is unusual for an experienced psychiatrist to report to a social work family therapist!

About three years into my tenure, the head of Catholic Charities, a much respected and long-serving social worker, retired. The archdiocese was now in serious financial trouble with bankruptcy looming ever closer. This may account for the board of trustees' strange decision to appoint a female attorney as the new head of Catholic Charities, someone with no formal training in mental health services. In addition, she lacked administrative skills and had an abrasive and unfriendly demeanor. Her office was adjacent to mine at one of the clinics, yet she never spoke a word to me.

It soon became clear that the attorney's mandate was to cut staff and costs. She introduced unpopular "productivity ratios" for the therapists and quickly got rid of anyone who challenged her authority. Morale declined, and I decided it was time to move on and concentrate on nurturing Faith in Recovery. (See "Faith and Recovery" in this piece.)

My decision was complicated by the difficulty of finding psychiatrists willing to take over my caseload, so I set a departure date some months ahead and began to work with clients and therapists to transfer care. I knew trouble was brewing when someone in Human Resources asked, "Why are you taking so long to leave?"

Some weeks later, on the eve of a vacation, I received a phone call demanding I go immediately to meet with the head of human resources. This involved significant time and a long drive to the archdiocese headquarters. So I asked why it was necessary. No explanation was forthcoming, and again, I was ordered to comply. When I declined due to the inconvenience and my impending vacation, I was told, "Come now, submit your resignation in writing, or be fired." I immediately called my supervisor who was as surprised and uninformed as I was. He called the head of human resources and was brushed off. I returned to

—

455

my office, wrote the resignation, and included a list of the patients left without a psychiatrist.

Over the next several weeks, I wrote to the board of trustees, including the archbishop, requesting an explanation but received none. The archbishop thanked me for my services. I called my erstwhile spiritual friend, the auxiliary bishop, who told me he knew nothing of the problem and felt it would be inappropriate to intervene.

A short time afterward, my boss was also fired, following many years of service and without any job prospect. We met for lunch; he was still bewildered, and I learned nothing had been done to help my patients find a psychiatrist to replace me. I agreed to write him a reference. At a second meeting some months later, he had found an excellent new job, all therapy and no administration, better suited to his skills and temperament.

So I learned the hard way, "No good deed goes unpunished."

Justice Deferred

More than a year after I left, the *Milwaukee Journal Sentinel* published a brief news article stating the executive director of Catholic Charities had resigned "during a closed-door meeting with the Chairperson of the Board of Trustees and another Board member." A statement was made that she "was not asked to leave," but the reporter noted that "efforts to reach her were unsuccessful." Perhaps she also fell afoul of the Chinese proverb, but a confidential source later alleged her abrasive management style had alienated both employees and board members; this was coupled with a budget deficit in 2008.

In 2012, a fellow resident at Saint John's has sponsored a visit here in support of her candidacy as a circuit court judge. I am torn between a desire to question her judicial temperament and adopting the church's strategy of hiding from controversy.

I stayed away but was relieved when she lost the election.

—

Faith in Recovery

When Winston Churchill failed in his bid for election as prime minister after winning World War II, his wife, Clementine, consoled him with the thought that defeat might be a blessing in disguise. Churchill responded, "If so, then it is very effectively disguised."

Faith in Recovery was conceived during the latter part of my time in the seminary. (See "Piece 18: Spiritual Pilgrimage.") The initial success of the program in several Catholic parishes led those of us involved to wonder how we could propagate it for people with mental illness in different faith communities and also preserve what we had learned. My friends put the latter concern in personal terms, "What will happen if you die?"

Taking the bait, I decided we should form a 501(c)3 not-for-profit organization to seek tax deductible funding from foundations to accomplish both propagation and preservation of the program. This would also allow us to develop a "tool kit" which included all the ideas and information necessary to start a Faith in Recovery program in new faith communities within an ecumenical framework.

With free advice from our local Law Society, I wrote an application which was approved by the Internal Revenue Service on its first submission. Our mission prospered initially due largely to a remarkable nun, who suffered from a bipolar disorder, well-controlled by medication. She was responsible for setting up the first homeless health clinic in Milwaukee, and, for over more than thirty years, had been an involved advocate for almost every initiative in the inner city devoted to meeting the housing and mental health needs of its citizens. Her brother designed and monitored our internet website (www.faithinrecovery.com) which contained the tool kit and other helpful material and contacts with existing programs. Sister used her own contacts to obtain free office space, a telephone, and computer in a Senior Service Center that raised money to support its programs from bingo sessions. My daughter-in-law designed a Faith in Recovery logo for our tool kit and the website.

In our new quarters, we set up a steering committee made up of folks with mental illness and family members. Sister followed me as

—

its chairperson. This freed me up to write grant applications, and we obtained over ten thousand dollars from two foundations supportive of mental health issues. This was used to support annual meetings to increase public awareness of Faith in Recovery, expand the number of affiliate programs from different faith traditions, and allowed us to host monthly half-day get-togethers at the Senior Center for representatives of the more than twenty affiliates we had acquired. Each of these programs was encouraged to offer twice-annual day-long seminars for the whole faith community in Mental Illness and Mental Health Awareness Months (May and October) to spread the word and stimulate recruitment to their support groups.

So far, so good. But serious problems began to emerge. The most significant challenged the fundamental premise of the Procovery concept on which Faith in Recovery was based; the extent to which people suffering from severe and persistent mental illness could manage and sustain the affairs of the organization unaided. Some psychiatrists had already challenged this concept, pointing out that the most serious disorders like schizophrenia often erode thought processes and motivation despite the best medication can do, corrupting a person's capacity and skills for independent living.

It was true that the most active members of Faith in Recovery were those with either less severe forms of mental illness or disorders well-controlled by medication. It was difficult to find members with the sustained energy and ability to plan ahead, manage a budget, organize or run meetings, and raise funds.

When attendance and enthusiasm at monthly meetings began to dwindle, we recognized that members were primarily committed to running the support groups and programs in their own faith communities with little time or energy left to devote to the organization as a whole.

Even at the individual church level, there were significant problems in recruiting new members. National data indicate that at least one in five of the population has firsthand knowledge of mental illness (as a patient or family member), but most groups had less than a dozen participants even in faith communities with several hundred members. New members came and went but seldom stayed.

Behind this reluctance lay at least three major factors: one was the stigma of mental illness, fear of discrimination, and concerns about confidentiality. Even in a faith-based community, many people preferred to "remain in the closet." Second is the problem of defining faith or spirituality; one expert likened the diversity to those of blind men groping different parts of an elephant in the room. How might spirituality best be nurtured in a group setting? Expert or personal testimony, Bible readings and exegesis, prayer, meditation, or support and advice?

No systematic effort was made to inquire and identify why some people came once or a few times and dropped out. What had they failed to get that they were seeking?

Finally were issues concerning group leadership. We had taken a position that this should be decided among group members rather than recruiting trained therapists from in or outside the faith community. This idealistic criterion failed to accommodate several concerns. How to deal with individuals who dominated a group or others who failed to speak up? What to do if someone was psychotic or suicidal? How to follow up when someone stopped coming? Was it all right to have patients and family members attend the same group?

Our philosophy was to turn these issues back onto the assumed wisdom of the group. Perhaps this was asking too much? But where was the energy to identify, train, and support successful leadership?

By now, I felt overwhelmed myself, like "Horatio on the bridge, whence all but he had fled." The nun's term as chair of the organizing committee had ended, and nobody was eager to inherit the job. Somebody did so reluctantly, but after I took a leave of absence, everything collapsed.

There was just enough energy and leadership remaining to wind up the 501(c)3 and distribute its remaining funds to kindred organizations. Once again, I was reminded of the dictum, "Experience is what you get when you don't get what you want."

—

The ghost of our website haunts the Internet but nobody answers the phone. A few of the Faith in Recovery programs may still exist, but I have not inquired. In the end the sources of failure often remain ambiguous, as Robert Browning says, "Fail I alone in words or deeds? Why, all men strive and who succeeds?"

Prison Doctor

If you want total security, go to prison. There you're fed, clothed, given medical care and so on. The only thing lacking is freedom.

—Dwight Eisenhower

Being fired by Catholic Charities and the collapse of Faith in Recovery coincided with my son's entry to medical school. Strategically, he applied for early admission and was accepted.

What specialty he might choose was undecided; he was blessed with manual dexterity (God knows from where), benevolence, and equanimity, so the field was open. Working at Saint John's retirement community, where his mother was president, he was much beloved by the elderly residents who awarded him a small scholarship toward his education.

I had secret hopes he might opt for family practice but knew that in today's world, medical students graduated with massive debts, up to one quarter of a million dollars, which seduced them into lucrative procedure-oriented specialties. Having funded his first education, we couldn't afford to subsidize another.

Then fate intervened. Fed up with Catholic misogyny and pedophilia, Kathie had transferred her faith affiliation to the next best faith tradition, the Episcopal Church. We became friends with an individual who was an associate pastor, a former Jesuit, a PhD psychologist, our realtor's spouse, and the head of Psychology in the Wisconsin Correctional System. He persuaded me to consider working as a psychiatrist in the prison system. This was far from an economic sacrifice; in one ten-hour day I could earn enough to pay my son's medical school tuition, $38,000

—

a year, increasing the chance he would feel free to choose whatever field he desired, including the lower paid "talking" specialties: family practice, pediatrics, or psychiatry.

The next opening available was in the women's minimum security prison in Waupun, a sixty-five-mile commute each way. I accepted, committing myself to one thirteen-hour day each week for the next four years, until my son graduated in May 2011.

Half the prison population of up to two hundred fifty women had a mental illness. As the only psychiatrist, I was therefore responsible for up to one hundred twenty-five inmates, depending on the census, amounting to fifteen to twenty patient visits a day. My main responsibility was medication management, and I worked with a very experienced and collaborative psychologist. I was situated in the Health Services Unit (HSU) with a small staff of nurses, none of whom were psychiatrically trained. There was no night or weekend call, which was provided by the psychology staff.

This proved to be one of the most rewarding and educational experiences of my career. In America, prison has always been a venue for those with mental illness, particularly since the mid-60s after closure of the mental asylums and failure to transfer funds into community care. I began with the belief this was plain wrong but soon changed my mind.

The stereotypical inmate with mental illness was incarcerated for one of several reasons. They suffered from a lifelong major mental illness but had never had health insurance or adequate care and so had treated their symptoms with drugs or alcohol, eventually coming into conflict with the law. Other common scenarios were repeat driving offenses due to alcohol abuse, including rare instances of vehicular homicide and retaliatory violence related to spousal abuse. A majority of inmates had suffered from emotional, physical, or sexual abuse as children, and many had posttraumatic stress.

Compared to life in the community, prison offered a safe and predictable environment, free of domestic stress, abuse, or responsibilities and absence of access to drugs or alcohol. In a minimum security prison, inmates also had the possibility of paid employment either in prison

—

(for only cents an hour) or outside in the community, where they were employed in factories, farms, or the Humane Society for at least the minimum wage and often considerably more.

Food in the prison was surprisingly good, and many women worked in the kitchens; staff ate the same food in the same dining hall. There was an excellent library, to which I contributed books, and a well-equipped gym. What was lacking was any chapel, meditational, or quiet space. There was good access to television and regular movies.

Most women shared a cell and upper or lower bunk bed with one other inmate; cell mates were not always compatible or considerate, and "special" (sexual) relationships were strictly forbidden. Makeup was also restricted. Infringements of the regulations resulted in a variety of penalties including "the hole," a period of days or weeks in solitary confinement at the women's maximum security prison in Taycheedah.

Security was maintained by two levels of guards: sergeants or "blue shirts" and two supervisory captains or "white shirts." I was impressed with the caliber of the correctional staff; the two captains were especially impressive in their ability to maintain firm discipline in a fair, predictable, and openhanded manner. Inevitably, there were a few blue shirts with mildly sadistic traits, but this was very much the exception. The warden was a woman, and, like the captains, I was impressed with her demeanor and relationship with the inmates who had access to her when requested.

The correctional system has a culture of its own, and my adaptation to it was not all plain sailing. The prison has a restricted formulary, partly to prevent abuse or addiction but also for financial reasons. Taycheedah, the parent women's institution, has been under court orders for several years following lawsuits brought by both the ACLU and the federal government for inadequate care. Prescribing practices differ from those in the community, mainly in relation to the use of sedative drugs (like Valium and other benzodiazepines) for anxiety and sleep disorders and stimulant drugs (like amphetamine) for attention deficit disorder. These conditions are treated instead with "off-label" use of nonaddictive compounds like the antihistamines, antidepressants, and beta blockers.

Initially, I was criticized for occasionally not complying with these stipulations and complaints were made behind my back to the medical director. This was handled by setting up a monthly staff meeting attended by the nurses, the warden, the captains, and the psychologist. This resolved the problem and became the foundation of a collegial working relationship. I was greatly helped by the advice and mentoring of my psychology colleague who understood the nuances of the correctional environment and how to negotiate them.

Another area of difficulty was the mildly sadistic attitude of one or two nurses who were inclined to assume inmates were malingering or manipulating the system. My background in psychosomatic medicine and family practice helped deal with this after I made the point that "everyone dies of something" and that it was wise to take complaints seriously. After I found some problems they had dismissed, this became less of an issue.

But probably the biggest problem and likely source of the nurses' attitudes was my opposite number in medicine. This was a former-pathologist-turned-internist who delighted in discontinuing all the medicines he considered "unnecessary" prescribed to inmates before transfer from Taycheedah to minimum security. This man was gay and boasted about the number of lawsuits filed against him by women inmates. He clearly was a misogynist who was eventually transferred to another male prison.

I was happiest seeing the women patients. Although my main job was medication management, and I only saw each patient on average every six weeks, I always took time to establish a personal relationship and deal with their psychological and personal as well as medical issues. Each week, I spent some time with my psychologist colleague, and we exchanged ideas about our shared patients. Although from different disciplines, our viewpoints were usually compatible. People who had an acute problem and needed to be seen more often filled out a "blue slip" and were seen at the next visit. I was required to dictate a record after every session but also kept meticulous written chart notes with more personal information that linked one visit to another.

—

Every three months, I went to Madison for a meeting with the thirty or more psychiatrists who worked in the correctional system throughout the state. Two of us were members of the ACNP and probably a third of all of them had held a faculty position in one of the two state medical schools. However, there was little evidence of any systematic attempt at quality improvement and during my four years—never a single visit by a supervisor to oversee my work. Nor was there any resolution of the thorny issues surrounding the appropriate treatment of insomnia among inmates. (See "Sleep in Prison" in this piece.)

I made my last visit to the prison two weeks after my son graduated from medical school and almost fifty years to the day since I myself became a physician. I hosted a carry-in lunch for the nursing, medical, and correctional staff; the warden thanked me for my work and said that the women had liked and would miss me, especially my English accent when I called them to my office on the overhead announcement system!

As I watch my son training to become a family doctor, I do indeed hope that Harry Truman was right when he said, "Deeds grow into destiny."

The poem below was written a few months after I began work in the correctional system and before I developed the more balanced view of the cost-benefit ratio of incarceration for people with mental illness.

The Prison Doctor's Dilemma

(With apologies to George Bernard Shaw)

In Minimum Security,
One third of women are marred
by abuse, breached boundaries,
Male brutality
And psychic scars.

Mean families and broken homes
Magnify each faulty gene.
Alone, burdened by childcare,
Illness quickens urban angst.

When sickness is dosed with
Liquor, crack, heroin or pot
Prison is one wrong day away.

Inside, inmates suffer DSM* disorders,
With substance abuse, "in forced remission."
Embroidered by penal epithets,
"Malingering" or "manipulative,"
Abusive echoes eclipse redemption.

Prescriptions take weeks to work,
From a formulary stripped of
"Potentially addictive" drugs
Offering safety over swift solace.

Denied solitude or sanctuary,
Primal fears and fractured sleep
Elude our panaceas.

*American Psychiatric Association's *Diagnostic & Statistical Manual*

—Barry Blackwell, January 2008

Although there are good aspects to treatment in prison, rehabilitation is not among them, as noted in the poem below.

Rehab

There's women jailed
That's done some wrong,
Whose minds have failed
And don't belong.

—

They broke our laws,
Got locked in cells,
Behind steel bars,
They're taking pills.

But once let out
They'll soon be back,
Revoked without
The skills they lack.

—Barry Blackwell, January 2010

*DOC "doc"

There's a prison doc I know well
With a bedside manner from hell.
Blind to feelings of every kind,
He tends bodies but never minds.

*DOC = Department of Corrections

—Barry Blackwell, July 2010

Thug

A violent man; a term derived from ancient Sanskrit describing followers of the Hindu goddess Kali who laid in wait to attack travelers in India.

—OED definition (modified)

The drive to and from the prison took around ninety minutes each way, adding three hours to a ten-hour work day. On those days, I ate no breakfast but stopped at a gas station on the way for a donut and worked through the lunch break. So by the time I set out around 5:30 p.m., I was hungry and in a hurry to get home, eager for the martini with which I rewarded myself. It was Kathie's kind job to have that ready and waiting.

You get the picture. About two years into my prison stint, I was driving through the town of Slinger halfway home and came upon four or five police cars huddled on the right-hand berm with their uniformed drivers chatting outside the vehicles. It was rush hour, the two lanes crowded with cars driving close to the speed limit. I sped past without changing lanes, never giving it a thought. Half a mile farther on, I noticed the flashing lights and siren of a police car behind me but didn't stop; I felt sure I had done nothing wrong and thought he must be after the car in front.

The police car caught up, drew alongside, and motioned me to stop. I pulled onto the berm and lowered the window coming face to face with a furious cop who ordered me to get out of the car. Did I know I had threatened the life of his fellow officers; why didn't I draw over into the left lane? Why hadn't I stopped promptly? Did I realize he could handcuff, arrest me, and take me to the station? By now he had a head of steam; there was spittle on his lips, he was clearly livid and repeated the threat to handcuff me several times in a loud, intimidating voice.

I felt terrified; what had I done? Didn't I know it was the law that a driver must draw over and away from a stationary police car by the side of the road? No, I hadn't heard of this. Was it a state or a federal law? This infuriated him more. It was a three-year-old state law I had never heard of. Recognizing an English accent, he asked where I was from, and, reassured I was not an illegal immigrant, he ordered me back into the car and returned to his squad car to phone in my plate number (EGO MD), check my driver's license, and write his tickets. There was no doubt I was going to get one.

I used the time to call my wife on my cell phone, explaining I would be late for the martini but would need a stiff one. This incident was very soon after an African-American Harvard professor got into an unpleasant altercation with a white Boston police officer who arrested him for breaking into his own home. The national press had turned this into a racial incident, so President Obama invited them to share a beer on the White House lawn and make peace.

—

Kathie and I agreed that I needed to be polite and respectful; she believed my license plate might have provoked the problem.

The officer returned, clearly still angry, and handed me three tickets, totaling $350 and nine points; my crimes were endangering the lives of the police officers, not stopping promptly, and hanging a handicapped sticker on my rear mirror, obstructing the view.

During our twenty-minute wait on the berm, I counted a dozen or more cars driving past without pulling over, all presumably ignorant of the fairly new and unadvertised law I had broken. I chose not to point that out before driving slowly home.

Three days later, I received an official letter in the mail from the Department of Motor Vehicles (DMV) informing me that an informant had filed a complaint that I was an elderly and impaired driver. I was required to take a special driving test within a month or surrender my license immediately. The test would include written and vision tests as well as an extended forty-five-minute behind the wheel examination. If I failed, my license would be revoked. And, incidentally, I would lose my job. So I phoned the DMV to obtain more information about the complaint. I learned it was from the policeman in Slinger, that it required no evidence in support other than the officer's opinion, and that there was no right of appeal. My contact was sympathetic but unable to help.

I boned up on the rules of the road and went to the local DMV testing center to take the visual and written tests on which I scored ninety-eight percent. I asked if they could recommend a driving instructor and a nice African-American man obliged. The instructor was also African-American, a former marine drill instructor, whose clients were mostly teenagers. I signed up for six sessions.

He badgered and bullied me while I made sure he understood that seventy-five-year-olds learned slowly by repetition, unlike speedy teens. I relearned a lot I had forgotten and became a far safer driver. It was almost sixty years since I first took the test in Britain when the woman examining me had concluded the test by saying, "I'm going to pass you, but thank god I don't have to drive home with you!"

—

When it was time to take the test, I was ready and passed with flying colors, this time with kind congratulations from, once again, a female examiner. I felt vindicated but for several weeks drove my wife's car to the prison, fearful my inquisitor might be lying in wait.

I never saw him again, but at our next monthly meeting, I told the story to the team, including the two captains. One of them nodded and smiled, immediately recognizing and naming the officer. He was well-known as an ambitious and obnoxious member of the Slinger police and had once dated the captain's daughter; she found him "overbearing and full of himself" and vowed never to date him again!

Several months later, my attorney negotiated with the Slinger Village Attorney for a reduction in points in return for paying the fine. What a deal! And what a thug!

Sleep in Prison

Sleep that knits up the raveled sleeve of care, the death of each day's life, sore labor's bath, balm of hurt minds.

—William Shakespeare (*Macbeth*, Act 2)

In the correctional system of medicine, there is no more refractory topic than the need for practice guidelines in the management of insomnia. There are several reasons why this is so.

A significant percentage of prisoners have abused sedative drugs on the streets and are appropriately suspected of seeking them in prison if only to blot out the tedium or stress of incarceration. Sleep is difficult to measure reliably as sleep lab studies have shown; correctional staff believe they have better things to do than attempt to determine if an inmate is asleep or awake behind closed eyelids. The alleged symptoms of insomnia are similar to the side effects of the drugs used to treat it, making it difficult to tease treatment from outcome. Many administrative, correctional, medical, and nursing staff hold strong opinions based on personal experience about how much sleep is enough and whether medical treatment is appropriate.

As a new doctor on the block, I ran into this buzz saw after the first few occasions I prescribed the kind of hypnotic drugs I used in community practice (Ambien, Lunesta, etc.). Brought to task, I was instructed to conform to the correctional use of sedative drugs without addictive properties. These included antihistamines, beta blockers, and sedating antidepressants which have not been studied adequately in insomnia, are not approved by the FDA for this indication, and, while free of addictive risk, have significant side effects of their own. This so called "off-label" use is officially frowned on in medicine but is not illegal; physicians' prescriptive rights are unrestricted. In Corrections, it had the added advantage of substituting cheap generic compounds for the highly expensive, widely advertised drugs used to treat insomnia in the general population.

I became intrigued by this dilemma and spent many hours of my own (unremunerated) time researching the medical literature. Even here opinion diverged and consensus was elusive; Ambien and Lunesta have become "blockbuster" drugs backed up by creative advertising, generating millions of dollars in sales, some of which trickled down into the palms of academic consultants, educators, and researchers.

What follows is the report I wrote with references redacted for ease of reading. It was submitted to the medical director at the Wisconsin Department of Corrections and shared with some staff in the prison where I worked. It failed to evoke a response or comment of any kind.

I attribute this to a combination of bureaucratic lethargy, unwillingness to challenge prevailing correctional ideologies, and an absence of intellectual curiosity.

Introduction

Humans sleep for up to a third of their circadian cycle. As Shakespeare noted, the reason is presumed to be restorative. Restful sleep shores up the ability to cope with the physical, intellectual, and emotional demands of the day. Inadequate or insufficient sleep (insomnia) is presumed to impair that ability, and for centuries, physicians have traditionally considered insomnia worthy of treatment.

—

Until the second half of the twentieth century the commonly used remedies were chloral hydrate, bromides, and the barbiturates. Addictive and lethal in overdose, these drugs were rapidly replaced by the benzodiazepines so that by 1970, retail pharmacies in America were dispensing over sixty-two million prescriptions for insomnia each year.

For a condition that is part of every person's life, so fundamental to well-being, and so frequently treated, surprisingly little is certain about sleep. This remains true despite the creation of sleep research institutes, sleep laboratories, a scientific journal (*Sleep*), and billions of dollars in pharmaceutical company profit derived from sedative-hypnotic drug sales.

The topic of sleep invokes a litany of questions to which science seldom provides unequivocal answers.

- How much sleep is enough?
- What are the measurable consequences of insufficient or inadequate sleep?
- What is the range of individual variation in sleep and effects of sleep deprivation?
- Is insomnia a treatable condition? If so, to what extent and with which drawbacks?
- Is it possible to measure sleep in an objective reliable way in a normal setting?
- What is the relationship of insomnia to physical and mental illness?
- Is insomnia a symptom, a cause of illness, or both?
- Why are nocturnal ruminations almost invariably negative and self-sustaining?
- What are the relative roles, benefits, and risks of drugs or cognitive strategies?

Prison poses additional problems and questions. Until Dorothea Dix advocated for asylum care, people with mental illness were at risk of incarceration. In recent times, the closure of mental hospitals, underfunded community services, lack of health insurance, and limited access to government programs have again exposed citizens with mental illness to jail or prison, often for crimes of survival or self-medication of their illness with alcohol or street drugs. Today, up to a third or a half of inmates have a mental illness.

Even well-designed or minimum-security prisons provide circumstances that can aggravate insomnia or mental illness. For those who have been the victims of physical, sexual, or emotional abuse, or who suffer from posttraumatic stress disorders, prison may not be a calming influence. Sharing a bunk bed in a small cell with an inconsiderate or disturbed roommate is seldom a tranquil experience. Crowded single-sex environments can aggravate social phobias and gender insecurities. Segregation or isolation for infractions is particularly harmful to inmates with mental illness and may contribute to suicide attempts or outcomes.

It is hardly surprising that the use of sedative-hypnotic drugs to treat insomnia in prison is controversial.

Competing Ideologies

Four ideologies contribute to the confusion and controversy surrounding this topic.

The Correctional Ideology

This emphasizes the problem of using potentially addictive drugs in a population at risk for abuse and diversion. In a rehabilitative environment, the benefits of drug-induced sleep may be considered subordinate to the risks of oversedation and accident-proneness on work productivity. Psychiatric symptoms and insomnia are almost entirely subjective, and, unlike medical disorders, are seldom amenable to validation by examination, tests, or procedures. This can create a high index of suspicion of manipulation, exaggeration, and drug-seeking behavior, presumably to ease the burden of incarceration.

These considerations impact on the drugs used to treat insomnia in a correctional setting. In America, benzodiazepines and related drugs that may produce dependency and are occasionally abused are frowned upon. Preferred is "off-label" use of drugs such as trazadone and tricyclic antidepressants, antihistamines such as diphenhydramine and clonidine, a beta blocker. Such drugs are sometimes prescribed in higher than usual amounts to capitalize on their secondary sedative effects. The price for avoidance of addictive potential is relative inefficiency and frequent side effects. But because these drugs are considered "safe" in a correctional setting, their use often becomes chronic. This sometimes creates an assumption in the minds of physicians and inmates that long-term treatment of insomnia is effective and acceptable.

Such opinions and practices thrive in the absence of data because there is very little contemporary research in prison settings. An exception is a series of studies conducted in Switzerland over the last five years.

The first is a study of the frequency, types, and causes of insomnia in a Geneva prison with three hundred to four hundred male and female inmates, a majority incarcerated for less than six months. Out of almost a thousand patients seen by primary care physicians, in one year, forty-four percent had insomnia. A history of substance misuse was three times as common among inmates with insomnia compared to those without (fifty-one percent vs. seventeen percent). When the author separated out inmates with insomnia but without substance misuse, twenty-nine percent had short-term insomnia attributed to the stress of incarceration, and fifty-nine percent had chronic insomnia (over three weeks), most often associated with generalized anxiety (thirty percent) or incarceration (eleven percent). Comparison of the nondrug-using insomniacs with inmates who had normal sleep found that sleep disturbance was associated with more frequent medical consultation, anxiety, and medical disorders, including diabetes and asthma.

In discussing these findings, the author notes that the frequency of chronic insomnia in prison is very similar to that in noncorrectional primary care settings.

A second study by the author in the same prison looked at the management and treatment outcome of insomnia in the nonsubstance misuse population treated by primary care physicians. Of the one hundred twelve patients with insomnia, all except one were treated with

—

hypnotics, eighty percent of which were benzodiazepines or zolpidem (Ambien) most often prescribed at the patients' request. Herbal and off-label drugs were used less often. Hypnotics were often prescribed for more than three weeks (sixty-one percent) and the dose was increased in nineteen percent of patients. Over half the patients received more than one hypnotic (fifty-five percent). Physicians' documentation of the type and severity of sleep disturbance, past history of hypnotic use, and daytime symptoms due to insomnia were all infrequent and limited.

Despite the extent of use, the outcome was not impressive. Just over a third (thirty-seven percent) reported complete improvement, less than a third (thirty percent) partial benefit, and a fifth (eighteen percent) no improvement. Patients with incomplete or no benefit took more hypnotics. These findings show a similar incomplete response to those reported in an earlier study by the same author. At the time of their release in this study, fifty-five percent of the patients left while still taking hypnotics. Compared to the others this group received more medications for longer periods with less improvement.

The first study concluded that the prevalence of insomnia in prison was comparable to the general population. This second study showed an overall hypnotic drug use of eleven percent compared to an estimated five to ten percent in the general population.

A recent review of these and other research findings in prison populations concludes that insomnia in prison is not only related to substance abuse and psychiatric problems. Its evaluation and management is inadequate. Because drugs provide only limited-term relief in some patients, nonpharmacological methods should be used more often. This article ends with a plea that "prison health services should develop clear guidelines based on research evidence about insomnia that contains treatment recommendations based on the principle of equivalence of health care outside and inside places of detention."

The Academic and Research Ideology

The above author's concluding comment is the natural prelude to exploring this arena. Studies investigate the nature of insomnia, its

—

consequences, and its treatment, and are the usual source of "best practice" paradigms.

A recent comprehensive review included thirty-six studies and surveys of insomnia and its consequences carried out between 1975 and 2003. Its conclusions included:

- Between ten and fifty percent of people surveyed reported some degree of insomnia depending on the criteria used and the population studied. A generally accepted estimate is that ten percent of the general population report a severe chronic sleep problem (twenty-five million people in the USA).
- Sleep problems include delay in falling asleep (sixteen percent), staying asleep (twenty-five percent), and waking early (fifteen percent), or some combination.
- Mild or transitory insomnia is more than twice as common as severe problems.
- Severe problems are more likely to become chronic and to produce daytime impairment.
- Insomnia is one and a half times as common in women as in men.
- Severe chronic insomnia is commoner in people with either medical or psychiatric disorders. Forty-four percent of people referred to a sleep center have a psychiatric problem.
- Insomnia may be a risk factor for depression, and depression is forty times as common in patients with insomnia as those without. Insomnia may persist after successful treatment of the mood disorder.
- Chronic insomnia has been correlated with impaired cognitive function, quality of life, mood disorders, daytime sleepiness, accident risk, and absenteeism from work.
- Untreated insomniacs report being easily upset, irritated or annoyed, too tired to function, and having impaired thinking or judgment.
- People with chronic insomnia consistently report reduced quality of life comparable to patients with chronic heart failure.
- Direct annual costs of insomnia in America have been estimated to be in the $15 billion range including health care utilization

($12 billion) and medication ($2 billion, half prescribed and half over the counter).

Other individual studies have tended to support or extend these findings.

A review reports preliminary data suggesting that two weeks of sleep disturbance may signal an increased risk of developing anxiety, depression, or substance abuse.

A study in France compared the quality of life on a standardized scale in severe insomniacs, mild insomniacs, and good sleepers after eliminating anyone with depression or anxiety. Impaired quality of life was significantly correlated with severity of sleep disturbance on eight dimensions of well-being. Insomnia was also correlated with worse physical health though the relationship was unclear.

A more recent study found that people who slept fewer than five hours a night were five times as likely to have hypertension.

Another French study found that absenteeism from work was more than twice as common in insomniacs as in good sleepers.

A recent study in the United States confirms that insomnia has a significant economic impact on both indirect costs (absenteeism and short-term disability) and direct (health care) costs.

The above data suggest that from both a quality of life and economic perspective, insomnia is appropriately considered a condition worth treating. But what does treatment accomplish and at what cost? An understanding of what drug research has to offer begins with an account of regulatory requirements and pharmaceutical company procedures.

In the wake of the thalidomide disaster, Congress enacted legislation to mandate that all medications be proven both safe and effective at about the time that psychopharmacology research reached its peak. The gold standard to accomplish this was the double-blind controlled study comparing drug to placebo. The FDA threshold for marketing

—

approval became a minimum of two such studies. Experience has revealed the inadequacies of this minimalist criterion. The studies are conducted on highly selected, relatively small, samples of healthy adults closely supervised to ensure compliance. They last just long enough to demonstrate statistical efficacy (which is usually four to six weeks), and the realities or risks of long-term use (often months or years) are overlooked. Rare or unusual side effects and addiction or dependency potential are seldom detected. Five years elapsed between marketing the first MAO inhibitor and the discovery of the potentially fatal "cheese reaction." To further compound matters, pharmaceutical companies almost never compare a new product to standard existing remedies and seldom, if ever, conduct postmarketing surveillance or "real world" effectiveness studies.

The resulting knowledge gap is nowhere more obvious than for the sedative-hypnotic drugs. The lack of scientific knowledge on long-term use is reflected in "small print" labeling found in package inserts and the dense pages of the *Physicians' Desk Reference* (PDR). For example, zolpidem is among the most widely advertised hypnotic drugs and similar but not identical to the earlier benzodiazepines. The PDR information on zolpidem (Ambien) is derived from two double-blind studies of chronic primary insomnia (DSM IV criteria) which lasted only three weeks. Primary insomnia is defined as lasting longer than a month but "Information to Patients" states: "Sleep problems are usually temporary, requiring treatment for only a short time, usually one or two days up to one or two weeks." This conflicts with both the research and the bulk of epidemiological data. There are no studies reported on any patients with psychiatric disorders which can cause secondary insomnia or in which insomnia may aggravate the primary condition.

Very recently, a longer-term study reports findings that call this labeling into question. A multicenter project by Duke University included 349 patients who also met criteria for chronic primary insomnia treated double-blind with either placebo or zolpidem taken "when necessary" between three to seven times a week for six months. Standardized measures were made of sleep latency, total sleep, awakenings, total wake time, quality of sleep, and next day function. Although more than half the placebo patients reported benefit, zolpidem was very

—

477

significantly superior on all outcome measures including reduction in daytime sleepiness and increased ability to concentrate. On this type of regimen, no rebound withdrawal symptoms occurred over three nights of drug-free discontinuation.

Large-scale metanalysis of all the short-term studies has yielded mixed conclusions. A review of eighty-nine randomized controlled trials comparing a benzodiazepine with placebo or another drug found forty-five studies that yielded acceptable data. Compared to placebo, active hypnotic drugs reduced sleep latency by only five minutes (not significant), although patients reported over fourteen minutes' reduction in time to fall asleep. Sleep duration increased by an average of over an hour. Several studies reported objective evidence of next day memory impairment, and patients reported daytime drowsiness, dizziness, or light-headedness.

A more recent review evaluated all studies between 1975 and 2004 that measured sleep maintenance and reached the conservative conclusion that "many of the currently available agents used to treat insomnia, including trazadone, non-benzodiazepines, and benzodiazepines, have not consistently demonstrated effectiveness in promoting sleep maintenance. The benzodiazepines with established efficacy are associated with next day sedation, the risk of tolerance or dependence or both."

A review article from Britain discusses the place of benzodiazepines in psychiatric practice. They note that it is standard practice in psychiatric hospitals to prescribe a benzodiazepine hypnotic to all newly admitted patients but comment this is appropriate only if "given on an occasional or intermittent basis." They note that dependency on benzodiazepines due to "rebound insomnia" on stopping can occur after only a few weeks' treatment, but they also cite evidence that more than half of long-term users are able to stop medication abruptly without difficulty. They comment that there are no other known adverse consequences of long-term treatment. Their concluding advice is, "Although benzodiazepines impair memory and other aspects of higher mental function, this does not always have much impact on discouraging

–

478

patients from continued use. In the current state of knowledge, it is too punitive to withdraw benzodiazepines from long-term patients who do not want to stop treatment." They point out that this may only be an exercise in futility by encouraging the patient to find a more lenient prescriber. Their final advice (which appears to apply to both hypnotic and daytime use) is to "avoid long-term use whenever possible, limiting use to no more than two weeks in regular dosage, or in intermittent flexible dosage."

An economic study in managed health care plans reported that drug treatment of insomnia significantly reduced other health care costs for some but not all medications.

The American Academy of Sleep Science has issued a statement on the use of over-the-counter and herbal sleep aids. They note that thirty percent of adults complain of sleep problems and that ten percent have used a sleep aid in the previous year. Double that number (twenty-one percent) do so if insomnia causes them daytime problems. They recommend that herbal remedies be used only when approved by a physician and that antihistamines be avoided except for short-term use in mild insomnia.

Successful nondrug treatments for insomnia also exist. Sleep hygiene measures include daily exercise, avoidance of caffeine, calming bedtime rituals, and a variety of psychological strategies. These include meditation; relaxation, and thought-control procedures that replace negative ruminations with pleasurable scenarios that disrupt "the ceaseless roundabout of painful thought" that usually occurs with insomnia.

A study conducted in primary care enrolled two hundred nine patients who had taken hypnotic drugs for at least a month and randomly assigned them to either six fifty-minute cognitive-behavioral training sessions or to a no-additional treatment control group. After three months, almost seventy percent of the treatment group had stopped taking medication. At six months, treated patients showed improvement in vitality, physical, and mental functioning. These improvements and reduction in drug use were maintained at one year.

—

Finally, in 2005, the National Institutes of Health convened a Consensus Conference of experts from throughout the United States. The concluding statement from the conference was as follows:

> Chronic insomnia is a major public health problem affecting millions of people, along with their families and communities. Little is known about the mechanisms, causes, clinical course, co-morbidities, and consequences of chronic insomnia. Evidence supports the efficacy of cognitive-behavioral therapy and benzodiazepine receptor agonists in the treatment of this disorder at least in the short term. Very little evidence supports the use of other treatments, despite their widespread use. Moreover, even for those treatments that have been systematically evaluated, the panel is concerned about the mismatch between the potential lifelong nature of this illness and the longest clinical trials, which have lasted one year or less. A substantial public and private research effort is warranted, including developing longitudinal studies of randomized clinical trials. Finally there is a need for educational programs directed at physicians, health care providers, and the public.

The Community Standards Ideology

As noted above, this is another yardstick used to develop treatment guidelines. Treatment comparable to that available in the community is often considered an ethical requirement that protects an inmate's right to equitable and competent health care. Infringement may become a basis for legal action against a correctional institution that fails to meet this standard. Two important issues are raised by this requirement.

Firstly, the absence of academic and scientific consensus in itself can result in the lack of community standards, contributed to by deficits in professional education. A recent review comments on the diagnosis and misdiagnosis of sleep disorders. Although sleep disorders are among the most common complaints in primary and specialty care, neither the public nor the profession are well-informed about them. During

—

five years of medical training, the average time devoted to sleep is five minutes with no evidence this deficiency is corrected by higher education even in those specialties where sleep disorders are common (pediatrics, psychiatry, and geriatrics). Physicians do not routinely inquire about sleep but reflexively prescribe. Daytime sleepiness is often misdiagnosed as "laziness, loss of interest, daydreaming, lack of motivation."

Not surprisingly, in the community there are wide differences of opinion and prescribing behavior among both primary care practitioners (who prescribe the majority of hypnotic drugs) and between psychiatrists. As the volume of prescriptions indicates, it is not unusual for community physicians (including those who also work in a correctional setting) to refill prescriptions on an indefinite basis without any adequate assessment of insomnia or treatment outcome.

Secondly, choosing a community standard begs the basic question of which community and of the comparability between community and prison populations. Compared to the general population, a prison population includes a disproportionate number of people with mental illness and an overrepresentation of drug abusers, ethnic minorities, and people of low socioeconomic status who often have a lack of health insurance and access to preventative health care. As noted, the correctional environment may also contribute to the frequency, severity, and chronicity of insomnia. Is it appropriate to assume that two such disparate populations need identical health care?

Taken together, these two considerations suggest that the most appropriate standard of care might be one developed to meet the unique needs of a correctional community. This suggestion also has pragmatic appeal. For the first two decades of modern psychopharmacology (1955-1975), significant amounts of drug research took place in prisons using paid volunteers to evaluate the safety of new medications. While this practice was ethically dubious, it had relevant practical advantages. A correctional setting provides an ideal environment to evaluate drug efficacy and safety. It combines the control associated with short-term double-blind studies and access to long-term stable populations that can be closely observed and carefully evaluated.

—

This difference between correctional and community environments is meaningful because sleep presents a unique clinical challenge. The symptoms attributed to lack of sleep are the same as the side effects due to treatment—daytime lethargy, accident-proneness, and mild cognitive impairments in memory and concentration. The correct balance between too little sleep and too much medication can be subtle, subjective, and difficult to determine. It requires rigorous evaluation of the kind that could be possible in a correctional setting.

Individual Ideologies

The absence of academic consensus and correctional or community guidelines creates an atmosphere which encourages strong personal attitudes and beliefs. These can result in idiosyncratic prescribing practices that vary between physicians and institutions. This, in turn, can create tensions between correctional, nursing, and physician staff; between practitioners and their supervisors; between patients and providers; and between institutions. It may also lead to detrimental outcomes that make the correctional system vulnerable to litigation.

A decision to develop mutually agreed on clinical guidelines for the management of insomnia could contribute to a mutual sense of purpose. It might not be easy but it might be worthwhile. As Mark Twain noted, "You can't throw an attitude out the window, you have to coast it down the stairs, one step at a time."

Conclusion

Despite an apparent lack of consensus between different ideologies and inconsistent or incomplete research findings, there is a significant knowledge base sufficient to develop practice guidelines for the management of insomnia in a correctional setting. The following are some principles that are supported by research evidence:

- All inmates who complain of insomnia should be evaluated by a standard rating scale that measures all aspects of the sleep cycle as well as daytime deficits attributed to insufficient sleep.

- Inmates taking sedative-hypnotics at the time of incarceration should be carefully weaned and the measures repeated to determine benefits or drawbacks of treatment. This would serve as a test of the alleged difficulties of weaning people with primary insomnia from long-term use of hypnotics. Rare exceptions could be made in individuals with bipolar disorder, major depression, psychosis, or serious medical problems where severe insomnia might worsen the primary disorder.
- All patients with validated sleep problems should be instructed in sleep hygiene and cognitive behavioral strategies for insomnia. These can be provided in written form, reinforced if necessary in clinical interviews or a group setting.
- Six to eight weeks later, the baseline rating scales should be repeated with additional data on the success of sleep hygiene and cognitive-behavioral strategies.
- Based on the above, inmates eligible for consideration of drug therapy would have:

Sleep and performance decrements, despite an adequate trial of nondrug measures, sufficient to impair the capacity to perform available work.

Poor sleep likely to cause or worsen a serious psychiatric or medical disorder.

- If indicated after the above observations, drug treatment of insomnia would comprise the following:

No herbal, over-the-counter, or "off-label" prescribed medications.

Use of a generic low-cost hypnotic within listed dosage limits, starting at the lowest dose.

Routine "drug holidays" on nights preceding work-free days (twice weekly).

Repeat ratings after four weeks for comparison to pretreatment baseline.

If incomplete benefit without side effects, consider dose increase within listed limits.

If insignificant benefit or worsening work performance, discontinue medication.

Repeat baseline ratings at three-month intervals to ensure continuing benefit.

Wean off drug prior to release to avoid dependency in the community setting.

No use of other hypnotic drugs based on cost and the absence of between drug comparisons for equivalence or superior efficacy.

The above principles could be modified and translated into clinical guidelines with input from clinicians, nurses, wardens, correctional officers, and forensic experts.

Economic Implications

A project of this proposed scope would impose a significant burden on psychiatric, medical, psychological, HSU, correctional, and administrative staff. An assessment of these costs should be made and included in applications for funding which might involve local, state, or federal sources and foundations, but not pharmaceutical companies. The study design should incorporate data collection on costs and savings that might be involved in setting up a program based on the study findings, which would have political and administrative appeal.

Experimental Caveats

- A combination of possible drug-seeking behavior by inmates and difficult to measure subjective endpoints makes this a

—

problematic area in which to obtain reliable results. It would be prudent to begin with a funded pilot study to ascertain and overcome these difficulties before seeking funding for a large-scale project. Consideration should be given to confining the use of sedative drugs to inmates with reliable documented absence of substance abuse or drug-seeking behavior in order to improve validity.

• Given the uncertain and unreliable nature of current information about sleep and hypnotic drug use, it is questionable whether the kind of study proposed would require informed consent or Institutional Review Board approval. Ethical and legal opinions would be helpful.

Author's Note:

The author's forensic experience consists of almost three years' work in a minimum-security prison. This review was carried out on personal (not DOC) time. It is based on Internet and library sources and may not be exhaustive. I am grateful to Adam Blackwell for help with data collection. Studies citied are available on request. Opinions expressed are the author's alone.

Mentoring

Perhaps a fourth "good deed" was my attempt at mentoring; a task that was an unusual union of social and professional motivations. This had a mixed outcome: part success, part failure.

A psychiatrist is not a mentor, although a mentor may be a psychiatrist. I learned the difference about fifteen years ago when I developed a mentoring relationship with two young men, Bobby and Jay, both in their late twenties and suffering from severe bipolar illness, each at times with psychotic symptoms. They were never my patients, and I met them in our Faith in Recovery support groups at our local Catholic church.

Perhaps the best example of mentoring is the work of Big Brothers and Big Sisters, an organization that provides volunteer surrogate parenting

—
485

to deprived children and adolescents. This can involve role modeling, advice, support and participation in all kinds of leisure activities.

As a psychiatrist mentoring these two men with mental illness, I needed to reexamine my boundaries. Many mentoring activities are proscribed to therapists and, by the same token, mentors should not meddle in therapy. The boundary between a recommendation and advice is narrow and must be defined. Crossing it might anger the real treatment providers and cause confusion and resentment.

So I got to know Bobby's parents and Jay's mother, to visit their homes, take them to movies and restaurants, swim in our pool, walk the dog, and just "hang out." In the course of all this, I gained a "worm's eye," bottom-up view of how people with a severe and persistent mental illness experience the world and the difficulties they encounter in life outside the doctor's office.

Both young men had been talented school kids; their cruel illnesses had not erupted until Bobby was almost through college and Jay was in high school. After their first hospitalization, they each began a lifetime of medication with ongoing ups and downs in mood and energy, occasionally leading to another spell in the hospital. Coping with the side effects of medicine was also a cross they had to bear, including weight gain, dry mouth, tiredness, slow thinking, and sometimes sexual dysfunction. Jay's recovery had been disrupted by drugs and alcohol, but he was now abstinent. Unfortunately the medication from which he benefited had a potentially fatal side effect that required monthly blood checks and needles he hated.

Bobby had no health insurance and refused to apply for disability benefits; he had a strong independent streak shared with a frugal father who was a corporate executive. Bobby stubbornly persisted in applying for jobs but was very seldom interviewed; he was not helped by a resume with illness gaps, quickly spotted by Human Resources. Jay opted otherwise; he and his mother survived on Medicaid disability benefits and food stamps, supplemented by rent support from wealthy family members. For several years, Jay was housebound, crippled by severe social phobias while his mother was chronically depressed.

—

Jay and Bobby shared the common handicaps of their illnesses: neither could emancipate from their parents or obtain employment or a life partner. Another difficulty was finding a competent well-trained psychiatrist willing to treat patients without health insurance or on Medicaid.

I did my best to help them deal realistically with these difficulties and handicaps. I began gently coaxing Jay out of doors to confront his fears, building on small successes until we were able to go together and obtain a new driver's license, after which I acted as a driving instructor until his competence and confidence were restored. I also introduced him to a psychiatrist I had trained and trusted to do a good job with medications.

I advised Bobby on revising his resume and job interview skills, including the enduring issue of whether or when to reveal a history of mental illness. He eventually found work as a hall monitor and basketball coach at a local high school where he also began a romance with a fellow teacher.

But it was not all plain sailing. Bobby began to experiment with the dosage of his medication in an attempt to reduce side effects without telling his parents or the psychiatrist he saw infrequently to control costs. His mental state deteriorated rapidly, and he became delusional. While Bobby's mother was out of town, his father spent the night at his daughter's house, leaving Bobby alone. The following morning, I visited the home to check on him and found Bobby in the kitchen. All the burners on the stove were lit, and the oven door was open, with burning newspapers inside and a golf club, glowing red, among the flames. I asked Bobby what he was doing; he was "reshaping a putter to help the American team win the Ryder Cup." When he refused to turn off the burners, I called his father on my cell phone, and he, in turn, called the police while I went to the back door to await them.

First to arrive was a burly police officer who brushed past me and refused to allow me into the house even after I explained I was a psychiatrist and family friend. Within minutes, the road outside was filled with squad cars, a fire truck, and an ambulance. In no time at all, Bobby was dragged out by the back door, his hands shackled behind his back, his nose broken and bleeding with a front tooth missing. The police officer had smashed Bobby's head against the stone floor, allegedly to subdue him. He was placed, kneeling on the grass, in full view of his father and the neighbors before being driven off to the hospital in a squad car.

Bobby spent several weeks in the hospital, during which time the local press reported that a new chief of city police was introducing training for police officers in how to relate to citizens with mental illness. Bobby's father, a former president of the village board, friendly with the local police chief and fellow member of the Village Men's Club, opted not to file legal proceedings.

Following this incident, the family and I took steps to see that Bobby saw his psychiatrist regularly and more often with an understanding we would all be more vigilant and communicate openly and readily if there were early signs of relapse. After this episode, Bobby lost his job, and the romance ended, although the couple remained friends. Bobby's illness and the medication regimen have now been stable for several years.

Recently his father retired, and Bobby became more purposeful in efforts to take the normal steps his age and life situation dictate. He found a female friend on the Internet, living in Texas, and visited her, returning with the news they were in love. Soon afterward, he moved in with her while she is helping him find a job. Bobby had finally decided to apply again for Medicare, but his move to Texas created problems. He was unable to keep the appointment to see an independent psychiatrist in Milwaukee to evaluate his claim, became discouraged, and informed the social worker he had decided not to pursue it. Interestingly and unusually, the worker tried, without avail, to change Bobby's mind. Imagine my surprise when Bobby called a few weeks later to tell me the claim had been approved *without* an independent evaluation, and he had received a backdated check for thousands of dollars with a monthly stipend of seven hundred dollars.

Shortly afterward, Bobby's parents drove to Texas, taking his dog to join him, and stayed at the girlfriend's house for several days. When they returned, I had lunch with Bobby's father and learned they approved

—

of his relationship, and the couple would be coming to spend several weeks at their home in Milwaukee during the summer months. I also learned that the father had earlier sent an unsolicited letter to Medicare in support of Bobby's application, and I asked to read it. It was a detailed unsentimental account of Bobby's illness, the many hospitalizations he endured, and his unrelenting but unsuccessful attempts to find long-term employment in the face of covert discrimination and despite his educational credentials. The letter was compelling and equal or better than many I had seen written by psychiatrists employed as independent assessors of disability on behalf of Social Security. I urged him to share it with other parents of children with mental illness, as well as the various mental health organizations who had failed to advocate on Bobby's behalf or help him find employment.

The father's action and its success were all the more remarkable because he had, at my instigation, met with the recently retired hearing commissioner who adjudicated Social Security claims in our area. His advice had been for Bobby to drop his application in favor of a more qualified applicant!

Jay's story has taken a more tragic turn. When he decided to find a new psychiatrist, the medication was changed and, in an attempt to treat his social anxiety, he began to take a benzodiazepine tranquilizer to which he soon became readdicted. At the same time, he gave in to his fear of needles and stopped taking the only medication that had suppressed his major mental illness. He quickly developed delusional and paranoid ideas toward immigrants, which were totally unlike his normal mellow temperament. To protect himself, he purchased a Glock 45 revolver and ammunition from a south side gun store—he had previously been beaten up by a street gang. Still delusional, he swallowed a bullet, which he later explained as "wanting to bond with the gun." Terrified that the bullet might explode, he tried to find a doctor who could remove it and, when this failed, reluctantly allowed his mother and me to take him to a psychiatric hospital. After sitting for several hours in a crowded waiting room, I insisted he be seen, and he was admitted.

A few days later, Jay passed the bullet and was discharged, still psychotic, before seeing several different outpatient psychiatrists, none of whom could persuade him to resume the medication from which he benefited or keep him in treatment long enough to improve from other drugs. Although we remained in touch, my ability to influence Jay dwindled as he remained delusional and his aggressive thoughts worsened. He began stalking foreign immigrants in the area in which he lived, eventually assaulting a man and was arrested.

He was incarcerated in the city jail and held without treatment. I spoke to both the prison doctor and public defender; eventually, after an independent evaluation, he was found not guilty by reason of insanity and sentenced to three years in the forensic unit of a state psychiatric hospital. Working in the correctional system myself, I was able to speak to the head of that unit, related Jay's treatment history, and urged he be placed back on the only medication from which he benefited. Nothing was done for six months but, when it was, he once again responded.

Jay's mother, the public defender, and I all urged him to apply for an early discharge in order to link up with community services before the sentence terminated, but Jay refused. When his mother and I visited him in prison to persuade him, it became clear that his social phobias had returned. He felt safer in prison and opted to stay there.

My attempts at mentoring, like other aspects of my career, met with limited success but were a learning experience. Severe and persistent (or intermittent) mental illnesses are cruel masters. They incapacitate the organ of discernment and reason in ways that can make even the most well-meaning attempts at assistance unproductive. Community care is underfunded and fragmented. Stigma and discrimination are alive and well in the workplace and sometimes even in faith communities. Inpatient care is too short (except in prison) to oversee full recovery; it is only funded by insurance until a person is safe to themselves and others. Outpatient care is also too brief and episodic to adequately monitor recovery or detect early relapse. The new medications, despite advertising hype, are no better than the old and impose side effect burdens that can threaten health and invite poor compliance.

I am not sorry that I tried and, if I was young enough, would start all over again!

—

"Good" Intentions

Good is only good
When what we do with others
Works for them, not you.

—Barry Blackwell, July 2012

Part Three: Personal

20. Taking Stock

The life of every man is a diary in which he means to write one story and writes another; and his humblest hour is when he compares the volume as it is with what he vowed to make it.

—James M. Barrie

At this time and place in writing my memoir, I realized something was not quite as I had imagined it. This piece was tentatively titled "Leftovers" and had grown to include fifty-five bits, compared to 132 bits in the preceding nineteen pieces. How could almost one third of what I had still to write be considered "left over?" That didn't sound very exciting!

When I reread Mark Twain's advice (see "The Book" in "Piece 1: Literary Considerations"), I was reminded that I had willfully violated his principle to "wander at will all over your life" in order to impose some chronological structure on the text. So next, I compared what was already set down with what I had waiting in the wings. The still to come bits were almost all nonwork topics, unconnected from my professional persona, but representing various other roles across my lifetime (marriage, domestic life, hobbies, etc.). There was also a disproportionate poem-to-prose ratio indicating emotion taking precedence over intellect in personal affairs. This was hardly surprising but consistent both with the material and the tardy arrival of poetry in my literary repertoire. So the remaining bits are no longer "leftovers" but assigned to pieces that acknowledge their provenance in the ongoing structure of life. This change is accompanied by dividing the entire text into three roughly

—

equal parts: Preparation (Pieces 1 through 8), Professional (Pieces 9 through 19), and Personal (Pieces 20 through 31).

Here are two short, rather dull bits that provide a framework to the remaining pieces.

Place Setting

I spent five years in India, twenty-nine in England, and (to date) forty-four in America. Born British, now I am an American citizen, but lately I'm beginning to think that was a mistake. (See "Then, Now, and Next" in "Piece 10: America.") Thirty-two of those forty-four years have been spent in Milwaukee, living in three locations, all on the east side. A large and elegant residence with a red-tiled roof in Shorewood for twenty-two years, sandwiched between a gastroenterologist and an anesthesiologist. Then an "empty-nester," two villages north in Fox Point, in a smaller ranch with a large yard and a swimming pool, for nearly nine years. Finally, all three physicians and former neighbors came to rest, till death do us part, in a brand-new, palatial twenty-one story tower—part of a retirement community on the shores of Lake Michigan. (See "Piece 31: In the End Zone.")

Dramatis Personae

In my seventy-eight years, I have lived with a large cast of characters. Intermittently, for eighteen years, with my parents during vacations from boarding school. In an army sergeants' mess for two years, and then in university dorms for four years with my college roommate, Wally. I married my first wife Mavis, a nurse I met in Cambridge, at age twenty-two, before I started medical school in London, and we sired three children (Sarah, Simon, and Martin) before we moved to America in 1968. We divorced in 1976. I met Kathie, also a nurse, in 1970, moved in with her in 1975, and married her (for the first time) in 1977. We have one son, Adam.

There are five grandchildren, Kris and Terris (by Martin and Ann), Tyler (by Simon and Laura), Jessica (by Sarah and Jayanta), and Oliver and Amelia (by Adam and Jessie). They range in age from newborn to the midtwenties.

Sarah (an immigration attorney), who is single after her former husband died, and Adam (a family medicine resident) and his wife Jessie (a graphic artist) all live in Milwaukee. Simon (an IT executive) lives on Bainbridge Island in Seattle and is now married to Juliana. Martin (a free spirit and entrepreneur) is separated from Ann and lives on the Big Island in Hawaii.

Family policy is not to tell tales about our children or their present or former spouses however proud or critical we may be. They have their own lives to share if and when they desire.

21. MARRIAGE

A successful marriage requires falling in love many times, always with the same person.

—Mignon McLaughlin

Few people can claim to have married the same spouse three times without a divorce in between.

The first occasion was planned in earnest but aborted due to cold feet brought on by income tax implications. We had lived together for two years, and divorce from my first wife had been granted with a price tag of $700-a-month alimony (current accumulated total, $330,000 and counting). Guilt is an expensive emotion!

Kathie's sister, Barbara, had persuaded a friendly Catholic priest to conduct our ceremony in another friend's house, without the bishop's knowledge or approval. After one failed marriage, I was phobic of white wedding gowns so Kathie wore a purple dress. I wore a matching tie and had a nerdy haircut. We did obtain a license from the courthouse and published an announcement in the *Cincinnati Enquirer* so that everyone present believed what they saw, including Kathie's devout Catholic parents and my three tearful children. Following the bogus ceremony, we drove across the border into Indiana for a rural honeymoon.

Exactly a year later to the day, we celebrated a repeat ceremony in front of a local judge without witnesses and went on the identical honeymoon a second time.

Our third ceremony, in 1991, took place in Milwaukee following the annulment of my first marriage and conversion to Catholicism, attended by all our children, grandchildren, and relatives. We paraded down the aisle of our local Catholic church; Kathie wore a gorgeous white gown, my children were cheery, and the priest seemed genuinely happy to bless us. The reception was held at the Pfister Hotel with dancing into the early hours of the morning until we retired to our room to find our youngest granddaughter, Jessica, had fallen asleep and peed in the wedding bed.

Marriage prospers and lasts longer between people of equal intellect, shared interests, similar ages, a sense of humor, and the wisdom to schedule time apart. Four out of five criteria may suffice. Society proffers no training for wedlock, and parents, like me, are often poor role models.

Here are several bits about marriage:

The Modern State of Matrimony

Matrimony is in more of a state than usual, and it would be a foolish spouse bold enough to comment on that. Being a psychiatrist confers no grant of immunity.

Nevertheless . . .

Today's statistics confirm the problem. Marriage is in decline; fewer people indulge, and those who do wait longer and cohabit more often without benediction. Single parents, those living alone, and the divorced now approach majorities in society.

Success at marriage is predicated on a happy blend of nurturance, sexual compatibility, and friendship. Freud gave precedence to the first two, and, when things go wrong, identified a whore-Madonna complex where men have problems reconciling their need to be nurtured by a saintly mother figure with the desire for a sexy bedmate. I suspect this was a misogynist view of a bisexual dynamic now aggravated by dual career tensions and pornographic cultural expectations.

A lengthening life span and Viagra may have added an end-of-life "last fling" to the already well-recognized "midlife crisis." I suspect this will appear soon in the medical literature or popular press and eventually find its way into the Diagnostic and Statistical Manual (DSM 5 or beyond).

When our biological clocks approach midnight, children emancipate, and sex loses its luster, I suspect friendship becomes the dominant element in sustaining a nuptial bond. Then mutual interests, matched intellects, a shared sense of humor, and skillfully titrated proximity determine the outcome until death intervenes.

Ode to Our Marriage

Thrice wed in thirty years.
First a sham ceremony,
Evading the marriage tax,
Leaving us single.
Deceiving but pleasing
Al and Eleanor.

One year to the day
We wed some more,
The civil, legal way.

Then third, betrothed
By Mother Church.
Clothed in wedding white,
Wrapped by family, friends,
With a weary flower girl
Who wet the bridal bed.

Multiple nuptials,
Symbols of perpetual love.
Built on what? I'll answer that!

Of Kathie as spouse,
A Lucy Stoner,
Assertive and strong.
An equal partner
In both yard and house.

Of Kathie as mother,
Three borrowed, one bred.
She nurtured all four,
And loved each alike.
We should have had more!

Of Kathie as friend,
Empathic galore.
Kind, generous and funny,
Letting me win
(Once or twice), at gin rummy.

Of Kathie as hostess
Always a hit.
Ever the mostess,
Hanging the walls
With her seasonal shit.

Of Kathie as lover,
We must be discreeter.
Don't think that it's over
At our time of life:
There's always Levitra.

—Barry Blackwell, New Year's Eve, 2006.

Physician Lifestyle and Medical Marriages

I wrote this article from material I gathered for talks I gave to the physicians and spouses who accompanied us on our tax deductible, allegedly "educational," foreign cruises.

Published in *Wisconsin Medical Journal*, April 1982:

> Whatever the stresses in a physician's life, their impact is either accentuated or attenuated by that person's preexisting vulnerability or coping capacity. This involves interactions between a physician's lifestyle, personality, and marriage as the major support system.

> Medical marriages are not a new area of interest; an article entitled "The Wives of Some Famous Doctors" catalogues the sufferings and supportive role of famous physicians' wives over the ages. Included was William Harvey's wife, Ann, of whom it was noted:

> > As their married life progressed, Ann's happiness became more and more clouded by anxiety for her husband; for, as you know, he used himself as an experimental subject and took terrible risks. He practiced wrestling with the bull the Queen had given him. He pursued and captured two escaped leopards; kept beehives in the conservatory and lived, with increasingly frequent attacks of angina, aided if not aggravated by the late effects of self-inoculated syphilis for which he took self-prescribed mercury treatments for a period of three years.

This in a capsule form was the life of a doctor-genius' wife.

William Osler's wife, Grace, is also discussed; during the time that he was organizing his department at Johns Hopkins, she persuaded him to delay their marriage until after he had finished writing his famous textbook; it is reported that on its completion he threw the book into her lap and exclaimed, "There, take the damn thing, now what are you going to do with the man?" Less you mistake this for an emancipated view of a wife's role, consider the following quotation from Osler's address entitled "The Student's Life," in which he writes: "What about the wife and babies if you have them? Leave them! Heavy are your responsibilities to yourself, to the profession and to the public. Your wife will be glad to bear her share in the sacrifice you make."

In 1893 a Mrs. Ellen Firebaugh published an article entitled "The Physician's Wife and the Things that Pertain to Her Life." In listing the desirable attributes of a physician's wife, she suggests that "she possess some tact and discretion, and that her bump of curiosity should not be too largely developed. When the doctor comes home, it is more probable that he will enjoy talking about something else than what has preoccupied his mind at the office." Mrs. Firebaugh goes on to note, "The physician husband is so accustomed to having his own way, and his say in the sick room, which is right, that he wants to be the autocrat at the breakfast table, the dinner table, the tea table and the time between tables, which is not right."

If these anecdotes seem quaint, they also illustrate the central theme connecting professional and personal life. This theme persists today, despite the social changes that Howard Rome describes in his article on *The Doctor's Wife:*

> The doctor's office is now seldom his home, telephone answering services have supplanted his wife as a buffer and first aid counselor, accountants provide relief from the burden of office bills, and the peer interaction in group practice protects her to some degree from the role of abreactor and the tedium of feigned attention to "interesting cases."

—

But coincident with these ameliorating influences have been other societal changes that serve to heighten tension; women now expect an independent and autonomous role in which they are liberated from the demands of their spouses' professional lives.

Although the historical and anecdotal information suggests that medicine and marriage make a difficult mix, only the data from control studies can reveal how complex the question really is and the degree to which medical marriages differ from others. George Vaillant and his colleagues at Tufts University have studied forty-seven physicians who graduated over thirty years ago and compared them to seventy-nine socioeconomically matched controls in other occupations with regard to marital breakdown and drug abuse. At first sight, the results appear to support the hypothesis that physicians have significantly more poor marriages (forty-seven percent compared to thirty-two percent of controls) and a higher incidence of drug abuse (thirty-six percent compared to twenty-two percent of controls). However, a close look at the data revealed that these outcomes depend more upon disturbed childhood psychologic status than on choice of medical career. Approximately half of the controls (forty-nine percent) had good childhood adjustments compared to only one-third (thirty-four percent) of physicians. When this variable was controlled for, there was no significant difference in frequency of drug abuse or poor marriages.

Several studies have approached the problem from the standpoint of the physician's wife who becomes psychiatrically impaired. Most of the wives were admitted with diagnoses of depression or suicidal preoccupation, but many were also enmeshed in alcohol or drug abuse and the pattern of marital interaction was strikingly similar in the different studies. The stereotypical marriage that breaks down appears to be between a dependent, histrionic woman with a large need for affection and nurturance who is married to an emotionally detached man. Initially, the phenomenon of "assortative mating" appears to be at play in which women with a need to be "looked after" marry physicians who select patients rather than partners. But a mismatch is also apparent; she speaks the language of emotion while he speaks the language of logic. While he may be the community's greatest

—

504

need-meeter, the wife does not get the warm available father figure she expected. One survey of physician's wives found that ninety-five percent felt neglected, fifty-three percent thought a medical marriage was demanding, and sixty-five percent reported that at least some member of the family had received counseling.

The personalities of the physician husbands in these studies appear to confirm Vaillant's findings; the men are described as often professionally competent and successful but also rigid, interpersonally distant, and covertly or overtly controlling. These are the features of the achievement-oriented obsessive-compulsive personality that correlates both with survival in medical school and success in practice. The negative aspects of this personality style sometimes prevent the male physician from obtaining the comfort and solace of marriage as a major support system. The pride in accomplishment and overproduction is coupled with an overdeveloped ability to postpone pleasure. Even though the physician arrives home emotionally drained, he cannot or will not ask for help; this tendency to repress feelings is part of the compulsive personality that is reinforced by the professional need to remain emotionally detached. Used to being in control, the physician is unable to unbend and to seek nurturance himself.

Once the marital relationship begins to deteriorate, the basic flaws that initiate its demise now accelerate it. In order to avoid conflict, the open expression of feelings, and what he experiences as excessive demands at home, the physician seeks increasing refuge in practice where the rewards are still present and compatible with his personality needs. In response to her husband's flight into work, the wife may devote herself to community affairs or less adaptively seek solace in the sick role with multiple somatic complaints that also invite overprescribing and drug abuse. Both partners may seek the affection they need elsewhere and the physician who feels disinclined to sex at home becomes vulnerable to erotic contacts with patients and office staff. Alcohol and drugs are usually only a final step along this path, but once initiated, they impair performance and gratification in both the personal and professional spheres.

—

In the end, physician marriages break down in the same areas as others; controversies over control, errors in communication, and unmatched needs for comfort and nurturance. But the personality profiles of the participants and the lifestyle of the physician make a considerable contribution. The deterioration in family life that is apparent at the time addiction becomes apparent is catalogued in the clues listed by Talbott and Benson. These include the physician's withdrawal from family, fights, and even child abuse, development of "spousaholism," abnormal or antisocial behavior by the children, sexual problems, and finally assumption of the surrogate role by the spouse or children with the institution of separation or divorce proceedings.

Like everything else in medicine, it is possible to portray too gloomy a prognosis by studying end stage or tertiary pathology and in doing so to miss preventative possibilities. A more hopeful aspect is that four out of five of the same wives who complained so bitterly in the survey quoted above also considered their marriages happy and said that they would marry the same man again. Divorce rates among physicians are actually lower in some studies than many other professional groups, and breakdown appears to occur after longer periods of marriage.

A number of suggestions for change have been made; one is that physicians use their compulsivity in a more creative manner to schedule their wives and families into their lives. Simply saying that family and practice are both important is not enough; this may create constant frustration and conflict if urgent practice needs gain priority over routine family plans. Time together must be scheduled and protected.

It would also help if medical students and physicians became more aware of the debit side of their otherwise successful personalities; this might give them permission to seek support and succor from their spouses without delaying their own needs indefinitely. A physician talking to medical students about the dilemma of professional demands and personal needs had the following to say:

> Let me change the expression "personal needs" to "personal demands" in order to emphasize the imperative quality of

self-identity as somehow distinct from professional identity. I suggest that there are two fundamental kinds of personal demands: cultivation of self-respect and support by loved ones. The critical quantitative requirement of these demands is free time. I'm talking about free time to sleep adequately, to stroll along the beach in bare feet, to hear the rustle of pine trees, to play the fiddle or build a cabinet and to learn how to love and grow with loved ones. I am convinced that a physician cannot provide optimal care for patients until as a person he has first learned how to care for loved ones and for himself; on purely intuitive grounds I do not believe the reverse will work at all.

Physician's Lib: A Midlife Reflection

Kathie and I like to think we have a liberated relationship. This means she has her own full-time job, is often out of town, and works to her own frantic schedules. We divide the chores and child care down the middle based on our skills and diurnal rhythms. I take Adam to school; Kathie puts him to bed. Still, there are some role specific imperatives that endure. Somehow I assume that my patients should preempt her customers while Kathie sabotages my attempts to plan the suppers.

Monday was Adam's first day at kindergarten. We went to bed early, but I was wakened at midnight to talk to the emergency room about a patient. Next morning, the patient called just as I was coaxing Adam out of bed from amongst his bears. As I dealt with the patient's questions, Adam dawdled over which clothes to wear. Tension began to mount as I fretted over taking him to school, dealing with my patient, and getting to morning rounds on time.

Old reflexes were triggered. An intern's insistent urge to be in the hospital took hold. A compelling sense of responsibility felt like a physical pain in my chest. Angry questions buzzed in my head. Why was it I who was taking Adam to school? What if I were late for residents' rounds? Who would see the new patient?

—

Displacing my discomfort, I nagged Adam to eat his cereal and chided Kathie for not coming with us to school. They ignored me as Adam picked up his new Jedi knight lunch box, and Kathie bundled us into the car with his nap blanket. Eyes brimming, she kissed Adam and wished him a happy day in his new school.

By the time I had dropped a calm but shy Adam at school and had reached the hospital, I was ten minutes early for morning rounds and wondering whether I would ever be liberated from the archaic imperatives of the physician role.

Night Owls and Early Birds

This essay is based on my own experience, both as a spouse and a psychiatrist doing repair work on other folks' marriages. I also thought it might make an interesting research project but, to my knowledge, its hypothesis remains untested. Ask around among your friends to see if it holds up.

Published in *Wisconsin Psychiatrist*, Winter 1994:

> Some people go to bed late and lie in, others sack out sooner but rise early. Why is this? As far as I can tell humans are split fifty-fifty with no gender difference, although most adolescents go through a night owl era at about the time their hormones kick in.
>
> An interest in diurnal rhythms was kindled thirty years ago by a fellow resident who had served on an Antarctic expedition studying physiologic fluctuations in relation to daylight hours. Knowing that melancholics often wake early, we discovered they had reversed physiological rhythms, including salivary flow which we measured every two hours (day and night) with weighed dental swabs. The pattern reverted to normal after treatment with ECT. This esoteric research has not had the slightest impact on psychiatric practice. It did, however,

raise my consciousness about the way body rhythms are physiologically determined and subject to change.

Lately I made an observation with more practical potential. Have you noticed how few married couples have synchronous sleep schedules? Virtually every spouse seems to have an opposing pattern—one a night owl, the other an early bird. Ask around; check it out for yourself.

Why is this? The literature suggests the opposite. Women prison inmates synchronize their menstrual cycles and male bomber air crew synchronize their cortisol rhythms. But we also know that environmental zeitgebers can desynchronize biological patterns—changing sleep-wake cycles in spelunking and jet lag for example.

Early in marriage I learned that the best time to read or write at home was in the early morning when nobody else cared a damn about what I did. Rising early was a facultative adaptation to domestic routine. Each couple may have similar but different reasons for seeking time alone. Living under the same roof is an art. There is a need to titrate intimacy, to minimize the brush of temperament, to share and yet to be apart. What better way for the mind and body to accommodate these needs than to desynchronize their diurnal rhythms. He sleeps late, she sleeps early or vice-versa.

There are some corollary questions. How does desynchrony correlate with marital bliss or discord? Is co-dependency associated with synchrony? Are divorce rates higher or lower in those with the same or different rhythms? You can probably come up with interesting questions of your own.

I'm offering this idea as a promising research topic to any young faculty member with the need to publish rather than perish. I even have a title for your proposed NIMH grant application—*Facultative Desynchronization of Diurnal Rhythms in Domiciliary Dyadic Relationships*. This should appeal to the

—

funding agency because it has no gender or sexual preference bias. It is also an archetypal biopsychosocial problem with lots of variables to correlate and data to collect.

Whatever you discover about this symbiosis between couples will serve to underline an ancient spiritual truth. Henri Nouwen in his book *Reaching Out: The Three Movements of the Spiritual Life* has a section entitled "Together, Yet Not Too Near," in which he comments: "The desire for protective boundaries by which man and woman do not have to cling to each other, but can move graciously in and out of each other's life circle, is clear from the many times that Khalil Gibran's words are quoted at a wedding ceremony":

> Sing and dance together and be joyous,
> but let each one of you be alone.
> Even as the strings of a lute are alone
> though they quiver with the same music.
>
> Stand together yet not too near together
> For the pillars of the temple stand apart,
> and the oak trees and the cypress
> grow not in each other's shadow.

Good Heavens
(I Can't Believe It)

Why does my wife insist?
There is no afterlife,
Where souls can persist?
Because
If heaven does exist
Our destiny could be
Wed for eternity.

—Barry Blackwell, August 2009

Saint's Day Savings

Valentine's Day thrift,
Is if man makes love to his wife,
Then calls it a gift.

—Barry Blackwell, February 2010

22. Parenting

Parentage is a very important profession, but no test of fitness is ever imposed in the interest of children.

—George Bernard Shaw

Like marriage, there is no formal training as a parent. No one should plan the size of their family until they have raised one infant, enjoyed the task, and know they have the temperament to do a good job. Then the next question becomes, is there enough love and patience for two or more despite inevitable sibling rivalry? I had three children by my first marriage and one by the second. Kathie and I sometimes wish we had more. Late-life parenting is easier when the burdens of work and ambition are relaxed.

This long, free-form poem is in two voices: a question a five-year-old son asks, answered by his father:

Duet

Dad,
If I'm good
Will I live a trillion billion years?
I wish I could.

I'm glad I'm not a girl;
They play with dumb dolls and dress up. Yuck!
Nana looks like she's sorry sometimes
And maybe Mom is too. Are you?

I wish each day was a weekend
'cause I could watch cartoons
and keep you all the time with me.
I'd paint pictures, do puzzles and play games
'specially with Mom. She lets me win.

Know what? If you're irritable or cross
It scares me. What did I do?
But when you laugh I like it lots.
Then I laugh too.
Why did the turtle cross the road?
To get to the shell station. See?

I know another riddle. Will you answer if I ask?
When do grownups die, and why?
Tell me,
Dad.

Adam,
You were carefully wrought, and rightly named,
The first for Mom, the final one of four for me.
Not an afterthought
Though after you we broke the mold
Tied our tubes and called it quits.
We've been lucky, us and you.

At birth you had a single blemish,
A strawberry splotch that faded so fast
No future lover will ever poke fun at it.
The time we picked was good, the seventies, not the fifties.
Sons and fathers bonded better.
Your mother's milk was copious but thin,
Making you a hungry runt, who needed holding.

—

It comes back now, as a bonus of family hugs
That will enter the generations.

You look like the milkman's child
With blond hair and blue eyes from God knows where.
Whatever the genes transmit we won't complain,
You catch balls and balance better
Than our own clumsy hands or wobbly feet permit.
In growth and girth you are an average child,
Someone who knows hunger so well
You can stop eating in mid-cookie.
Both parents were too busy to bribe you
With unnecessary ice cream to eat unwanted cabbage.

At two we tested wills;
One parent was good at limits, the other love.
Line-treading between indulgence and independence
We came out right this time.
Nana says you don't respect the rights of elders
But you know your own, and that's better.

You were four and fed up with coy queries
Whether your aunt's baby would be a boy or girl.
Impish, you asked if it might be a medium.
At five the three most important things, you said,
Were liking yourself,
Getting lots of sleep (so as not to be grouchy),
And knowing God was stronger than anybody.
Echoes; or your own ideas?
Is anything original, even sin?

Added up, it's turned out well
So far.
But all the accidents of upbringing that work
Don't drown the pit-stomach future fears of
Child molesters, malignant cells, drunk drivers and divorce.
Soon you'll be in latency, a limbo
Between Oedipus and adolescence.

A boy with a token doll
Waiting for your glands to work.

Creating the chemicals,
Exciting the world outside our windows,
Urging the species
To separate. To mate.
Go gently then, but come back later in our lives,
Adam.

—Barry Blackwell, circa 1983

Daddy

First acts of love
that bond a baby
to the breast
impose their trust
upon an eager
primal thirst.

But men start dry,
begin another way,
by breeding kids
whose unmet needs
and hungry eyes
are always asking why?

Men parched at birth
or thrust away
have little left.
Need echoes lack.
Bereft, giving nothing,
Some get nothing back.

Others, amply fed,
Bestow the orbit
of their loving arms
in lingering hugs,
quell the ebbing anger
and reap beginning love.

—Barry Blackwell, circa 1995

Doubt

Published in *Jazz Street*, Vol. 3, No. 1 and 2, 1986

You wonder why I worry?
well I wonder too
Maybe it was Dad
whose rivetgun eyes
poked holes in your ego
my ego, I mean
Sorry, but
images of Him
pop in and out

Of Him
expecting
correcting
inoculating
my thoughts
with
should
oughts
and doubts

So my shrink said
   get off the carrousel
   cut out this mind fucking
   she said
   it's all in your head
   she said
I try, I really do
   try, I mean
   but

—Barry Blackwell, 1986

This free-form poem has short staccato lines between four and six syllables with an irregular rhyme scheme between the three stanzas. The adverbs in the last four lines of the third stanza suggest something slipping away. The poem's form creates a feel of urgency, unpredictability and loss.

Taboo

Some gentle magnet lured me to his lap
and coaxed my pudgy limbs and petalled skin
inside his tweed-sleeved arms. Aromas trapped
in woolen pores rouse memories again,
of instant pain at just the moment when
I heard my daddy say, "You're much too grown."
No sooner said than done; he pushed me down.

Those first-grade smiles and budding social graces
were frantic recompense to fill the void
which earned me friends, but none of them replace
a forlorn sense of loss, of him annoyed,
of feeling bad inside, almost destroyed,
but never sure what error I had made,
what act of mine had made him feel afraid?

—Barry Blackwell, circa 1990

517

The above poem is the result of an assignment in poetry class. We were asked to write a poem on a topic of our own but in a classic form where each line had ten syllables and each stanza had an unusual end rhyme scheme, AC, BDE and FG. This task embodied the challenge and excitement of melding emotion and intellect; of finding a way to express powerful feelings within a preordained poetic structure. This contrasts with free form poetry where the content of the poem determines its form.

Turnpike Prayer

A multi-ton truck
Thunders by, overtaking me
In dusty triumph.
The radio fades in and out
As scenery slides past
Too fast to view;
Tuning me to new wavelengths.

Once, the sun rose and set
For reasons still unknown.
Soil was tilled and seeds sown,
Certain the seasons would prevail.
Navigators set sail
Hoping their ships would not fall
Off a flat earth.

The world aged as
Knowledge and doubt
Grew together;
Discovery explained mystery
In astronomy, physics and chemistry.
Science replaced blind faith,
Minting new coinage.

The crucifix at my neck
Is a security blanket
To unseen love.
I fondle it, asking God
Not to mend my life,
But strengthen my faith
And stifle my doubts.

I brake to slow,
Dig coins from my pocket,
Throw them in the toll,
And speed on toward
My son and grandson,
Whose love I cannot feel,
Yet know for sure is real.

—Barry Blackwell, circa 1994

Quit that Scat!

Kids bring home to Mum
Words they first heard from school chums;
"Shit, crap, piss, and turds!"

—Barry Blackwell, May 2012

Imagine being a parent, sitting down to supper, when your seven-year-old son serves up words never heard before. This haiku shows how an ancient and sedate Japanese poetic form can meld with the scatological humor and vulgarity of the English language. Those attributes contribute to its poetic form with both rhyme and assonance.

23. Divorce

Divorce is the psychological equivalent of a triple coronary bypass . . . it takes years to amend all the habits and attitudes that led up to it.

—Mary Kay Blakely

Divorce is ugly—hard on everyone, especially unemancipated kids who bear the brunt in the short term when it breeds sadness and anger and, later in life, when it may be reenacted in their own marriages. Love takes effort to sustain, and divorce teaches no skills, only disappointment and failure.

Divorce, British Style

The New York Sunday Times (April 8, 2012) reports that "Britain, unlike every state in America, does not have a no-default divorce law . . . instead one party has to accuse the other of acting so unreasonably that living together has become intolerable." A divorce lawyer, campaigning to change the law, joined with her fellow lawyers to compile a list of complaints filed with the courts.

This is a scenario that lays bare the superficial architecture of marriages gone wrong, of ruined dreams and diminished hopes, told in a curiously funny but odd way. The foundations of these breakdowns are obscure to the audience and perhaps for the couples themselves. Not everybody is psychologically minded, and in therapy, insight is first base. Here are the complaints, some mildly edited:

A woman complained that her husband insisted she wear a Klingon costume and speak in Klingon.

A man felt his wife was malicious because she kept serving him tuna casserole.

A husband refused to speak to his wife and for fifteen years, communicated by Post-it notes.

A wife wanted her husband to sleep separately, but he insisted on sharing the marriage bed and keeping his pet tarantula on the bedside table.

A man complained his wife flirted with every tradesman, saying she couldn't stop herself.

A husband took control of the TV remote and kept flipping through the channels, ignoring his wife's request to stop.

One husband had an atrocious body odor; another complained he hated the way his wife breathed.

A woman complained her spouse paid obsessive attention to detail, including combing the fringes of a rug.

One spouse demanded sex every night.

A wife alleged her husband was cross-dressing and stretching all her best outfits. He was six feet three inches tall.

A spokesperson for the justice department stated that the government had no plans to reform the law. An attempt to do so in 1996 failed, for fear it would make divorce too easy—available on demand.

—

Till Death Do Us Part

Kids become
Collateral damage
In broken marriages.

Deceived by ancient oaths
They never made
And vows that don't persist.

Let's pray they perceive
Commitment only lasts
As long as love exists.

—Barry Blackwell, August 2008

Heartbreak

With fractured hearts
Each partner knows
Love ebbs and flows
In fits and starts.

First the heart aches
Under cover;
Blames the other,
Before it breaks.

Folks don't admit,
Are loath to name
Oaths they defame,
Sins they commit.

Sometimes its age,
And messy rows
Or unkept vows
That turn the page.

—

Time is a thief
That robs the brain
Till what remains
Is loss and grief.

The stuff folks take
To soothe the soul
Exerts its toll,
On hearts that break.

So, in the end
They split apart;
A broken heart's
Too hard to mend.

Barry Blackwell, March 2012

This poem is in an "old-fashioned" form; each line has only four syllables and each stanza only four lines. The first and last lines end with a rhyme, as do the second and third lines. This form is not predetermined; each poem finds its own best form as it takes shape. This is an unhappy theme dealt with in a terse and ironic manner.

Endangered Species

Primal laws dictate
Species perpetuate.
When coded chromosomes
Urge them to mate
They propagate.

Conceived in fervent passion,
Raised with tender care
Love and lust entwined
Preserve the human race.

—

When fate mutates
Their lust to distrust
And love to hate,
The children born
Decline to mate.

—Barry Blackwell, March 2012

24. Sex

There may be some things better than sex, and some things may be worse. But there is nothing exactly like it.

—W. C. Fields

Give me chastity and continence, but not just now.

—Saint Augustine

For most folks sex is taboo or only a topic for private conversation. Here are a couple of funny poems that should offend nobody.

I'm Potent!

Nobody knew
Or even suspected
What pills might do
When, limp and dejected,
We were re-erected.

—Barry Blackwell, July 2008

This poem has a clever title (a literary "double entendre") and is a spoof on the modern Viagra variety of drugs. It is unpublished, censored by Kathie from the annual Christmas letter to friends and family. It has short lines, which contribute to its vertical (erect) feel with a rhyme scheme that comes to a swift conclusion.

Doubles Trouble

Mascular Feminate
Masters and Johnson mate
Folk who've forgotten what
Needs to be done.

There are some who get worse,
Polymorphousperverse,
They never discover
Sex can be fun.

—Barry Blackwell, September 1986

This poem is written in an unusual form in the same genre as a limerick. It begins with two misspelled nonsense words which must convey the content of the poem and rhyme with the second line. Known as a "double dactyl," this poem was published in the *Journal of Irreproducible Results* (Sept.-Oct. 1986), a medical version of the satirical lay newspaper, *The Onion*.

Seek and We Shall Find

The male Holy Grail,
Found not in guys, only gals,
Disguised: the **G**-spot!

—Barry Blackwell, May 2012

The traditional Japanese haiku form is embellished with Anglo-Saxon rhyme coupled with both alliteration and assonance based upon the letter *G* and its sound.

Sex in Britain

During our family trip to India (see Piece 3: India), we occasionally kept in touch with world events by reading the *India Times*. It is an English-language newspaper with an impeccable reputation for scrupulous reporting. One day, early in January 2002, we were astonished to read the following verbatim report:

> LONDON: One in four Britons has had sex in the car park after the office Christmas party, according to a survey, which said more than 80 percent of British people admitted to enjoying saucy in-car activity.
>
> Women in Cheshire, northwest England, have sex in cars most often, with 20 percent saying they do it once a month or as often as possible.
>
> Meanwhile, 22 percent of women in Newcastle upon Tyne, northeast England, said they had had sex in the back of a cab. Nearly 40,000 people replied to questions in the survey, which found that men from southeast England were the most sexually inept—18 percent of them admitted injuring themselves while trying out their favorite position.

I am aware of no cross-cultural studies that provide comparative data. America's love with the automobile suggests we should be able to compete.

Fair Trade

It amazed him how different cities could be from one another around the world. Just the small things. In Toronto, cars stop whenever a walker steps off the curb. In Adelaide, the traffic lights emit a steady beep that tells the blind (and the sighted) if it's safe to cross. In Cairo, it takes the speed and agility of a road runner to evade the donkeys and Rolls Royces.

—

527

In this city, all commerce ceased at noon on Saturdays, leaving him bored and frustrated, isolated and lonely, in an international hotel room identical to dozens he had stayed in elsewhere. He had seen the same pictures on the walls in other countries and smelled the same musty disinfectant on carpets everywhere. The conference had ended that morning and with it the excitement and hospitality, dumping him into a twenty-four-hour limbo before the next leg of a ten-city lecture tour that would pay his way around the world.

Conferences bruised him. There was too much uninvited closeness in the audience and never quite enough applause at the podium. The academic grooming rituals made him feel edgy and competitive. He had planned to cure himself with a spending spree looking for a pair of expensive earrings for his wife. The city was famous for the black opals that were mined in the hills that surrounded it. When he discovered the shops were closed, he drifted toward the hotel wondering what to do with the day.

Back in the room, he pulled a local beer from the well-stocked bar above the refrigerator and dropped several ice cubes into it. Sipping slowly, he flipped the pages of a booklet on the coffee table, looking for a movie he hadn't seen or an ethnic restaurant for supper that evening. The page in front of him caught his attention. It was another difference he'd noticed. In America, they were called massage parlors, in Canada, health clubs. Here, it was escort services. There were several to choose from. "Dial-A-Lady," "Les Amorettes," "Top Shelf," "Night Shift." Suggestive names with different phone numbers but the same message. For seven days a week, twenty-four hours a day, you could buy company in your home, hotel, or motel. They promised distinction, discretion, and attractive companions who catered to your "every taste" for "any event." Most of them took credit cards.

As soon as he read them and wondered, "Why not?" the thought excited him. His pulse skipped a beat as he picked up the phone to dial one of the numbers. A ringing tone but no answer. The next attempt drew a recorded message to call back later. The third time was lucky. A woman's cockney voice asked what he wanted and quoted the rates. Half an hour for sixty dollars, an hour for ninety. Not a real bargain when he considered his own limited capacity for prolonged or repeat performances. He put the phone down without making a decision, but he was too excited to doubt the outcome. After another sip or two of beer, he called back and said he'd take an hour. The same cheery voice asked for his first name, his hotel, the room number, and told him to expect a call back in twenty minutes. It came earlier. Another upbeat voice and an accent he couldn't place. She called him by his first name and told him hers. It was the same as his youngest daughter's name.

Between the call and her arrival, he had time to shower and put on a bathrobe so that when the knock came and he opened the door, he felt warm and relaxed, although he couldn't bring himself to say her name. She had jet-black hair, olive skin, and almond eyes that smiled quickly and often. He offered a drink and poured the soda she asked for before fixing a stiff brandy for himself.

They sat together on the bed and though her first moves were tentative and even shy, she quickly became skilled and passionate. He was surprised at her aggressive enjoyment and the excited noises she made. He wondered if it was done to urge him to an earlier end, but the thought held no delaying power, and they quickly came to a frenzied halt in a duet of deep-throated sounds.

In the collapsed afterglow, she gently rubbed the skin of his back and the small talk began. She was Malaysian and guessed he was American. This was a second, part-time profession. Something she did on Saturdays to earn enough to support a partnership in her real job. She sold personalized photo albums to the parents of children in kindergarten. When he told her he was a psychiatrist, she giggled and said it made her nervous that he might be analyzing everything she said. But as the hour eroded, the flow of talk became one-sided. She told him more about herself and asked him less. Used to listening and content with the work of her hands, he said only enough to encourage her to prattle on.

She told him about her double life. She was divorced, and there were two miscarriages but no children. One day she hoped to have a love child, but finding a man who would give you a rose or buy you chocolates was hard. Most just wanted sex. The irony of this seemed to escape her as she went on to explain how secrecy had cost her friends. They were puzzled when she no longer came to lunch or visited their homes. If they persisted, she became angry or irritable, pushing them away to protect her privacy. When she was on call for her second job, it wasn't safe to go among her former friends—what would she say if the pager in her purse went off? All this was becoming too difficult, and she was thinking of moving to another city where she could start over.

When it came time for her to stop, she eased herself off the bed and began to put her clothes back on. He picked up his wallet from the bedside table and gave her a one hundred dollar bill. She smiled and said perhaps she should pay him for listening. How much did he charge? He laughed and said their rates were the same—except that for ninety dollars, you got only fifty minutes of talk. Ten minutes were for writing notes. Not so different, she said, when you counted the time for taking your clothes off and putting them on.

Before she left, she telephoned in to report the job was done. He heard her say she was ready for another and would be having supper somewhere. He wondered if he should invite her to eat with him and was about to suggest it when a thought entered his mind that stopped him. If they went somewhere together and her pager went off, she would leave, and he would have to deal with the loss. He decided it would be better to eat by himself, so he showed her to the door and said nothing. As she slipped past him, he whispered his thanks, calling her by name for the first time.

25. DOMESTICITY

Home is the place where, no matter where you're sitting, you're looking at something you should be doing.

—Popular saying

Most men today share the burdens of domesticity; in addition to my love of cooking (particularly Indian food), I (occasionally) do the laundry or shop at the grocery store or pharmacy where I became familiar with lost socks and long lines. In the third poem, you are invited to guess the identity of what is used up! (Hint: *dental, not mental.*)

Sole Mates

Socks live
Sad lives;
Identical twins
Forced apart.
Never sure
If they are
Left or right.

Laced inside
Dark shoes,
Stifled by
Sweaty odors;
Holey from
Torn toenails,
Darned by needles.
When one is lost
In the wash
Then its mate is
Tossed in the trash.

—Barry Blackwell, circa 1996

Checkout

The fast lane never is:
The man in front
Has lost his coupons.
The checker asks,
"Endive or chicory?"
Then, "What's it cost?"
The register
Runs out of change.
The bagger takes
A bathroom break.
Liquor needs someone
Over twenty-one.

The next lane
Is always quicker.
Its customers
Are gone . . .

—Barry Blackwell, circa 1998

Used Up

Shelf fresh and shiny,
Eye appealing,
Stretched plump.
Seductive as a ripe plum,
Cozy in the palm,
Urgent to be squeezed.

Twisted and wrinkled,
Brutally furled,
Bent at the end.
Uncapped and empty,
Congealed and tacky,
Garbage can ready.

—Barry Blackwell, *Wisconsin Psychiatrist*, Winter 1998

Grooming

Periodically my spouse conducts a loving inspection of my fitness to appear in public. This includes a check of my outerwear to determine I am spot-free (I have a floppy lower lip) and a review of my exoskeleton (hair and nails) to ensure everything is well-trimmed. In tough economic times, people perform these chores themselves, giving the manicurist and hairdresser a break.

Cut Short

We groom and clip
Whatever grows.
First the fingers,
Then the toes.
We call them "cures"
With Latin names,
Although we know
(It's such a shame),
That only death
Stops them grow.

—Barry Blackwell, March 2010

26. Hobbies

Get interested in something. Shake yourself awake. Develop a hobby.
Let the wind of enthusiasm sweep through you. Live today with gusto.

—Dale Carnegie

As individuals and family, we indulge in hobbies and pastimes that temper our work or school lives. Like fashions, they flower and fade, often depending on ability, opportunity, or life circumstance. Here are some of mine that have come and gone; only writing and cooking survive and, as I burn fewer calories with age, I recall Benjamin Franklin's warning to "beware of a hobby that eats."

Fitness

For over twenty years, beginning at age eleven, I played vigorous rugby at a high competitive level—for my school, Cambridge University Sixty Club, Guy's Hospital (the oldest rugby club in the world), and the Saracens, now a leading London semiprofessional club. Before women began to indulge—an unthinkable idea in my time—rugby was known as "a ruffian's game played by gentlemen," while soccer was "a gentleman's game played by ruffians." Fitness is a fleeting concept; I suffered concussion at least a dozen times, developed cauliflower ears (see Piece 7: Guy's Hospital), and had a cartilage removed from my knee (two weeks in hospital for what is now an outpatient procedure).

I quit rugby when I came to America at age thirty-four, just as the game was beginning to be popular here. So, symbolically, I never played "my last game." Well past midlife, I decided it was time to indulge the fantasy and persuaded a young faculty member to negotiate a brief "on-field" appearance in the closing minutes of a game at the lakefront. Watched by a terrified Kathie and Adam, I dove into the scrum and flailed around, a twenty-year-old mind in a fifty-year-old body. I escaped serious injury, limped off, and licked my wounds for the next couple of weeks.

As an undergraduate, I also rowed in a college "eight" during the summer and competed in the May "bumps." These are races conducted on the River Cam in June; because the river is narrow, the boats line up prow to stern, a fixed distance apart, and begin to row like crazy at the sound of a starter gun. A boat that catches up and bumps the one in front is declared the winner and both boats draw to the bank. Next day, the winner and loser switch places, and the process is repeated for four days. If a boat secures a "bump" on each of four days, every member of the crew is awarded a trophy. Oarsmen receive a twelve-foot long oar engraved with the names and weights of crew members and the colleges they bumped. I was fortunate to win two of these trophies, exported them to America, and gave them to my kids when we no longer had space to hang them.

In America, I played racquet ball until I began to suffer the delayed consequences of two decades' pushing in the scrum; today I have an artificial hip, two severely arthritic knees, and spinal stenosis. Nonetheless, Kathie and I still play an occasional game of golf (plus a cart) at which we both lift divots and lose balls, refusing to keep score and enjoying "one hole at a time." With lifetime access to a heated indoor pool, I now indulge in "water aerobics," relieved to know that submerging yourself takes forty percent of your weight off arthritic joints. I can build up muscle without wrecking the joint.

Cooking and Recipes

On social occasions, when friends visit on the weekends, Kathie and I share the cooking, but during the week, when she works, I am the principal chef de cuisine. I learned to cook from my mother, not because she taught but because I watched. She was a natural cook of traditional Lancashire regional dishes, some of which are not popular in America, such as pig's trotters, tripe, and kidneys. I learned to like kidneys as a young lad during the war years. Unlike muscle meat, offal was not rationed, and I was delegated to make the rounds of the local butcher shops scrounging for lamb's kidneys. They are difficult to find in America but, once in a while, when Kathie is out of town, I manage to find and cook some for myself. The last time I did this, I fed the leftovers to our black lab, Stanley, who took a bite, spat it out on the kitchen floor, and took a drink from the toilet bowl.

Try to forget kidneys and enjoy the following four recipes from my mother's repertoire; they are guaranteed to delight your family and friends.

Potato Pie

For this, you need a crock pot or some other form of very slow cooking. The ingredients are as basic as you can imagine for a dish that tastes, and smells, so divine. This makes enough for four to six people.

> *About 2 lbs. Idaho potatoes*
> *About 2 lbs. of Spanish onions*
> *About 3 lbs. of stew beef*
> *About 2 lbs. of mushrooms*
> *Two double pan frozen pie crusts*

You can vary the amounts depending on the size of the crock pot and the number of people. You will have a better idea after you have made it once.

Peel and slice the potatoes and onions into about quarter-inch-thick slices and slice the mushrooms also.

Lay the sliced vegetables and the meat in separate layers, beginning at the bottom with the potato (sprinkle some salt), then onion, then meat, then mushroom (sprinkle some pepper). Repeat the layers in order until the ingredients reach to within a half inch of the top. Try to finish with a layer of potato.

Add one tablespoon of water or broth (not more; the ingredients produce ample juices).

Put the crock pot on high and leave for several hours until there is an unmistakable appetizing smell, then turn down to low and leave until time to serve. (Eight hours or so.)

Make a pie crust from the two double pan pie crusts (thawed). Roll them out with a pin to fit the top of the crock pot. I prefer to cook the crust separately in the oven on a cookie sheet and place it on the crock pot when I serve the meal. If you try to cook the pastry on the pot itself, you will need to prop it up with a pie crust support. Even then, it often collapses.

Serve this with either frozen peas or the carrot and turnip dish below (or both).

I usually provide hot English mustard (Coleman's) and Branston pickle (made by Crosse and Blackwell, available in most grocery stores).

Shepherd's Pie

Almost inevitably ethnic foods are modified by American cooks, not always in helpful ways. Two things to know about the "genuine article": true shepherd's pie is made from ground lamb and cottage pie from ground beef. Otherwise, they are identical. They do not need added vegetables which, if served, should be cooked separately. (With the exception of some grated carrot—see recipe.)

About ½ lb. of top quality ground chuck or lamb per person
One large Spanish onion
About 2 lbs. of Yukon potatoes for mashed potato topping
Beef broth
One packet of powdered gravy mix (to make 1 ½ cups)
Liquid gravy browning (optional)

Fry the onions in a small amount of oil until light brown and then add the meat and fry until thoroughly browned. I usually grate one medium-sized carrot into the mix—this gives it a slightly sweet taste.

Make the gravy by mixing the powder with the correct amount of beef broth. Heat as directed until gravy thickens. Add a tablespoon of liquid gravy browning to darken.

Pour the gravy over the meat and onion mix and cook on medium for about forty minutes. Season with salt and pepper. Allow to cool and place in fridge until ready to add topping, reheat, and serve.

Make mashed potato topping; boil potatoes till soft (about twenty to twenty-five minutes), drain, add enough melted butter and warm milk, salt and pepper to taste, and then mash with a whisk.

Spread the mashed potatoes onto the meat and decorate with tines of a fork.

Place in medium oven to rewarm (about forty-five minutes) and then turn on broiler to brown the potatoes. Watch closely and serve when the mashed potatoes are browned (usually five to ten minutes).

I serve with the same vegetable(s) and condiments as the potato pie.

Carrots and Turnips

This highly compatible mix of two common root vegetables is not often served in America but is very popular in the UK and tasty.

Equal amounts of large sweet carrots and turnips (about one of each per person)

Chop the carrots and turnips into inch-square pieces and cook in boiling water until soft (about twenty-five minutes). Drain and puree with a potato masher and a knob of butter; add salt and white pepper. The pepper is important; enough to notice but not overwhelm the flavor.

English Trifle

This is a very popular, delightful, and attractive desert. It does contain sherry or masala in modest amounts, something you should tell your guests. The calorie content can be kept down considerably by using "Lite" ingredients.

Large glass or china bowl
Jar of raspberry jam
Medium sherry or dry masala
Trifle sponges—round or fingers—enough to cover the sides and bottom of the bowl
Two cans of Lite sliced cling peaches
Sugar-free packet of vanilla pudding mix and required amount of skim milk
Cool Whip topping
Crystalized cherries
Whole almonds

Spread a thin smear of raspberry jam on the inner sides of the sponges and lay them along the bottom and sides of the bowl. You can put more than one layer on the bottom.

Trickle the sherry or masala onto the sponge so that it absorbs the liquor and is damp but there is no free fluid (about half a cup).

Empty the peach slices and place throughout the bowl, on top, and alongside the sponges, using a small amount of the juice.

Make the vanilla pudding and pour over the sponges and into the bowl. The top of the pudding should come to just over an inch below the rim. (If necessary, make more.)

Place in the refrigerator and allow to set. If necessary, leave overnight.

Thaw Cool Whip in the refrigerator according to instructions and then spread evenly over custard in a layer, up to rim of the bowl. Place back in refrigerator for a few hours.

Remove from refrigerator and decorate with cherries and almonds. I usually place one cherry each in the center of the bowl and at the twelve, three, six and nine o'clock positions, allowing enough space away from the rim to place five almonds around each cherry in a circle.

Dietary Dislikes

Obviously, I am a meat and potato person who shuns fish. Except for salmon, fish is colorless and complicated by skin and bones. It is tasteless until it becomes "fishy" when it is inedible. Meat is never "meaty" and may even improve with maturity (fowl and game). When we dine out, if my wife orders a whole fish with its head on, I place the menu between it and myself to avoid having to gaze into its reproachful eyes.

"Fishee"

Tofu of the sea
Its diminutive describes
What it must not be.

—Barry Blackwell, 2009

Cooking Shows

TV cooking shows have become an invasive part of American life, with an almost hypnotic and addictive quality. This coincides with an epidemic of obesity that is sweeping America. As a psychiatrist, I have pondered a possible relationship between these two phenomena that reaches beneath the obvious and is reflected in the following parody and poem.

NEWS FLASH!

The Iranian Government has awarded the Noble Piece Prize to Professor Barry Blackwell for his discovery of the Benign Oral Sublimation Syndrome (BOSS), a condition that allows women to avoid weight gain, consistent with Sharia Law. Criteria for diagnosis (DSM X) are:

- Watching cooking shows continuously or intermittently for a minimum of two hours on at least two TV sets in separate rooms.
- Failure to gain weight due to optical sublimation of oral needs.
- Weight loss confirmed by a significant male authority figure.

Caution: Results based on a crossover study in a single subject related to the investigator; claim not approved by the FDA.
Black Box Warning: Watching the same show on two TV sets may cause astigmatism or diplopia.

"No Wait Loss"

Watching cooking shows
Switches fat to images,
Swapping pounds to sounds.

—Barry Blackwell, December 2011

Libations

Whenever wine is lacking, medicines become necessary.

—The Talmud

Better to pay the tavern keeper than the druggist.

—Spanish saying

I chose the title *Libations* advisably. Liquor or booze sound vaguely derisive, alcohol too medicinal, drinks too generic, and wine too exclusive.

The British are somewhere between the French and the Americans in how they introduce their children to alcoholic beverages. For the Gallic folks, wine is an integral part of a family meal, and no one of any age should be denied a taste. Americans enacted Prohibition, a disastrous example of religious intrusion in federal policy; a Puritan sentiment that lingers on in some state jurisdictions where young adults, under twenty-one, must sit outside the tavern door while their parents imbibe inside. Most Brits allow minors to quaff beer or sip wine on special occasions, but pubs are less permissive than parents.

The two quotations above offered sound advice at a time when alcohol was more potent than most materia medica. But modern medications are often toxic, even in modest dosages or brief ministrations. Consistent with their prescriptive authority, psychiatrists often issue routine draconian injunctions that patients avoid any drop of alcohol to avoid an unspecified drug interaction. Aware that people often ignore doctors' orders if advice seems arbitrary, unexplained, or inconsistent with a person's opinions or daily habits, I took a different tack. I explained that if the drugs I prescribed and alcohol shared sedative effects, it would be wise to titrate their use against that outcome. If they normally drank two glasses of wine or a couple of beers, they should pause after the first drink and accept or reject the second based on the results of their own experiment. My patients were not immune from side effects, but alcohol was never a problem.

—

For myself, relaxing at home after a hard day at the office, I enjoyed wine, beer, or an occasional weekend martini (white rum, not gin). Not an expert oenophile (Greek for "wine lover"), I lack the sensory equipment to be a wine snob. My tongue and nose have no receptors for those nuanced flavors on the label or the descriptors listed in the wine magazines; pepper, leather, tobacco, etc. My mouth has only a single ten-point scale of opinion from 0 (undrinkable) to 10 (buy it).

For me, the impulse to buy is also heavily influenced by price. The most compelling lesson learned over a lifetime is that the correlation between cost and flavor for wine is wildly inconsistent. I like finding gems priced for less than ten dollars which, when presented in a cut glass wine decanter, fool my friends into making wildly inaccurate estimates of price and provenance. Even better, but irritating, is seeing my inexpensive selection appear on a classy restaurant's wine list at five times the price I paid in my liquor store.

My mother's favorite beverage was cheap gin, consumed to excess and concealed behind the kitchen curtains or underneath the sink. Gin is an ancient beverage which originated in the Middle Ages as a patent medicine and used as a remedy for the Black Death; obviously ineffective, it may have eased the terminal agonies of its victims. In the eighteenth century, gin became an inexpensive and popular drink of the poorer classes in England, when the government allowed its unlicensed manufacture at a time when a heavy duty was imposed on all imported liquor. During this time, known as the "Gin Craze," over half of the 15,000 taverns in London were gin shops, and it became known as "mother's ruin." In America, "bathtub" gin was also popular during Prohibition because of the ease with which it could be manufactured.

Just as England was exploring the social charms of gin, she was also expanding the bounds of Empire in hot climates. The mosquitoes fought back, and gin found a new medicinal use. Flavored with the juniper berry, gin cut the bitter taste of quinine used to treat malaria and, in doing so, serendipitously introduced its sufferers to the tasty blend of gin with tonic water. It was a successful marriage of medicinal and social utility.

Later on, in Vienna, Freud's personal dalliance with cocaine did not lead to the medical discovery he craved to advance his career in neurology—somebody else beat him to the punch, discovering its local anesthetic effects. Later, in America, Timothy Leary and his Harvard pals enjoyed the mind-expanding effects of LSD, but those who followed never identified a medical use for hallucinogens, although some felt it held promise in the treatment of alcoholism.

Neither of my parents was a devotee of wine; my father preferred scotch whiskey but, despite her love of gin, my mother did have a favorite wine. Unsophisticated though she was, she developed a strong liking for Chateau d'Yquem, probably the world's most expensive and adulated wine. It belongs in the classification of the sweet white wines, Sauterne and Barsac. The Chateau and its vineyards where it grows in France belonged to Eleanor of Aquitaine who married Henry II of England in 1154, making it a royal British estate until it reverted to France at the end of the Hundred Years' War in 1453.

How my mother's strange enthusiasm for the world's most celebrated wine came about is a mystery. My parents could afford to dine in fine restaurants, and my father never stinted in paying for the best of what my mother wanted if it was available. The wine is sweet, seductive, and voluptuous; the kind that appeals equally to sophisticated and naïve drinkers.

February 14, 2006, was the centennial of my mother's birth; Valentine was her middle name, so my father called her "Val," the only person who did. I decided to plan and cook a meal in my mother's memory, inviting the grandchildren as guests. The menu included the dishes for which she was famous. (See *Cooking and Recipes* in this piece.) I also scanned the Internet to find her favorite wine and ordered two bottles of Chateau d'Yquem from different vintages at a cost of $250 a bottle. I considered this a very reasonable price until the mailman delivered a smaller-than-expected package containing two *half* bottles!

Over forty years ago, my wife and I began to save the corks from wines we drank on celebratory or joyous occasions. Written on each cork was the date, place, and names of those present. The corks are gathered in an elegant crystal glass bowl in a place of honor in our living room. This week I took them all out, placed them in chronological order and traveled back in time to when we were engaged; living together but not yet married in Cincinnati. A thirty-year-old nurse and a forty-year-old psychiatrist, working together on the same academic teaching unit at the university. Here is the inventory of our life together told in wine corks!

The corks date from over forty years (1971-2012), and the earliest was drawn from its bottle on January 29, 1971. There are a total of two hundred, and every year is represented by at least one cork, average five per year. Twenty percent are champagne corks and the remainder almost all red wines, including a few vintage ports and distinguished (a.k.a. expensive) burgundy (Beaune) or clarets (Latour and Beaucastle). But most corks were drawn from run-of-the-mill, thirty-dollars-or-less a bottle at today's wine list prices.

The wines were consumed in England, Wales, Australia, Spain, India, Mexico, South America, and throughout the United States in Cincinnati, Dayton, Milwaukee, Washington, D.C., Hawaii, Disneyworld, Door County, Chicago, Phoenix, New York, Las Vegas, San Francisco, New Orleans, Boca Raton, and on two family cruises to Alaska and the Caribbean.

The occasions celebrated among friends and family included anniversaries, birthdays, graduations, weddings, a wake, homecomings, baby showers, Easter, New Year, Christmas, Mardi Gras, sporting events, promotions, new jobs, and my college roommate's golden wedding anniversary held in London's Apothecaries Hall.

Although this is an impressive inventory, I cannot escape knowing we have thrown away many more corks than we kept!

Gardening (a.k.a. Yard Work)

According to family mythology, the first words out of my mouth were "pretty flowers," an assertion supported by a faded photograph of a blonde curly-headed infant, circa eighteen months, reaching for a flower in the yard of the house where I was born. Although gardening was my father's favorite avocation and an Englishman's vice, I spurned its lure in youth. Perhaps, like Alzheimer's, our brains are programmed to express the disorder late in life.

Nor did the opportunity present until, as empty nesters, we downsized to a smaller bungalow with a larger yard and swimming pool in 2002. The half-acre grounds were desolate and neglected, without a bush or flower in sight—only a yellow and green blanket of dandelions and weeds. Temporarily retired and with time on my hands, I set to with a passion; designing a garden is like painting on a blank canvas, choosing your palette and blending the colors, but waiting two or three years for the full picture to emerge. Almost like birthing a family, but with the added advantage that you can pull up and throw out whatever fails to please or develop. After a while, you learn which plants need sun or shade and where they can find it.

Over the course of the nine years we lived in that house, I turned the yard into a floral and herbaceous wonderland with a shade and lily garden, perennial flower beds, a hosta garden, rose bushes, purple, white, and yellow magnolias, and an English rock garden with a fountain. Kathie was an admirer but not a weeder, even for her herb garden!

As the yard matured, so did I; with arthritis spreading though my limbs like a creeping vine, I was reduced to horizontal gardening, lying on the turf to wield a trowel. Thus doth nature ease us from one life passage to the next; from doing to contemplating, from planning to remembering.

Flowers for Life

Published in *Labors Of Love,* Noble House, 2005:

Barry to Kathie, Sweetest Day, 2003

This garden is my gift,
Planted for you.
Fragrant and perennial
From spring through fall,
Hellebore to Columbine,
Valentine's till Sweetest Day,
An annual recollection
Of lives entwined.

Herbs to kiss your lips,
Scents to flood your senses,
Weeds to remind us
Love best be blind
To imperfection.
When we are joined forever
It will remain
Our gift to others.

Camping

We were avid campers of the cultivated kind. In our younger days we owned a VW camper with a pop-up top that slept four comfortably and possessed endless nooks and crannies in which to store provisions, as well as a refrigerator, a stove, and a sink. When the kids went to college, the camper was retired, and we reverted to hotels, but happy memories linger.

Camp Out

This waterlogged weekend
pent up kids and tent trapped grown ups
incubate cabin fever under
shrinking canvas, dripping like
a ticking clock into soggy ground.

Parents cluster like damp crows
round a smoking campfire,
cawing their garden fence chat,
cloakroom jokes and gossip
that kills time and office enemies.

One fresh scratched girl says
climbing fences is a waste of skin,
except how else can she get to
exciting places that say
"KEEP OUT," when they invite her in.

Two scrawny boys swap
penis tales and sexy stories,
giggling and bragging each
knows best how to make his prick
stiff and tall, like a giraffe's neck.

A madder 'n' hell Mom stacks
muddied jeans and puddled shoes,
cussing kids and idle dads,
wishing she'd packed sparklers,
marshmallows and more band-aids.

On sunny Monday morning
not a single soul admits
they quit their sodden site
and scurried home to dry suburbia,
earlier than they usually do.

—Barry Blackwell, circa 1994

The poem is structurally interesting and unusual. In addition to limited rhyme *(suburbia-earlier)* and off rhyme *(kids, dads, aids)*, it contains a lot of alliteration *(crows, cawing, chat, cloakroom)* and assonance *(stiff, giraffe)*. Much of this is not deliberate but slipped off the tongue and pen as the poem evolved.

Operas and Arias

When it comes to describing opera audiences, there isn't an adequate adjective less than "fanatic." Not even "lover" or "enthusiast" quantifies the zeal. At the opera meccas, the Metropolitan and the Lyric, single seats are seldom sold and can fetch a king's ransom.

These are rich and smart people, and my inability to join with them makes me feel inferior and paranoid. Here's why:

Most of the repertoire is in strange languages: Russian, German, French, and Italian. Sometimes a translation flashes overhead—reading it is like watching a vertical tennis match with the proscenium as net. Seldom-used neck muscles become strained.

Much is lost in translation. In English, the lyrics lack subtlety, meter, and rhyme. Humor is feeble but the audience titters dutifully on cue. The themes seem sentimental and the story line often turgid and banal.

Audiophiles find the music and arias celestial, which I can concede even though I am tone deaf. So altogether, for me, opera and enjoyment are an oxymoron. I like peanuts but not the shells and candies without the wrappers. An occasional aria is enjoyable but, inside, the opera is indigestible. And definitely not worth the price of admission.

Pink Paperweights

To the extent that I engage in introspection, I consider myself mildly obsessional because I do tread on the cracks in the sidewalk, but I don't hoard things. In fact, I'm more likely to give them away; after reading a novel, I either donate it to the library or give it to a friend. Who needs crowded bookshelves in the age of Amazon, Google, and the Internet?

Obsessional because, once in a while, I have an urge to collect things. As a child, it was postage stamps, but there were too many, and I couldn't afford the rare ones. The lesson learned was you best collect something that was not so common as to be boring but not so rare it was unaffordable.

This lifetime need was satisfied professionally by doing research; gathering information about matters of significant concern that could be studied without a need for extravagant funding.

In the domestic realm, I settled for corks from wine we consumed (see "Libations" in this piece) and pink paperweights. Paperweights because I coveted the intricate designs and unique shapes lodged in sparkling glass; unmanly pink after it became my favorite color when my college roommate was elected to the elite English Leander Rowing Club in recognition of coxing the first college eight. His badge of office was a pink blazer.

Recently I became a member of the Milwaukee Brewers "pink-tie club" after we were invited to a charitable fund raiser, at which the tie rewarded a significant donation.

In forty years, the paperweight collection grew to more than eighty pieces, elegantly displayed in our living room. When the time came to downsize, I winnowed the collection to my favorite twenty and gave the rest as gifts to my friends and family.

27. Pets

If a man could be crossed with a cat, it would improve man but deteriorate the cat.

—Mark Twain

The more I see of men, the more I like dogs.

—Madame de Stael

Animals, especially dogs and cats, are easier to like and love than people, even perhaps for psychiatrists. Or should it, more honestly, be *especially* psychiatrists. No one knows better than we do how fifty years of effort to translate animal brain research into finding cures for human mental illness have failed miserably compared to other areas of medicine. (See "Sea Change or Tsunami?" in "Piece 12: Psychopharmacology: Then, Now, and Next.")

Closely examined, this is hardly surprising although it is slow to be acknowledged. Of all the body's systems and functions; cardiovascular, neuromuscular, gastrointestinal, etc., the gap between human and animal is widest when it comes to the central nervous system. This is true for both good and bad attributes, all of which are exclusive to mankind. On the asset side, speech, prescience, dexterity, imagination, spirituality, and more; on the debit side, mental illness, psychosis, personality disorder, criminality, drug abuse, and more.

Of all professions, except perhaps for criminal justice, psychiatrists are most exposed to the darker side of humanity. No wonder it is a relief to get home to a welcoming pet whose kinder side is almost always up and on display. No sulking, temper tantrums, unreasonable demands—just a daily walk, bowl of food, and a tummy tickle, with affection and loyalty received in return.

Published in *Wisconsin Psychiatrist*, Vol. 42, No. 3, Summer 2002:

Genomic Eugenics

God's architectural plan
For making man
From genes
Now stands revealed.
Divine mistakes
Can be repealed;
We know the mode
That replicates
Selected templates,
Corrects the errors,
And eradicates
The imperfections
In His faulty code.
Rightly aligned, certain chromosomes
Make canines kind.
Inserted in our genome
Traditional emotion
Would be converted
To unconditional emotion.
Then happy smiles
Plus wagging tails
Could duplicate the joy.

> But grimmer folks
> Who don't enjoy a joke
> Won't hesitate;
> They'll amputate.

—Barry Blackwell, 2002

Of course, there are drawbacks; veterinary medicine has adopted almost all the moneymaking procedures of the human kind without the benefit of insurance coverage, but doubtless there soon will be deductibles, copays, and preexisting conditions. My son's lovable dog, Sprecher (named after Adam's favorite beer), came from the Humane Society free, but later in life required surgery for each of his front knee joints at a cost of $6,000.

Our own two pets, Stanley (a black Lab), and Fuzzy (a long-haired black cat), both lived to be seventeen. Here are their eulogies:

Requiem for Stanley

1989-2006

> Stanley came the way most dogs do;
> A puppy, begged for by my son,
> Bequeathed back when walking him
> Became too big a burden
> For a busy child to bear.
>
> Pure black Lab, bred to fetch
> Sticks, bones, balls or frisbees.
> Stanley's arctic island genes
> Custom made him for his daily swims
> In our icy northern lake.

Tightly muscled, an ornery alpha dog,
Stanley perfumed lamp posts, fire hydrants,
Tree stumps, garbage cans, and parked cars,
Cocking his leg even when
His tank was on empty.

Stanley had the appetite of an elephant,
The table manners of a two-year-old,
The menu of a starving goat,
A mouth like a vacuum cleaner
And iron-clad innards.

A disgusting significant other,
Stanley passed gas without guilt,
Ate cat shit and smiled,
Stole my supper from the kitchen table,
Teased me with torn socks and chewed shoes.

Stanley liked to lick my naked toes,
Unleashing feelings not linked
To sex, skin color, or bribery.
If people had tails or wagged their faces
There'd be fewer divorces.

Seventeen years of loyalty and love
Have left an aching void,
Bereft of walks, licks, barks, or laughs.
Only his ghost and scattered ashes
Guard Stanley's much beloved yard.

—Barry Blackwell, June 2006

Fuzzy

A Christmas kitty
Left on the shelf in
Feline foster care,
Bereft, by herself,
Home with our son from
The Humane Shelter.

Coal black, shiny fur,
Slits for emerald eyes.
A ravishing coat
With a lion's mane,
She swishes her tail
In female disdain.

By a shrink's guidelines
A borderline cat.
She's cuddly and close
Till she starts a fight,
When an overdose
Makes her scratch and bite.

Daring outdoor cat,
Until she met that
Ginger bully boy
With sharper claws
Who scared her home,
For refuge back indoors.

A sister to Stan,
She misses him now.
A sibling who helped
Make a morning row
That wakened us up,
For their breakfast chow.

Her fur's turning gray,
She's nearing her end
With Adam and Stan
Gone away from home
We three are alone
A cat with two friends.

—Barry Blackwell, August 2009

28. TRAVEL

Twenty years from now you will be more disappointed by the things you didn't see than the ones you did. So throw off the bow lines. Sail away from the safe harbor. Catch the trade winds in your sails. Explore. Dream. Discover.

—Mark Twain

Of all the pieces in this book, none has evolved so much as travel. Extended journeys are a feature of modern times. When my father was born in 1900, the Wright brothers were still earthbound and Ford had not yet mass produced the car; travel from your place of birth by train or ship was primarily a privilege of the rich and idle. Among that category, if you suffered an unhappy or broken engagement to be married ("engyesis"), your psychiatrist prescribed a sea voyage lasting six months, the average time it took for a serious depression to go into spontaneous remission before the days of effective treatment. (ECT was discovered in 1934, the year I was born.)

In 1938, our trip to India was by boat, accompanied by our goods and chattels; in 1943, when my mother and I were repatriated to England, it was wiser to risk the German submarines than fly. Only after the middle of the twentieth century did air travel become safe, affordable, and available to the average citizen. Since then flight has had a checkered history from its early days as a pampered and luxurious interlude to the contemporary cramped and uncomfortable experience. Oddly enough, Milwaukee provides a fascinating case history of that deteriorating transition.

In 1948, the Kimberly Clark Corporation (KCC) in Neenah, Wisconsin, began providing private air transportation for employees visiting its mills throughout America. Thirty years later, in 1978, just before we moved to Milwaukee, Congress passed the Airline Deregulation Act. With only two DC-9s and eighty-three employees, KCC decided to expand their fleet and make it accessible to the public. Increasingly popular, especially with business travelers, KCC went public in 1984 as "Midwest Express" with the motto *The Best Care in the Air*. That claim was supported by planes with two-aside leather seating, ample legroom, gourmet meals on starched white tablecloths with china, real cutlery, and warm chocolate chip cookies, baked on board.

Not everything went smoothly; fifteen months after its virgin flight, the airline experienced a first and only fatal incident when Midwest Flight 105 crashed shortly after takeoff, killing all on board.

At the time I was enrolled in my first poetry class at UWM, when we were given a homework assignment to write a poem in which the form matched the content. Here it is:

Countdown from Takeoff

They flew an arc before they met the earth
Clad in metal sheets and tender skins
Held by tendons, bolts, ribs and struts.

Pounding hearts and powerless jets
Welded into clumps of
Flesh and tarnished steel.

A ruddy gray
Collage on
Fresh green
Fields.

—Barry Blackwell, 1982

Each line of the poem is reduced by one syllable, from ten to one, as the plane crashes.

Despite this tragedy, Midwest Express went on to become a highly successful and popular airline. It changed its name to Midwest Airlines to reflect an expanding market and became the largest, longest-standing operation at Milwaukee's Mitchell Field, serving twenty-one cities with nonstop flights. During this period, it received more awards for exceptional cabin service than any other U.S. airline from *Condé Nast Traveler* magazine.

The Twin Towers terrorist attack on September 11, 2001, set in chain events that would change everything for the airline industry in general and Midwest in particular. Oddly enough, it was Midwest Flight 7 from Milwaukee to Dayton that was in a near-midair collision with hijacked United Airlines Flight 175 one minute before it hit the South Tower.

Two months later, in November 2001, Kathie and I made a previously planned trip to New York on a Midwest flight and visited the devastation at Ground Zero.

November First

Published in *Wisconsin Psychiatrist*, Winter 2002:

> Seven weeks past September eleven
> Marathon runners, Diamondbacks
> And curious out-of-towners
> Crowd the canyons of New York.
>
> Some come looking for new heroes
> Patriotism on their sleeves,
> Others to help repair the sabotage
> With caring hearts and open wallets.

Voyeurs atop the Empire State
Gaze across an urban collage
Southward, toward ground zero,
Disappointed by distance and haze.

Kamikaze cabs (terrorists in training?)
Careen crazily downtown
Shedding their fares in posh places
Where spending is spectator sport.

At St. John (knits, not holy saints),
A blue-suited man from Memphis
Watches his daughter, no bulge in sight,
Model impeccable twinsets.

Uncomplaining and indulgent
Dad pays, speculating that
"Full Alert," plus anthrax unleashed,
Means more cash than time remaining.

—Barry Blackwell, November 2001

Phone Home

Published in *Wisconsin Psychiatrist*, Winter 2002:

Cell phones silenced
By crushed concrete,
Fractured steel,
Falling dust and ash.

Images fester
Infecting minds.
Hearts tremble
Awash with fear.

Folks respond,
Finding comfort,
Bonding to friends
And calling home.

—Barry Blackwell, November 2001

A drop-off in air travel after 9/11 had an insidious impact on Midwest's profit margins and the quality of the services provided. The airline reconfigured its planes, installing cloth seats and a two by three arrangement with decreased width. Gourmet meal service disappeared. These changes were sugarcoated as a "Saver Service" offered as an alternative to "Signature Service" which retained some two-across leather seats but not the gourmet meals.

Adding to its problems, Midwest's fleet of McDonald MD-80 jets were gas guzzlers in a time of Mideast turmoil and rising fuel costs, so the planes were decommissioned. At the end of 2006, a bidding war began for control of Midwest, first by Air Tran and then by a TPG and Northwest Airlines consortium. Although the latter takeover succeeded, it lost ninety-three percent of its investment ($419 million) in less than two years. As a result, in June 2009, Republic Airways acquired Midwest assets in a fire sale for only $31 million, a few months before its FAA operating certificate as an independent airline expired. All that was left of the original dream was the chocolate chip cookies, and even these eventually disappeared.

On April 2, 2012, the front page of the *Milwaukee Journal Sentinel* announced, "The cookie has crumbled," explaining in a short article that Frontier Airlines (the latest iteration of Midwest Airlines) was "removing the complimentary warm cookies from in-flight service." They were to be replaced by Goldfish or animal crackers, for which economy class passengers would have to pay one dollar.

Nationwide, air travel became an ordeal, especially for the elderly, infirm, and people with metal joints (like me); long lines, pat downs at security, vast distances between gates, immigration and customs, skimpy or no food on board, and surly flight staff who claimed they were "happy you

–

chose us" but made that difficult to believe with surcharges for baggage, pillows, blankets, and legroom.

The most difficult challenge for older folks is often psychological; the humiliation of a wheelchair because there is no available alternative. Every airport has parked and empty people movers for from six to ten passengers without a driver in sight. It remains a mystery why the airlines don't use them to routinely shuttle the infirm between gates, security, immigration, and customs for a small fee. This would be cost-effective, perhaps garner a small profit, and make travel immeasurably more comfortable for people in need of less help than a passive push in a wheelchair.

Travel Choices

Buying a pig in a poke.

—Popular idiom

This idiom refers to a confidence trick originating in the Middle Ages when meat was scarce and street vendors sold suckling pigs in sacks, often substituting puppies or cats to unwary customers who failed to examine the contents. Hence also the related idioms, "buying or selling a pup," and "letting the cat out of the bag." Almost every language has a version of these sayings.

Waiting everywhere are the con artists, frauds, tricksters, and slick salesmen seeking to expose, exploit, or leverage our naïveté and vulnerability. Some of the smartest and most energetic of them cluster like human locusts at the airport, luxury hotels, and time-shares along the Cabo Peninsula in Mexico. Here is where the wealthiest citizens migrate to meet the neediest—those with the most to give and the most to gain.

Entrepreneurs have transformed thousands of acres of barren sand and desert into exotic time-shares, condos, luxury hotels, designer golf courses, and million-dollar mansions. Basking in a temperate climate, they look out on a sky blue ocean, migrating whales, pristine beaches, and Technicolor sunsets. An impoverished population has been trained to serve and soak the itinerant visitors, earning a much-needed and well-deserved improvement in their own lifestyles.

Kathie and I, innocents abroad and refugees from the frozen and humid Midwest, fell easy prey, both to the lure of the region and the means of getting there by air.

On our first visit to a Cabo hotel, recommended by a trustworthy travel agent, we were seduced into the impulsive purchase of a time-share at the owner's neighboring "Sunset Beach." Now, after our third enjoyable visit, we know that the Pacific Ocean is too cold and dangerous to swim in (which is why the beaches are pristine). After a quarter of a century as "One of the World's Best Resorts" (*Condé Nast Traveler*), the long-promised Jack Nicklaus golf course and grocery store still do not exist, and the cost of the new "all-inclusive meal plan" almost doubles the price of admission.

All told, however, we had a pretty good idea of what was in the poke and have only ourselves to blame for not scrutinizing its contents more fully. But on our latest trip to Cabo, we learned a new wrinkle on the idiom from the airline that flew us there. Like most retired folks on a fixed income and no longer eligible for corporate largesse, we could not afford business class but were attracted by an offer of "choice" seating in economy for an additional $76 dollars per person. This promised more legroom and, other than access to a bathroom, was about the only onboard amenity not already up for sale. Pillows, blankets, meals, and booze already had their price.

But choice is only what it claims to be when you make it for yourself. In this case, neither the pig nor the poke was on view until we received our boarding passes at check-in. On the first leg, we were seated in bulkhead seats separating steerage from first class by a vanity curtain. Our knees were protected, our legs could stretch, and weak bladders did not inflict an unwelcome lap dance on us en route to the bathroom.

The second leg (Phoenix to Cabo) was problematic. Seats 7 D and E were several rows behind the bulkhead and in front of the exit row. Our knees were at risk of being crushed by the seats in front, and we were at the mercy of the bathroom demands of the passenger next to the window. The cabin hostess was a veteran of the old-fashioned kind: friendly, well-groomed, and past middle age. When I inquired how these were "choice" seats, she smiled and quickly responded, "They're on the aisle and near the front." It was not the first time she had been asked that question. Only one of the two seats fulfilled both those criteria and neither added to our comfort except for a faster escape at the end of our incarceration.

I settled down to read my book but, within minutes, the overhead light bulb gave up the ghost. So I quit reading and waited patiently for the beverage cart to arrive, pushed down the aisle by the same friendly hostess. Tongue in cheek, I asked if free liquor was part of the "choice" deal? Again she laughed as she served me a small bottle of wine and charged me seven dollars. She seemed to enjoy passengers with a sense of humor in difficult times.

Shortly before landing, I woke from a doze to find her standing beside me. She had snuck back from first class to offer each of us a glass of wine concealed in a paper napkin.

As we trooped in line toward the exit door, the hostess stood next to the captain thanking us for choosing their airline, wishing us well, and inviting us to come back. I thanked her for changing a bad choice into a better one and, once again, she smiled.

For less than the price of this pig in a poke, you can now buy a gadget to carry onboard the plane which can be affixed to the seat in front, preventing its occupant from crushing your knees. It sounds like a better deal and a genuine choice.

Time Travel

In April 2012, we stayed at our time-share in Cabo San Lucas for the third time. Arthritis had migrated from hip and spine to invade both knees so, coupled with ataxia, a cane became mandatory for walking at even a modest pace. The floors in the corridor outside our apartment were of shiny black tile, scrubbed clean daily by our Mexican maid and left to dry in the sun. Leaving our room en route for the pool, my cane slipped on the surface; stumbling, I just managed to maintain my balance, avoiding a nasty fall that would put my aging bones in jeopardy.

Lifting the cane, I noticed the rubber ferule had eroded, exposing a bare wooden tip to the slick wet tile. It needed replacement, but where was I to search for such an esoteric item in a foreign language? Our guest, my oldest son, Simon, knew at once. Ace Hardware in America sells ferules. A day or so after our return to Milwaukee, I visited a nearby outlet. Ace had cornered the niche market, offering a selection of black or white ferules in assorted sizes. Black, three quarters of an inch across fit snugly.

Later that day, I had a flashback of memory from an earlier holiday, nineteen years before. In summer 1993, Kathie and I took our youngest son Adam, aged fourteen, to visit all the places in England that marked my early life. It began and ended in London, (medical school and psychiatry training), then Canterbury (boarding school), Salisbury (British Army), Chard (first boarding school), and Cambridge (university).

On our way to Cambridge, we had lodged at "Blackwell Grange," an old manor house, now a bed and breakfast. On Monday, June 28, it was Adam's turn to write the daily log that documented our travels. Here are his own words, "We left Blackwell Grange today. We first went to Stow and looked at all the antique shops. I bought a gift for dad and he told me he hated it, it was ugly." Next to the word "ugly" is an asterisk and, at the bottom of the page, in my handwriting are the dismissive words, "A rubber ferule for my walking stick." I had purchased an elegant cane that took my fancy for decorative, not practical, purposes, and when Adam gave me the ferule as his gift, I responded in a teasing, insensitive, and ignorant manner, confusing beauty with utility.

—

With these memories and feelings in mind, I went to bed the evening I purchased the replacement ferule. The next morning the haiku below was fixed in my brain, coupled with a sense of wonder at the intuitive insight of a young lad who has become, not surprisingly, a nurturing father and empathic family physician.

Adam's Rule

Canes with bare tips slip;
There's no fool like an old fool
Who shuns a ferule!

—Barry Blackwell, May 2012

Humans have always explored time and place in search of new insights and information, an archeology of the mind. Science fiction turns the clock backward and forward with Rube Goldberg machines, Einstein's formulae and novel dimensions. Psychoanalysis employs the couch and the analytic "blank screen" to plumb the unconscious for novel meanings and repressed memories from childhood and beyond. Whatever is unearthed must muster truth by passing Freud's acid test of wisdom, "When is a cigar just a cigar?"

Two vacations on different continents and almost twenty years apart have taught me that a ferule is more than an ugly rubber tip to an elegant cane. According to Adam's Rule, it may have lifesaving properties.

Putting aside these senile pet peeves, there are plenty of pleasant memories of foreign lands to share. Most of them took place when travel was still a civilized and enjoyable experience that was part of the academic life, and my joints functioned painlessly. Here are five poems that attempt to convey the essence of those countries: (See also "Piece 3: India.")

Pharaoh's People

This
is a place
of sand and
smells, scratching
membranes and seeping
into skin folds, nooks and
crannies. Everything crumbles.
Dwellings are ramshackle sheds. So
people laugh a lot and put their hope
in the life hereafter. The pharaohs did
it divinely. Their impudence commanded the
pyramids and sphinx. Willing subjects toiled in
massive servitude for nothing now. Only the promise
of resurrection and God Osiris to give safe passage to the
other side. So they could slave again as servants to the king.

Then
came a
time of decay
and desecration.
Memphis shrank to
adobe huts among the
date palms and mud colored
stains on the desert. Sand
silted the tops of their tombs.
Pharaoh's bribes and comforts to ease
the voyage to eternity were dust consumed,
defiled by thieves, put on display. His barge
to reach the sun hangs suspended in a shed. Five
pounds a peek. Unswaddled mummies were bacteria infected
and burnt. Today the dwindling dug up assets are explained to
tourists by a new hieroglyphic. The graffiti of light and sound.

These
are a people
not readily discouraged.
The papyrus reed and the
lotus flower still bloom in the
Valley of the Nile. Pharaoh's subjects
don't complain they were misled. (Nobody in
this country speaks ill of the dead.) Instead
poverty is softened by all time smiles. Endless street
greetings make even aliens feel safe. When spring holiday comes
the crowds picnic at pharaoh's tomb under table cloth tents. Nowadays
faith is where it belongs, with Islam, and perseverance is spent on
bargaining or baksheesh. The people don't build pyramids anymore.

—Barry Blackwell, 1986

Holy Land

This is thirsty land,
Strewn with rocks and bones,
Layer upon layer
Of truth and faith,
Told by relics and holy ruins.

This is blood soaked ground
Fed when ancient armies
Fought at Megiddo;
There knights and martyrs
Shed life for new beliefs.

This is fertile soil
Where twisted olive trees,
Millennia old,
Cast friendly shade
Upon the Son of God.

This is sandy shore.
Here pilgrims gather;
I and others,
Seeking footprints
Left behind, long before.

—Barry Blackwell, 1999

Tango

Porta La Plat has a craw
Wide enough to swallow
The sailors of the world,
Lured ashore by the whores
Of Buenos Aires.

Here men pluck guitars
To a carnal beat.
Gender innuendo
Throbs to the tempo
Of an Argentine tango.

Autocrats in tuxedos
Stole the duet,
Swapped the sailor's slut
To strut and glide
With scant-clad Madonnas.

There is rhythm and desire
In gesture and glance,
Posture that speaks
Primal fantasies
Of must or chance, love or lust.

Its beat is unrelenting,
But everyone knows
The tango is ending
To the sound of a sailor's
Drowned feelings.

—Barry Blackwell, April 2007

Fado

The Portuguese today
Know centuries of sorrow;
Once captains of the ocean,
Owners of an Empire,
Now washed away.

Slim coastal strip, Iberia's face,
Fertile, fecund, domain;
Once invaded and defiled
By envious neighbors;
Now regained.

Grapes, olives, almonds,
Grow in shale and shallow soil
On dizzy sun-burned slopes;
Ripe fruits in terraced rows,
Picked clean by calloused hands.

Fall harvest's home,
Hard labor done;
Across the nation
The melancholic Fado
Is sung in celebration.

—Barry Blackwell, October 2011

The Panama Canal

Over three decades and more
Thirty thousand died to join
The quadrants of the compass,
East to West and sea to sea.

The French failed nobly, foiled by
Jungle, hard rock, death and debt,
Leaving just a half-dug trench.

Next, the Yankees toiled like moles,
Shifting tons of sod and soil,
Stifling deadly disease,
Blasting through a mountain chain,
Damming rivers, flooding the trench.

Fifty miles of lake, cuts, locks,
Made the Panama Canal;
Open on the eve of war.*

Today it conveys vessels
Of the world, in peaceful trade.

—Barry Blackwell, February 2009

*The "Great War" between Britain, France, and Germany was declared two weeks before the Canal opened. America joined the Allies three years later. In 1916, the Battle of the Somme raged across twenty miles of slit trench and three hundred thousand troops were killed in five months, ten times the number who died from accidents, malaria, and yellow fever during thirty years of digging fifty miles of deep trench to create the Panama Canal. Many who died were buried in, or close by, the trenches they helped dig. The First World War, "to end all wars," spawned a humiliating peace treaty that ushered in the Second World War twenty years later. Almost a century after completion, the Panama Canal has provided safe passage to a million ships.

Ode to Merrie England

England is a lovely land,
Filled with friendly chaps.
On the other hand . . .

The toilets never flush
Enough to wash
Your turds away.

Public loos charge users fees;
At Harrods in the city
It costs a quid to pee.
(It used to be a penny.)

Air conditioning's a window, plus a fan,
Which makes for sweaty sex
That wrecks your nuptial plan.

We love the pubs, the bitter beer
And dishes which they sell,
Like fish and chips.

Steer clear of posher places
That bill for bottled water;
Tap water oughta do.

Yes, England is a lovely land,
Filled with friendly chaps.
On the other hand . . .

Take a Yank's advice,
Don't push the Brits too far,
Never ask for ice!

—Barry Blackwell, 1993

Cold to Hot and Back Again

I doze in humid shade
Fanned by the palm tree's
Windmill sails;
A sticky witness
To beach gossip.

Chubby men with skinny mates
Frolic in the shallows.
Grownups build sand castles
Or issue orders:
    "Spit out that gum."
    "Be kind to your sister."
    "Don't pee in the pool."
Tots in Technicolor swimsuits
Oscillate like
Molecules under a microscope.

Home cold in Milwaukee
Burned skin
And sand-trap toes
Shed hot memories
Of Boca Raton.

—Barry Blackwell, 2009

29. BEAUTY

Everything has its beauty but not everyone sees it.

—Confucius

One might expect a five-year-old child at boarding school within sight of Mount Everest to grow up enthralled by nature; perhaps familiarity breeds, if not contempt, then indifference. All I can report is a fear of heights. I stand well back from the railing of our fifteenth-floor balcony and feel extremely anxious if my grandson ventures close to the edge.

Still, I have seen some of the world's best natural and man-made delights; the Taj Mahal, the Parthenon, the Eiffel Tower, America's parks, Alaskan glaciers, the pyramids and the Sphinx, the Suez Canal, Milwaukee's own Calatrava Art Museum, more Gothic cathedrals than I can count, and much, much more. I visited, but failed to see, Machu Picchu when we went there as a prelude to our South American cruise. Done in by microbes and air hunger, I spent two days bedridden, wrapped in diapers, while Kathie went sightseeing. The postcards were terrific! Late in life, our black Lab introduced me to the splendor of early morning at the lakefront, glistening with ice crystals lit by the rising sun in winter. (But spoiled by the odor of rotting alewives in the summer.)

Work of Art

A blank page,
Unmolded clay,
An empty stage,
The unlived day.

Shaped God's way,
Primal material
Placed on display
Becomes celestial.

—Barry Blackwell, 2000

Lake Effect

Tepid steam
Rising
From ice floes:
A bronze sun
Glistening
On frigid snow:
Barren branches
Spawning
Newborn icicles.
Divine alchemy,
Forging
God's gold.

—Barry Blackwell, 2000

Early Spring

A slow melt
strips the bare earth
of cold skin,
naked to a sensate sun
that breaks its
mellow shafts
on furrowed ridges
of frigid soil.

Somewhere below,
thirsty seeds swell
bursting from
a parched winter,
breaking blind
toward the trickling light.

Tonight a
frost might come.

—Barry Blackwell, 2002

God's Quilt

Harvest Gold
Sown between
Green turf
and tilled
Brown earth.

—Barry Blackwell, 2002

577

Cathedral

Pindrop echoes
Of organ pomp,
Slow files
Of hooded monks,
In metered steps
With muffled chant,
Shuffling
Down wind tunnels
Of frigid stone.

Brute sepulcher
Of quarried slabs,
Mute columns
That prop apart
Vaulted roof
From flagstone floor.
Bleak altar,
Worn flat
By pilgrim's prayer.

—Barry Blackwell, 2002

This free-form poem obtains a vertical sense from ultrashort horizontal lines with four or fewer syllables. It owes a coldness to terse adjectives and hard consonants (frigid, bleak, brute). A musical and ghostly feel is created by subtle assonance (shuffling, muffled) and scattered rhyme (mute, brute, vaulted, altar).

30. AGING

One of the many pleasures of old age is giving things up.

—Malcolm Muggeridge

Growing old is inevitable and easy—simpler than the expectations that accompany it. As the only creatures prescient of death, the longer we go the more imminent the end.

Belief in an afterlife, living one day at a time, or adopting the Serenity Prayer may all help. Slow erosion of body or brain, the accompanying decrements of age, loss of a spouse, or living in solitary poverty may not.

Whatever our own expectations, those of others are often well-intended but idealistic or unrealistic. Praised for our accomplishments or wisdom, we are urged to keep busy, exercise actively, espouse causes, live in community, adopt a vibrant hobby, and enjoy a strong faith.

Life at Saint John's On The Lake tilts toward the positive pole. But we are a select, successful, wealthy, and relatively healthy cohort provided exceptional care from independence to dependence and death. So let me dwell awhile on the shadow side.

The decrements bestowed on us by age are inexorable. They may be mitigated by a congenial environment, denied by temperament, or reduced by a hardy physique, but they are never entirely avoided, except by death. Surprisingly, they are seldom studied or catalogued, perhaps because scientists of any stripe have little interest in what they themselves will endure and for which there is no remedy or money to be made. This is the perfect "Don't Ask, Don't Tell" topic to replace homosexuality, now that it is out of the closet.

Before I put pen to paper, I consulted the Internet, source of contemporary wisdom (a step up from Twitter), and typed in "Behavior changes with age." Back came lists of deteriorations in elderly dogs, cats, and rabbits. Perhaps this is part of a "stiff upper lip" syndrome that lasts until rigor mortis sets in. Humans seem to take pride in denying mortality even when we gather together in retirement homes to watch it happen. It's the noble thing to ignore.

I don't deny there are Chinese menus of failing functions in body parts and systems, but there is almost nothing about subtle changes in behavior and social interactions. The sole exception is Alzheimer's dementia and its seven stages—Shakespeare's ages of man in reverse. Here the functions of the brain are stripped away like the layers of an onion until we resemble babbling infants in diapers. Its official name is "retrogenesis," literally returning to the beginning. Even so, it's a crude catalogue, scary enough to overlap with "normal aging." It's okay to occasionally misplace your spectacles but not to hide your dentures in the fridge. You can forget the name of a casual acquaintance but not your spouse.

If I had any say in public policy, I would outlaw research on telomeres—the tail end of the chromosome alleged to modulate aging. Some scientists are claiming they may be able to extend the life span to one hundred fifty or beyond by fiddling with it. This is unethical and should be illegal until we have a way to prevent or treat dementia; imagine the economic and emotional burden of a totally demented population of super old citizens.

Decrements of Age

I am soon to be seventy-eight, a year beyond the average age of male death in America, so I have begun to notice a few decrements on nobody's list. They may not be unique, so I'll share them with you in the hope you might dodge or diminish them:

- Senile technophobia: A fear of and inability to cope with rapid advances in mobile phones, iPods, computers, and associated paraphernalia. An associated symptom is appeals to youthful relatives to stop by and fix things.
- Clutter complex: Most successful folks are compulsive and tidy; they put things away or chuck them out. Nowadays I notice them lying about, out of place, scattered across tabletops, and even the floor. Maybe it's because fewer people are calling or coming to dinner, so there are less spectators, but I wonder if it's a subtle neurological defect in perception or just plain not caring as much.
- Gero-photophobia: Not traditional shunning the light, but a reluctance or refusal to take photographs due to realizing they are destined to gather dust in the basement or attic and make an unwelcome estate gift. A further cause of the syndrome is digital cameras that have multiplied the rate of accretion logarithmically.
- Late-onset agoraphobia: Distances traveled from home become inversely related to age. This applies to restaurants, movie theaters, and vacation destinations. We become homebodies partly due to the brutal inconveniences of travel (unless you can afford first class) but also, perhaps, because there is less that is new to eat or see.
- Proxemic overload: Healthy humans need time apart. An honest answer to "What will you do after you retire?" might be "Hide from my spouse." Failure to plan time apart can lead to the syndrome below.
- Irascibility: This is one step up from irritable and tends to be outwardly directed in response to perceived or imagined unkindness, incompetence, or intrusion by those who live closest.

—

- Personality quirks: The human cortex functions as a straitjacket to restrain basic instincts, behavior, and emotions. When it weakens with age, out pop new manifestations previously repressed or hidden. These can be funny or sad, good or bad, but don't be surprised by them.

- Cerebral calisthenics: Popular opinion maintains the brain can be exercised like a muscle. I have fallen for this myth and start each day by completing the "Word Game" in the local paper (next to the comics). Do you realize that many words with only seven letters can spawn over fifty smaller words? Although I can beat the average score (many Brits have larger word banks than Yanks) I still forget the names of people and places. This is because our vocabulary is laid down in childhood long before the things we forget. Another example of this is that I more often miss medical words (ulna and acne) than lay words (luna and cane). This is because doctors double their vocabulary in medical school, learning strange names with Latin and Greek roots. This confirms that what is learned last is lost first and indicates I am beginning to fade. It's also why doctors should retire before they forget what they are prescribing.

- Dwindling appetites: Forget sex because Viagra and its relatives can take care of that. But I do worry about eating. Since arthritis prevents me from exercising, eating less is necessary to avoid the current plague of morbid obesity and its prevalence on cruise ships and at lunch and brunch buffets. I am helped by having gout which proscribes all the delightful delicacies that contain uric acid (shrimp, organ meats, and red wine). I also want to take into account my preferred manner of death. I'd like to go quickly; just enough time to say good-bye but less time to suffer. This means I should load up on cholesterol but how to do so without gaining weight is an unsolved problem. It's getting late; soon nature will take the matter out of my hands and mouth.

- Multitasking: Doing two or more things at once becomes difficult or dangerous. If you put something on the stove to cook and then turn on your computer, I guarantee the pot will boil over while you are immersed in the Internet.

- Toilet paper: Consumption of this item increases with age. Frequent peeing and terminal dribbling in men may be due to a large prostate and in women to childbirth and uterine prolapse. Both genders poop with the same lifelong frequency but weakening sphincters prolong the act of cleaning up.

- There are certainly many more undefined, subtle, and unexamined decrements of age, and if I were younger, I would want to collect and describe them.

Amazed

Now an old man in failing health, struggling to cope with its decrements, I am lost in the maze of modern medicine. Here is an example:

En route to our time-share in Mexico, I was bored enough to feel for my pulse. It was irregular, as it had been for several years, but now it seemed remarkably slow; about forty beats a minute. An elite athlete might feel proud, but with crippling arthritis and a cane, I couldn't even work up a sweat. Something was wrong.

Two weeks later, the morning after our return to Milwaukee, an EKG in my doctor's office confirmed atrial fibrillation complicated by bradycardia. My internist, Dr. V., ordered a twenty-four-hour-hour Holter monitor to be read by my cardiologist, Dr. L. He also stopped the beta blocker I was taking to control my blood pressure because it might contribute to the slow heart rate, and I was to take my own blood pressure twice daily.

Five days later, my chest was plastered with electrodes and my shirt stuffed with wires leading to a monitor strapped to my belt. Now my blood pressure was way up, more so in the mornings, directly after sleep, around 160/100. Dr. V. started me on a new type of blood pressure medicine; over the next five days, the pressure seemed to be responding, but the following morning it jumped to 180/98 and the day after to 180/115.

My wife and I get up at 6:00 a.m. and, while she goes to Curves to exercise her body, I read the paper and do the Word Game to flex my brain. It was too early to call Dr. V.'s office, and rather than wake the

—

on-call physician, we hustled to the emergency room, five minutes away from our apartment. Soon I was flat on my back in a hospital gown, hooked up to a monitor again. Blood and kidney tests were ordered, and over a couple of hours, my pressure dropped to safe levels and all the tests came back normal. Dr. L. had not yet read the Holter monitor report but prescribed an additional medication to control hypertension. I was to call his office for an appointment to see him.

I did so, only to learn he was too busy to see me soon, but I could make an appointment a week away with his nurse practitioner. I had not seen Dr. L. for several years but liked him. He seemed more interested in me as a person than as a case or source of revenue. So I agreed to wait two weeks to see a person who knew me, had read my Holter monitor report, been briefed by the emergency room, and had prescribed new medication in an emergency.

Now I realized that trouble loomed: months before, I had planned an annual visit to my eighty-five-year-old brother in England and purchased plane tickets for a flight in four weeks' time. It was likely to be a stressful occasion; in addition to the vicissitudes of travel, both he and his wife were in poor health, struggling with the possibility of assisted living but not yet ready to accept it.

My blood pressure was still erratic and, if I needed a pacemaker, there might not be time to accomplish that before my planned visit. Communicating with your primary care physician is not easy. Understandably, they don't take phone calls during a busy schedule. The clinic policy is not to give out e-mail addresses for confidentiality reasons, even though your entire medical record is accessible in the database. The only remaining option was a polite, carefully worded letter; hand carried by me and dropped off at his office asking for advice and assistance. Could he ask Dr. L. if a pacemaker was indicated and, if so, could it be implanted in time for my trip?

Dr. V. called back later that day to tell me that Dr. L. was only responsible for my blood pressure, not my pulse rate. (So why was he asked to read the Holter monitor?) For that, I would need to see Dr. P., an electrophysiologist whose team handled all pacemaker needs. He had a nurse practitioner who would be willing to see me at short notice. Dr. V. also expressed concern at the delayed conduction time in my heart and seemed rightly upset that the emergency room had not consulted him during my visit. (Although they were given his name and it appears on the discharge summary.)

I called Dr. P.'s office and spoke to Heather who took all the details; I explained I was Dr. Blackwell, a patient of Dr. V.'s, spelled my name and gave my date of birth. I mentioned the time concern and my wish to see the nurse practitioner as soon as possible. Heather downgraded me automatically to "mister" and informed me that new referrals were only seen by Dr. P. who was very busy. She would have to research my case on the database, discuss it with the team, and call me back.

Next morning I called again and Heather was gone, replaced by Melanie. Once again, I introduced myself as Dr. Blackwell. Melanie was helpful and well-informed about my predicament. There were questions to be answered, followed by an assurance they would do their best to fit me in before Dr. P.'s next open appointment, three weeks away. The call ended with Melanie thanking Mr. Blackwell and promising an early call back. It came less than two hours later, while I was in the pool doing water aerobics; a voicemail message told Mr. Blackwell he had an appointment with Dr. P. in ten days' time; please call back to confirm.

This time Heather answered, and the dialogue repeated itself. Self-identified yet again as "doctor," I was responded to as mister. After I gave them my wife's date of birth, I tackled the name issue head on. I explained that I was not seeking special treatment but wanted to ensure I was dealt with as a person seeking help and not as a case to be fixed. This was not a personal criticism but a reflection of repeated experiences in settings with providers at all levels. Naturally enough Heather became defensive and blamed the earphones she wore when answering the phone but she did offer to share my feelings with Melanie and began to call me Dr. Blackwell.

Talking to elderly and retired physician friends, I know mine are not unique experiences, and I wonder why. I can think of two reasons: treating patients as the people they are, and not as problems to be

—

fixed, takes time and breeds intimacy. Those who perform invasive or dangerous procedures and those who work with them may prefer to keep their distance, perhaps to preserve their equanimity. I am struck by the absence of this defensive maneuver in medical students who, instead, tend to identify themselves with the body they are about to dissect. It is easier to wield the knife on dead tissue rather than living flesh.

The poems that follow also tilt toward the pessimistic pole, reflecting my skeptical temperament. The first poem is not my own and I have chosen four out of its twelve stanzas. It is well known and often quoted.

Excerpted from *"Too Soon Old"*

What do you see nurses? . . . What do you see?
What are you thinking . . . when you're looking at me?
A crabby old man . . . not very wise,
Uncertain of habit . . . with faraway eyes?

I'm now an old man . . . and nature is cruel.
'Tis jest to make old age . . . look like a fool.
The body it crumbles . . . grace and vigor depart.
There is now a stone . . . where I once had a heart.

But inside this old carcass . . . a young guy still dwells,
And now and again . . . my battered heart swells.
I remember the joys . . . I remember the pain.
And I'm loving and living . . . life over again.

I think of the years, all too few . . . gone too fast.
And accept the stark fact . . . that nothing can last.
So open your eyes, people . . . open and see
Not a crabby old man . . . Look closer . . . see ME!!

—Attributed to Dave Griffith
Often misquoted as "Crabby Old Man"

Growing Old

Growing old gracefully
Is oft an oxymoron.
As decrements abound
And dwindling abilities
Betray life's aspirations,
A melancholia of living
Supplants a fear of dying.

A slim minority
Cope with equanimity,
Bearing the inevitable
In acceptance and hope,
Sparing onlookers their pity.

The majority grouch and groan,
A chorus of creaking joints
Or aching appendages,
Which tire the caring touch,
Mocking oaths about
Cherishing their spouse
"till death do us part."

In life's finality
Senility is wedge, not bond,
Driving folks asunder.
Fragile, living longer,
They wonder; what's to come?

—Barry Blackwell, 2007

"Deus ex Machina"

Once kept secret, now body organs
Are open for inspection;
Some malignant part,
A fetus sucking thumb,
The beating heart.

Technical names or acronyms
Describe the apparatus
For each prescribed intrusion.
"Echocardiogram" is new for me;
My heart, the part in question.

Prone on my left side,
Electrodes glued to breast,
Wide-eyed, I view the screen
Reflecting flickering images
The roving probe provides.

I see my heart pump blood,
Flooding each chamber in turn.
I hear the swoosh of valves parting
Like leaves in summer's breeze;
Pushing life to destined places.

My able heart has kindly worked,
More than three score years and ten,
Without spare parts or intervention.
Despite belief in Evolution
It makes design seem debatable.

—Barry Blackwell, May 2012

The Golden Years

We who have aged,
Outgrown a misspent youth,
Are oft portrayed as
"Sage," "mellow," or "serene,"
When in reality
"Moody," "touchy," or "mean"
Reveal a harsher truth.

—Barry Blackwell, September 2005

Bonus Time

I crossed the Rubicon this year,
Past three score years and ten.
Then invaded borrowed time,
Stretched my allotted span
Beyond the limits God allowed.

I wonder if the decrements
And ravages of age
Can be viewed instead
As sacraments of living,
Or testaments of thanks?

Slow stiffened gait, creaking joints,
Impediments to speed,
Now tend to gentler tasks,
Lend themselves to strolling
In sylvan groves; minding the soul.

—Barry Blackwell, July 2004

Dwindling

In a slow foot race
Between body and mind,
Mobility and memory,
I ponder; which decrement
Matters most?

Bone and muscle wilt,
Worn joints feel like
Treading on broken glass;
This wobbly gait's
Like balancing on stilts.

Or is it "senior moments";
Lost names ridiculed
To ease my fear of brain decay?
Either way, I can't deny
I'm dwindling away.

—Barry Blackwell, September 2006

Corked

If growing older
Was a flavor or odor
Men would age better.

—Barry Blackwell, July 2011

Brighton Gardens

. . . Is a white lie.
Residents know
It's not the seaside,
Snared in wheelchairs,
Trapped inside.

Dumped by
Busy kids hoping
The family wealth
Outlasts their parents'
Dwindling health.

Demented minds
In rooms stuffed
With antiques and odors.
Caring staff, unasked,
Mask them with scented smells.

"Never mind, Dearie,"
They say kindly.
In the wreckage of life
Self esteem
Is a salvage operation.

—Barry Blackwell, 2007

31. In The End Zone

Who knows whether, in retirement, I shall be tempted to the last infirmity of mundane minds, which is to write a book.

—Archbishop of Canterbury Geoffrey Fisher

A History of Saint John's

Saint John's Home for Friendless Old Ladies was founded in 1869 at the instigation of Episcopal Bishop Henni, later (from 1875) archbishop.

Its initial site was 682 Van Buren Street, in a dwelling supported by voluntary contributions, staffed by a superintendent, nurses, cleaners, a cook, and four physicians who volunteered their services. The initial home housed nineteen women, increasing to twenty-five after it moved to new quarters in 1877 at 640 Cass Street. In 1922, this building was razed and replaced with a larger facility built on the same site. The house rules at that time convey a verbal picture of the institutional climate. They included:

- Each member will regularly attend Divine Service and Holy Communion.
- Each member will attend punctually at meals.
- No persistently discontented or dissatisfied member can be retained in the Home Family.

- Members will not criticize the Superintendent who shall be treated with respect and her wishes complied with.

In 1977, the home had outgrown its space and moved to the present location at North Prospect Avenue on the shores of Lake Michigan, a site with a distinguished history of elite mansions.

In 1899, the president of the former Wisconsin National Bank built the Petit mansion with a ballroom (for two hundred fifty couples), a billiard room, and a gymnasium, along with stables for four horses and assorted broughams and carriages. This building was severely damaged by fire in 1938 and replaced the following year on a somewhat smaller, but still impressive scale. I was able to purchase a 1940 photograph of this porticoed structure on eBay for ten dollars!

This building became the home of the American Legion Alonzo Cudworth Post. When Saint John's moved to the site in 1977, a new building was commissioned on the north side of the existing structure, and it remains in place today as the North Tower.

In 1994, the board of trustees for Saint John's purchased the right of first refusal to the Cudworth property to its south, which was successfully invoked when the Post closed and moved to a suburban location. Eventually the building was razed and temporarily converted to a parking lot until Saint John's developed its plans to build a twenty-one-story South Tower on the site. Ground was broken in 2009 and the building completed in 2011.

Modern Saint John's On The Lake

We moved into our "final resting place" a few days after my seventy-seventh birthday; on the fifteenth floor of the new tower looking to the east and south with a view of Lake Michigan, the Calatrava Art Museum, the Henry Maier Festival Grounds, and the city lights. Each day, we are treated to a Technicolor sunrise and the sun setting above and beyond the tall buildings that obscure the view of its descent from ground level. In the summer, we can watch the fireworks light the night sky over each ethnic festival from our bed or the patio.

This is truly "the home that Kathie built" in her final two years as president of Saint John's retirement community. When she moved from president to resident, the board of trustees named the conference room in the fitness center in her honor.

But there is a great deal more than the view: an indoor pool for water aerobics and lap swimming; a workout room looking out on the lake, with state of the art equipment and resident trainer; an in-house art museum with quarterly displays installed by the Wisconsin Art Museum; a bistro with a pizza oven and gelato ice cream; a magnificent chapel; and, finally, a continuum of lifetime health care.

Behind the architecture and services are a culture and philosophy which seeks to replicate an "in-home" environment, minimizing any institutional tendencies. Residents have a well-developed system of governance with advisory input to management and two representatives on the board of trustees. Each month the president hosts an open forum for dialogue and exchange of ideas with the residents.

This community of lifelong "movers and shakers" continues to dance, organizing and offering a dizzying variety of daily activities difficult to decide among. This is an end zone that invites you to do the "Lambeau Leap."

Still, there's a part of me surprised to find myself living in community again. For most of the first twenty-five years of life I did that: in boarding school, the army, and at university. When I finally escaped into a private world, I vowed never to return to the enforced intimacy of a communal existence. Especially one whose members watch and wait for others to die, undiluted by younger friends or neighbors.

But the life trajectory in the "Bits and Pieces" of this memoir has been one of change and challenge, of choosing the "road less traveled." Why not do it again, one last time?

Caveats on Community Living

Anybody contemplating community living would be well-advised to reflect on their psychic soft spots. Hopefully you will have lived long enough to know what they are. In my own case, I was mildly phobic of institutional living. Having visited friends in like circumstances, I felt particularly averse to cafeteria-style dining, especially when its pretensions outdid its performance (which was customary). I also fought shy of communal activities, preferring solitary or domestic amusements and pastimes to group activities among relative strangers.

After a year at Saint John's, I have learned enough to confront and attempt to deal with my premonitions and misgivings. Two examples follow.

Gender Disparity

Sometimes I wonder if men and women really suit each other. Perhaps they should live next door and just visit now and then.

—Katharine Hepburn

Anyone who opts to join an elder community must realize that women outlive men. For single, recently bereaved, or handsome and wealthy males, this might provide an opportunity. Our marketing representatives occasionally field questions that make them feel like a *sub rosa* dating service.

Whatever your needs, once installed, you will face the reality of a feminist enclave where a majority rules and the two most recent presidents have been women, my wife being the first.

Among an impressive, almost overwhelming, repertoire of community activities, I chose only two: water aerobics and book club.

The first was determined by rapidly advancing osteoarthritis in one hip (now replaced), both knees, and my spine, the sequelae of a vigorous rugby career. I had passed the point of no return for working out on the Rolls Royce machines in our well-equipped fitness room; a "good" workout only made matters worse.

Exercising in water takes forty percent of your weight off the joints. So I signed up for a twice-weekly water aerobics class. Our pool is wheelchair accessible, gently sloped, a comfortable eighty degrees, and safely shallow. At one end it says, "Depth: 1 ft.; No diving"; we older folks can be forgetful!

At the first class, I was surprised to find myself the only man in the water among nine women. Arthritis is an equal opportunity ailment, so even allowing for differential mortality rates, some males must be in hiding, who knows from what.

Our instructor began promptly on the hour as latecomers drifted slowly in. She is tall, lithe, and poised, with a well-versed repertoire of moves, some stipulated by the Arthritis Foundation and others improvised, for a total of precisely forty minutes. Moving with the elegance of a ballet prima donna, the instructor models each move at poolside while we mirror her in the pool. Even though water tempers the burden on my joints, I have the added challenge of a late-life lack of balance and lifelong motor incoordination. Four feet of water conceal much of my clumsy posturing, but occasionally it becomes so obvious that the women laugh; this doesn't disturb me because it lacks the derisive edge of male merriment. We are having fun together.

Forty minutes later, I haul myself out of the pool to discover that my water-borne ease of movement does not transfer itself to dry land, and the pain that haunts my joints has returned. But I hope that the muscles I am trying to build will eventually help prop me up.

The women gossip quietly during our sessions while I tend to ruminate. Recently a strange idea settles in my mind; as retrogenesis of old age moves me inexorably backward through childhood, why not to infancy and before? Imagine what it would be like to relive the lot of a fetus, happily underwater, safe inside the womb but free to push, kick and shove; with a willing, eager, loving mother waiting to pull me from the pool once I was ready to live and learn to walk again, free of pain.

—

The Book Club

My other choice, the book club, was set to read a selection of the Greek plays, something that, despite my classical English education, I never accomplished. Once again I found myself the onion in a petunia patch: the only male amidst upward of fifteen women.

What fun this was! The Greeks, mercifully unfettered by Sigmund Freud, attributed all the angst and retribution wrought by their bad behavior and strong emotions to the gods, with a chorus to announce the stakes and penalties. Much more entertaining than the id, ego, and superego invoked by an inscrutable, out of sight, analyst.

Two of the plays, *Medea* and *Lysistrata*, evoked strong feelings linked to gender, reminding us that misogyny and paternalism were alive and well two millennia ago, continuing on until women in America were the last segment in our society to win emancipation. A few of our female residents were born before that got fixed.

My fellow pupils were a feisty and well-informed bunch; late in the series, one of my classmates noted that I often raised issues different from those women were more interested in. I didn't take the bait because it was demonstrably true. They were wrapped up in the powerful emotions portrayed in the plays while I inquired more about the plays' provenance, poetic forms, and translational veracity. Our text of *Lysistrata* was purged of obscenity apart from a smattering of mildly suggestive footnotes. But another of our classmates had downloaded a salacious version from the Internet, replete with four-letter words and sexy allusions too risqué to cite in this memoir.

As I reflect on these experiences at Saint John's, I realize that my reluctance to commit to life in community is ameliorated by an unanticipated paradox. Almost my entire childhood, adolescence and early adult life, from ages five to twenty-three, were lived in all-male communities; in boarding school, the army, and at university with hardly a female in sight. Not surprisingly, I reacted by preferring what I had missed: the company of women. Now I can luxuriate in an environment in which they predominate! The men, for reasons unknown, prefer to lurk in

—

their private places; perhaps the golf course or gone fishing. They don't know what they're missing! Or perhaps they don't care?

Closed-Door Community?

In practice master plans fail. They are too rigid; they cannot easily adapt to the natural and unpredictable changes that inevitably arise in the life of a community.

—Christopher Alexander

Community cannot for long feed on itself; it can only flourish with the coming of others beyond, their unknown and undiscovered brothers.

—Howard Thurman

June had arrived, summer was just around the corner, global warming was already upon us, and it was a sunny seventy-five degrees. Time to eat outside on the Bistro balcony where comfortable chairs, clean tables, and colorful umbrellas had been chained to the railing all winter long, waiting for the residents to emerge from hibernation, poking their noses out like the groundhog.

Getting there was a feat: self-service sans a waitress or a tray meant discarding my cane, balancing two plates, a soft drink, and cutlery, pressing keypads to open two automatic doors, dodging them as they swung open, and exiting without spilling my vittles on the floor. I managed all that proudly despite arthritis, ataxia, and a decidedly wobbly gait.

It was worthwhile; the sun shone and there I was looking out over Prospect Avenue, connected to our neighborhood, part of the larger community.

After a leisurely meal of turkey meat loaf dunked in sticky gravy, I rose to return inside, balancing my empty utensils and pressing the keypad. Nothing happened. I pressed again. Again, nothing. I was locked out!

Peering through the window, I spied a fellow resident and knocked loudly to attract attention. She pushed the pad and kindly let me in.

Mildly miffed, I approached the food counter to inquire why the patio was locked and off limits. Nobody knew; I would have to speak to "administration." Chance intervened; close by was a mammoth Morrison man (our subcontracted food service). His first response was, "We haven't started to service that area yet." I pointed out they didn't service any area—it was self-service. This invited a back-up explanation that we "need to keep the public out." So "Why didn't I just use the keypad code?" I pointed out these were codeless keypads. He was surprised and would have to "look into it." What was my name? Staff does like to identify the troublemakers.

All this got me thinking; it was time somebody did. Wed to the former president of Saint John's, I recalled some relevant history. Folks in the old North Tower had lobbied to keep the second "not-so-fine dining" venue where they felt it belonged, in the basement. Management, allied with the architects, favored the new South Tower looking out on Prospect Avenue, fostering a sense of integration with the larger community. To implement this concept, they designed a balcony linked to the street below by an open staircase. Inviting the neighbors to dine with us was never part of the plan. There was no sign outside facing Prospect Avenue advertising "the Bistro" to seek hungry customers (though that might be a worthwhile commercial enterprise given the amount of food often left over).

If a street person was bold or well-informed enough to seek sustenance, the Bistro staff, who now call me by name, would quickly recognize an alien, request an apartment number, and ask the person (kindly I hope) to please leave.

Now a stray thought crosses my mind. These two doors, connecting directly to the street, are the only means of entry to Saint John's that does not admonish concealed weapon aficionados to leave their heat outside. But it gets odder still. The Bistro is just a few strides away, around a corner, from our now famous art gallery, advertised as "open to the public." So the enemy is already within our gates!

—

What does all this mean? First, there is not a lot of common sense at work and, secondly, we should decide to which community we belong. Are we a privileged minority hiding in a wealthy enclave or part of a larger community that welcomes neighbors into an elegant and safe environment?

The morning after my "lockout," I visited the scene of my incarceration to check the facts. Stuck to the outer glass door and facing inward was a newly posted sign, "This door is locked for security purposes. It will be opened on June 28." It is disturbing to learn that eating outside and the threat of invasion are dealt with by a date on the calendar, rather than flexible and rational criteria.

Institutional swimming pools open and close on Memorial and Labor Day, but homeowners with pools (I was one) do so when the weather dictates. June 28 is eight days after the first day of summer. Somebody misread the groundhog!

Institutional Indigestion

Strange to see how a good dinner and feasting reconciles everybody.

—Samuel Pepys

There's no love sincerer than the love of food.

—George Bernard Shaw

Even Camelot had its shortcomings; here is one at Saint John's I find difficult to swallow!

However hard Saint John's struggles and often succeeds in converting "institutional" into "in-home living," it continues to be baffled by the food service. This is despite an exquisite dining room, "Taylor's," named after a resident couple who endowed it.

Two adjectives I find difficult to define are "spiritual" and "institutional" despite spending four years as a seminary student and a lifetime eating in institutions: first a childhood in boarding schools, then an army mess hall followed by university dining, and a long line of hospital cafeterias. Fortunately, like pornography, everyone recognizes these twin terms when they encounter them.

The modern Saint John's has two dining venues: Taylor's, dedicated to "fine dining," and the Bistro, serving everyday food, cafeteria style. Neither lives up to the aspirations of its name, to rise significantly above "institutional," in service or menu. The Bistro is self-service and Taylor's is unsophisticated service.

Taylor's blurs its image with a menu offering twice-weekly "Blue Plate Specials," a term borrowed from the drugstore counter. The same daily soups are served in both places with monotonous predictability, often thin and devoid of whatever gives the soup its name or intended flavor. These offerings don't begin to compete with what comes off the grocery store shelf or is available for a modest price at local bistros (North Star, North Shore, The Knick, Harry's).

Growing up in India and accomplished in its cuisine, I am troubled when the word "curry" appears on the menu to describe overcooked chunks of chicken covered in a flour-based white sauce, faintly flavored with store-bought curry powder and served over sticky rice without any appropriate condiments (naan, chutney, raita). I feel tempted to invite the cook (I'm not ready to use the word chef) to join me for a "fine" dinner at either of the two Indian or three Thai restaurants within walking distance of Saint John's. I could multiply this example many times but to little purpose. You know what I mean.

In a recent attempt to upgrade quality, a new menu was introduced along with comment cards available for completion at every meal. After several weeks, one staff member reported that all but one was negative. But nobody seems to know who reads them and nothing changes. I indicated I was willing to meet someone face to face, but no one has taken me up.

—

As an occasional host and greeter at Taylor's, I notice that attendance seems to be dwindling. I took a guest to lunch recently, and when we arrived promptly at noon, there wasn't a staff person in sight. Eventually seated, we ate in solitary splendor. When my guest asked for the list of the salad dressings, the waitress couldn't remember them.

I suspect that people are beginning realize it is better, and not much more expensive, to eat at one of the excellent restaurants in our neighborhood. You would certainly avoid Taylor's if you wanted to impress even a modestly sophisticated guest and avoid embarrassing yourself. Nevertheless, residents are still obliged to buy $200 worth of institutional food a month per apartment. And if you are too infirm to wander abroad and graduate to nursing home care, "lifetime health care" does not include food which costs extra on a per diem basis.

Not to mix metaphors, but institutional attempts to solve this problem seem unduly constipated. In all other areas, administration does an excellent job—whether it is maintenance, infrastructure, marketing, health care, or building a magnificent new South Tower. There is a residents' food committee, but it also seems impotent. Now I *have* mixed my medical metaphors!

Here is a suggestion I believe might relieve both constipation and impotence. A two for one!

Immediately implement a system of continuous quality improvement (CQI) as follows:

- After every meal, invite each resident to fill out a short, simple rating scale appropriate to each venue that has only two simple items to be checked: one for service, the other for food. Completion would be encouraged by placing these on every dining table. In Taylor's, the ten-point scale would be from 0 (institutional quality) to 10 (fine dining). In the Bistro, it would be from 0 (institutional quality) to 10 (meets community standards).The rating sheet would include space for optional, more specific, comments on food or service.

- The director of Food Services would be responsible for tabulating the survey results and presenting them in written and numerical form (brief training might be necessary) to a monthly meeting with the president (or designee) and chair of the residents' food committee. The chair of the residents' food committee would share the findings with the full committee for comment and feedback at the next monthly meeting.
- After three months, to identify trends, the average score on each scale would be adjusted upward as a target for improvement in service and food quality to be met within a designated time period. Achievement of these goals would be rewarded by a bonus for cooking and waitstaff distributed annually. Success or failure to meet CQI goals would be documented in the director's personnel file to be available at annual performance and salary review.

This is a simple and easily implemented proposal with the following advantages:

- It focuses on the specific goals of improving service and food quality to achieve fine dining (Taylor's) and meet community standards (the Bistro).
- It avoids the impossible task of satisfying every individual dining expectation in a very diverse population of residents. Instead, it provides consensus-based definitions (fine dining and community-based quality) which may differ between individuals but which strive toward common goals.
- It places responsibility squarely where it belongs on the director of Food Services and ensures regular, documented communication between that person, administration, and residents.
- It provides specific, timed, and measurable dining outcomes tied to employment incentives but preserves the autonomy of the food services to implement improvements in a broad scope without dictating detailed alterations. These would be influenced by the open-ended detailed comments from residents. The proposal encourages effort and creativity!

Caveat: One additional suggestion would be that no person with executive responsibility in Food Services should be hired without understanding and agreeing to this system of CQI unless, of course, they have a better idea.

Food for Thought

One man's way may be as good as another's, but we all like our own the best.

—Jane Austen

"Know thyself" is a good saying but not in all situations. In many it is better to say "know others."

—Menander

New residents began to move into the new South Tower at Saint John's on my seventy-seventh birthday, and exactly a year has passed since then. The previous bits in this piece reflect some of my ambivalent experience in adapting to life in community. Others took to the environment like a duck to water.

For all the amenities and luxuries available, this is still an institution so that living here and feeling content demands some sacrifice of personal autonomy in favor of communal consensus. Nowhere has this been more obvious than in the area of food service. Catering to the wishes and appetites of several hundred individuals is inevitably the road to mediocrity. The outcome of my attempt to achieve change in this with the previous bit ("Institutional Indigestion") is still unclear, but on further thought and discussion with other residents, I am almost persuaded that "fine dining" in an institution is an operational oxymoron. Those with the ability to cook for themselves or who have the affluence to seek fine dining elsewhere will shun the institutional venues.

But food for thought is about more than fine dining; it extends to all aspects of community life. Here I have to confess a handicap derived from a childhood and early adult life spent almost entirely in boarding schools, the army, and university. This stifled any desire for affiliation and turned most of my peers into rivals rather than friends. So we shall see if, in this current setting, the present can outdo the past. I hope so.

Last Wish

When life is dwindling
Choose the road less traveled for
A joyful ending.

—Barry Blackwell, November 2011

Unsound Advice?

Geoffrey Fisher was archbishop of Canterbury from 1945 to 1961, overlapping the time I was in boarding school (1945-1952), high on a hill outside the city walls, looking down on his cathedral. Geoffrey presided at the wedding and coronation of Queen Elizabeth and was the first archbishop of the Anglican Communion to meet with a Pope (John XXIII) since Henry VIII broke from Rome.

Educated at Oxford (his family preferred Cambridge), Fisher became headmaster of Repton, a prestigious boarding school founded in the sixteenth century, at the young age of twenty-seven. When he retired in 1961, he visited the prime minister, Harold Macmillan, to advise on his successor. Fisher was a consummate politician and head of the English Freemasons. His advice was as follows:

> Whoever you choose, under no account must it be Michael Ramsey, the Archbishop of York. Dr. Ramsey is a theologian, a scholar and a man of prayer. Therefore he is entirely unsuitable as Archbishop of Canterbury. I have known him all my life. I was his head master at Repton.

The prime minister's wry reply was as follows:

—

Thank you, your Grace, for your kind advice. You may have been Doctor Ramsey's headmaster but you were not mine.

I am happy to be in such good company when it comes to rejecting the archbishop's advice about the unwisdom of writing a book in retirement. The prime minister appointed Ramsey!

"Closer to Thee"

Our tower in the sky
Is where old folks can gather
Together to die.

—Barry Blackwell, November 2011

Afterthought

When reading is done
This book's covers will be shut,
But thinking goes on.

—Barry Blackwell, May 2012

And with this I bid the reader a fond and thankful farewell!